TUNEUP & TROUBLE SHOOTING

TUNEUP &

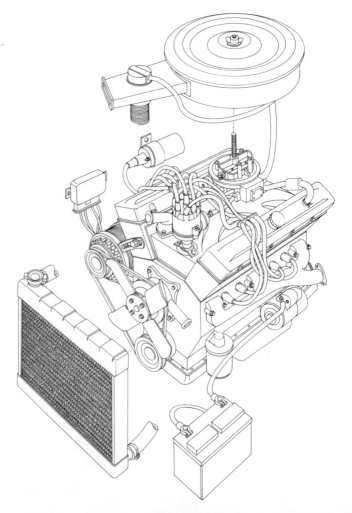

TROUBLE SHOOTING

Hearst Books
The Hearst Corporation
New York, New York

SATURDAY
MECHANIC

Other
titles
from

BASIC CAR CARE ILLUSTRATED
BODYWORK & PAINTING
CAR CARE GUIDES
Chevy
Chevelle
Cutlass
Nova
Vega
Ford
Pinto
Torino
Dart
Valiant
Datsun
Toyota
VW Beetle
VW Rabbit

Library of Congress
Catalog Card No. 79-66361

Soft Cover ISBN No. 0-87851-512-7
Hard Cover ISBN No. 0-87851-513-5

Printed in the United States of America

Designed and produced by: For Art Sake, Inc.
Automotive Books Division, 36 West 89th St., New
York, New York 10024

The information herein has been compiled
from authoritative sources. While every
effort is made by the editors to attain
accuracy, manufacturing changes as well as
typographical errors and omissions may
occur. The publisher and the editors cannot
be responsible nor do they assume responsibility for
such omissions, errors or changes.

STAFF AND CONTRIBUTORS

John B. Miller
Director of Design and Production, President, For Art Sake, Inc.

Lynn Capehart
Mechanical Artist, Specifications

Michael Eastman
Layout Artist and Picture Research

Cliff Gromer
Editor, Technical Specifications

Jeff Mangiat
Contributing Illustrator

Eileen Bossong-Martinez
Production Assistant and Editor of Troubleshooting by the Numbers

Phillip Nochlin
Text Editor

Ruth Plave
Mechanical Artist, Troubleshooting by the Numbers

John Samanich
Technical Consultant

Hannah K. Selby
Managing Editor

For Art Sake, Inc.
Cover Design

ACKNOWLEDGMENTS

The editors are grateful for the assistance provided by the following individuals, manufacturers, and organizations.

AC-Delco Division
General Motors Corporation

Ace Pontiac, Bronx, NY

ACF Industries, Inc.

American Motors Corporation

Berk Trade School, Automotive Books Division, Brooklyn, NY

Allen Bragdon, Editor in Chief, Hearst Books

Donald H. Bray, Instructor, ITT Technical Institute, Automotive Division, Chelsea, MA

Carter Carburetor Division

Chrysler Corporation

Chrysler Manhattan

Champion Spark Plug Company

Concord Typesetters, Inc., NY, NY

Courtesy Oldsmobile, Bronx, NY

Ford Parts and Service Division
Ford Motor Company

Lou Fourier, Editor, MOTOR Auto Repair Manuals

General Motors Corporation

Gumout Division of Pennzoil Company

Holley Economaster Carburetors courtesy of Holley Replacement Parts Division, Colt Industries

Claude Milot, Assistant General Manager, MOTOR Publications

Daniel Oates, Production, POPULAR MECHANICS

Joe Oldham, Editor, MOTOR Magazine

Publishers' Design and Production Services, Composition and Film

Rochester Products Division
General Motors Corporation

Springfield Electrical Specialties, Inc.

Volkswagen of America, Inc.

CONTENTS

FOREWORD

So you want to tune up your car! You're not alone. Welcome to the growing number of car owners who now perform their own tuneups. Surveys show that more than one-third of all tuneups are done by home mechanics, and the figure is climbing. With the cost of a tuneup at a service station ranging anywhere from $50 to $85, and a gallon of gas breaking the $1 mark, more and more car owners are asking themselves: "Can I do it myself?" Let us reassure you, the answer is an emphatic "Yes." All you'll need is the illustrated, step-by-step, how-to instructions in this book, the basic tools (pictured in Chapter 1), the essential tools listed at the beginning of each chapter, and the manufacturer's specifications for your car's engine, which you can find beginning on page 202 or on the decal in your engine compartment. We've left some room on page 10 for you to keep a permanent record of your car's "vital statistics."

The tuneup defined

Where do you begin? Let's first define what a tuneup is because the word can have different meanings for different mechanics. Basically, it's a series of procedures that restore optimum performance, reduce exhaust emissions, increase fuel mileage, and prolong the useful life of your engine. A tuneup can save you a long walk home or an expensive tow and repair job, or both. Since an engine tuneup is one of the most important elements of proper car care, it should be performed at regular intervals rather than after a failure occurs. When it is performed regularly, it is called a maintenance tuneup. When it is done to track down a problem or after a failure, it is diagnostic. In either case, the result is the same: The engine's driveability, power, and performance are restored by replacing defective parts and adjusting everything to manufacturer's specifications.

Not all motorists are alike

Ideally, you would perform a maintenance tuneup on your car regularly. But recognizing the frailty of human nature and the fact that many owners neglect their cars until a problem develops, this book has been prepared with both the industrious and the indolent motorist in mind.

For the person who has pledged to perform the basic maintenance tuneup faithfully and regularly, we have provided nine chapters of easy-to-follow, numbered Job Steps, each step fully illustrated. Each chapter deals with a single engine system. For example:

Chapter 2, Battery and Cable Service, introduces the reader to the role played by the battery, and explains how to buy, how to test, how to service, and how to replace, not to mention tips on how to work on this potentially explosive item without getting killed.

Chapter 6, Distributor Service—cap and gap, reluctor and rotor—has 12 illustrated Job Steps clearly outlining general distributor service, plus 11 pages (with almost 60 illustrations) which unravel the mysteries of troubleshooting five different electronic ignition systems including the new Hall-Effect type.

Chapter 9, Carburetor Service, explains the servicing of the air cleaner, the vacuum motor, and the snorkel, and describes adjustments you can make within the carburetor itself. In addition, photos of 16 models of Carter, Chrysler, Holley, Motorcraft, and Rochester carburetors, accompanied by a list of adjustment procedures, show you where to find what has to be adjusted.

Besides these, there are six other chapters of solid tuneup information. But before plunging into your tuneup, study Chapter 1, The Fundamentals, which gives you a broad overview of what a car is, what a tuneup is, and how they go together.

Troubleshooting

The second major part of the book, "Troubleshooting by the Numbers," is for the car owner who opens the hood of the car only to investigate a problem. The word "maintenance" is not part of this driver's active vocabulary. "Quick-fix" and "jump-start" are. If this is you, the Troubleshooting section offers a series of easy-to-follow, illustrated diagnostic and repair charts. You'll find descriptions of your car's symptoms accompanied by several hundred cross references to service procedures in the tuneup chapters. By zeroing in on your problem, you can easily run through a diagnostic tuneup "by the numbers" that will improve performance.

The special section on "When Your Car Talks, Listen!" is designed for the car owner who believes, and rightly, in "talking" to his or her car. And the diesel section describes step-by-step, illustrated maintenance procedures for the Olds 350 V8 diesel and the Volkswagen Rabbit diesel.

The Specs section

109 pages of technical specifications follow the Troubleshooting section. Don't let the austere look of this Appendix put you off. These charts contain much useful and—for the do-it-yourselfer— much vital information on just about every American make and model passenger car, plus light trucks and vans and the most popular imports. The Specifications list everything from where to find

your engine number to the firing order of your cylinders and your carburetor's settings. And with the world turning to the metric system, you will find the Conversion Table, Inch Fractions and Decimals to Metric Equivalents (pages 311–312), particularly useful.

Everything in this book is at your fingertips if you make full use of the overall table of contents on pages 6 and 7, the individual chapter tables of contents, and the Index at the end.

When not to do it yourself

If you don't find instructions in the tuneup chapters for a repair job you want to tackle, or the Troubleshooting section recommends that you see a pro, it means that the technical experts who prepared this book feel that the job is too difficult for a do-it-yourself mechanic to handle.

One final word. When you do undertake a job, be sure to work slowly and carefully, and observe the cautions about potentially hazardous or tricky procedures which are printed in *italic type*. Remember that in working on your car, you carry two big responsibilities: the first for your own safety while making a repair and the second for the safety of passengers and fellow motorists after the repair is completed. Good luck!

THIS BOOK BELONGS TO:	
CAR MAKE AND MODEL:	
VEHICLE IDENTIFICATION NO:	ENGINE:
Cylinder firing order:	Timing rpm:
Oil capacity:	Choke setting:
Fuel tank capacity:	Fast-idle rpm:
Radiator capacity:	Curb-idle rpm:
Spark plug type:	Battery amperage:
Spark plug gap:	Alternator output amperage:
Ignition timing:	Distributor rotation:

CHAPTER

THE FUNDAMENTALS

How can you tell when to tune up your car? If you're an average driver, every 12 months or 12,000 miles is a good rule-of-thumb schedule for performing a maintenance tuneup. If you use your car less frequently, let's say 4000 or 5000 miles a year, then you must base your tuneup on time rather than miles. In this case, a tuneup once a year should keep your car running at peak efficiency. If, on the other hand, you drive 40,000 or 50,000 miles a year, your tuneup schedule should be every 15,000 miles or so. Different driving conditions will also call for different servicing schedules. If you do a lot of driving under dusty conditions or in the city where there's a great deal of stop-and-go driving, even if you use your car infrequently, you should perform a tuneup more than once a year.

If all these schedules confuse you, an easier and better way to determine if and when your car needs a tuneup is to keep a regular record of your car's running history: Maintain an accurate record of gas mileage; be aware of your car's behavior; and take note of any changes in the way your car runs. Be on the lookout for problem conditions, such as stalling, loss of power, rough idle, engine knocking or pinging, black smoke from the exhaust, hard starting, misfiring or dieseling. If any of these problems occur frequently, there's a good chance your car needs a tuneup. But keep in mind that some cars have poor fuel mileage and are hard to start, even when they are well tuned. If you're driving a car like that, a tuneup won't solve the problem. In addition, if your car has a major mechanical problem in the engine (piston or ring damage, for example), a tuneup will be almost useless.

Before starting to tune up your car, carefully read through the instructions and study the illustrations in each chapter two or three times to get an overview of what you will be doing and what you can expect next as you proceed from Job Step to Job Step. Also, be sure you have the right tools, equipment, and parts on hand before you begin. It's frustrating to begin a job and then find out that you do not have everything you need to complete it.

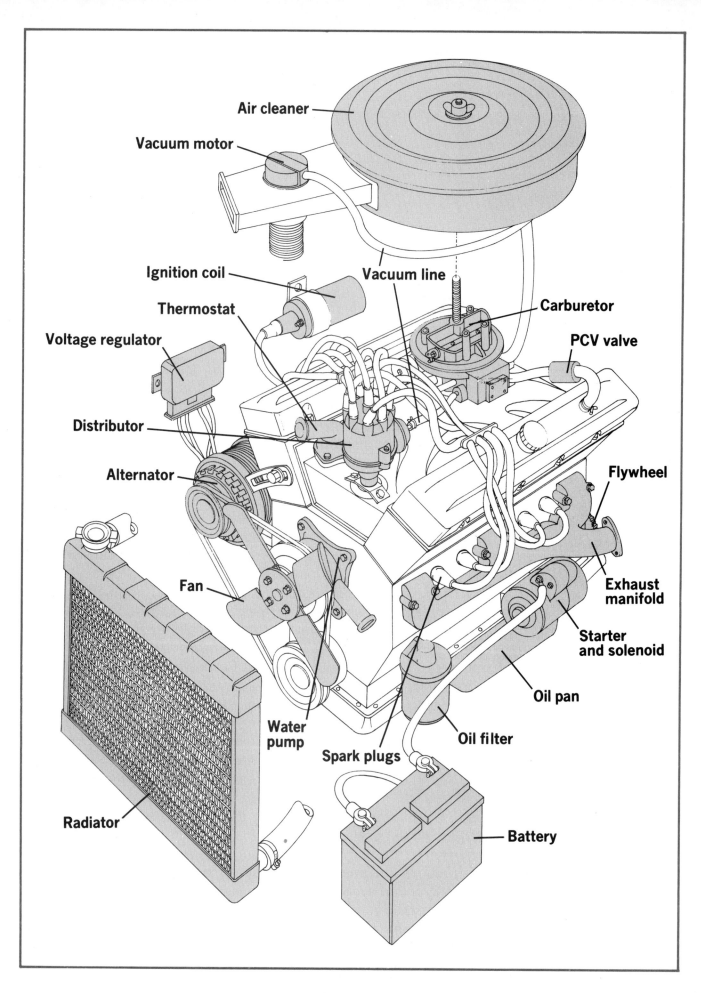

Air cleaner

Vacuum motor

Ignition coil

Vacuum line

Thermostat

Carburetor

Voltage regulator

PCV valve

Distributor

Flywheel

Alternator

Exhaust manifold

Fan

Starter and solenoid

Oil pan

Water pump

Spark plugs

Oil filter

Radiator

Battery

TUNEUP FOR MILEAGE

One sure way to make tuneups a snap and extend the life of your car is to perform maintenance services regularly. While a new car usually requires less-frequent service, it's a good idea to get into the habit of periodic maintenance right from the start if you buy a brand-new car. It's also easier to keep up with the service schedule when you start with a new vehicle. With the cost of cars soaring out of sight, you'll want to keep your present one trouble-free for as long as possible. With the proper care, 100,000 miles is not an unreasonable goal.

No other single maintenance service will help your car reach its 100,000-mile birthday more than frequent oil changes. How frequent? Never exceed the mileage suggested by the manufacturer in your owner's manual. However, if you read this recommendation carefully, you will see that it is only a guide. The oil-change interval should be adjusted to the type of driving you do and the area in which it is done. Engine longevity is directly related to how often the oil is changed.

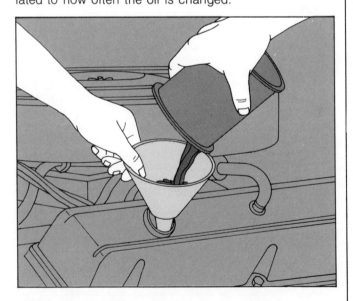

Use an oil made by a reputable company and make sure it meets API (American Petroleum Institute) recommendations for your car's model and year. If you decide to add a synthetic oil to the engine, you can probably extend the interval between oil changes. Most synthetics are advertised as able to provide proper lubrication for 15,000 miles under normal conditions. However, never exceed the manufacturer's mileage recommendation if the vehicle is under warranty because you will void it. The section in your owner's manual on oil is important.

Read it carefully. It will explain mileage requirements and what oil to use in your car for your weather.

Should an oil filter be replaced every other oil change, as car manufacturers suggest, or every oil change? The fact is that one quart of dirty oil is contained in the old filter, and four quarts of clean oil plus one quart of dirty oil equal five quarts of dirty oil. Whether or not you go along with the manufacturer's recommendations, you will have to replace the oil filter sooner or later. An oil filter is a blind item. You can't look inside to judge quality, so buy a filter made by a reputable company.

One advantage in knowing how to service your car is that you can check the important things as often as you like, such as the carburetor and ignition timing settings. These settings change as mileage accumulates, and there is no guarantee they are going to remain accurate. Most car owners verify settings when doing an engine tuneup. But just to make sure, it is a good idea to check the carburetor and timing adjustments every 5000 miles. And sometime within the first 10,000 miles you're going to have to clean the carburetor air cleaner, and replace the fuel filter and maybe the anti-freeze.

The emission-control devices you'll most likely be dealing with during tuneup are the Positive Crankcase Ventilation (PCV) system; the Fuel Evaporation Control system; the Exhaust Gas Recirculation (EGR) system; and the catalytic converter. Keep in mind, however, that not all emission-control systems require servicing during the 10,000- to 20,000-mile period. Check your owner's manual for the exact service intervals.

A malfunction in the PCV system will have an adverse

effect on the calibration of the fuel mixture. For this reason, PCV parts should always be kept in good working order. These parts include hoses, an air-intake filter, and a regulating (PCV) valve.

The Fuel Evaporation Control system uses a vapor separator to collect fuel tank fumes. Some fumes are condensed into a liquid and returned to the fuel tank. The remainder are transferred to the intake manifold through a charcoal canister. In American-made cars, the only scheduled service for this system is to replace the filter in the charcoal canister every 12,000 miles.

The Exhaust Gas Recirculation system limits the formation of oxides of nitrogen by diluting the intake charge, which reduces peak combustion temperature. Oxides of nitrogen will be formed only with high heat.

A metered amount of exhaust gas is injected into the combustion chamber with the intake stroke by the EGR valve. The exhaust gas entering the combustion chamber is inert and cooler than combustion temperature. Since the gas won't burn, the peak temperatures of the gases in the combustion chamber are lowered. Note:

EGR systems are very complicated, consisting of a number of parts in addition to the EGR valve. If this valve loses calibration, a number of engine problems can occur, notably stalling and poor acceleration. Most car makers recommend that the EGR system be serviced between 15,000 and 30,000 miles.

The catalytic converter changes hydrocarbon and carbon monoxide exhausted by the engine to water vapor and carbon dioxide. Never use leaded gasoline in a car with a catalytic converter. In a short time it will make the catalyst ineffective. There is no periodic maintenance for a converter. The catalytic element or the entire converter should be replaced when the catalyst is no longer effective. This occurs at about 50,000 miles.

Sometime between the first 10,000 and 20,000 miles you're going to perform a complete tuneup on your car. If it has an electronic ignition, the tuneup should be done during the second 10,000 miles of your car's life, and every second 10,000 miles thereafter. If your car has breaker points, tune it up sometime after the first

10,000 miles and every 10,000 or so miles after that. In any case, during the tuneup you will probably have to replace the spark plugs.

As the odometer approaches the 30,000-mile mark, you'll probably have to replace the hoses in the cooling system. The period between 30,000 and 40,000 miles are the carefree miles, because by this time, most of the wrinkles that may have afflicted your car in its earlier years should have been ironed out. However, there are still some chores you may have to do other than regular maintenance. You should inspect the spark plug cables

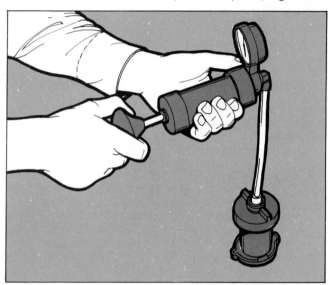

and replace them if necessary. Also, you should test your car's battery. It has done yeoman service for about three years now and may be ready for retirement.

As a car heads toward the midway point in its first 100,000 miles, it enters a transition period. Up to 40,000 miles, your car mainly requires regular maintenance: that is, lubrication, tuneup, and adjustment and inspection. Minor repairs may be needed, but the emphasis is on the services that lay the foundation for long life. But between 40,000 and 60,000 miles, the emphasis begins to change. Some critical parts start to wear out and need to be replaced or overhauled. It is during this period that

COMPARISON CHART: MM VS. INCHES		
6 mm	½″	¾″
¼″	13 mm	20 mm
7 mm	14 mm	13/16″
5/16″	9/16″	21 mm
8 mm	15 mm	22 mm
9 mm	5/8″	7/8″
¾″	16 mm	23 mm
10 mm	17 mm	15/16″
11 mm	11/16″	24 mm
7/16″	18 mm	25 mm
12 mm	19 mm	1″

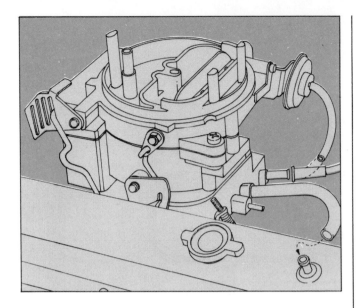

the home mechanic's skills really begin to pay off. One repair your car is likely to be ready for at 50,000 miles is a carburetor overhaul. A new carburetor can be expensive. But with a zip kit you can overhaul your old carburetor for a fraction of the cost. A typical overhaul kit contains a new needle and seat, an accelerator pump, gaskets, a float-level gauge, and instructions. You will also need a container of carburetor-cleaning agent to soak parts that can be reinstalled. The instructions that come with the kit are explicit and complete, so there is no need to repeat them here.

The stretch from 70,000 to 80,000 miles presents a rewarding lull to the home mechanic who has been doing his automotive homework diligently. Just as dur-

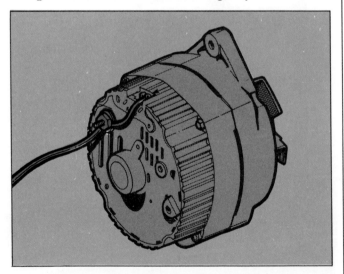

ing the earlier carefree miles, your car requires little service work, just periodic maintenance.

''How about electrical components?'' you might ask. What about the alternator, starter motor, and voltage regulator? Alternators and starter motors do not require maintenance and they are probably two of the most reliable components in your car. In fact, the alternator and starter motor may not give you trouble for more than 80,000 and then some.

An electrical problem that is being caused by a faulty alternator won't escape you for long. The generating system light or gauge on the dashboard will either light

up or point to discharge, or the engine won't start at all. Voltage regulators fail more often than alternators, with opposite results. A malfunctioning alternator leads to undercharging, while a faulty regulator usually results in overcharging. In most cars, overcharging is easily detected. The battery will require water too often. Furthermore, you will probably sense an odor resembling rotten

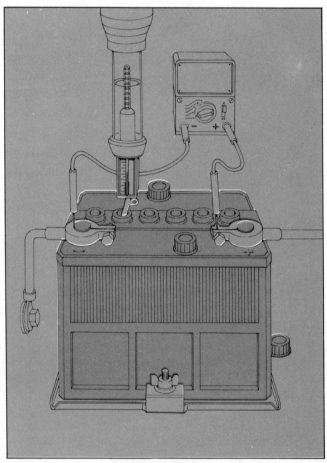

eggs when you remove the battery caps to check the water level. On maintenance-free batteries, the state-of-charge indicator will be yellow if the battery needs to be replaced and black if it needs to be charged.

In the 80,000-to-90,000-mile stretch, your car is entering its golden age. It's a period when you begin to admire your vehicle's strength and to congratulate yourself on keeping it in top condition. However, your car should continue to receive the attention you have given it from mile one. In addition, you may be faced with such repairs as replacing the water pump, the radiator or the thermostat. But this is no problem. This book tells you the tools you'll need and gives you the step-by-step instructions you will follow.

If you treat your car right, it should have no trouble reaching the 100,000-mile mark and maybe more. Several facts attest to this: The average age of cars on the road today is 5.7 years, up from 4.1 years in 1971. Over 93 million cars are now three years old or older. Is yours one of them? Will it still be alive at 100,000 miles? A well tuned car will.

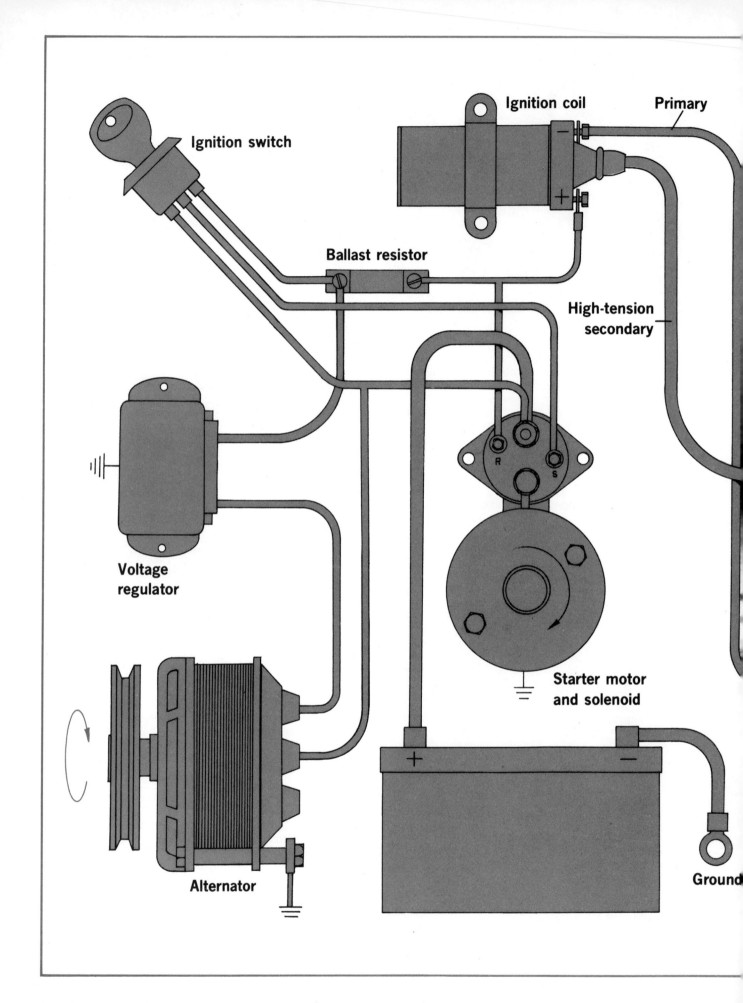

Ignition switch

Ignition coil

Primary

Ballast resistor

High-tension
secondary

Voltage
regulator

R

S

Starter motor
and solenoid

+

−

Alternator

Ground

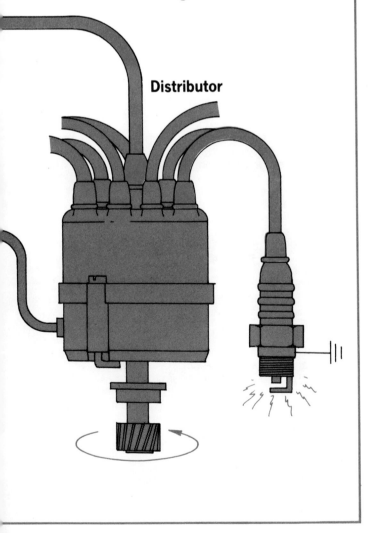

Electronic ignition

Distributor

THE ELECTRICAL SYSTEM

Your car actually has three electrical systems: cranking, charging, and ignition.

The cranking circuit gets the engine started so that it can begin to run on its own. The system consists of an ignition switch, a battery, its cables, a neutral safety switch, a starter relay and/or starter solenoid, and a starter motor. Activated by the car key, the ignition switch, along with the neutral safety switch, starts the flow of electricity from the battery to the cranking circuit and the charging circuit, as well as to the car's ignition system. The neutral safety switch, which is found either on the steering post or on the transmission or clutch linkage, prevents the engine from starting when the transmission is in gear. The starter solenoid connects the battery to the starter motor and engages the starter motor to the engine's flywheel. The starter motor is designed to crank the engine. The starter relay, usually mounted on the firewall or the inner fender skirt, is an electromagnetic switch connecting the battery to the starter motor. The battery is the car's basic source of electrical power.

The charging circuit keeps the battery charged and provides power for the car's electrical systems. It is composed of an alternator, a voltage regulator, an ignition switch, a charging indicator (a warning light or an ammeter), the wires connecting all the components, and a battery and its cables. The alternator, driven by the engine, produces electrical power to supply the car's needs once it's started and also keeps the battery charged. The voltage regulator controls the output of the alternator. The ignition switch electrically connects the voltage regulator to the alternator.

The ignition circuit produces a high voltage (secondary circuit) which is delivered to the spark plugs at the proper time to ignite the compressed fuel-and-air mixture and fire the cylinders. The system is made up of a primary and a secondary circuit. The primary circuit includes a battery, an alternator, a charging indicator (a warning light or an ammeter), an ignition switch, a ballast resistor, a coil, and a magnetic pickup assembly (or points and condenser in a breaker-point system). The secondary circuit consists of a coil winding in the coil, a high-voltage coil wire, a distributor rotor and cap, and spark plugs and their wires. The ignition switch starts the ignition circuit in two ways: It engages the starting circuit for engine cranking, and it supplies battery voltage to the positive side of the coil. The purpose of the ballast resistor is to reduce heat buildup in the coil by lowering the battery voltage going to it. This prolongs the life of the coil and the points. The ballast resistor also reduces primary voltage to the positive side of the coil. The coil is basically a step-up transformer. It raises primary battery voltage to secondary voltage, which is necessary to ignite the fuel-and-air mixture. The points, which open and close the circuit, and the condenser, which prolongs the life of the points, are replaced in electronic ignition systems by a magnetic pickup assembly. A reluctor, attached to the distributor shaft, replaces the cam. The rotating reluctor is never in contact with the pickup assembly, so neither is subject to wear. The pickup assembly sends an electrical signal to the electronic control module, where a transistor makes and breaks the primary circuit, allowing the coil to produce a high or secondary voltage that ignites the compressed fuel-and-air mixture in the cylinders.

TROUBLESHOOTING YOUR ELECTRICAL SYSTEM

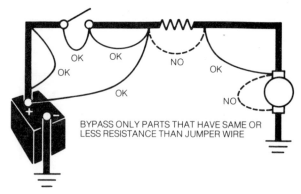

BYPASS ONLY PARTS THAT HAVE SAME OR LESS RESISTANCE THAN JUMPER WIRE

FIG. 1 USING A JUMPER WIRE

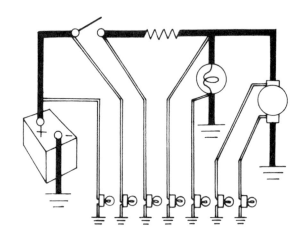

FIG. 2 USING A TEST LAMP

Electricity is a law-abiding phenomenon. If you obey the same rules and regulations that electricity does, you should have no trouble solving electrical problems.

The first law of electricity is Ohm's Law. It concerns various units of measurement such as quantity (amperes), pressure (volts), and resistance (ohms) in relationship to each other. These measurements are defined as follows: The movement of electrons is electrical current. The quantity of current flow in a given time (rate) is measured in amperes, much like gallons per minute for water flow. For your information, 6.28 billion-billion electrons per second equal one ampere. The unit of pressure that moves these electrons is called a volt. The unit of measurement used to express the resistance of a given object (conductor) to the flow of electricity is called an ohm. The resistance of a conductor is affected by its material, length, and thickness. The larger the conductor, the less the resistance and the more total current can flow. Ohm's Law states that electric current varies exactly as voltage varies so long as the resistance remains the same. By the same token, the current varies inversely with any change in resistance so long as voltage remains unchanged. In other words: If the voltage goes up and the resistance remains the same, then the amperage will also go up. And, if the voltage remains the same and the resistance increases, then the amperage will be reduced. Translated mathematically: Amperes equal Volts over Ohms. Or, Volts equal Amperes times Ohms. Or, Ohms equal Volts over Amperes. Another good formula to keep in mind is: It takes one volt to push one amp through one ohm of resistance in a circuit.

What is a circuit? Any usable circuit must have four elements: 1) a source of electrical energy; 2) the means for making and breaking a circuit (a switch); 3) a resistance (a lamp, starting motor, fan, etc.); and 4) a route (wiring or conductor) to and from the resistance and the source of energy. This source can be a battery or a generator (alternator). The switch can be manual (headlight switch) or mechanical or transistorized (distributor points). Resistance can be a light motor or any object that electricity can flow through. The route between these units can be wire, the frame of the car or the engine. Keep in mind that in all circuits, electricity must get back to its source. If electricity starts at the battery, then it must return to the battery.

The three major electrical troublemakers you are likely to come across in the automobile are an open, a short, and a grounded circuit (see Figs. 3, 4, and 5). A complete break or interruption in the normal current route is called an open. This condition can also be caused when there is a break within the unit itself. In a sense, a break is high resistance in the circuit. Any abnormal resistance reduces the current flow in a circuit and leaves the unit working intermittently or not working at all. An open or high-resistance circuit may occur as the result of a broken wire within the wiring harness, loose connections at the terminal of the electrical unit, broken leads or wiring within the unit or, poor connections between the unit and the ground.

A short is a circuit that is completed in such a way that current bypasses part of the normal circuit. This can be caused by two wires touching each other. Bypassing part of the normal circuit results in less resistance and higher current (amperage) flow, leading to overheating in the wiring or the unit, which could possibly burn part of the insulation.

A grounded circuit is similar to a short circuit in that current bypasses part of the normal circuit, but instead of going to other components, it goes directly to a ground. This can occur when a wire touches a ground or part of a circuit within a unit or units and comes into contact with the unit's frame or housing. Grounded circuits can also be the direct cause of oil, dirt, and moisture around connections or terminals.

There are three basic instruments any home mechanic who wants to troubleshoot electrical problems must have: an ammeter, a voltmeter, and an ohmmeter. Each is designed to handle a specific job.

An ammeter must be connected in the circuit according to polarity; that is, in series, *before* any electrical load. When connecting the ammeter this way, all the current to be measured will pass through the tester. The

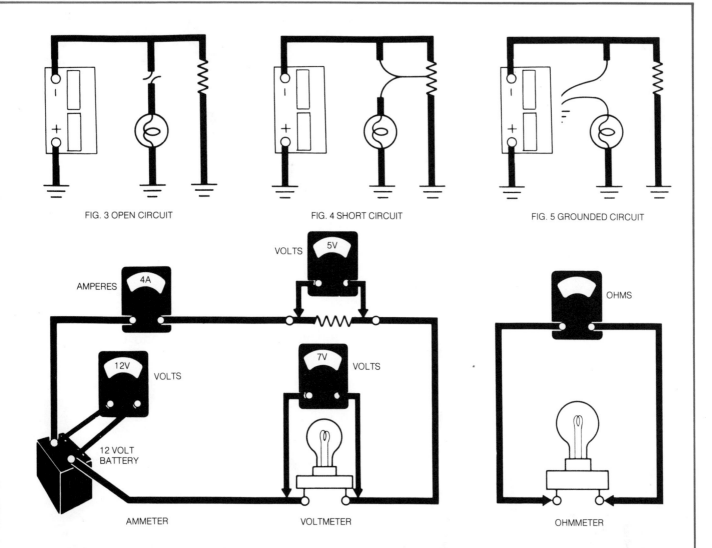

FIG. 3 OPEN CIRCUIT   FIG. 4 SHORT CIRCUIT   FIG. 5 GROUNDED CIRCUIT

VOLTS   5V

AMPERES   4A

12V   VOLTS

7V   VOLTS

OHMS

12 VOLT BATTERY

AMMETER   VOLTMETER   OHMMETER

home mechanic can then compare the reading with specs to determine if the circuit is functioning properly. It is important that you always use a meter large enough to handle the amperage to be measured. Remember, the ammeter measures current flow or amperes and is always used in a closed circuit in series.

A voltmeter must always be connected in parallel in a circuit or part of a circuit. The voltmeter measures voltage drop, which is the difference between voltage at its low terminals in a closed circuit. Use a meter large enough to handle the voltage to be measured.

An ohmmeter can be used only when the unit or circuit to be tested is disconnected. It has its own power supply. An ohmmeter measures resistance directly on its own meter. This reading should then be compared with manufacturer's specifications.

To do electrical testing accurately, you will also need a jumper wire, a test light, a compass, and a circuit breaker. A jumper is simply a piece of wire fitted with an alligator clip or a probe at each end. It is used to bypass parts of a circuit by serving as a substitute for wires or switches (see Fig. 1). If a resistance unit operates when a jumper wire is used, this indicates that the wire or switch portion of the circuit between the leads of a jumper wire is faulty.

Test lights come in two varieties: One that needs an outside source of power and a second that has its own

source of power. When you use the second type, always disconnect the energy supply to the circuit being tested. The type of test light that uses an outside source of power is usually a 12-volt bulb with a pair of wires. It uses the car's battery as a source of power. A test light can be fabricated by using an insulated 2-wire socket and bulb with wires acting as probes. Test lamps are used in parallel with parts of a circuit so continuity may be checked (see Fig. 2). When one lead of a test lamp is grounded and the other lead is moved from one circuit connection to another, the lamp is being used in parallel to locate an open circuit, which is between the last point of light operation and the point where the test lamp no longer glows.

An ordinary magnetic compass is a valuable tool for locating a grounded circuit. It operates on the principle that a wire carrying current creates a magnetic field. In circuits protected by a circuit breaker, a short or a ground should be easy to locate with a magnetic compass. Just turn the circuit on and follow the wiring with a compass. The needle of the compass will fluctuate each time the circuit breaker closes. When the point of the short or ground is passed, the compass needle will no longer kick. Thus, the problem can be pinpointed without removing the trim, cover plates or tape. If a circuit is fused, the problem can be found in the same way, but a circuit breaker will have to be substituted for the fuse.

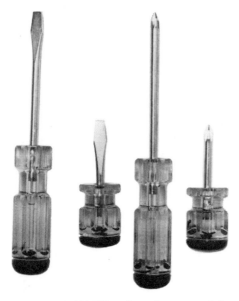

Flatblade and Phillips-head screwdrivers

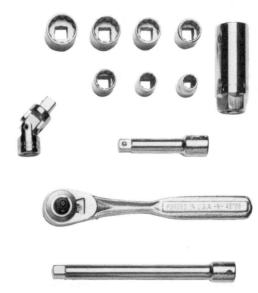

Rachet, sockets, handles, and universal joint

Slip-joint, long-nose, and locking-jaw pliers

Adjustable wrench

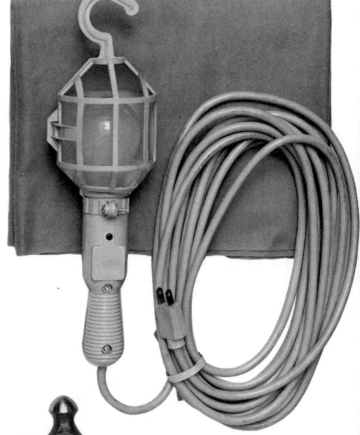

Droplight and fender cover

Ball-peen hammer

BASIC TOOLS

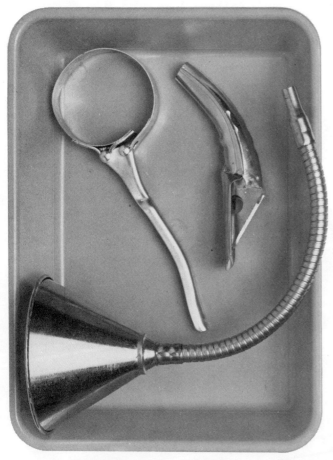

Combination box- and open-end wrenches

Oil changing gear

Check your toolbox and compare its contents with the tools shown at the left. You may already own most of them. But if you're missing any, fill in those you don't have before attempting to work on your car.

Since most home mechanics work on their cars to save money, you'll want to buy the least expensive tools that will *effectively* do the job. As a rule of thumb, you'll find that the very cheapest tool is almost always so inadequate that buying it is a waste of money. And the very best is so superadequate for your purposes that buying it is also a waste of money. Your best bet, then, is the moderately priced tool.

Any specialized tools should be purchased as they're needed. When you think you need a special tool, first ask yourself if there's a way to get the job done—and done right—without it. If there is, you don't really need it. When buying tools, strive to be a money-saver, not a tool collector. Let's run down the list of basic tools:

Screwdrivers. You need at least three flatblade types—small, medium, and large. A short or stubby screwdriver helps you work in tight places. You can get by with two Phillips-head screwdrivers—a #2 and a stubby one.

Pliers. Don't buy cheap pliers. They are awkward to use—they slip, spread their jaws, do not work smoothly, break—and are dangerous to use. Buy a few good ones, rather than a lot of poor-quality ones. Your toolbox should have at least three: a 6- to 8-inch long slip-joint steel pliers; long-nose pliers about six inches long; and a pair of locking-jaw pliers.

Adjustable wrench. One's enough. Use it when you can't carry a complete set of fixed-opening wrenches with you or for turning nuts and bolts of odd sizes.

Ratchet wrenches and sockets. Actually you'll need only one or two ratchet handles to turn your many sockets. Sockets come in standard depths for most nuts and deep sizes for removing spark plugs and nuts that have a lot of bolt sticking out from them. Check your car's plugs and then get the right socket—$13/_{16}$-inch or $5/_8$-inch—to handle them. A universal socket is handy when a bolt or nut is difficult to reach.

Combination wrenches. One end is a box wrench, the other an open-end wrench. With a box wrench, you can apply more torque to a tight nut or bolt without the risk of the wrench slipping off. An open-end wrench, however, slips easily over a nut or bolt and does not have to be lifted off every time it is repositioned. It pays to buy a set of wrenches.

Ball-peen hammer. This is the basic hammer for auto mechanics. Get a good one with an 8-, 12-, or 16-ounce head. Never hit a hardened surface with it, which can chip or split the head.

Droplight. For working directly on your car, you need either a standard droplight (shown) or one of the newer fluorescent tube droplights, which are much more expensive, but easier and safer to work with.

Fender cover. It's expensive, but useful to have. If you don't want to spend the money for the professional type, use an old shower curtain, blanket or beach towel.

Oil changing gear. You'll need a drain pan (get one large enough to hold all your car's oil and then some), an oil filter wrench, a flexible-neck funnel (for transmission fluid), and a combination opener and pour spout.

BASIC MAINTENANCE TUNEUP

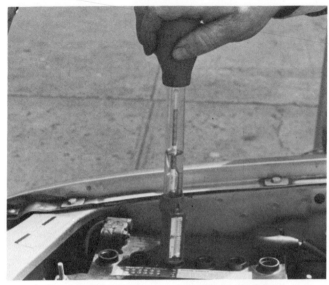

1 Service battery and battery cables

Before getting into the specific operations of a basic engine tuneup, it will be helpful for you to know the steps involved. While the definition of tuneup may vary from home mechanic to home mechanic, the following 15 basic steps should be included in any good maintenance tuneup. The tuneup outlined in the first ten chapters of this book is more comprehensive and covers a greater number of engine components and systems than the 15 Photosteps shown here. No explanatory text is included with this basic tuneup outline as each step will be discussed in detail in its proper place in the ensuing chapters. Since an engine tuneup must follow a definite procedure, it is important that the do-it-yourselfer carry out the steps in the order given. If your car is equipped with an electronic ignition system, it will have no points or condenser. Therefore, exclude the steps for point service. All other service procedures should be followed.

4 Check and service distributor

TOOLS FOR A BASIC MAINTENANCE TUNEUP

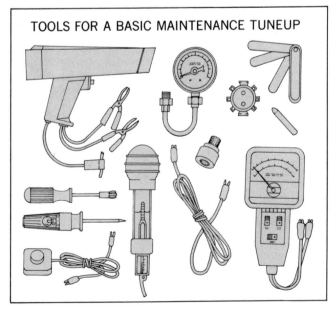

7 Check and adjust ignition timing

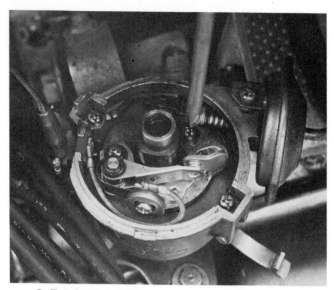

2 Perform compression and vacuum tests

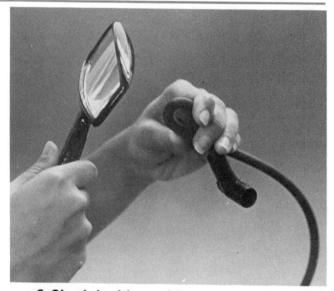

3 Replace breaker points and condenser and adjust points

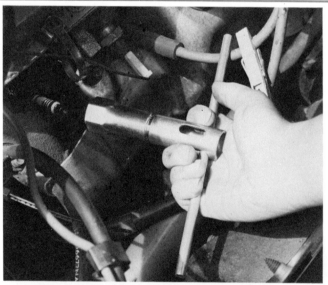

5 Remove and service spark plugs

6 Check ignition cables

8 Inspect air filter

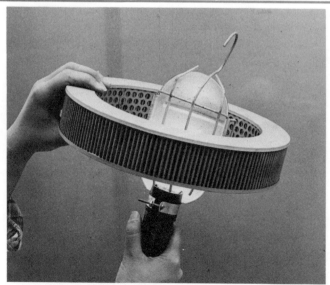

9 Check air cleaner operation ⟶

10 Replace PCV (Positive Crankcase Ventilation) valve and filter

11 Replace fuel filter

12 Check and service carburetor choke and linkages

13 Check idle speeds

14 Check all vacuum lines and hoses

15 Check emission control components

CHAPTER

BATTERY AND CABLE SERVICE

Battery failure is one of the leading causes of no-start problems year after year. According to the American Automobile Association, road service calls to revive dead batteries account for nearly 50% of its emergency service. During cold weather, this figure jumps to nearly 70%. Every winter dead batteries leave almost 40 million motorists stranded on the road or in their driveway. Although it is the heart of the automobile—if it fails, you don't move—it's also one of the most neglected components. Yet, there is no part of the car that's easier for you to maintain.

If you're serious about tuning up your car—and you wouldn't be reading this book if you weren't—you must start with the battery. It must be in good condition in order for you to test and service the other systems that keep your car running.

Knowing how the battery works, what it does and, just as important, what it *doesn't* do, is the first step toward good battery housekeeping. The battery is basically an energy bank. It stores electricity deposited by the alternator which changes the turning action of the engine into electric power. If the alternator does not make enough electricity, all the energy will be withdrawn from the battery and it will fail. To keep your battery alive and well, check its electrolyte level every time the gas tank is filled. Look for cracks, leaks, bulges, and dirt. See that the terminals are making good contact with the battery posts, and that the battery is fully charged.

Spot these early warning signs that signal something could be wrong with your battery: You're having trouble starting your car. The lights are dim when the engine is running. Your flashers and blinkers are sluggish. Your engine doesn't have any spunk. You've been jump-starting your car too many times lately. Any one of these symptoms could mean a problem in the battery or the charging system.

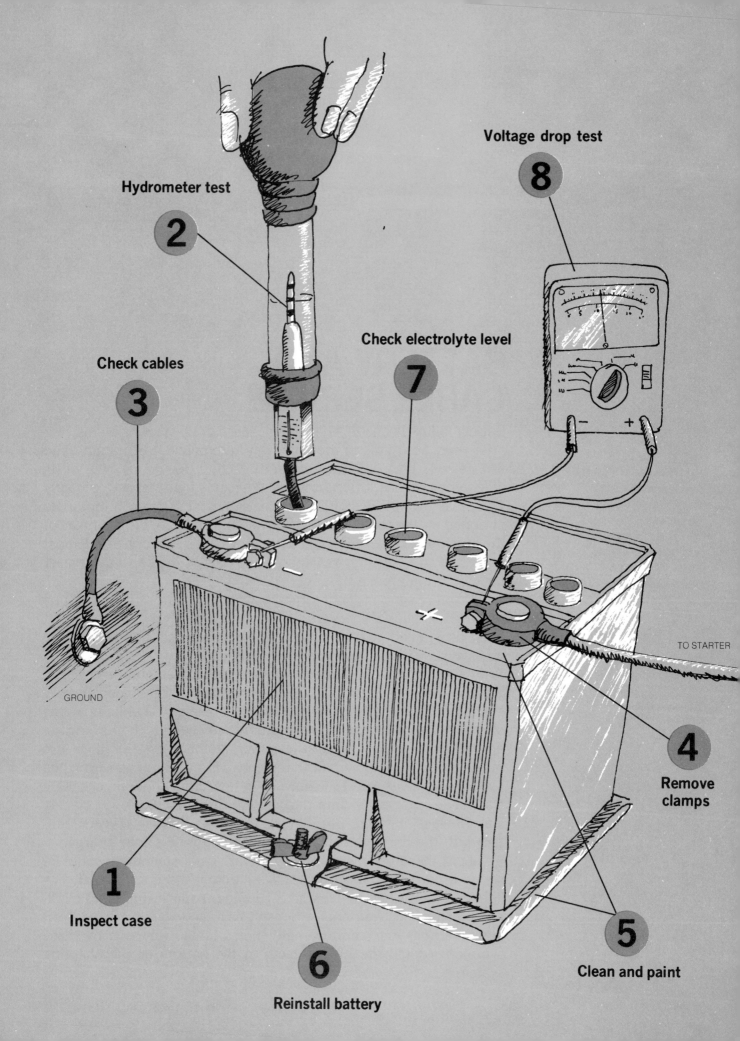

Hydrometer test

2

Check cables

3

Check electrolyte level

7

Voltage drop test

8

GROUND

TO STARTER

Remove clamps

4

1

Inspect case

6

Reinstall battery

5

Clean and paint

Job Steps

Battery and Cable Service

1 **Inspect case.** Place a fender cover near the battery and inspect the case and top for cracks, leaks, bulges, warpage, and dirt (p. 28). Perform battery leakage test (p. 28).

2 **Hydrometer test.** This measures the specific gravity of the battery's electrolyte, which is a mixture of water and acid in the cells (p. 28). A reading above 1.225 means the battery is OK for further testing (p. 29), as long as the individual cell readings don't vary more than .035 points from each other. If they do, replace the battery (p. 31). If the specific gravity is below specs, fast-charge the battery (p. 32) and retest with the hydrometer (p. 28). If the battery fails the test again, replace it.

3 **Check cables.** Inspect the cables for breaks and wear. Replace, if necessary (p. 29).

4 **Remove clamps.** Remove the cable clamps from the battery posts. Inspect them and the terminals for deposits and corrosion (p. 29).

5 **Clean and paint.** Remove the hold-down clamps and lift out the battery with a lifting strap (p. 30). Set the battery on a solid surface away from the car and clean the case, top, clamps, and posts. Replace parts as needed (p. 30). Clean the battery shelf (box) and hold-down clamps and paint with an acid-resistant paint (p. 30).

6 **Reinstall battery.** Return the battery to the box and reinstall the hold-down clamps and battery cables (p. 31).

7 **Check electrolyte level.** Remove all cell caps to make sure all plates are covered with electrolyte. If not, add distilled or mineral-free water to each cell needing electrolyte. Fast-charge the battery to mix the water and acid (p. 32). For maintenance-free batteries, check the visual state-of-charge indicator (p. 32).

8 **Voltage drop test.** To find out if your battery is putting out enough power to start the car under all conditions, perform a cranking voltage drop test with a voltmeter (p. 32). If the reading is above 9.5 volts (9 volts on a small battery), the battery is OK. If it's not, charge the battery and retest (p. 32). Slow-charging is best, but if you're in a hurry, fast-charge it (p. 32). If the battery still fails the voltage test, you may have to replace it. But before you do, check the starter (p. 49). A battery must always be charged after a voltage drop test. A 15- to 30-minute fast-charge at a medium rate should do the job (p. 32).

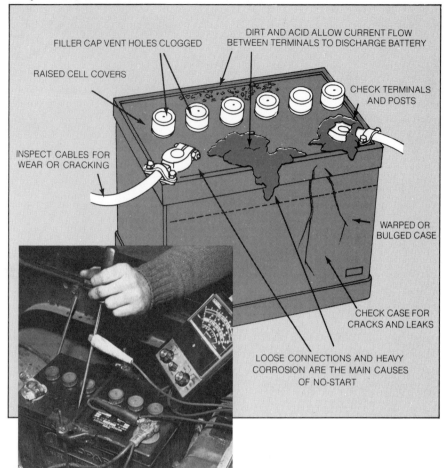

TOOLS

Essential. Basic tools (p. 20) ·
Goggles · Jumper cables · Fender
cover · Hydrometer · Wire brush ·
Water (distilled or mineral-free) ·
Baking soda or ammonia · Petroleum
jelly · Towels or clean rags ·
Voltmeter · Terminal spreader.
Handy. Cable terminal puller ·
Battery post cleaning tool · Terminal
adapter (for side-terminal batteries) ·
Battery charger · Lifting strap ·
Battery pliers · Remote starter switch.

Step 1 Inspect Case

FILLER CAP VENT HOLES CLOGGED

DIRT AND ACID ALLOW CURRENT FLOW
BETWEEN TERMINALS TO DISCHARGE BATTERY

RAISED CELL COVERS

CHECK TERMINALS
AND POSTS

INSPECT CABLES FOR
WEAR OR CRACKING

WARPED OR
BULGED CASE

CHECK CASE FOR
CRACKS AND LEAKS

LOOSE CONNECTIONS AND HEAVY
CORROSION ARE THE MAIN CAUSES
OF NO-START

Leakage test. Sometimes your battery
will have such a slight hairline crack, you
won't be able to notice it with the naked
eye. If it goes undetected, it can cause
the battery to discharge. To check for
this type of leakage, hook up a voltmeter
to the battery, negative-to-negative.
Attach the positive voltmeter lead to a
screwdriver blade. Move the screwdriver
around the entire battery case, taking
care not to touch the positive battery
terminal. At the same time, watch the
voltmeter needle. If the needle moves, it
means the battery is discharging. Clean
the battery thoroughly and retest (p. 30).
If the voltmeter needle still moves, the
battery has a crack and should be
replaced.

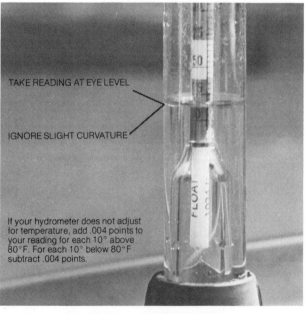

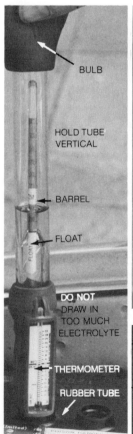

BULB

HOLD TUBE
VERTICAL

BARREL

FLOAT

DO NOT
DRAW IN
TOO MUCH
ELECTROLYTE

THERMOMETER

RUBBER TUBE

TAKE READING AT EYE LEVEL

IGNORE SLIGHT CURVATURE

If your hydrometer does not adjust
for temperature, add .004 points to
your reading for each 10° above
80°F. For each 10° below 80°F
subtract .004 points.

Step 2 Hydrometer Test

The tool. A battery's acid and water
mixture, called electrolyte, is checked
with a hydrometer, which measures
specific gravity (density or weight). The
tool consists of a glass tube with a
rubber bulb on one end and a hose on
the other end. When electrolyte is drawn
into the tube, a calibrated float measures
specific gravity. A good hydrometer is
designed with a thermometer to
compensate for variations in
temperature. It's inexpensive, so get the
best and save yourself the trouble of
correcting for temperature.
The test. Remove all caps from the
battery cells. First squeeze the
hydrometer bulb, then insert the rubber
hose into the first cell, keeping the
hydrometer straight up. Release the bulb
and draw fluid into the tube until the float
rises freely. *Caution: Don't let acid drip
on you or your car. Wearing protective
clothing and goggles when working on a
battery is a good idea.* Make a note of
the number or letter on the float. Empty
the electrolyte into the same cell it was
drawn from. Test all cells and write down
the results. A fully-charged battery
should read 1.280, a half-charged
battery should read 1.220, and a dead
battery will have a reading below
1.190. These figures depend on the
temperature. All the cells must be within
.025 of each other. If they're not,
replace the battery.

PERCENTAGE-OF-CHARGE TABLE		
STATE OF CHARGE	STANDARD SPECIFIC GRAVITY AS USED IN TEMPERATE CLIMATES	SPECIFIC GRAVITY IN CELLS BUILT WITH EXTRA WATER CAPACITY
Fully charged	1.280	1.260
75% charged	1.250	1.230
50% charged	1.220	1.200
25% charged	1.190	1.170
Discharged	1.130	1.110

Step 3 Check Cables

When the insulation is frayed, the exposed wire encourages corrosion, which builds up resistance in the cable and causes hard starting. Frayed cables should be replaced.

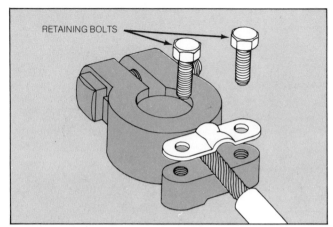

If only the terminal clamp is damaged, as a temporary repair, don't bother replacing the whole cable. Just cut off the damaged clamp, strip off about ¾ inch of insulation, and install a replacement clamp, as shown.

Step 4 Remove Clamps

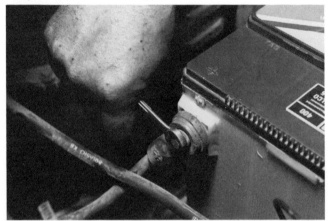

On side-terminal batteries, loosen the negative (−) cable retaining bolt first and then remove the cable at the point where it's grounded. This will prevent arcing (electricity leaping the gap between two electrodes).

On some other types of batteries, loosen the cable retaining bolts with the proper wrench. Then lift the cables off the battery posts. Again, remove the negative cable first at the point where it's grounded.

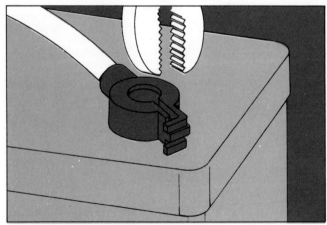

Spring-type terminal clamps, usually found on older General Motors cars, can be removed by squeezing the tabs on the terminals with pliers and lifting the cable off the battery posts.

Use a cable terminal puller if the cable terminals are difficult to remove. Place the legs of the puller under the cable terminal and tighten the puller screw until the clamp comes off.

Step 5 Clean and Paint

1 To remove the battery from the box, disconnect the cables from the battery, and then remove the hold-down clamps. Before you can budge the clamps, you first may have to remove any rust with a wire brush and apply penetrating oil to the bolts. The safest way to remove the battery is with a lifting strap.

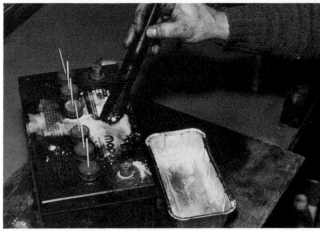

2 Now mix a solution of baking soda or ammonia with water. To prevent this solution from getting into the cells, plug each cell cap vent hole with a toothpick. Then brush the mixture on the battery and the box. Scrub vigorously with a brush, then rinse thoroughly with clean water and wipe dry.

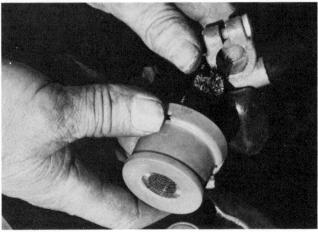

3 Clean the cable terminals and battery posts with a special tool. The one shown above is for top-terminal batteries. There is also a special cleaning tool for side-terminal batteries.

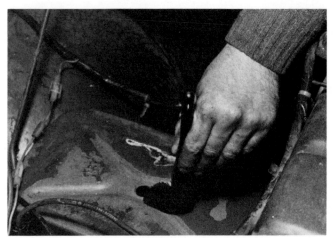

4 After cleaning the box and the hold-down clamps, paint them thoroughly with acid-resistant paint or undercoating. This step is important because when the box is covered with dirt or acid, contamination can cause battery discharge.

Check Your Ground

Many of today's cars use a pigtail wire as the battery ground between the negative post of the battery and the body sheet metal. The ground path for parts of the electrical system, such as headlights, horn, and heater blower motor, is from the battery negative post through the pigtail to the body sheet metal. There may be a poor ground because of loose or dirty connections at the area shown in the illustration, resulting in dimmed headlights and on-again-off-again accessory performance. Check for a bad ground with a voltmeter. With the engine off and the headlights on, check the voltage reading between the alternator bracket and the fender. A reading other than zero indicates a poor ground. Check that pigtail. It may just be corroded or rusted. Scrape it clean and reinstall it, making sure the fit is tight.

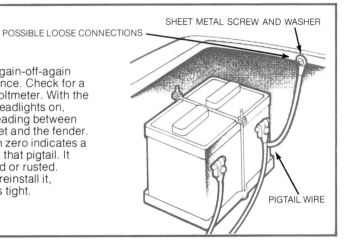

POSSIBLE LOOSE CONNECTIONS

SHEET METAL SCREW AND WASHER

PIGTAIL WIRE

Step 6 Reinstall Battery

1 To reinstall top-terminal cables, you first may have to spread the terminals with a special spreading tool, shown above. Always replace the positive (+) terminal first.

2 After tightening the bolts with the proper wrench, making sure the terminals are tight on the battery posts, coat the terminals with petroleum jelly to retard corrosion.

Jump'er

1 Read the precautions on this page first.
2 Connect the red jumper cable to the positive (+) terminal of the battery to be jumped and to the positive (+) cable of the jumping car's battery.
3 Connect the negative (−) or black cable to the negative (−) cable of the jumping car.
4 Connect the other end of the negative (−) jumper cable to a good ground, the alternator bracket or a nut or bolt on the engine of the car to be jumped. Do not connect this end to the negative (−) battery post!
5 Start the engine of the car with the boosting battery and turn on the ignition of the car with the disabled battery.
6 When the disabled battery has been boosted, disconnect the cables, reversing the above order.

Jump-starting an engine with the battery from another car is a common procedure, but it can be dangerous if precautions are not taken. Follow these do's and don'ts before hooking up the cables:
Do turn off your ignition and all electrical accessories to avoid draining any power that might still be left in your battery.
Do put your transmission in Park (automatic) or Neutral (manual) and your parking brake on.
Do wear eye protection, gloves, and other protective clothing to guard against splashing acid.
Do remove all cell caps from the disabled battery and cover the openings completely with a damp cloth.
Do check the electrolyte level in the cells and add water, if necessary.
Don't jump the battery if the electrolyte is frozen. The battery could explode.
Don't smoke or hold a flame near the battery.
Do be sure the two cars are not touching.
Do throw away all acid-soaked cloths.

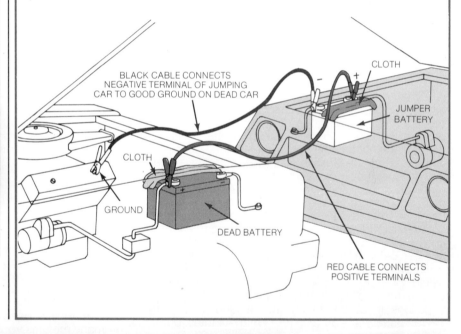

BLACK CABLE CONNECTS NEGATIVE TERMINAL OF JUMPING CAR TO GOOD GROUND ON DEAD CAR

CLOTH

JUMPER BATTERY

CLOTH

GROUND

DEAD BATTERY

RED CABLE CONNECTS POSITIVE TERMINALS

How Not to Blow Up Your Battery

The battery in your car is a potential bomb. If you don't take the proper precautions, it could blow up in your face. The danger is greatest when you are using a charger, boosting a dead battery, and boosting a frozen battery.

A battery always has hydrogen gases around the top. Any spark could ignite and explode these gases, so never smoke when working on a battery, and always ventilate the area around it. Remove all the vent caps and cover the openings with a damp cloth. This will act as a flame arrester and allow the gases to pass out. Turn on the charger switch only after all hookups have been made. Connect the positive clamp to the positive post first. Connect the negative clamp to a good ground at least a foot away from the battery. Make sure all electrically-operated components are turned off. After charging, switch off the charger before disconnecting the clamps.

When boosting, open the hood of the car to be boosted to allow gases around the battery to blow away while you're getting out the jumper cables. Take the vent caps off and cover the holes with a damp cloth. Hook up the positive clamps first. Hook up the negative cable on the car to be jumped to a good ground—an engine bolt or the alternator bracket. Remove the cables in reverse order.

A good way to blow up your battery is to boost it while the electrolyte is frozen. Let the ice melt first, and make sure each cell is free of ice.

Step 7 Check Electrolyte Level

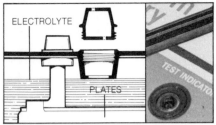

Check the electrolyte level of your battery every time you fill the gas tank. If it needs fluid, fill each cell with distilled or mineral-free water. Make sure the water covers the plates inside the cells up to a point just below the bottom of the lip at the base of the filler hole, never higher. If your car has a maintenance-free battery, it does not have removable cell caps. If the water level is low, the battery must be replaced. A sight glass on the top of the battery lets you check the state-of-charge. Green means OK—the battery is ready for further testing. If the indicator is dark, the battery should be charged until the green dot appears. Light or yellow means the battery must be replaced.

Step 8 Voltage Drop Test

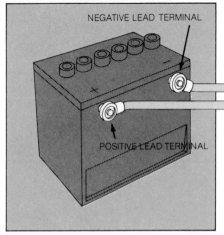

The cranking voltage drop test checks the battery's capacity and its ability to deliver and hold the least amount of voltage needed to start your car under all conditions. Before proceeding with this test, make sure the battery has a specific gravity of at least 1.220 and its electrolyte is temperature-corrected (p. 28). Next, remove the air cleaner, unhook the high-voltage coil wire from the center tower of the distributor cap so the car won't start while you're cranking the engine, and ground the coil wire. Now connect the positive lead terminal of the voltmeter to the positive post of the battery and the negative lead terminal to the negative post. Connect a remote control starter switch to the solenoid or the relay (p. 44). Crank the engine with this switch for about ten seconds and, at the same time, observe the voltage reading. It should not drop below 9.5 volts. If it does, the battery may have a weak or defective cell. To check, recharge the battery and then retest. If it still reads below 9.5 volts, replace the battery.

Charge It!

If your battery is dead but the electrolyte meets specs, the battery can be recharged. The best way to do this is with a trickle or slow-charge. There is less wear and tear on the battery and it will take a fuller charge. A slow-charger is one that charges about five or six amp and takes over 16 hours to fully charge a battery. Before charging, prepare the battery by adding water, if needed, and removing the vent caps. Now connect the positive (+) clamp of the charger to the positive (+) battery terminal and the negative (−) clamp to the negative (−) terminal. Charge until the electrolyte's specific gravity does not increase on three consecutive 1-hour readings. If it does, cut the charge rate down to its minimum and charge one hour longer. Don't let battery temperature exceed 125°F (51.6°C), and don't forget to compensate for temperature. If battery temperature exceeds 125°F, reduce the charging rate. Unplug the charger before removing the clamps to avoid sparks.

Prepare a battery for fast-charging the same way you would for slow-charging. To set the charging rate and time period, follow the equipment manufacturer's instructions. If you don't know the rate and time, charge a 12-volt battery at a 35-amp rate for 20 minutes, but don't let the electrolyte temperature go above 124°F (51°C). Control the rate so it does not cause excessive gassing and loss of electrolyte. Don't fast-charge a battery for more than one hour without checking the specific gravity. If specific gravity shows no significant change after one hour, revert to the slow-charge method.

FAST-CHARGE TIMETABLE		
FAST-CHARGE TIME	STANDARD SPECIFIC GRAVITY AS USED IN TEMPERATE CLIMATES	SPECIFIC GRAVITY IN CELLS BUILT WITH EXTRA WATER CAPACITY
1 hour	1.150 or less	1.135 or less
¾ hour	1.150 to 1.175	1.135 to 1.160
½ hour	1.175 to 1.200	1.160 to 1.185
¼ hour	1.200 to 1.225	1.185 to 1.210
*slow charge	above 1.225	above 1.210

*In order to fully charge a battery, the period of fast-charge recommended above should be followed by a period of slow charge until the specific gravity reading indicates a fully-charged battery.

All About **Buying a Battery**

Now that you're pretty sure you need a new battery, how do you decide the right one for your car? The big question you should ask yourself is: Will the battery deliver on the coldest morning? The amount of power a battery puts out on a zero-degree day is called *cold-cranking performance* and it is that rating you should be looking at first when shopping for a battery. When the mercury dips to zero, a 60-month battery can shoot around 500 amps to your starter. An 18-month unit, on the other hand, will ooze only 240 amps.

How can you tell what your car's cold-cranking requirement is? Simple. Just take the engine's displacement figure and match it with the battery's cold-cranking rating. In cold climates add 20 percent. For example: You live in Minnesota and drive a Torino with a 351-cubic-inch V8. You'll need a battery with a basic cold-cranking rating of at least 350 amps. And since you live in Minnesota, you'll have to add the extra 20 percent or 71 amps. Therefore, in this case, buy a battery with a cold-cranking rating of not less than 422 amps.

Another rating that tells you about a battery's performance is *reserve capacity*. That number tells you how many minutes your car can keep running at night if your alternator dies on you. If a battery has a reserve capacity of 100, it means you can drive for 100 minutes on a balmy night without an alternator before the battery stops working altogether.

Once you've checked out cold-cranking and reserve capacity, your next considerations when buying a battery should be warranty and price. If you think you'll keep your car longer than the cold-cranking rating dictates, then by all means go to a more generous warranty. The longer the warranty, the higher the price.

Battery warranties come in various forms. The most common offer an initial free replacement period of 90 days. After that, the rest of the warranty is broken down and prorated by months. If you buy a 36-month battery for $36, each month is worth $1. So if your battery fails at 24 months, you have $12 worth of credit toward another battery from the same store.

CHAPTER

CHARGING SYSTEM SERVICE

Simply put, the charging system replaces the power that the car uses up. It also operates the car's electrical system after the battery has done its job in starting the engine. But it can't do its job unless three conditions are met: The charging system, particularly the alternator, must be in good working order; the drive belt must have proper tension, and the engine must be running.

The alternator is really a generator that manufactures electricity to charge the battery. It's much like a city reservoir, which must always be ready to replace the water consumed by the city's population. If the reservoir ran dry, the city would soon cease to function. If the alternator stopped making electricity, the battery would soon run down and the car would also cease to function.

The alternator can only do its job if the engine is running. It takes the mechanical power created by the engine via the fan belt and turns it into electrical power, which it then puts into the battery. A voltage regulator, acting like a faucet, controls the amount of electricity going into the battery, based on demand.

How can you tell if your alternator is not keeping up? One of the early warning signs is a sluggish battery. You'll probably be troubled by hard starting. The alternator warning light will come on or, if your car has an ammeter, it will indicate no charge or discharge. Once you've satisfied yourself that the battery is in good working condition, check out the drive belt and the charging rate of the alternator. If you find you have to replace the alternator, make sure you get the right one for your car. Alternators are rated according to their amperage output—45 amp, 55 amp, and so on—so ask for one that way when making your purchase. If the alternator, voltage regulator or battery fails repeatedly, it means something is wrong in the charging system. Remember the system is designed for a particular electrical load. So if you've added an accessory to your car, it could be drawing more power than your alternator was built to deliver.

The only maintenance for the charging system is to keep the drive belts at the proper tension and in good condition, make sure all mounting bolts are tightened correctly, and that all connections are tight and free of corrosion and dirt.

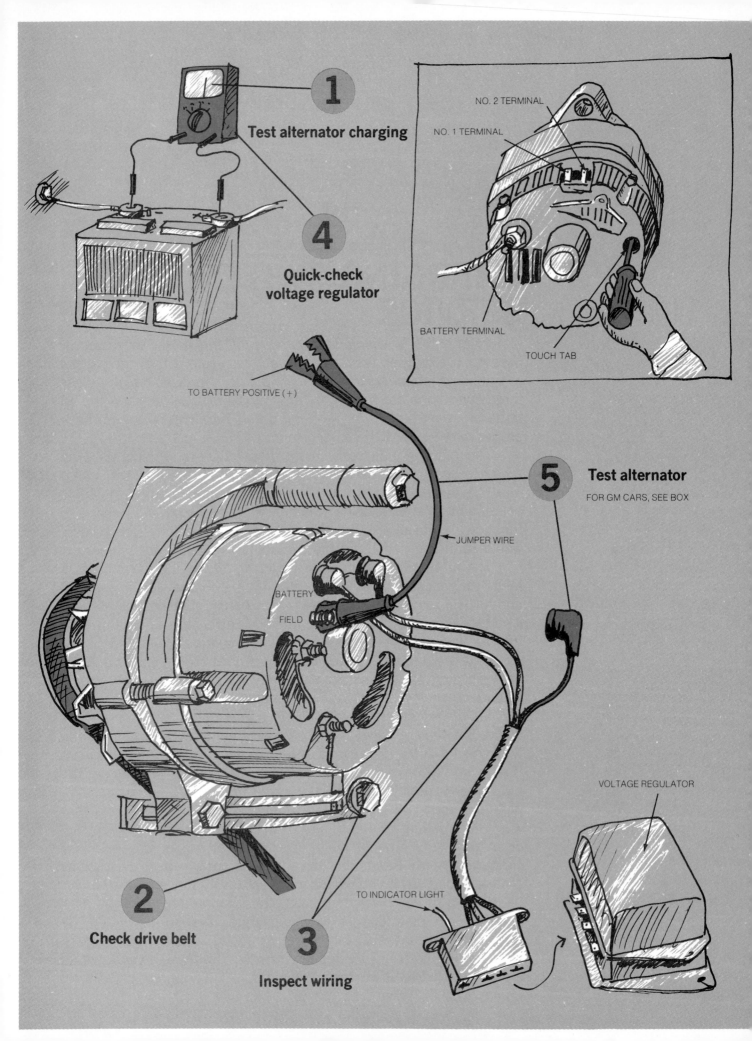

1

Test alternator charging

4

**Quick-check
voltage regulator**

NO. 2 TERMINAL

NO. 1 TERMINAL

BATTERY TERMINAL

TOUCH TAB

TO BATTERY POSITIVE (+)

5 **Test alternator**

FOR GM CARS, SEE BOX

JUMPER WIRE

BATTERY

FIELD

VOLTAGE REGULATOR

2

Check drive belt

3

TO INDICATOR LIGHT

Inspect wiring

Job Steps

Charging System Service

Prep: Check the battery. Make sure it's in a good state of charge (p. 28).

1 Test alternator charging. First connect a voltmeter to the battery and note the voltage (p. 36). A battery in a good state of charge should read at least 12 volts. Then start the engine. The voltmeter should now read close to charging voltage for your car, or about 13.8 to as high as 15.0 volts. If the charging rate is below specs, shut the engine off and go to Step 2.

2 Check drive belt. Turn the alternator pulley by hand. If it moves easily, the belt is slipping and should be adjusted (p. 36). Repeat the test in Step 1.

3 Inspect wiring. Check the alternator and regulator wiring for looseness and corrosion. Make sure all the connections are clean and tight (p. 37), and that the alternator and regulator are well-grounded (p. 37).

4 Quick-check voltage regulator. Run the engine at fast idle, 1500 to 2000 rpm, and note the voltmeter reading. If it's more than two volts higher than the battery voltage reading (see the reading in Step 1), let the engine run until the voltage reading reaches its highest value. If the voltage keeps climbing, the regulator is faulty and you should replace it (p. 38).

5 Test alternator. Check the field (F) terminal(s) on the alternator (p. 38). If improperly grounded, the alternator will not charge. Disconnect the field terminal for a minute or two, run the engine at fast idle and note the voltmeter reading (p. 38). If it drops, the field is OK, but the regulator may be faulty (p. 38). If it doesn't drop, check the field wiring in the charging system by connecting a jumper wire between the battery positive (+) terminal and the field terminal on the alternator. Make sure the regulator plug has been disconnected. Now read the voltmeter. At fast idle, it should read 14 volts or more. *Caution: Do not allow the voltage to exceed 15.5 volts. If it does, it could cause damage to the alternator.*

Essential. Basic tools (p. 20).
Jumper wire with female spade
terminal • Jumper wire • Straightedge •
Ruler • Spring clothespin • Voltmeter.
Handy. Fender cover • Droplight or
flashlight • Belt tension gauge •
Fuse puller.

Step 1 Test Alternator Charging

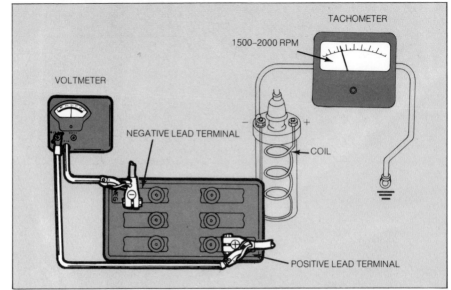

If your ammeter gauge or alternator light
shows a low charge, no charge or
discharge condition, perform this quick
test to see if the problem is in the
alternator or regulator. First connect a
voltmeter to the battery, with the red
lead going to the battery positive (+)
terminal and the black lead to the battery
negative (−) terminal. Make a note of
the battery's voltage. Now start the
engine and run it at fast idle, about 1500
to 2000 rpm. Note the voltage reading
and compare it with the battery voltage
reading. The reading with the engine
running should be about two volts
higher. If it is, the alternator and
regulator are probably OK. See Step 4
for a further check. If the reading isn't
higher, go on to the next step.

Step 2 Check Drive Belt

The drive (alternator or fan) belt must be adjusted to the
correct tightness or torque. If it's too loose, your battery
may not charge, or it may lose its ability to start the engine. If the belt is too tight, it can damage the alternator
bearings. Belts will usually tell you they're too loose by a
loud squealing noise. A loose drive belt usually makes
this kind of noise when a cold engine is started or when
the car is suddenly accelerated. To check the drive belt
for looseness, turn the alternator pulley by hand. If it
moves easily, the belt is probably slipping.

To check drive belt tension, place a
tension gauge halfway between the
alternator pulley and the fan pulley.
Instructions for the use of the gauge will
usually be found on the tool itself. If you
don't have a belt tension gauge, you can
check belt tightness with a straightedge
and a ruler. Bridge the alternator and fan
pulleys with the straightedge, and press
down on the belt halfway between the
two pulleys with the edge of the ruler.
If the belt sags more than half an inch,
it's too loose.

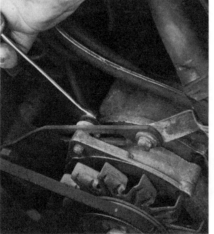

Adjusting drive belt tension. Drive belts
are usually adjusted by moving the part
that is driven by that particular belt.
However, the water pump and fan belts
are adjusted by moving the alternator.
Locate and loosen the adjusting lock
bolt on the alternator. Loosen the pivot
bolt as well. The adjusting bolt is usually
found in a slotted bracket. The pivot bolt
is at the bottom of the alternator on the
front. *Caution: When you want to move a
part with a pry bar, be careful where you
position the bar. Never lean it against*

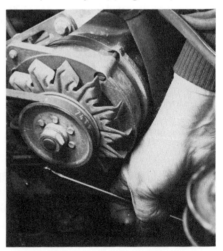

*another part, such as the power-steering
pump reservoir. You could easily loosen
or break off the part. To tighten an
alternator belt, hold the alternator in a
taut position with a pry bar and pry
against the alternator case or the engine
block. Do not lean the bar against the
alternator fins. Check the belt's tension
and, when it's correct, tighten the
alternator's adjusting bolt, and the pivot
bolt. Then recheck.*

Inspect the underside of belts by twisting them. If they are cracked, cut, frayed, glazed or covered with grease, you should replace them.

Replacing Drive Belts

While the instructions in this chapter deal primarily with the belt attached to the alternator, they also apply to the other belts in the engine compartment: the air conditioner, power steering, and air-injection belts. These should be checked periodically and replaced when necessary. To replace any belt, move its accessory toward the engine and slip the belt over the pulleys. To replace a belt near the engine, you must first remove any other belts in front of it. Loop the new belt over the fan or crankshaft pulleys, then over the accessory pulley. Finally, adjust belt tension as shown opposite.

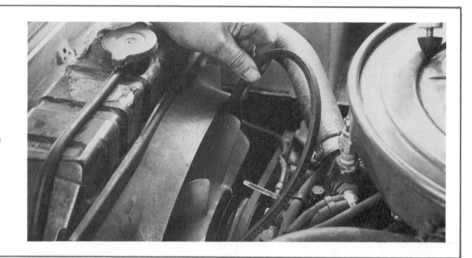

Step 3 Inspect Wiring

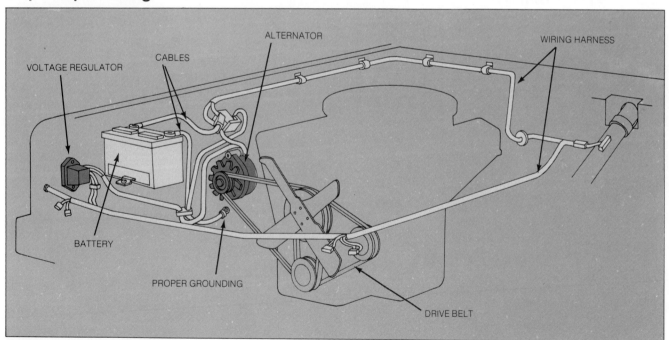

Check all connections at the alternator, the voltage regulator, and the wiring harness for looseness and corrosion. Make sure the alternator and the regulator are grounded properly. Wires are insulated, so check them for cracks, breaks or fraying. Frayed wires may accidentally ground, causing the charging system to short out or to work overtime. Make sure the alternator mounting bolts are tight and properly grounded.

Step 4 Quick-check Voltage Regulator

With the voltmeter hooked up to the battery (positive-to-positive, negative-to-negative), take a reading with the engine running. If it's more than two volts higher than the battery voltage reading (see Step 1), let the engine continue to run at fast idle, between 1500 and 2000 rpm, until the voltage reading reaches its highest value. If the voltage keeps climbing, the regulator is faulty and you should replace it. The job of a regulator is to decrease the voltage from the alternator to the battery when the battery is sufficiently charged.

Replacing the external voltage regulator. Disconnect the wire plug attached to the regulator terminals. Some regulators have a locking clip that must be released before you take out the plug. With the correct socket or screwdriver, remove the regulator screws or bolts. Then install the replacement regulator, tighten the screws or bolts securely, and reconnect the wire plug. Start your engine and test the regulator as described previously.

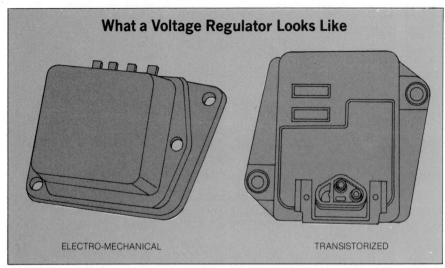

What a Voltage Regulator Looks Like

ELECTRO-MECHANICAL   TRANSISTORIZED

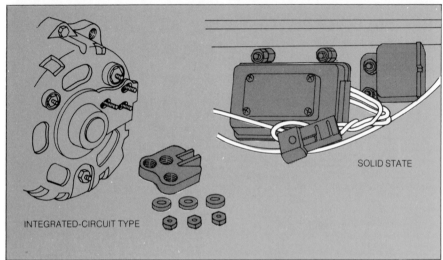

INTEGRATED-CIRCUIT TYPE   SOLID STATE

Step 5 Test Alternator

Testing the Delco-Remy alternator with an external regulator. Disconnect the F-R plug located at the top rear of the alternator housing by pulling the plug straight up. Connect the voltmeter positive lead to the BAT terminal of the alternator and the voltmeter negative lead to a ground. Connect a special jumper wire with a female spade terminal to the F terminal of the alternator. Hook up the other end of the wire to the BAT terminal. *Caution: A spark may occur when you connect the jumper lead to the BAT terminal.* Start the engine and operate it at fast idle, 1500 to 2000 rpm, then observe the voltmeter reading. If it's 15 volts or higher, the alternator is OK. If the voltmeter reads only battery voltage, the alternator is not charging, and should be replaced. But before condemning the alternator, check the fuse. It could be blown. If it is, replace it (p.40), and retest. If the alternator still is not charging, you should replace it. *Caution: Do not operate the alternator under these conditions longer than it is necessary to take a voltmeter reading because the alternator is now running unregulated and could overcharge the battery.* Switch off the engine, disconnect the voltmeter and the jumper wire, and reconnect the F-R plug.

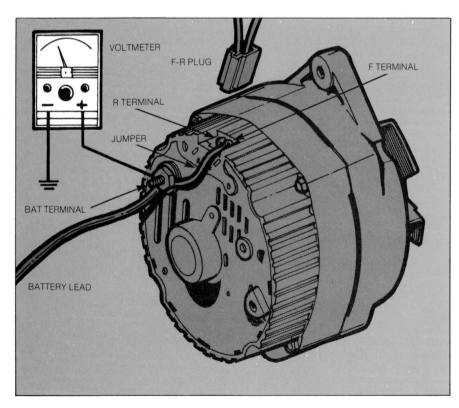

VOLTMETER
F-R PLUG
F TERMINAL
R TERMINAL
JUMPER
BAT TERMINAL
BATTERY LEAD

Replacing the Delco-Remy alternator. If your test indicates that the alternator is not putting out enough power to the battery and the car's electrical system, replace it. Disconnect the battery's negative cable, then remove the F-R plug at the alternator and the BAT wire from its terminal at the rear of the alternator. Now loosen the adjusting bolt and the pivot bolt(s). Push the alternator toward the engine to free the fan belt from the alternator pulley. Remove the belt, the bolts, and the alternator itself from the engine. Reverse this procedure to install the replacement alternator. Adjust the fan belt tension and reconnect all the wires, including the negative battery cable. Start the engine and test the alternator's output (p. 36).

ADJUSTING BOLT

Testing the Chrysler Corporation double-field type alternator. This type of alternator has two field (F) terminal connections. Check the fan belt tension and then connect a voltmeter to the alternator as shown in the illustration. Disconnect both F terminal wires at the rear of the alternator and connect a jumper wire from one F terminal to a ground. Carefully connect a second jumper wire with a female spade terminal (see page 38) from the BAT terminal of the alternator to the second F terminal of the alternator. *Caution: To prevent a short circuit, be sure the second jumper wire touches only the BAT and F terminals. Also, sparks may occur when you connect the second jumper wire.* To test, start the engine and run it at fast idle, about 1500 to 2000 rpm. The voltmeter reading should be 15 to 16 volts for a properly functioning alternator. Switch off the engine and disconnect the two jumper wires and the voltmeter, then reconnect the two F wires. *Caution: Do not run the alternator longer than it is necessary to make this test, since it is operating without the regulator and this could overcharge the battery.* If the voltmeter reading indicates that the alternator is defective, you must replace it. Use the same removal and installation procedures as for the Delco-Remy alternator.

Testing the Chrysler Corporation single-field type alternator. After checking the fan belt for correct tension, connect the positive lead of the voltmeter to the alternator's BAT terminal and the negative lead to a good ground. Remove the F-terminal plug and connect a special jumper wire with a female spade terminal (see page 38) to the F terminal. Connect the other end of the wire to the BAT terminal. *Caution: Sparking may occur at this point, but this is normal.* Now start the engine and run it at fast idle, about 1500 to 2000 rpm. The voltmeter should read at least 15 volts if the alternator is putting out enough power. If it doesn't, the alternator is defective and should be replaced. Follow the same removal and installation procedure as for the Delco-Remy

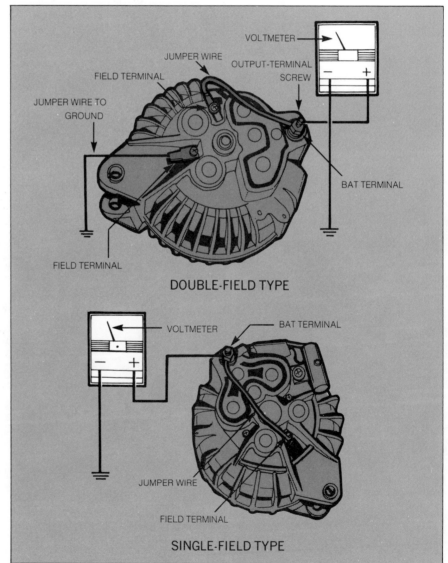

DOUBLE-FIELD TYPE

SINGLE-FIELD TYPE

alternator. However, on some Chrysler models you may have to remove or loosen the power steering pump or air-conditioning compressor to get the old alternator out and the new one in. *Caution: Do not operate the alternator under these conditions longer* *than is necessary to take a voltmeter reading because the alternator is now running unregulated and could overcharge the battery.* Switch off the engine, remove the jumper wire, reconnect the F wire plug, and remove the voltmeter.

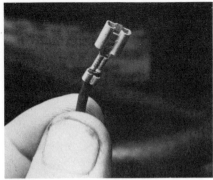

This is a jumper wire with a female spade terminal. Terminals can be bought from a hardware store or auto supply outlet. The do-it-yourselfer can easily fabricate this kind of jumper wire by crimping the terminal on the end of a piece of wire.

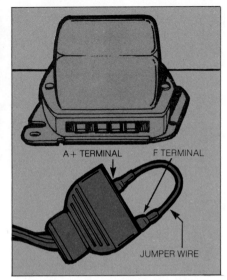

Testing the Ford-type alternator. Locate the regulator, which is usually found on the radiator support near the fender well or on the fire wall. Then release the wire harness plug from the regulator by

loosening the clips on the side of the plug and prying it out with a screwdriver. Locate the F terminal and the A+ terminal of the plug. With a special jumper wire, a short wire with two male plug inserts which look like the terminals of the regulator, connect the F terminal with the A+ terminal of the plug. Connect the positive lead of the voltmeter to the positive post of the battery and the negative lead of the voltmeter to the negative post. Start the engine and operate it at a fast idle, about 1500 to 2000 rpm. The voltmeter reading should indicate 14 to 16 volts. If it does not, the alternator is defective and you should replace it. Remove and install the Ford alternator in the same way as the Delco-Remy alternator (p. 39). When disconnecting the electrical connections, keep in mind that a push-on stator and field connectors are used on the rear-terminal alternator. They should be pulled straight off to prevent damage to the terminal stud. Side-terminal alternators use a push-on blade with a lock tab. Push the tab in before you pull the connections off their terminals.

Replacing Fuses

1 Locate the fuse panels. They are usually attached to the firewall on the driver's side, underneath the dashboard, or in the glove box. Some are located under the hood. Check your driver's manual for the location of the panel and the particular fuse protecting the circuit you are concerned about.

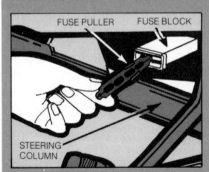

2 Remove the blown fuse. First make sure the ignition is off. Then remove the fuse with a fuse puller, if you have one. If you don't, you can pry it out with half a spring clothespin. To avoid breaking the fuse, use firm, steady pressure. If the fuse is a ceramic one, it can be removed by hand. *Caution: Do not pry fuses out with a screwdriver. This can cause a short or break the fuse in the panel.*
3 Position the new fuse against the retaining clips in the panel. Then press both ends of the fuse inward against the clips until the fuse snaps into place.
4 Check the operation of the circuit which the fuse you replaced was protecting. If the fuse blows, there is a short in the circuit and you should see a professional mechanic.

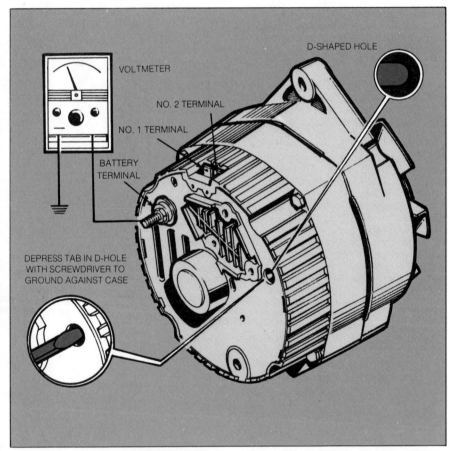

Testing and replacing an alternator with an internal regulator. On alternators with internal regulators, the No. 1 and No. 2 plug terminals are parallel with the rear of the alternator. Check the fan belt tension, then connect the positive voltmeter lead to the alternator's battery terminal. Connect the negative voltmeter lead to the negative post of the battery. Start the engine and allow it to operate at a fast idle, 1500 to 2000 rpm. Insert a screwdriver or straightened cotter pin

into the D-shaped hole in the back of the alternator. If the voltmeter indicates 15 to 16 volts, the alternator is good, but the internal regulator is defective. Remove the cotter pin, switch off the engine, and disconnect the voltmeter. The alternator's defective regulator must be replaced. This should be done only by a qualified alternator rebuilder. Remove the alternator and take it in for servicing.

STARTING SYSTEM SERVICE

The starting system has a brief but important role to play in the operation of the automobile. Its job is to turn the crankshaft until the engine is able to do this under its own power. After the car begins to run, the starting system, with the exception of the battery, disengages itself and is not called on again until the car's engine stops and the driver attempts to restart it. In a well-tuned car, the starting motor and its components are used for only a fraction of a minute each time the engine is started. The starting system is probably the least-used major system in a car. But when it doesn't work, the car simply doesn't move.

The do-it-yourselfer will find it easy to test and replace most components of the starting system, but he should not attempt to repair them. A few components—the starter switch and the 1974–75 GM seat belt interlock system—we feel are beyond the ability of the average home mechanic. So if a problem develops in one of these areas, you should see a professional mechanic.

The starting system works this way: The starter switch releases battery power by way of the starter relay and/or solenoid to the starting motor, which turns the engine crankshaft by engaging a large gear attached to the flywheel.

If you're having a problem starting your car, a quick and easy check is to turn on the headlights. If the lights don't burn brightly, the problem is probably in the battery. If they do burn brightly, crank the engine. If the lights go out, there's probably a weak connection somewhere in the starting circuit (p. 49). If the lights dim, there may be a mechanical problem in the starting motor (p. 49). If the lights stay bright but the engine won't crank, there's probably a circuitry problem in the starter or starter solenoid (p. 48).

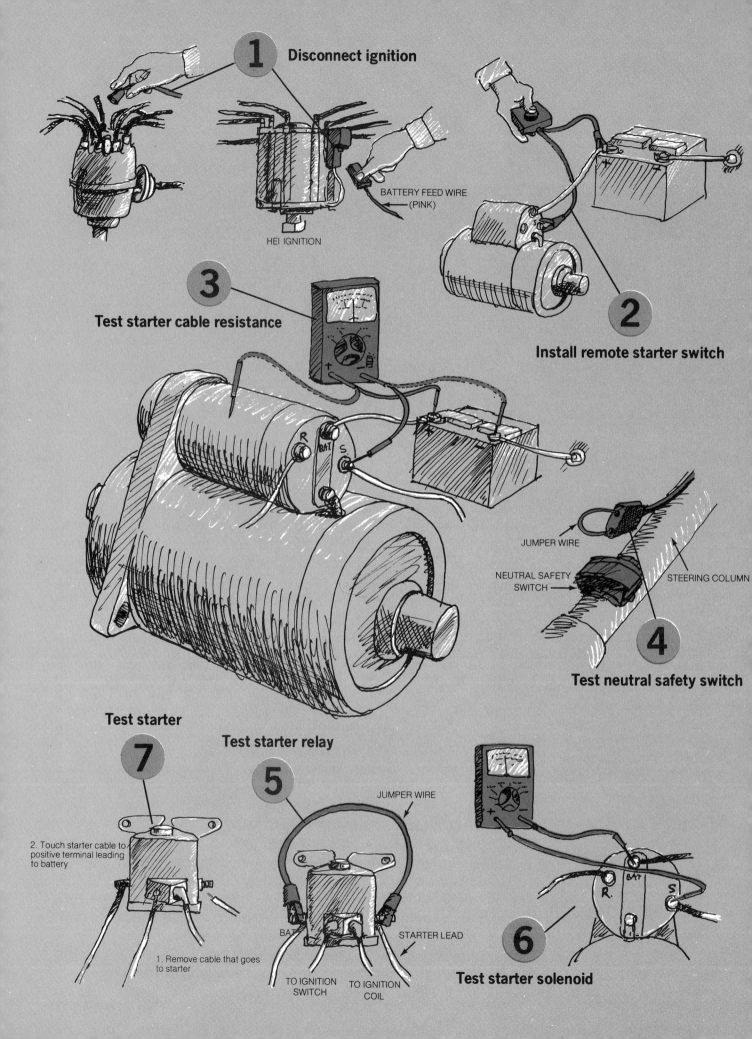

1 Disconnect ignition

BATTERY FEED WIRE
(PINK)

HEI IGNITION

2 Install remote starter switch

3 Test starter cable resistance

JUMPER WIRE

NEUTRAL SAFETY
SWITCH

STEERING COLUMN

4 Test neutral safety switch

7 Test starter

2. Touch starter cable to positive terminal leading to battery

1. Remove cable that goes to starter

5 Test starter relay

JUMPER WIRE

BAT

TO IGNITION
SWITCH

TO IGNITION
COIL

STARTER LEAD

6 Test starter solenoid

R. BAT S.

Job Steps

Starting System Service

Prep: Make sure the battery is in a good state of charge and the cables are tight and free of corrosion (p. 29). Put the transmission in Neutral (manual) or Park (automatic). Then set the parking brake.

1 **Disconnect ignition.** To prevent the engine from starting during the test, remove the coil wire from the center of the distributor cap and ground it with a jumper wire (p. 44). Most cars with HEI (High Energy Ignition) do not have a coil wire, so in these cases disconnect the battery feed wire from the side of the distributor.

2 **Install remote starter switch.** If you don't have a helper to crank the engine from inside the car, you'll need a remote starter switch (p. 44).

3 **Test starter cable resistance.** Use a voltmeter calibrated in tenths of a volt (p. 45).

4 **Test neutral safety switch.** If the engine doesn't crank in either Neutral or Park, it may be due to a faulty neutral safety switch. To test, you'll have to bypass it (p. 45). If the engine starts in any drive gear or in Reverse, the neutral safety switch should be repaired immediately (p. 46). If your car has a manual transmission with a safety start switch on the clutch, this should be tested in the same way as a neutral safety switch is tested (p. 45).

5 **Test starter relay.** Connect a jumper wire on the starter relay between the battery terminal and the ignition terminals on the relay. If the engine cranks, the relay is OK. If it does not crank, the relay is faulty. Replace it.

6 **Test starter solenoid.** There are three different tests for this component, depending on the make of the car you have (p. 47). If the solenoid is faulty and can be removed from the starter, then replace it (p. 48).

7 **Test starter.** It's not easy to check out the starter while it's in the car, but you can do this without removing it by using the starter relay (p. 49).

Essential. Basic tools (p.20). Jumper wire • Voltmeter • Safety stands • Chocks • Drain pan • Jack • Test light.

Handy. Droplight or flashlight • Fender cover • Wire brush or sandpaper • Starter switch.

Step 1 Disconnect Ignition

This is a safety measure to make sure the engine doesn't start during the test. Remove the coil wire from the center of the distributor cap and ground it with a jumper wire. The coil wire is the one that goes between the coil and the distributor cap. *Caution: Never remove the wire from the coil's high tension tower because the spark arcing to the coil primary side could ruin the coil.* Connect the jumper wire between the distributor side of the coil wire and any metal part of the engine. (Some coils are marked DIST. or −.)

To disconnect the HEI ignition system used on some 1974 and all 1975 and later GM cars, disconnect the pink (+) battery feed wire from the side of the distributor cap. On some models, the feed wire is a 2-pronged connector; on others it's only a single wire. Carefully note the terminal the wire belongs on. Putting it on the other terminal will damage the module.

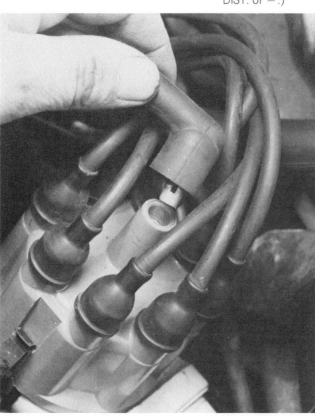

HEI IGNITION

Step 2 Install Remote Starter

Since you'll want to observe the starting system components as you test them, you'll need a remote starter switch to enable you to crank the engine from under the hood if you don't have a helper to sit in the car and crank it. The switch is connected between the positive (+) terminal of the battery and the S terminal of the starter relay or solenoid.

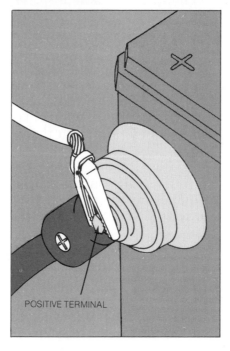

POSITIVE TERMINAL

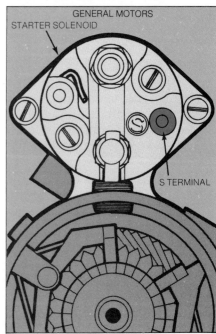

GENERAL MOTORS

STARTER SOLENOID

S TERMINAL

Starter Switch Hookup

FORD

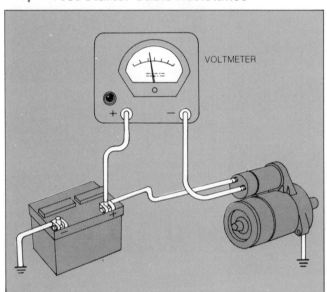

REMOVE THIS WIRE AND ATTACH REMOTE STARTER SWITCH HERE

If your starting system uses a starter relay instead of a solenoid, there are two different hookups for installing a remote starter switch. If your starter relay looks like the one at the left, connect one lead of the remote switch to the battery positive terminal and the other lead to the relay terminal indicated in the drawing. If your relay looks like the one at the right, then the remote switch is connected to the relay's battery and solenoid terminals.

CHRYSLER

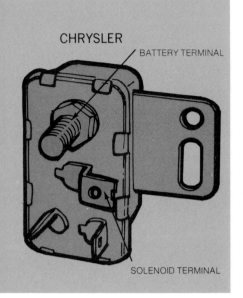

BATTERY TERMINAL

SOLENOID TERMINAL

Step 3 Test Starter Cable Resistance

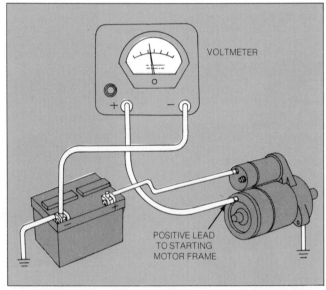

VOLTMETER

VOLTMETER

POSITIVE LEAD TO STARTING MOTOR FRAME

To test the starter cables for resistance, you'll need a voltmeter calibrated in tenths of a volt. Hook up the voltmeter between the battery's positive post and the battery terminal on the starter (positive to positive, negative to starter).

Then check the cable from the battery's positive post to the starter. Crank the engine. If the reading is higher than 0.1 volt, replace the cable. To check for high resistance on the grounded side of the starter circuit, connect the voltmeter

between the battery's negative post and the starter motor frame, then crank the engine. A reading of more than 0.1 volt means there's a lot of resistance in the ground cable and you should repair or replace it.

Step 4 Test Neutral Safety Switch

On American Motors, GM, and some Ford cars, the neutral safety switch is on the steering column inside the passenger compartment between the steering wheel and the floorboard. To test this type of switch, unplug the wires that are attached to the left side, the side facing the parking brake pedal. If the plug has two wires, hook up a jumper wire across the two contacts and turn the ignition to the start position. You have now bypassed the safety switch. If

the starter now cranks the engine, the neutral safety switch is defective and must be replaced. If the plug removed from the neutral safety switch has four wires, attach the jumper wires to the two contacts on the left side of the plug, the side nearest the parking brake pedal. Test the safety switch by cranking the engine. *Caution: With the jumper wire connected, the engine can be started in any gear, which could cause the car to lunge forward or backward.*

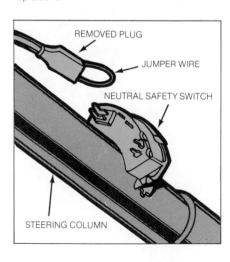

REMOVED PLUG

JUMPER WIRE

NEUTRAL SAFETY SWITCH

STEERING COLUMN

On Ford cars, the starter relay is usually on the inner fender pan close to the battery. First, place the transmission in Neutral or Park and set the parking brake. Then make sure the ignition is in the off position. Pull out the wire connected to the ignition switch terminal. That's the small terminal closest to the positive post of the battery terminal. Connect a jumper wire to the battery post terminal of the relay and touch the other end of the jumper wire to the ignition switch terminal of the relay. If the starter cranks the engine, the neutral safety switch is defective and must be replaced.

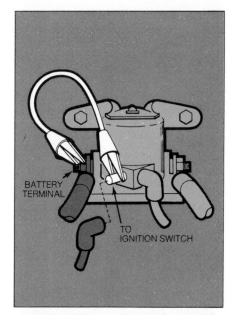

BATTERY TERMINAL

TO IGNITION SWITCH

On Chrysler cars, the starter relay is mounted on the firewall or the inner fender pan. Position the transmission in Park or Neutral and set the parking brake. Connect one end of a jumper wire to the battery terminal on the starter relay and the other end to the ignition terminal. If the engine cranks, the starter relay is OK. If it doesn't crank, connect a second jumper wire on the starter relay between a ground terminal and a good ground. If the engine now cranks, the starter relay is OK, but either the transmission linkage needs adjustment or the neutral safety switch is defective. If the engine does not crank, the relay is defective and must be replaced.

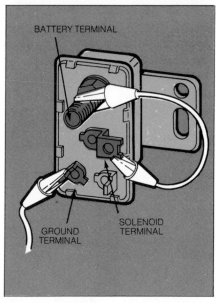

BATTERY TERMINAL

GROUND TERMINAL

SOLENOID TERMINAL

Adjusting the Neutral Safety Switch

Sometimes the screws attaching the neutral safety switch to the steering column become stripped and will not hold the switch in proper adjustment. A worm-type hose clamp can be used to anchor the switch in position. To provide clearance for the projections on the steering column, notch one side of the clamp. Put the shift lever in Neutral and set the parking brake. Remove the stripped screws from the

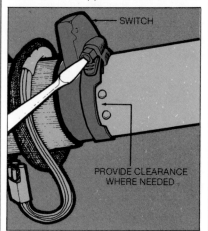

SWITCH

PROVIDE CLEARANCE WHERE NEEDED

switch, then hold the selector level against the Neutral stop, full left of the Neutral position. Install the clamp and test switch operation. The engine should start with the selector lever in Neutral or Park, but not in Drive or Reverse. Readjust the switch if it does not function correctly. If the starter does not crank the engine when the transmission is in Park, loosen the screws holding the neutral safety switch and move the switch slightly clockwise, toward the accelerator pedal. Tighten the screws and try the starter again.

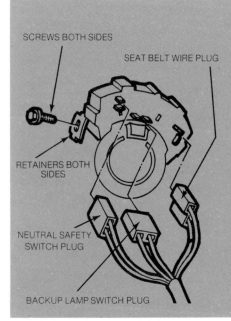

SCREWS BOTH SIDES

SEAT BELT WIRE PLUG

RETAINERS BOTH SIDES

NEUTRAL SAFETY SWITCH PLUG

BACKUP LAMP SWITCH PLUG

Replacing the Neutral Safety Switch

To replace the neutral safety switch mounted on the steering column, unplug the wires that are plugged into it. Now remove the two screws holding the switch to the column, and take out the switch. Install the new switch and plug the wires into it.

To replace the neutral safety switch mounted on the transmission, jack up and support the front of the car with safety stands and place chocks behind the rear wheels. If the neutral safety switch is screwed into the transmission case, place a drain pan directly below the switch to catch

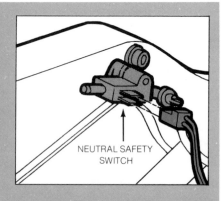

NEUTRAL SAFETY SWITCH

any oil that may drip when it is removed. Unhook the wire(s) connected to the switch and remove it. Now install the new switch and connect the wire(s). Remove the safety stands, lower the car, and replace any transmission fluid that may have been lost.

Testing the Clutch Start Switch

Cars with manual transmissions have a switch that prevents the driver from starting the engine in any gear but Neutral, or with the clutch depressed. It is similar to the neutral safety switch on cars with automatic transmissions, but is called the clutch start switch. To test this switch, have a helper depress the clutch pedal and follow the same procedures described on these pages for automatic transmissions.

Replacing the Starter Relay

Disconnect the negative battery cable from the post, and identify the wires you remove from the relay so you can reconnect them to the new relay correctly. Now install the new relay and reconnect all the wires. Reconnect the negative battery cable to the post and test for cranking.

Step 5 Test Starter Relay

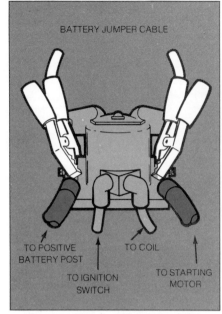

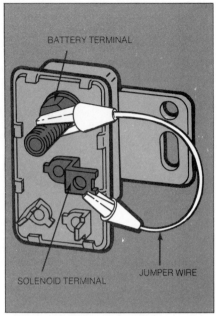

To test the starter relay on Ford cars, set the transmission in "Park" or "Neutral," and set the parking brake. First connect a battery jumper cable to the battery terminal of the relay—the terminal which is connected to the battery with a cable. Touch the other end of the jumper cable to the starter side of the starter relay. If the engine cranks, the relay must be replaced.

To test the starter relay on Chrysler products, for cars equipped with automatic transmissions position the transmission gear selector in "Park" or "Neutral." Connect a jumper wire on the starter relay between the battery and solenoid terminals. If the engine cranks, the starter relay is good.

Step 6 Test Starter Solenoid

On GM cars, connect the voltmeter positive lead to the solenoid starting motor terminal and the voltmeter negative lead to the solenoid battery terminal. Set the voltmeter to the high scale, then crank the engine. Now switch the voltmeter to the low scale and, still cranking, take a reading as fast as possible. Switch the voltmeter back to the high scale and shut off the engine. If the voltmeter reads more than 0.2 volt, you should replace the solenoid.

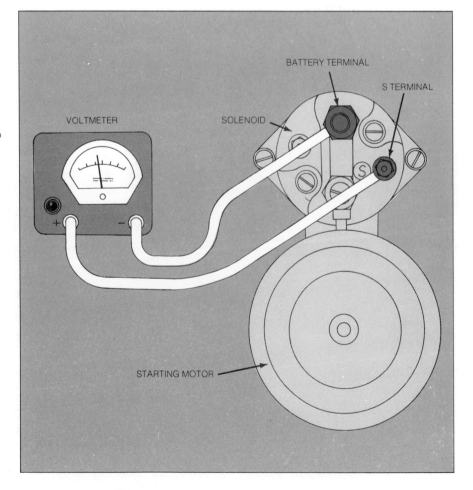

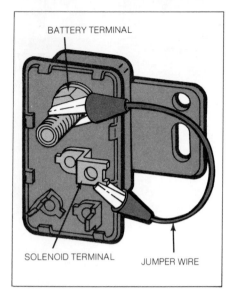

BATTERY TERMINAL

SOLENOID TERMINAL

JUMPER WIRE

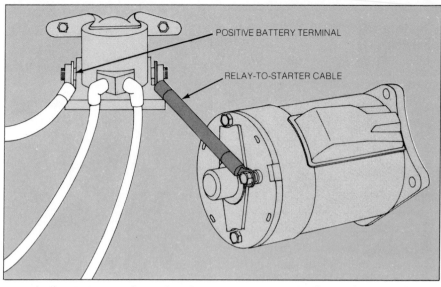

POSITIVE BATTERY TERMINAL

RELAY-TO-STARTER CABLE

On Chrysler cars, connect a heavy jumper wire on the starter relay between the battery and solenoid terminals. If the engine cranks, the starter solenoid is good. If it doesn't crank or the solenoid chatters, check the wiring and the connections from the relay to the starter for looseness or corrosion. Pay particular attention to the connections at the starter terminals. Repeat the jumper wire test. If the engine still fails to crank

properly, the starter must be replaced, since the solenoid on Chryslers is built into the starter and cannot be removed for replacement without disassembling the starter.

On Ford cars, remove the relay-to-starter cable from its terminal on the starter relay and touch it to the positive battery terminal on the relay. *Caution: Make sure the car is in Neutral or Park. Also,*

wear eye protection as there may be arcing when you do this. The engine should crank. If it does not, inspect the wiring and connections from the relay to the starting motor for looseness and corrosion. If they're OK, then the starter or the solenoid is faulty. To isolate the problem, you must remove the starter and bench-test it. This is best left to a professional mechanic.

Replacing the Starter Solenoid

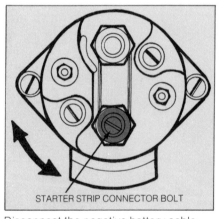

STARTER STRIP CONNECTOR BOLT

strip to the solenoid. Press the solenoid inward, toward the starter, and twist it either right or left to release it from the starter. Remove the solenoid, but do not remove the plunger return spring.

Install the new solenoid by placing it against the return spring and

pushing inward toward the starter flange. Twist the solenoid either right or left until the bolt holes are aligned, then attach the bolts and tighten them securely. Connect the starter strip to the solenoid with the bolt or nut and install the starter. Lower the car and reconnect the negative battery cable.

Disconnect the negative battery cable from the post, then jack up and support the front of the car. Remove the starting motor (see Replacing the Starter, p. 50), and take out the nut or bolt that connects the starting motor

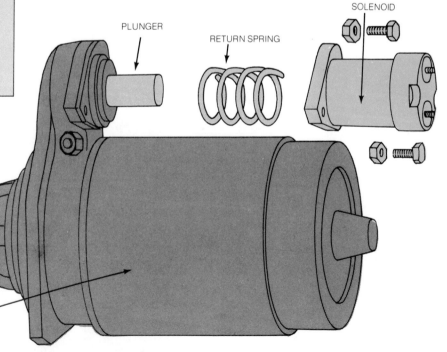

PLUNGER

RETURN SPRING

SOLENOID

STARTING MOTOR

The Starting Motor

When the ignition switch is turned on, a small amount of electricity from the battery is sent to the solenoid, which is located above the starter. This creates a magnetic field that draws the solenoid plunger forward, forcing the shift yoke attached to it to move the starter drive so its pinion gear engages the engine's crankshaft flywheel. As the plunger moves forward, it touches a contact that allows more electricity to flow from the battery to the starter motor. The motor then spins the starter drive and turns the pinion gear, which turns the flywheel. After the engine starts and the ignition key is released, the starting circuit is broken. The plunger goes back, shutting off the motor and disengaging the starter drive. The flywheel is now rotating as a result of engine combustion and the brief but important role of the starting motor has ended.

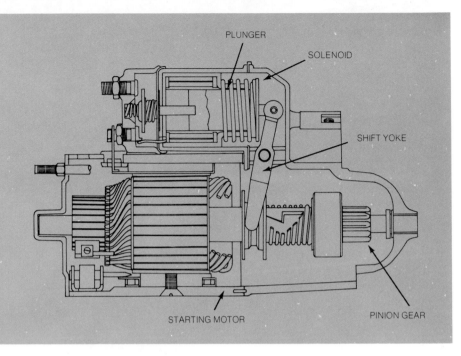

Step 7 Test Starter

To test the GM starter, the engine must be at normal operating temperature (at least 150°F). Make sure the battery and cables are in good condition. First, disconnect the ignition (p. 44). Then connect the voltmeter positive lead to the starting motor terminal on the solenoid, and connect the voltmeter negative lead to a good ground (an engine mounting bracket, for example). With the ignition switch on, crank the engine and take a reading as quickly as possible. *Caution: Don't operate the starter for more than 30 seconds at a time, and always allow the motor to cool off for at least two minutes before cranking again. Continuous cranking can cause overheating and damage to the starting motor.* If the starter turns the engine at normal cranking speed (200 rpm or more) with a voltmeter reading of at least nine volts, the starting motor and the solenoid switch are OK. If the cranking speed is below normal and the reading is nine volts or higher, provided the connections are good and the starter is properly grounded, then the starter is defective and must be replaced. Cranking speed can be determined by hooking up a tachometer.

On Chrysler and Ford cars, testing procedures for the starting motor are the same as for testing the solenoid (p. 48).

Starts and Stops

If you're having trouble starting or if your engine inexplicably conks out on the highway, one very good possibility is a loose wire in your primary circuit.

To make sure everything is OK in this area, do the following:
1 Tighten down the wire on the side of the coil toward the distributor.

2 Trace this wire over to the distributor and tighten it down there too.
3 Check the wire that goes from the ignition switch to the coil for tightness.

Also, if either of these wires shows cracks in the insulation, replace it.

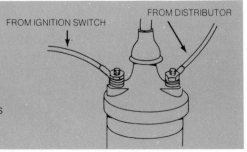

Replacing the Starter

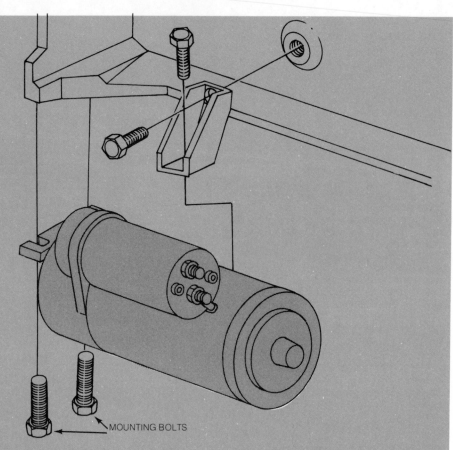

First disconnect the negative battery cable from the post, then jack up and support the front of the car. Disconnect and label all wires attached to the starter, so you can reinstall them correctly. *Caution: The motor is heavy, so we suggest that when you are removing the last bolt, hold the motor against the engine with one hand and remove the bolt with the other. Reverse this procedure when you are reinstalling the starter.* Remove the mounting bolts and the starter. On some cars you have to disconnect the exhaust system or an engine mount to get at it. On some GM V8 engines after 1973 there is a heat shield protecting the solenoid. To disconnect it, remove the upper bolt of the supporting bracket.

To install a new starter, first clean the starter and engine-housing mounting surfaces. This provides the ground circuit for the starter. If you don't have a good ground, the starter will draw off more current than it should and run down the battery. A poor ground can also prevent the starter from cranking. Continuous cranking under these conditions can burn out the starting motor. Position

MOUNTING BOLTS

the starting motor on the engine and install the mounting bolts, torquing them to 45 lb./ft. Replace all the wires you removed and tighten the

nuts. Reconnect any components that you had to remove to get at the starter, then reconnect the battery negative cable.

All About Seat Belt Interlock Systems

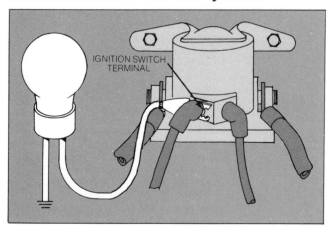

IGNITION SWITCH TERMINAL

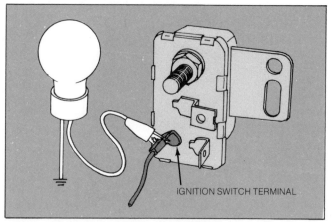

IGNITION SWITCH TERMINAL

If your car was built in 1974–75, it has a seat belt interlock system that controls current flow to the solenoid/starter relay, which in turn activates the starter. This means, if your car won't start, you're going to have to check out the interlock in your search for the problem. Testing the Ford and Chrysler interlock systems is within the scope of the average do-it-yourselfer. But the GM system is more complicated. Therefore, we suggest that you check out the other components of the GM starting system and, if they prove to be in working order and the car still won't start, have the interlock tested by a professional mechanic.

To test the Chrysler and Ford interlock systems, connect one lead of a test light to a good ground and the

other lead to the ignition switch terminal on the starter relay. Have a helper seated in the driver's seat with the seat belt properly hooked up. If the test lamp lights when he turns the ignition switch to start, the interlock is operating properly. If the light doesn't go on, remove the interlock connectors and briefly connect the red wire (which goes to the battery) to the yellow wire (which goes to the starter relay) with a jumper lead while cranking the engine. If the engine cranks, the interlock unit is defective and must be replaced. If the engine does not crank, check for voltage by hooking up the test light between the red wire and a good ground. If there is no voltage, the wiring has an open circuit. If there is voltage, check the yellow wire for an open circuit.

CHAPTER

COMPRESSION AND VACUUM SERVICE

Compression and vacuum tests tell you what's going on inside an engine without tearing it apart. They are quick ways to determine if an ignition tuneup can improve your car's performance and gas mileage. Basic to the performance of any engine is its mechanical condition. An engine works by drawing a gasoline and air mixture into the combustion chamber. This mixture is then compressed and ignited. The burning of the mixture creates expanding gases which provide the power. The burned mixture is then discharged into the exhaust system. Several key elements are necessary: 1) the mixture must contain the correct amount of air and gasoline to burn completely and efficiently, 2) this mixture must be drawn into the combustion chamber, 3) the mixture must be compressed and ignited at the proper time, and 4) the spent gases must be pushed out of the combustion chamber. All the mechanical pieces of the engine must be in good condition for this to happen efficiently.

By removing a spark plug and inserting a compression gauge, the actual ability of the engine to compress the mixture is measured. If the engine isn't mechanically capable of compressing the mixture, inefficient combustion results. Restoring an ignition system to its optimum operation, in this case, will have little effect on the performance and gas mileage of the engine—until the mechanical problem is taken care of.

A compression test takes you to the heart of the engine and tells you how the valves and pistons are doing.

A vacuum test tell you what happens to the mixture before it reaches the combustion chamber. It is a method to determine if the engine is mechanically capable of drawing in the correct mixture. Even if the pistons and valves are operating correctly, vacuum leaks at the intake manifold or carburetor will cause the mixture to be wrong. Again, inefficient combustion is the result, with a corresponding loss of performance and gas mileage.

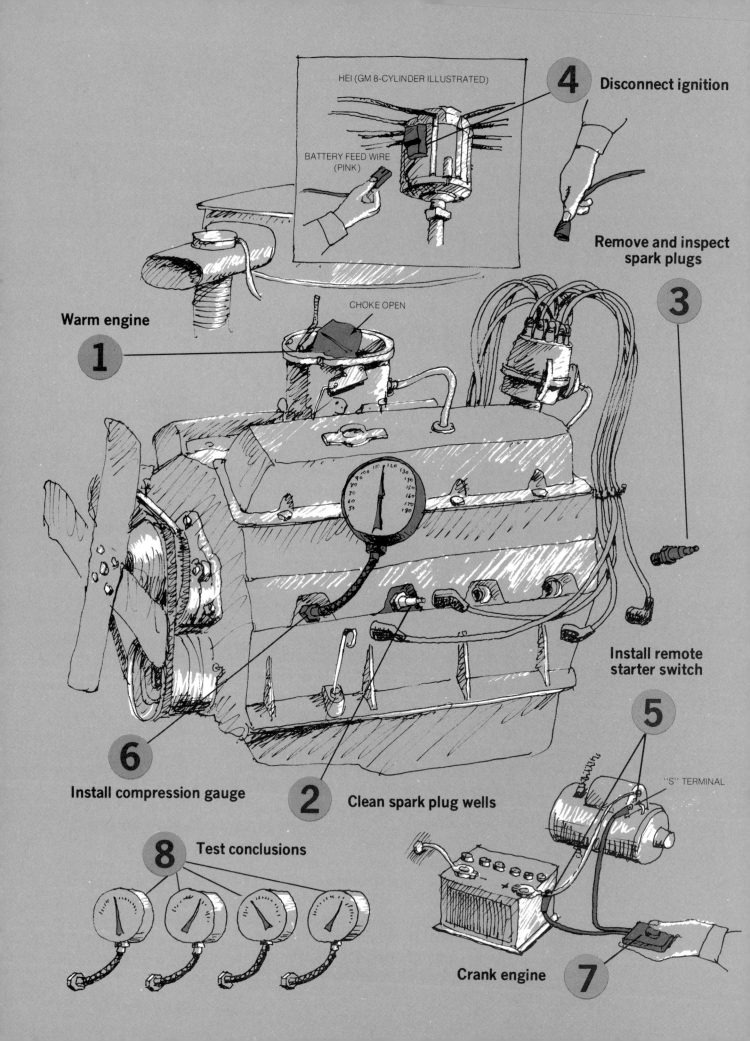

HEI (GM 8-CYLINDER ILLUSTRATED)

BATTERY FEED WIRE (PINK)

4 Disconnect ignition

Remove and inspect spark plugs

3

CHOKE OPEN

Warm engine

1

Install remote starter switch

5

"S" TERMINAL

6

Install compression gauge

2 **Clean spark plug wells**

8 **Test conclusions**

Crank engine

7

Compression Test

Prep: Check the engine oil. If it is very old, dirty, diluted with gasoline or not at the proper level, the compression readings will be wrong (p. 125). Check the battery. The starter cranks the engine during a compression test, and a weak battery can't keep the engine cranking fast enough to give accurate readings (p. 28).

1 **Warm engine.** The test should be performed with the engine at normal operating temperature (at least 150°F) (p. 54). Also remove air cleaner (p. 107).

2 **Clean spark plug wells.** This is a precaution which prevents dirt from entering the cylinders when the spark plugs are removed (p. 54).

3 **Remove and inspect spark plugs.** Remove the plugs from the cylinder head, marking them with a code (p. 54).

4 **Disconnect ignition.** To prevent the engine from starting during the test, remove the coil wire from the center of the distributor cap and ground it with a jumper wire (p. 54). Most cars with HEI do not have a coil wire, so in these cases disconnect the battery feed wire from the side of the distributor.

5 **Install remote starter switch.** If you don't have a helper to crank the engine over from inside the car, you'll need a remote starter switch (p. 54).

6 **Install compression gauge.** Install the gauge according to the manufacturer's instructions (p. 55).

7 **Crank engine and take readings.** Crank the engine for four compression strokes to obtain the highest reading. An easy way to count compression strokes if you're using a gauge with a grommet seal is to watch the needle. It will move every time there is a compression stroke. If you're using a screw-in type, the gauge's hose will move each time the engine goes through a compression stroke. Write down the cylinder number and the compression reading. Repeat the test for all cylinders, making a special note of the first and fourth cylinders (p. 55).

8 **Test conclusions.** Compare your readings with the reading for the highest cylinder. If all the readings are at least 75% of the highest reading, the compression is OK. If the readings are not OK, see What the Readings Mean (p. 55).

Danger: Hot Stuff

The compression test is performed on
a warm engine (some surfaces, the
intake manifold for example, can
exceed the temperature at which
water boils), so take care not to burn
your hands. And make sure the
ignition system is disconnected
during the test so the engine can't
start.

Step 1 Warm Engine

CHOKE VALVE OPEN

Let the engine run until it reaches
normal operating temperature (or at
least 150°F). On cars equipped with a
temperature gauge, watch the needle.
On cars without a temperature gauge,
wait until you can kick the fast idle down
to the normal idle speed (see the
chapter on carburetors, p. 110). The
heater should be warm and the choke
valve fully open. This should be done
with the air-cleaner cover off. Once the
engine is warm, turn it off.

Step 2 Clean Spark Plug Wells

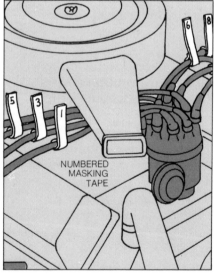

NUMBERED MASKING TAPE

Dirt and grease that gather around the
base of the spark plugs can fall into
the cylinders and cause damage.
Professional mechanics use
compressed air to blow the dirt away.
Another way is to let the engine do it for
you. First, remove the spark plug cables.
Then, using masking tape, number each
cylinder and code each cable for easy
identification when reconnecting them.
*Caution: Remember the engine is warm:
Don't burn your hands.* You will probably

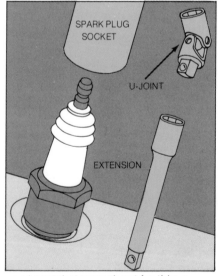

SPARK PLUG SOCKET

U-JOINT

EXTENSION

need a ratchet-wrench set for this: a
handle, an extension, a U-joint, and a
spark plug socket. Loosen all the plugs
one turn and reconnect the cables.
Leave the identification tags on. Start the
engine and let it run for one minute.
Engine compression leaking past the
spark plugs should blow away any dirt in
the plug wells as well as clean the
carbon from the spark plug threads.
Now shut off the engine.

Step 3 Remove and Inspect Spark Plugs

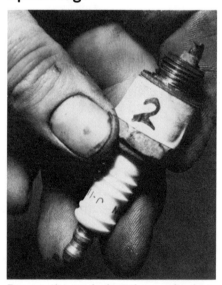

Remove the spark plug wires again, then
take out the plugs, marking them with
the same code as the cables. Inspect the
plugs (p. 89).

Step 4 Disconnect Ignition (See p. 44)

Step 5 Install Remote Starter Switch (See p. 44)

Step 6 Install Compression Gauge

First, open the carburetor throttle. Your helper can do this by pressing the accelerator pedal to the floor. The pedal can also be held down with a brick or similar object. Do not pump the pedal during the test or gasoline will get into the cylinders and wash the oil off their walls. Now install your compression gauge. Follow the manufacturer's instructions for installation. There are two types of gauges. The more expensive type screws into the spark plug hole. The other type has a rubber grommet on the end and is held over the spark plug hole.

Step 8 Test Conclusions

Compare your readings with the reading in the highest cylinder. If all the readings are at least 75% of the highest reading, the compression is OK. The above readings of 110 and 89 psi are within an acceptable range. Good compression

means that the piston rings and valves are mechanically capable of compressing the fuel-and-air mixture. If the readings are not within specs, see What the Readings Mean.

Step 7 Crank Engine

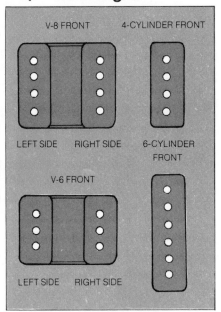

Have a pencil and pad ready for recording the compression readings. Draw a chart of the engine's cylinder sequence. With the gauge in place, crank the engine for four compression strokes (approximately four seconds) to obtain the highest reading. Record the cylinder number and reading. Repeat the test for all cylinders.

What the Readings Mean

If one or more cylinders read low when compared to the others, squirt a couple of drops of oil into the spark plug hole. Don't inject more than a tablespoon. Turn the engine over three or four times, then recheck the compression. If it is now higher, your piston rings may be worn. If the compression doesn't improve, you may have a burned or sticking valve or a blown head gasket.

If two cylinders next to each other show readings of more than 20 pounds lower than the others, and injecting a tablespoon of oil doesn't change the readings, the head gasket could be bad. A good rule of thumb. If there is popping (backfire) through the carburetor or if the engine is overheating, suspect a blown head gasket. A compression test will verify this. However, faulty head gaskets are rare on late-model cars.

If all the cylinders read exceptionally high, then it's likely there are excessive carbon deposits inside the combustion chamber. To confirm this, warm up the engine, ground the distributor wire from the ignition coil, and then crank the engine. If it attempts to start, then it's carbon for sure. See a professional mechanic.

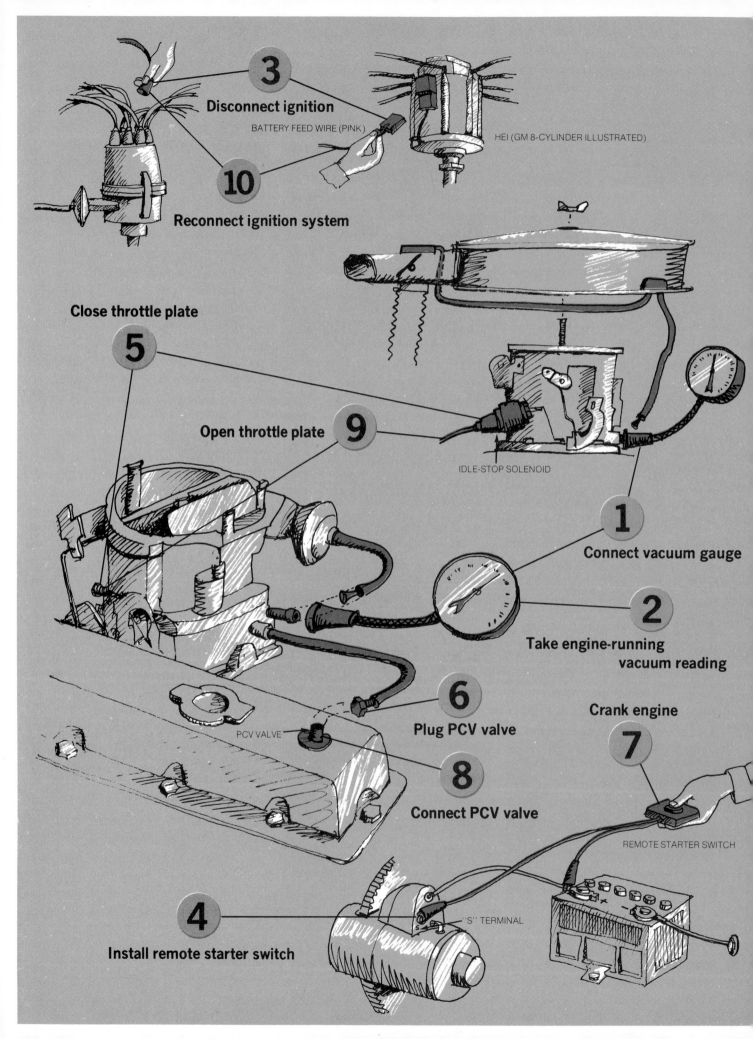

3
Disconnect ignition

BATTERY FEED WIRE (PINK)

10

HEI (GM 8-CYLINDER ILLUSTRATED)

Reconnect ignition system

Close throttle plate

5

Open throttle plate

9

IDLE-STOP SOLENOID

1
Connect vacuum gauge

2
Take engine-running
vacuum reading

6
Plug PCV valve

PCV VALVE

8

Connect PCV valve

Crank engine

7

REMOTE STARTER SWITCH

4

Install remote starter switch

"S" TERMINAL

Job Steps

Vacuum Test

Prep: Check the battery. It must have sufficient charge to crank the engine (p. 28). Warm the engine. It should be at normal operating temperature (at least 150°F) (p. 54). Check the oil. The engine oil should be at the proper level and in good condition to properly seal the rings (p. 125).

1 **Connect vacuum gauge.** The gauge is attached to a source of manifold vacuum. See sources of manifold vacuum (p. 58).

2 **Take engine-running vacuum reading.** Record this reading for later comparison with the cranking vacuum reading. A normal cranking vacuum reading should be within one inch of the reading you have just taken. See What the Readings Mean (p. 58). Shut off the engine.

3 **Disconnect ignition.** This is done so the vacuum reading may be taken with the engine cranking, not running (p. 59).

4 **Install remote starter switch.** If you don't have a helper to crank the engine, you'll need a remote starter switch. Before hooking it up, find out if you have a starter-mounted or fire-wall mounted solenoid (p. 59).

5 **Close throttle plate.** To close the carburetor throttle plate, disconnect the idle-stop solenoid if your car has one, and/or back off the throttle screw (p. 59).

6 **Plug PCV valve.** Remove the PCV valve and plug the line between the valve and the intake manifold (p. 59).

7 **Crank engine.** Observe the vacuum gauge while cranking the engine (p. 59). A normal reading is six inches or more. If your readings are not within specs, see What the Readings Mean (p. 60).

8 **Connect PCV valve.** The PCV valve should be reinstalled (p. 60).

9 **Open throttle plate.** The engine must idle at the normal speed (p. 60).

10 **Reconnect ignition system.** Remove the ground from the coil wire or hook the HEI's feed wire back to the distributor (p. 60).

Essential. Basic tools (p. 20).
Jumper wire • Manifold vacuum
gauge.
Handy. Fender cover • Remote
starter switch.

Step 1 Connect Vacuum Gauge

Attach the gauge to a source of intake
manifold vacuum. Follow the gauge
manufacturer's instructions. All engines
have at least one of the two following
sources of intake manifold vacuum;
hook the gauge up to the most
accessible one.

(a) The choke vacuum pull-off,
sometimes called the vacuum kick, is
mounted on the side of the carburetor
and actuated by intake-manifold
vacuum. Disconnect the rubber hose
between the choke vacuum pull-off and
the base of the carburetor and connect
the gauge to the carburetor base.

(b) The heated-air intake system is a
flapper-type valve mounted in the
snorkle of the air cleaner. Most are
operated by intake manifold vacuum.
Trace the rubber hose that is connected
to the valve, back to the base of the
carburetor. Disconnect the hose and
attach the vacuum gauge to the
carburetor.

Step 2 Take Engine-running Vacuum Reading

A high, steady vacuum reading (between
14 and 22 inches of vacuum) as the
engine idles tells you that you have a
mechanically sound engine, good rings,
properly sealed combustion chamber
and intake manifold, the valve guides are
not leaking, and the starter is cranking
the engine at the normal speed (200
rpm). Note: Acceptable vacuum
readings vary because the design
characteristics of different engines vary.

What the Readings Mean
Engine-Running Vacuum Test

If your engine is operating perfectly at
sea level, the gauge needle will
remain steady at the acceptable
vacuum reading for your particular
engine. This reading can range all the
way from 14 to 22 inches of vacuum.
Generally the reading will decrease
one inch for every 1000 feet of
altitude above sea level.

Gauge dropping one inch or more
indicates valve leakage. You can
make this test at idling speed. Each
time the valve closes but doesn't seat
properly, the vacuum reading will
drop an inch or more. This happens
as each leaky valve fails to seal. The
valve or valves causing this can be
located by using the compression
gauge test.

Gauge dropping sharply ten to 12
inches indicates cylinder head gasket
leakage. With your engine running,
the vacuum reading will drop sharply
each time the leak occurs, from a
steady reading to a reading of ten to
12 inches or less. When the leak is
between two adjacent cylinders, the
drop will be much greater. The
location of the leak can be found with
the use of a compression gauge.

Almost identical low readings will be
found in adjacent cylinders if the leak
is between them.

Gauge fluctuating between three
to eight inches below normal
indicates an intake system leak. With
the engine idling, this type of vacuum
leak will make the gauge needle
fluctuate between readings of three
to eight inches lower than normal.
This kind of a reading indicates a leak
through the intake manifold gaskets
or any vacuum-operated accessories
such as vacuum power brakes,
vacuum transmission control or a
modulator valve.

Gauge vibrating one inch above or
below normal indicates general
ignition problems. With the engine
idling, you get continued needle
vibration about an inch above or
below an acceptable reading. This
could be caused by defective spark
plugs, improper spark plug gap, faulty
point adjustment, spark plug wire
leaks, bad distributor cap or weak
ignition coil. Further testing with
electrical test equipment is required
in this case.

Step 3 **Disconnect Ignition**

Cranking vacuum is a valuable diagnostic test that can be used to determine the condition of the engine and the intake system. The vacuum reading is taken with the engine cranking, not running. Use the same procedure to disconnect the ignition that is listed for the compression test (p. 44).

Step 4 **Install Remote Starter Switch** (See p. 44)

Step 5 **Close Throttle Plate**

On cars equipped with an idle-stop solenoid, disconnect the electrical feed wire. This closes the carburetor throttle plate. If the plate is held open during cranking, the vacuum reading will be inaccurate. On cars without an idle-stop solenoid, turn the idle-speed adjustment screw counterclockwise until the throttle is completely closed. Count the number of turns necessary to do this so you can reset the idle later.

Step 6 **Plug PCV Valve**

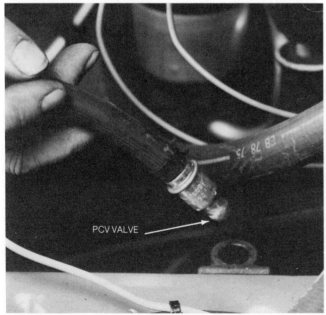

PCV VALVE

Remove the PCV valve from the valve cover and hold your thumb over the end of the valve. You can also slip the valve out of the rubber line and substitute a bolt of the same size in its place.

Step 7 **Crank Engine**

REMOTE STARTER SWITCH

Observe the needle of the vacuum gauge while you are cranking the engine. The test will monitor the level of the vacuum in the intake manifold and its consistency. Now compare your readings with What the Readings Mean.

Step 8 Connect PCV Valve

Remove the bolt from the hose, if necessary, and put the PCV valve back in. Then snap it back into the rubber grommet in the valve cover.

Step 9 Open Throttle Plate

In order for the engine to idle at the proper speed, it's necessary to reconnect the idle-stop solenoid (p. 59). On cars without an idle-stop solenoid, turn the idle-speed screw clockwise the same number of turns that you backed it off in Step 5 (p. 59).

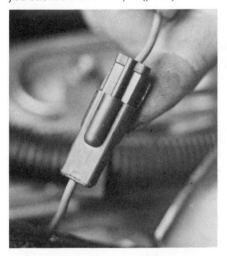

What the Readings Mean
Engine-Cranking Vacuum Test

Readings may pulsate slightly, especially if the vacuum gauge is not connected to the center of the manifold in 8-cylinder engines and in-line 6-cylinder engines. Generally V8 engines read lower than 6-cylinder engines.

Uneven, pulsating gauge needle movement means: Faulty valves, rings, pistons, head gasket or uneven cranking speed.

Low, even gauge needle movement means: Slow cranking speed (rpm), overall low compression, incorrect valve timing, throttle valves not closed tightly, vacuum leaks at intake valve guides or vacuum leaks at manifold or vacuum-operated accessories.

Cranking speed below normal (low rpm) means: Excessive battery cable resistance caused by poor connections or sulphated cable at terminal ends, faulty starter or excessive drag in the engine.

Uneven cranking speed means: Uneven compression or defective starter or drive.

Note: When you find your engine has low or uneven cranking vacuum, make a compression test if you haven't already made one. You cannot successfully tune your engine until compression or vacuum leaks are corrected.

Step 10 Reconnect Ignition System

Remove the jumper wire from the coil wire and snap the coil wire back into the center of the distributor cap. On General Motors cars with HEI-type ignitions, hook the pink battery feed wire back into the side of the distributor cap.

Replacing Gasket on Rocker Arm Valve Cover

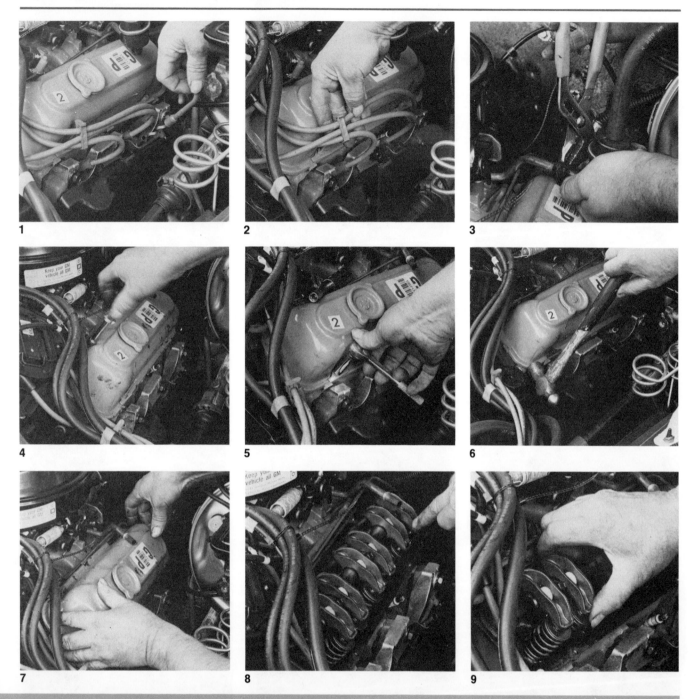

1 Take out the oil dipstick to allow you room to remove the valve cover.

2 Remove the spark plug cable bracket from its support on the valve cover by pulling up. Note: Cables on this car are routed in sequence, making it unnecessary to tag them for identification.

3 Slip the spring-type wire clamp off the booster check-valve hose with pliers before removing the hose from its vacuum source. Leave the clamp on the metal tube so you do not lose it.

4 Remove the valve-cover retaining bolts with a screwdriver-type drive socket.

5 A deep socket ratchet is necessary to remove the front left valve-cover retaining bolt because of the support that holds the spark plug cable bracket.

6 Break the gasket loose from the engine block by striking the valve cover sharply with a hammer.

7 Remove the rocker arm valve cover. Be careful not to tear the gasket when lifting the cover off.

8 View of the engine valves with the cover removed. Note: All valves are the same height (closed), a design characteristic of this particular engine. These valves are not adjustable, but the valves in other engines may not all be closed at the same time.

9 Check between the rocker arm and the valve stem for looseness. Too much lash (play) could mean excessive wear in the valve train (push rod, valve stem, rocker arm or shaft).

Replacing Gasket on Rocker Arm Valve Cover

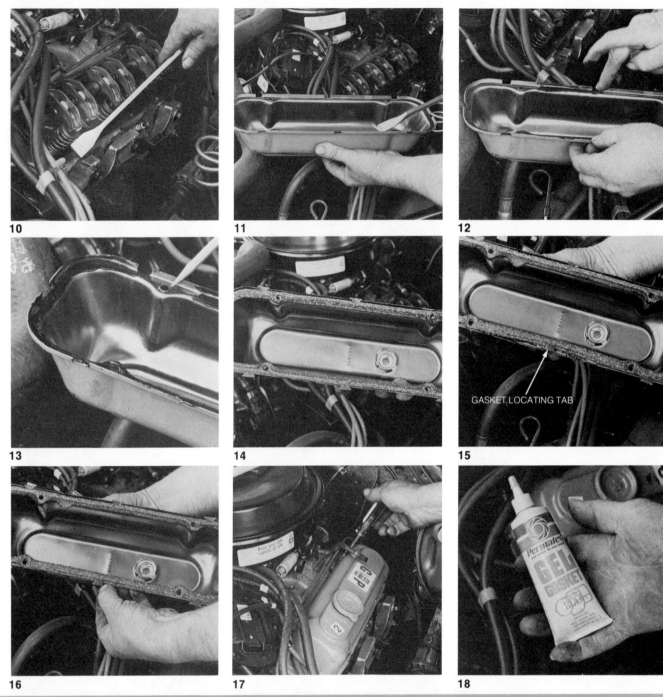

10

11

12

13

14

15
GASKET LOCATING TAB

16

17

18

10 Clean off any remaining gasket material from the engine lip with a scraper or putty knife.

11 Scrape all old gasket material off the valve cover lip as well.

12 Spread gasket sealant sparingly around the rocker-arm-cover lip surface.

13 The pencil points to the valve-cover retaining bolt hole. Make sure the holes are not deformed, since this can cause a poor seal when the cover is installed.

14 This new gasket is improperly placed. The holes in the gasket do not line up with the valve-cover bolt holes, which can cause a poor seal.

15 This new gasket is improperly installed. The gasket-locating tab is not set in the valve cover notch, which can cause a poor seal.

16 This correctly installed gasket shows the holes lined up and the tabs in the valve cover notches.

17 Carefully seat the rocker arm valve cover on the engine block and tighten the retaining bolts until they are snug. Then turn the bolts an additional one-half turn.

18 Gel can replace a cork gasket. Many late-model cars use only gel, because it can withstand underhood temperature better than cork.

CHAPTER

DISTRIBUTOR SERVICE

The ignition system supplies the spark that ignites the fuel-and-air mixture in the combustion chamber. It takes relatively low battery voltage and transforms it into high voltage that jumps across the plug gap. A basic ignition system consists of: a battery to provide the initial electricity; an ignition switch to activate it; a ballast resistor to limit primary current; a distributor to fire the coil and direct the spark to the plugs; a coil to transform low voltage into high; the wires connecting the coil to the distributor and the distributor to the plugs; and finally, the spark plugs that ignite the mixture.

The distributor is the system's brain. It tells the coil when to fire, then directs the spark to the correct plug. Both the quality of the spark and its timing are important for engine efficiency. The faster an engine goes, the earlier the spark must be introduced into the combustion chamber so the mixture burns completely. If the mixture doesn't burn completely, the engine loses power and gas mileage is lowered.

The distributor has two electrical circuits and several component parts. The electrical circuits are called the primary and the secondary. The primary circuit is the low-voltage side that triggers the coil. The secondary circuit is the high-voltage side that receives the stepped-up voltage from the coil and delivers it to the plugs.

Older ignition systems have a distributor which uses a mechanical method to trigger the coil. These are known as breaker-point systems because they have contact points that open and close by rubbing against a cam. The adjustment of the point gap—the amount of space the points open—is crucial to spark timing. As the points get older, wear changes the adjustment. In extreme cases, the points wear so much that the distributor cam no longer opens them and the car won't start. Recently, manufacturers have replaced the mechanical contact points with non-mechanical electronic triggering devices. This eliminates point wear and increases the reliability of the system. These electronic ignition systems still use a distributor but now there is a sensor and trigger wheel instead of contact points and no adjustment is required.

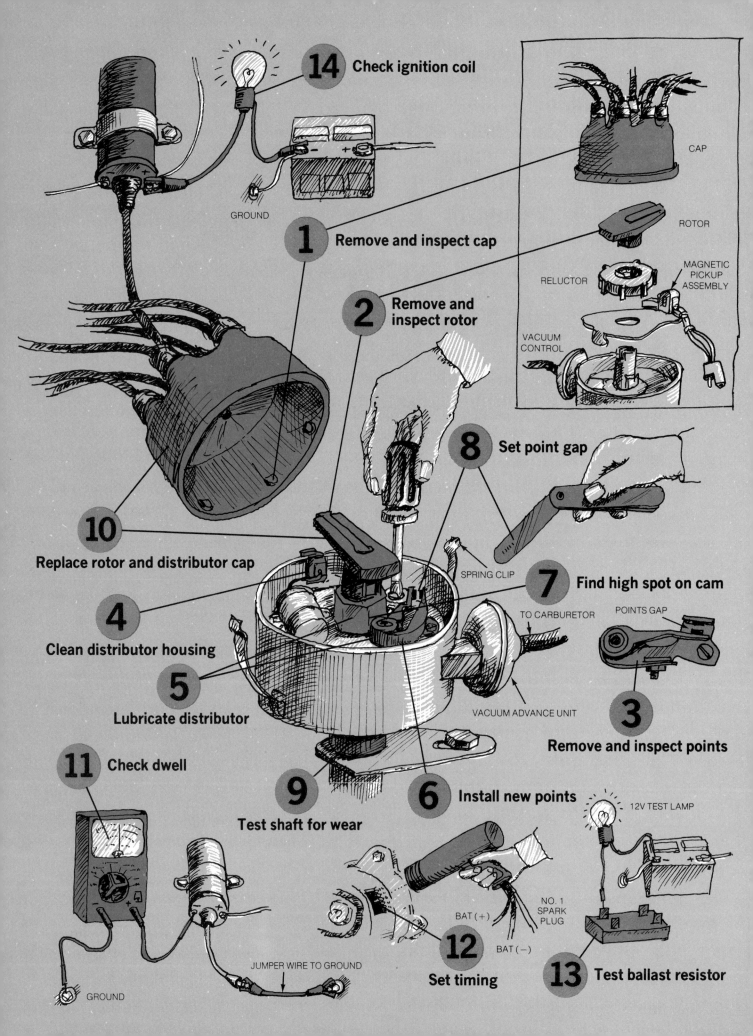

14 Check ignition coil

GROUND

CAP

1 Remove and inspect cap

ROTOR

2 Remove and inspect rotor

RELUCTOR

MAGNETIC PICKUP ASSEMBLY

VACUUM CONTROL

8 Set point gap

SPRING CLIP

10 Replace rotor and distributor cap

7 Find high spot on cam

TO CARBURETOR

POINTS GAP

4 Clean distributor housing

5 Lubricate distributor

VACUUM ADVANCE UNIT

3 Remove and inspect points

11 Check dwell

9 Test shaft for wear

6 Install new points

12V TEST LAMP

JUMPER WIRE TO GROUND

GROUND

BAT (+)

BAT (−)

NO. 1 SPARK PLUG

12 Set timing

13 Test ballast resistor

Distributor Service

1 **Remove and inspect cap.** Look for cracks and burned terminals (p. 66). Remove the cables and inspect the towers (p. 66).

2 **Remove and inspect rotor.** Look for cracks, corrosion, and burns (p. 66). If your car is equipped with an electronic ignition, proceed to Step 10 (p. 70).

3 **Remove and inspect points.** If they are pitted, burned or the rubbing block is worn, replace them (p. 67). Replace the condenser when replacing the points (p. 67).

4 **Clean distributor housing.** Wipe the breaker plate and cam clean (p. 68). Check the cam for excessive movement (p. 68).

5 **Lubricate distributor.** Apply a light coating of cam lube to the cam (p. 68). Apply a drop of light oil to the distributor lubrication locations (p. 68).

6 **Install new points.** Position the points on the breaker plate and tighten the holding screws finger-tight (p. 68).

7 **Find high spot on cam.** Install a remote starter switch (p. 44), have a helper crank the engine or turn the engine over by hand (p. 69).

8 **Set point gap.** Adjust the gap with a feeler gauge and tighten the holding screws (p. 69). See Appendix, Specifications by Make and Model (p. 202).

9 **Test shaft for wear.** Push the distributor shaft from side to side. If the point gap increases or decreases, the distributor is worn (p. 70).

10 **Replace rotor and distributor cap.** Make sure the rotor is properly seated. Position the cap correctly and fasten it to the distributor (p. 70).

11 **Check dwell.** Measure the point gap with a dwell meter (p. 71). On cars with electronic ignitions, dwell is not adjustable. Proceed to Step 12.

12 **Set timing.** Connect a timing light to the number 1 spark plug wire and set the timing (p. 72). Check the vacuum advance (p. 73).

13 **Test ballast resistor.** This can easily be done with a test light (p. 74). There are two types of ballast resistors: internal and external. If the internal type is faulty, see a professional mechanic. If the external type is bad, replace it (p. 74).

14 **Check ignition coil.** Clean the coil tower when servicing the distributor (p. 75). Replace the coil if it is damaged (p. 75). A breaker-point ignition coil can be checked with a test light (p. 75).

TOOLS

Essential. Basic tools (p. 20).
Towels or clean rags • Cam lube •
Light oil • Feeler gauge • Timing light •
Ignition wrench • Flashlight •
Tachometer • ⅛-inch Allen wrench
(for GM cars).
Handy. Remote starter switch •
Dwell meter • Magnetic screwdriver.

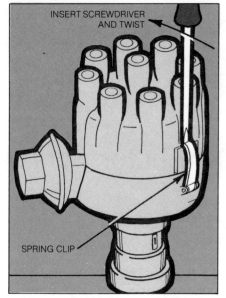

INSERT SCREWDRIVER AND TWIST

SPRING CLIP

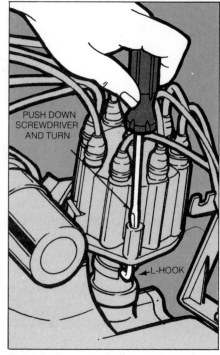

PUSH DOWN SCREWDRIVER AND TURN

L-HOOK

Step 1 Remove and Inspect Cap

Start your distributor service by
removing the distributor cap. Caps are
attached to the distributor base with
spring clips, L-hooks or screws. Most
Ford and Chrysler cars use spring clips.
To remove this type of cap, insert your
screwdriver blade between the cap and
the spring clip and twist. Most GM cars
use L-hooks. To remove this type of cap,
hold the screwdriver on the head of the
hook, push down, and then turn the
hook one-half turn counterclockwise so
the L-hook comes away from the
distributor base. GM cars with point-type
ignition systems have two L-hooks

opposite each other that hold the
distributor cap on. Some cars use
screws to hold the cap on. To remove
this type cap, turn the screws
counterclockwise until it is free of the
distributor base.

**Once you have removed the distributor
cap,** clean it to remove grease and dirt
from the outside. Use a flashlight when
inspecting the cap. Check the outside
and inside for cracks, carbon tracks,
and burned terminals. If you find any of
these, replace the cap. Now look at the
center electrode to make sure it hasn't
worn away. Next, gently remove the
spark plug wires one at a time from the
top of the cap and clean and inspect
them. *Caution: Never pull on the wire.*

*Twist the boot one-half a turn in each
direction to free it from the tower and the
wire ends.* Both the tower and the wire
ends should be free of corrosion. You
should replace them if they are not. A
worn cap can cause hard starting,
engine misfiring or even prevent starting altogether.

**1977 and later Fords equipped with the
Dura-Spark electronic ignition** use a
silicone dielectric compound on the tip
of the rotor and on the electrodes on the
distributor cap. Leave this white grease
on. It helps eliminate radio interference.

Step 2 Remove and Inspect Rotor

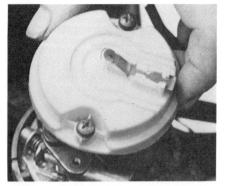

Roters are press-fitted or screwed to the
center shaft of the distributor. Unscrew
or lift off the rotor and inspect it for
cracks, chips, corrosion, burns or weak
spring tension. Be sure to turn it over
and inspect the underside with a
flashlight for electrical tracking
(indicated by black lines on the surface).
You should replace a rotor with any of
the above conditions. Always replace
the cap and rotor in pairs. If your car is
equipped with an electronic ignition,
proceed to Step 10.

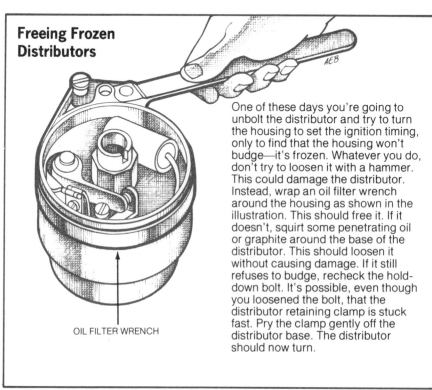

Freeing Frozen Distributors

OIL FILTER WRENCH

One of these days you're going to
unbolt the distributor and try to turn
the housing to set the ignition timing,
only to find that the housing won't
budge—it's frozen. Whatever you do,
don't try to loosen it with a hammer.
This could damage the distributor.
Instead, wrap an oil filter wrench
around the housing as shown in the
illustration. This should free it. If it
doesn't, squirt some penetrating oil
or graphite around the base of the
distributor. This should loosen it
without causing damage. If it still
refuses to budge, recheck the hold-
down bolt. It's possible, even though
you loosened the bolt, that the
distributor retaining clamp is stuck
fast. Pry the clamp gently off the
distributor base. The distributor
should now turn.

Keep the Feeler Clean

Everyone doing his own engine tuneup knows that the distributor breaker points should be kept as clean as possible. Otherwise, they burn prematurely. However, sometimes do-it-yourselfers make a slip and use a feeler gauge which looks as if it had been used as an oil dipstick. Oil or grease is then deposited on the points, and before you know it, you are wondering why the points have gone pf-f-ft. Before slipping the feeler gauge between the points, wipe it off. And if the blades

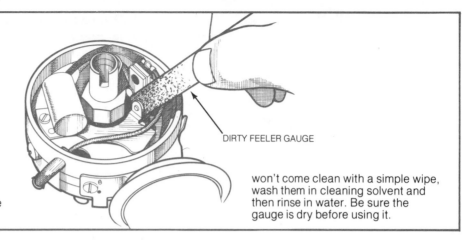

DIRTY FEELER GAUGE

won't come clean with a simple wipe, wash them in cleaning solvent and then rinse in water. Be sure the gauge is dry before using it.

Step 3 Remove and Inspect Points

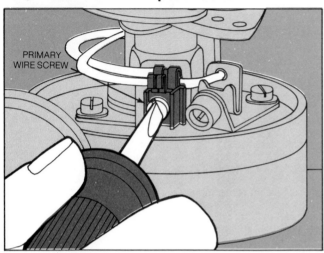

PRIMARY WIRE SCREW

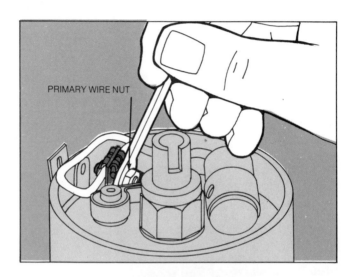

PRIMARY WIRE NUT

To remove the points, first take out the wires that are attached by a screw, nut or spring clip. Note: Some older GM cars may have a radio interference shield over the points. This should be removed before you attempt to remove the points. To take off the shield, take out the two screws that hold it to the breaker plate. Be careful not to drop the screws into the distributor.

After taking out the wires, remove the hold-down screw from the base of the points. Be careful not to drop the screw

into the distributor. A magnetic screwdriver is handy here. Inspect the contact points for wear. If they are pitted, worn, loose or blue in color, the rubbing block worn or the pivot point damaged, you should replace them. If the points are replaced, also replace the condenser. Note the position of the old condenser in the hold-down clip before removing the screw. Position the new condenser in the same place. If the points are light gray and have a smooth surface, they can be reused.

SCREWDRIVER   SPRING CLIP

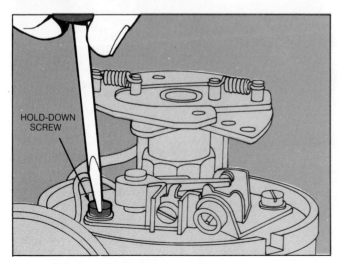

HOLD-DOWN SCREW

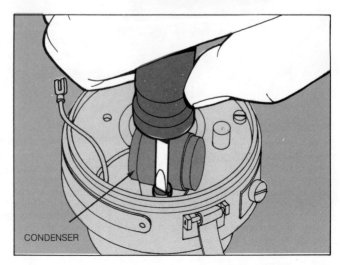

CONDENSER

Step 4 Clean Distributor Housing

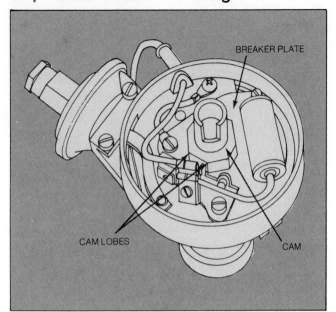

Wipe the breaker plate and cam clean of dirt and old cam lube. Check the cam lobes for roughness or pitting. If the cam is rough, the points will not stay in adjustment. You should replace the distributor if the cam is damaged. Also, check the side play in the distributor shaft by moving it from side to side. If the shaft moves more than .010 inches, you will probably need to replace the distributor. But before you do, have it checked out by a professional mechanic.

Step 5 Lubricate Distributor

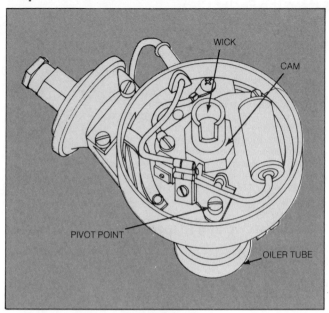

Apply a light coating of cam lube to the distributor cam. Spread not more than two match heads worth equally around it. Wipe off any excess. Apply a drop of light oil to the wick in the center of the distributor shaft, the advance weight pivot points, and the oiler tube on the outside of the distributor body, if necessary on your car. On distributors with cam oiling wicks mounted on the breaker plate, rotate the wick 180 degrees. On older cars, where engine heat has dried out the wick, replace it.

Step 6 Install New Points

Place the points on the distributor breaker plate and tighten the attaching screw(s) finger-tight. On Ford cars, the ground wire goes on top of the point set, not under it. Be sure the tab on the bottom of the point set lines up with the hole in the breaker plate and that the point set sits flat. Be careful that no grease or dirt gets on the point surfaces.

Now install a new condenser. On Ford and Chrysler cars, be sure the tab on the breaker plate lines up with the hole in the condenser bracket. On GM cars with a radio interference shield, be sure the condenser is positioned exactly like the old one or the shield won't fit. Some GM cars are equipped with a point set that has the condenser built into it. On these

cars, a separate condenser isn't necessary.

Reconnect the primary and condenser wires to the point set. Make sure the wire terminals don't touch the breaker plate or the distributor base. Also, make sure that the wires don't rub on the cam or breaker plate.

Step 7 Find High Spot on Cam

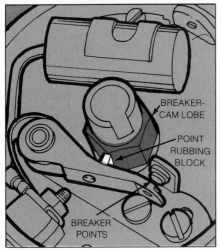

BREAKER-CAM LOBE

POINT RUBBING BLOCK

BREAKER POINTS

Position the distributor cam so the high spot is against the point rubbing block. Now install a remote starter switch (p. 44) or have a helper crank the engine, with short bursts, until the high spot of the cam is in position. The high spot is the position in which the points are open widest. On some cars, the engine can be turned over by turning the fan by hand.

Step 8 Set Point Gap

Measure the gap between the two point faces with a clean feeler gauge. Adjust the gap until it meets specifications (see the Appendix, Specifications by Make and Model, p. 202). The point gap is changed by moving the points toward or away from the distributor cam. Insert a regular screwdriver in the distributor slot. Some GM cars use an Allen head screw to adjust the point gap. These cars have an external adjustment for the point gap which is made while the engine is running (see Step 11, p. 71). Make sure the points are open at the high spot of the cam and closed on the flat spot. This is necessary so the engine starts, allowing the running adjustment. Tighten the point attaching screws when the gap is correct. After tightening the screws, recheck the gap to make sure it hasn't moved.

Cam Lube

A little part mechanics often ignore during an engine tuneup is the cam in a non-electronic ignition distributor. Failure to lubricate it will lead to excessive wear that causes the ignition timing setting to change considerably over a few thousand miles. Failure to lube also increases the possibility of damaging the distributor, which can result in overhauling the entire distributor if the damage is serious enough. To lubricate the cam, use distributor cam lube—no other—available at auto parts and accessory stores. Apply it sparingly. Overuse can cause the lube to melt and splash on the contact points so that they burn prematurely.

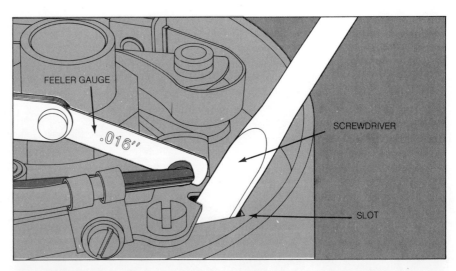

FEELER GAUGE

.016"

SCREWDRIVER

SLOT

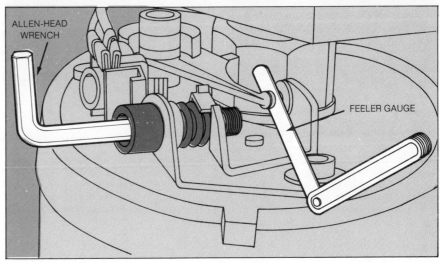

ALLEN-HEAD WRENCH

FEELER GAUGE

Step 9 Test Shaft for Wear

Push the distributor shaft in the direction of the rubbing block. If the point gap increases, the distributor is worn and should be replaced. But before replacing it, have it checked by a professional mechanic. Reinstall the radio interference shield on GM cars which have them.

Step 10 Replace Rotor and Distributor Cap

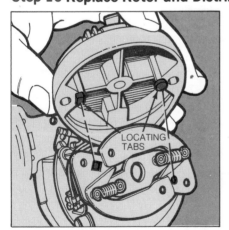

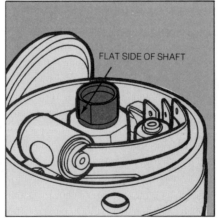

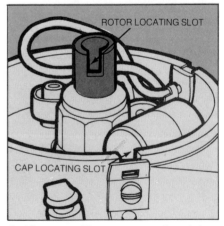

On Ford and Chrysler ignition systems, add one drop of oil to the wick in the center of the distributor shaft. On GM ignitions, add one drop of oil to each of the two pivot points for the advance weights. On all systems, replace the rotor. Chrysler and Ford rotors have square locating tabs that fit into slots in the distributor shaft or over a flat side of the shaft. GM rotors have square and round locating tabs that line up with holes. Be sure the rotor is properly seated.

Replace the distributor cap. Distributor caps have either a locating tab or a slot that lines up with a corresponding slot or tab on the distributor base. Make sure the cap is in the correct position, then fasten it with the L-hook, spring clips or attaching screws. If your car is equipped with an electronic ignition, proceed to Step 12, since dwell is not adjustable on electronic ignitions.

Step 11 Check Dwell

Attach a dwell meter according to the manufacturer's instructions, then start the car and observe the reading. If it is within specifications (see the Appendix, Specifications by Make and Model) (p. 202), proceed to the next step. If the dwell is off, the point gap must be reset. See Step 8 (p. 69). On GM external adjustment-type distributors, insert the Allen wrench through the access window and turn the adjustment screw. Turning the screw counterclockwise opens the points and decreases the dwell. Turning the screw clockwise closes the points and increases the dwell.

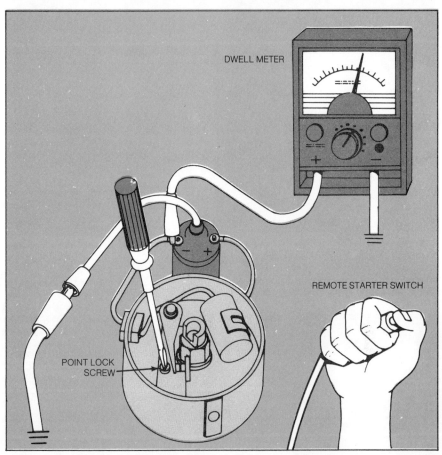

DWELL METER

REMOTE STARTER SWITCH

POINT LOCK SCREW

WINDOW

ALLEN WRENCH

All About Dwell Meters

A dwell meter electronically determines how long the points remain closed and converts that information into the number of degrees of distributor rotation. The point gap directly affects dwell. A dwell reading greater than specifications means that the point gap is too narrow and the space between the points needs to be opened up. A dwell reading of less than specs means the point gap is too wide and the space between the points needs to be closed. Correct dwell is important for ignition system performance. If the dwell is off, the coil won't operate as efficiently as it should.

A dwell meter has two wires. One is hooked to the coil at the primary terminal marked (neg), (−) or (Dist). The other wire is hooked to a ground such as the negative (−) terminal of the battery or a metal part on the engine such as a manifold bolt head. Once the wires are hooked up, select the proper scale for representing the number of cylinders the engine has by turning the switch

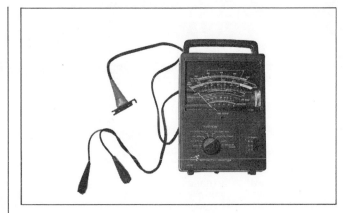

to 4-, 6- or 8-cylinders. Start the car and observe the needle. A good dwell reading is within engine specs and the needle is steady.

Step 12 Set Timing

Ignition timing is one of the most important adjustments you can make on an engine to improve performance and gas mileage. Timing is adjusted so the spark occurs a specified number of degrees before top dead center (BTDC) or after top dead center (ATDC). Top dead center is the highest point of piston travel in the cylinder.

Both mechanical (centrifugal) and vacuum spark advances are based on the specified timing adjustment. If the initial timing position is off, all the subsequent timing adjustments that are made automatically by the distributor will also be off. After the timing is correctly set, shut the engine off.

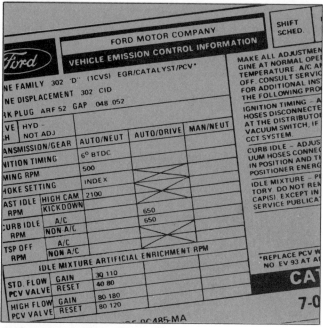

1 Wipe clean the timing marks that are located on the crankshaft pulley or harmonic balancer, then check the timing specifications (see the Appendix, Specifications by Make and Model).

2 Compare the timing specs with the EPA (Environmental Protection Agency) sticker that is under the hood. EPA stickers are located on the engine valve cover, the inner fender wells, the underside of the hood or the radiator support, depending on the model. The sticker gives you the basic timing specs and the exact setting procedure. The proper idle speed is also specified. Follow the procedure on the sticker. Timing is usually set on a warm engine, at idle or a specified rpm with the vacuum advance disconnected and the line plugged.

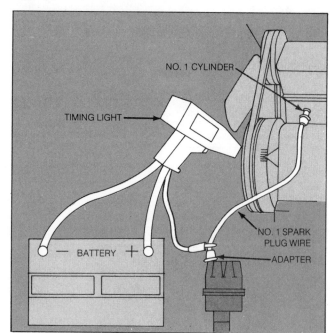

3 Connect your timing light to the engine, following the manufacturer's instructions. A typical timing light has three leads. One is connected to the number 1 spark plug wire, one to the positive (+) terminal of the battery, and one to a ground or to the negative (−) terminal of the battery.

On Timing Lights

TIMING MARKS

A timing light flashes a bright beam of light every time the spark plug wire it is connected to delivers high voltage to the spark plug. Timing lights are usually powered by the car's battery. Three connectors are necessary, one to the positive (+) terminal of the battery, one to the negative (−) terminal or other ground, and one to the number 1 spark plug wire. The light is pointed at the timing marks on the front of the engine, usually located on the bottom engine pulley, and every time the plug fires, the light flashes. The mark that is illuminated is then compared to a specification given by the engine manufacturer. Make sure the timing light is aimed in such a manner that it goes through the center of the pulley.

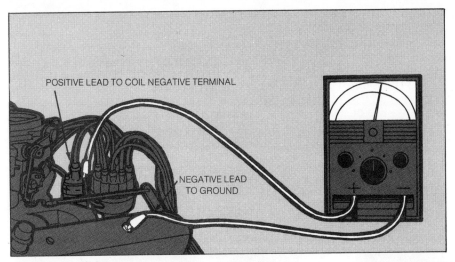

POSITIVE LEAD TO COIL NEGATIVE TERMINAL

NEGATIVE LEAD TO GROUND

4 Next connect your tachometer to the engine, following the manufacturer's instructions. A typical tachometer has two leads. One is connected to a ground such as the negative battery terminal. The other lead is connected to the distributor side of the coil. On breaker-point ignition systems, this is the terminal of the coil that goes to the distributor. It is usually marked (−) or (Dist). On Ford cars with electronic ignitions, the coil is marked either (DEC) or (Tach/test). Chrysler cars are marked (Dist). GM cars with HEI have a terminal on the distributor next to the pink battery feed wire marked (Tach). Start the engine and allow it to reach normal operating temperature (150° F).

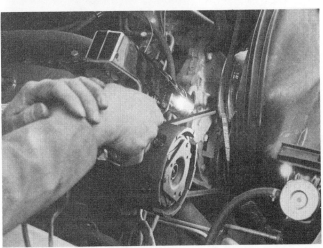

5 Check the tachometer for correct engine rpm and aim the timing light at the timing marks. Compare your reading with the specifications.

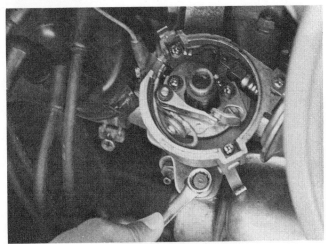

6 If the timing is not within specs, loosen the distributor hold-down bolt and turn the distributor until the correct timing is indicated. Retighten the hold-down bolt and check the timing to make sure it hasn't moved.

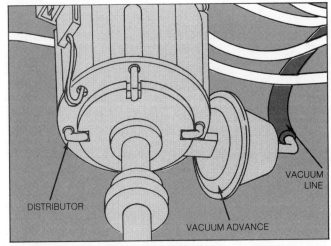

DISTRIBUTOR

VACUUM ADVANCE

VACUUM LINE

7 After the timing is properly set and the distributor is bolted down, reattach any vacuum lines to the distributor vacuum advance. A quick check of the vacuum advance can now be performed. With the timing light pointed at the timing marks, briefly accelerate the engine.

8 If the advance is working properly, the timing will advance beyond the initial setting. The timing mark on the crankshaft pulley will move off the scale as the engine accelerates. If the timing mark does not advance, a defective vacuum advance unit or vacuum supply line is the likely cause, and you should see a professional mechanic.

Step 13 Test Ballast Resistor

Most cars have a device called a ballast resistor which limits the amount of current that goes to the ignition system, thus increasing distributor point life. In cars with electronic ignitions, which have no points, it is the coil which reaps the benefits of the ballast resistor. There are two commonly used types: external and internal. The external one is a white porcelain rectangle, housing two or four terminals, which is usually mounted on the firewall, depending on the car's make and model. The internal ballast resistor is actually a high-resistance wire which is built into the wiring harness somewhere between the ignition switch and the positive (+) terminal of the ignition coil. A car with a bad ballast resistor will almost start with the key in the "start" position and the engine turning over, but when the key is returned to the "on" position, the engine will stall. The easiest way to check a ballast resistor you have doubts about is with a test light.

On cars with an externally mounted ballast resistor (Chrysler, some GM, and AMC), check both sides of the resistor for current. The test light should be hooked up to the negative (−) terminal of the battery or another ground and applied to each terminal of the resistor with the ignition key in the "on" position. Be sure the probe of the test light is applied to the copper terminal, not the plastic insulating cover. If the bulb doesn't light on both sides of the resistor, you should replace the resistor.

Chrysler cars equipped with electronic ignitions have a four-terminal ballast resistor. With the key in the "on" position, there should be current at all four terminals. If the bulb doesn't light at every one, first make sure the light is good by touching the probe to the positive (+) terminal of the battery. The light, if properly grounded and working, will go on. If it does, but you still get nothing when you touch the probe to the terminal, the ignition switch or wiring is defective and you should see a professional mechanic.

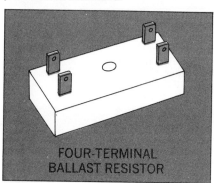

FOUR-TERMINAL
BALLAST RESISTOR

On Fords and other cars without an external ballast resistor, the resistor is built into the wiring. To check it, hook the test light to a ground, such as the negative (−) terminal of the battery and the positive (+) or (BAT) side of the ignition coil. The battery side of the ignition coil on cars with non-electronic ignitions is the side that doesn't go to the distributor. With the key in the "on" position, the bulb should light. If it does not, there is a defect in the wiring or in the ignition switch, and you should see a professional mechanic.

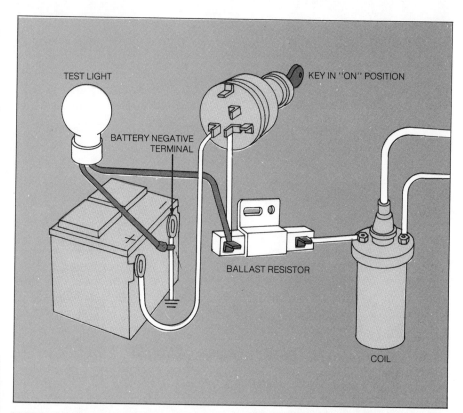

TEST LIGHT

KEY IN "ON" POSITION

BATTERY NEGATIVE TERMINAL

BALLAST RESISTOR

COIL

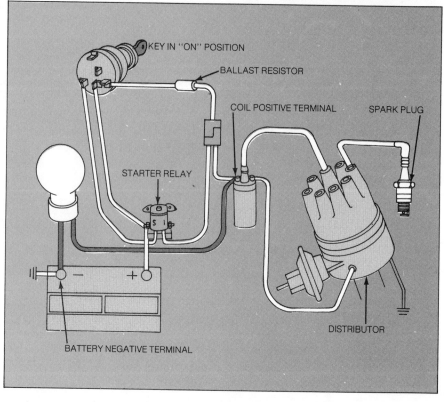

KEY IN "ON" POSITION

BALLAST RESISTOR

COIL POSITIVE TERMINAL

SPARK PLUG

STARTER RELAY

DISTRIBUTOR

BATTERY NEGATIVE TERMINAL

Step 14 Check Ignition Coil

The ignition coil transforms low battery voltage into high. While there is no prescribed maintenance for a coil, you can help keep it efficient by cleaning the tower of dirt while you are servicing the distributor. Remove the high-tension wire from the center of the coil and wipe the top clean. Inspect the top for electrical tracking between the center tower and the positive (+) and negative (−) terminals. Replace the coil if it is physically damaged or if there is evidence of tracking. Make sure the positive (+) and negative (−) wires are securely attached.

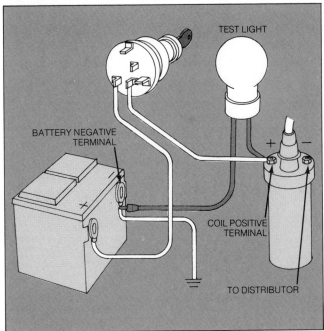

On breaker-point ignition systems, you can check the coil on a no-start car with a test light. For electronic ignition coils, see Testing: Electronic Ignition Systems, starting on p. 76. First perform the 13 steps described already in this chapter. If the car still doesn't start, turn the key to the "on" position and check for current at the battery terminal of the coil (BAT) or (+) with a test light as follows: connect the test light to a good ground, such as the negative (−) terminal of the battery, and touch the probe to the positive (+) terminal on the coil. The light should go on. If it doesn't, see the section on ballast resistors (p. 74). If the light goes on, move the probe to the negative (−) side of the coil. With the key in the "start" position and the engine turning over, the test light should flicker on and off. If it does not, and all of the steps in this chapter have been performed, you should replace the coil. If the light flickers, remove the high-tension lead between the coil and the distributor cap from the distributor cap side and hold it ¼-inch from a ground such as the engine block. Now crank the engine. If there is a spark, the coil is most likely OK, but you don't know for sure since the spark may be too weak to fire the spark plugs. Check for fuel in the carburetor (p. 100) and check the condition of the spark plugs (p. 90) before replacing the coil. If there isn't any spark, you should replace the coil.

Replacing the Ignition Coil

To remove the ignition coil, disconnect the wires from their terminals and mark them for easy reinstallation. Carefully grasp the rubber boot of the coil tower cable and twist it gently to the left and right. Carefully ease the cable out of the coil tower by holding the boot between your fingers. Do not pull or yank on the cable. Now remove the coil from the bracket mounted to the engine or remove the bracket itself.

To install the new coil, insert it into the bracket and tighten the bracket down. Hook up the wires to their correct terminals. The wire from the ignition switch and ballast resistor is connected to the terminal marked (BAT) or (+). The wire going to the distributor is connected to the terminal marked (DIST) or (−).

Testing Electronic Ignition Systems

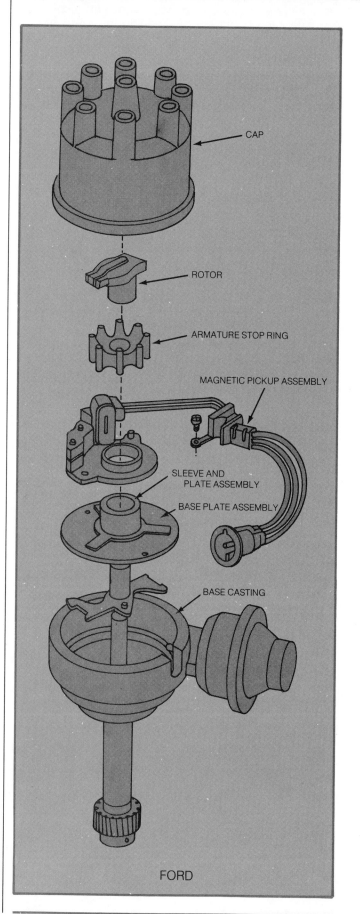

In an electronic ignition system, the points and condenser have been replaced by a non-mechanical triggering system, usually a reluctor and pickup assembly, installed where the breaker set would be in a conventional system. The primary voltage is no longer routed through a distributor, but through an electronic control unit where a switching transistor, activated by the reluctor and pickup, makes and breaks the primary circuit. Since there is no physical contact between the parts of the triggering system, only magnetic oscillations, parts do not wear out. The elimination of point wear has three advantages: greater output, increased reliability, and less service and maintenance.

Higher voltage output is necessary to fire the lean mixtures in today's low-compression, emission-controlled engines. When working on the electronic ignition system in your car, keep in mind that it is possible for your system to develop up to 47,000 volts. This higher voltage has a wearing effect on the secondary components that is only partially offset by the use of new materials. When problems develop in your ignition system, such as increased resistance from worn spark plugs, the high voltage supplied can burn holes in the distributor cap and rotor. In cases of electronic ignition-system failure, however, it's usually something other than the cap or rotor that's to blame. And you would be wise to carry spares of those parts most likely to fail in your car's electronic ignition system. As it happens, all these items lend themselves to replacement by a do-it-yourselfer. Now, what parts are we talking about?

If you're driving an American Motors car, the sensor assembly would be your best bet. It would be the most likely to fail and it's relatively inexpensive.

If your car is a Chrysler product, you should carry two items: a ballast resistor and a magnetic pickup. Make sure they fit your particular make and engine. For Ford Motor cars, carry a modulator stator for the model and year you're driving.

On General Motors cars, the pickup coil is most likely to fail, so be sure you have a spare when far from home.

And in every electronic ignition system, the spark plug cables can age before their time because of the high voltage and under-the-hood temperatures. So when you replace them, make sure you get the right ones, which are usually insulated with silicone.

The following pages present step-by-step photo sequences on service and testing procedures for the major electronic ignition systems found in today's cars.

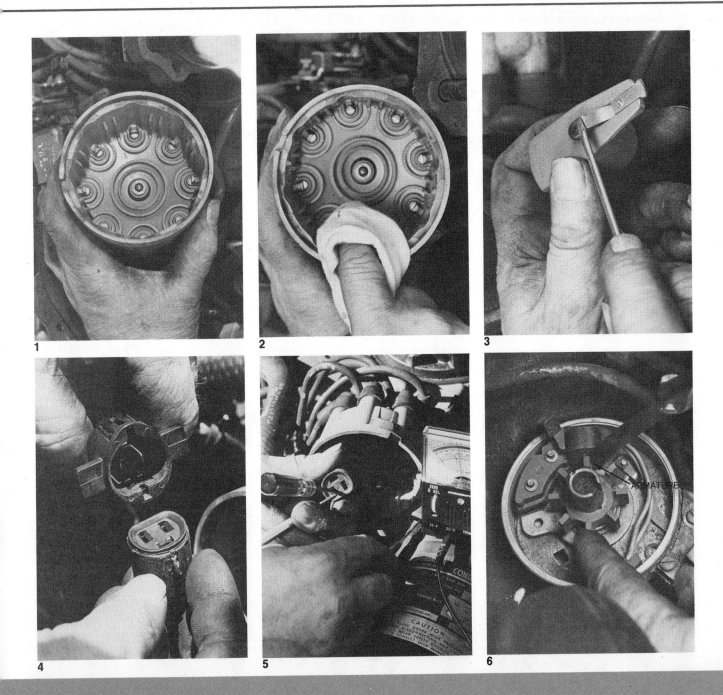

1 Remove the distributor cap and inspect the underside for arcing across the terminals, cracks on the side of the cap, and signs of rotor blade contact with the distributor spark plug terminals. Make sure the center carbon button is in good working order. It should move down when pressure is put on it and up when pressure is released. Replace the cap if necessary.

2 Wipe away any signs of contamination or moisture with a clean cloth.

3 Inspect the rotor blade and spring contact for wear, burns, and breaks. Replace the rotor if necessary.

4 Disconnect the triggering device from the distributor wire harness connector. Inspect both sides for corrosion, broken leads, and shorting. If the device shows any of these signs, replace the magnetic pickup assembly or the amplifier module, depending on which side of the 3-wire connector is defective.

5 Hold the female side of the connector facing you with the single terminal on top. With the ignition switch on, attach the positive voltmeter lead to the lower left terminal of the connector and the negative lead to a ground. The reading should meet specs. If it does not, replace the wiring harness and the amplifier module.

6 Make sure the armature is not making contact with the pickup coil. Use a feeler gauge to check for proper clearance.

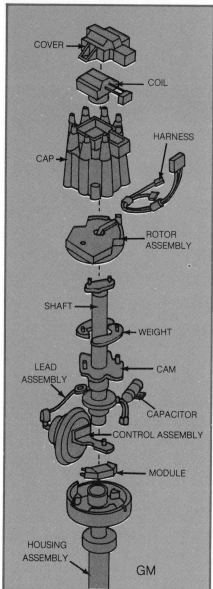

COVER

COIL

HARNESS

CAP

ROTOR ASSEMBLY

SHAFT

WEIGHT

LEAD ASSEMBLY

CAM

CAPACITOR

CONTROL ASSEMBLY

MODULE

HOUSING ASSEMBLY

GM

LUG HOOK

1

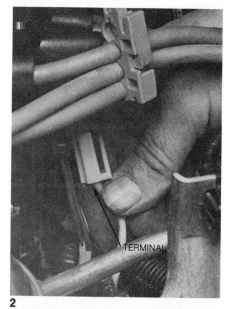

TERMINAL

2

1 To inspect the HEI system, first remove the air-cleaner wing nut. Then remove the distributor cap by pressing down on the spring-loaded lug hook with a screwdriver and rotating the hook about one-half turn.

2 Remove the battery terminal from the connection on the distributor cap marked BAT. When removing the terminal, hold it by the plug, not by its wire.

3 Disengage the distributor harness from the coil assembly by inserting a screwdriver between the terminal and its lock and pushing down.

4 To remove the circular spark-plug-wire holder, insert a screwdriver between the holder and the ignition coil cover and then pry up. Carefully remove the holder and move it aside so you can inspect the distributor. Turn the distributor cap over and inspect the spark plug terminals for any heavy deposits and corrosion. Also, check for signs of rotor blade contact. If there are deposits or blade contact, replace the rotor and cap.

5 Remove the rotor and inspect its spring contact for tension and wear. Replace the rotor and cap if necessary.

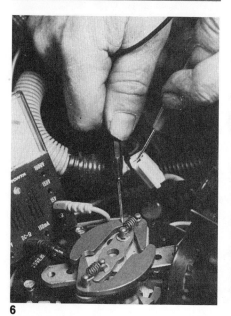

6

7

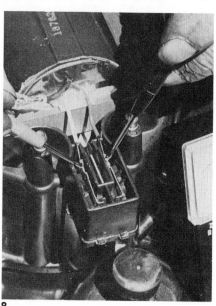

8

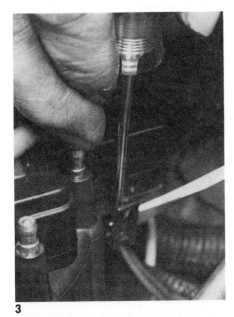

3

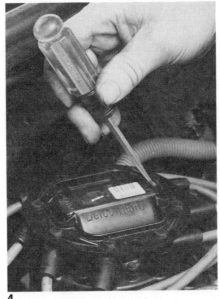

4

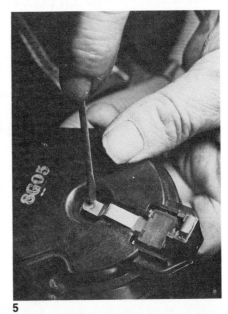

5

6 Touch the voltmeter negative lead to a ground and the positive lead to the white battery connector. Make sure the ignition switch is on. The voltmeter should read battery voltage. If it does not, check the ignition switch lead from the battery to the switch, and from the switch to the distributor battery terminal that connects to the coil. The voltmeter should read battery voltage.

7 To check the secondary resistance of the coil, touch one ohmmeter lead to the distributor high-tension terminal and the other lead to the coil wire. Make sure the ignition switch is off. The reading should be within specs. If it is not, replace the coil.

8 To check coil primary resistance, remove the three screws that attach the coil cover to the distributor cap and lift off the cover. Touch one lead of an ohmmeter to the battery terminal and the other lead to the coil wire. Make sure the ignition switch is off and the battery source is disconnected. The reading should meet specs. If it does not, replace the coil.

9 To test the distributor pickup coil, connect one lead of an ohmmeter to one connector terminal and the other lead to the second connector terminal. The reading should be within specs. If not, replace the pickup coil or see a professional mechanic. Inspect the connector wires for chafing, breaks or loose connections.

10 To replace the module, first unplug the two connectors, one on each side of it. Note that the module terminals are of different sizes to prevent improper installation. Now remove the two hold-down screws from the module and lift it out.

11 With a timing light, set the correct timing at the proper rpm. The vacuum line should be disconnected and plugged. Then adjust the idle speed to specs.

9

10

11

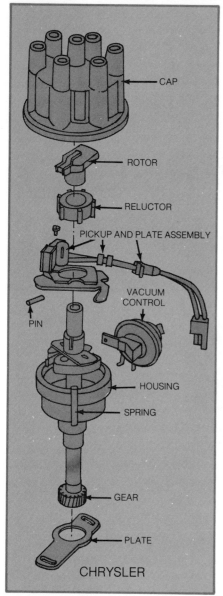

CAP

ROTOR

RELUCTOR

PICKUP AND PLATE ASSEMBLY

PIN

VACUUM CONTROL

HOUSING

SPRING

GEAR

PLATE

CHRYSLER

1

2

6

1 Remove the Phillips-head screw holding the multiple-wire connector to the electronic control unit. Note: Whenever this unit is removed or reconnected, the ignition must be off.

2 Connect the positive voltmeter lead to cavity No. 1, and the negative voltmeter lead to a ground. The reading should be within one volt of battery voltage with all accessories off and the ignition switch on.

3 If there is more than one-volt difference, test the circuit shown with a voltmeter at each connecting point until the problem is found.

4 With the ignition switch still on, touch cavity No. 2 with the positive voltmeter lead and ground the negative

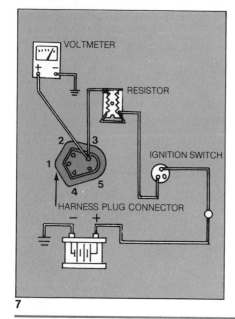

VOLTMETER

RESISTOR

IGNITION SWITCH

2 3

1

4 5

HARNESS PLUG CONNECTOR

7

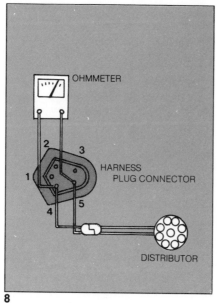

OHMMETER

2 3

1

4 5

HARNESS PLUG CONNECTOR

DISTRIBUTOR

8

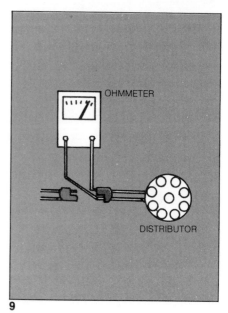

OHMMETER

DISTRIBUTOR

9

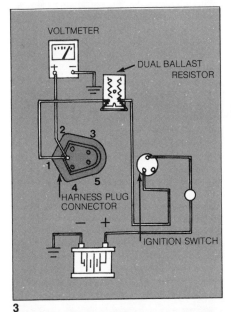

VOLTMETER

DUAL BALLAST RESISTOR

2 3

1

4 5

HARNESS PLUG CONNECTOR

IGNITION SWITCH

3

4

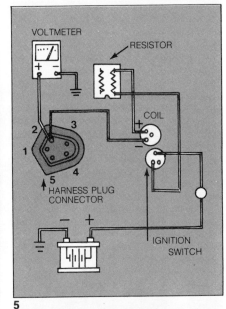

VOLTMETER

RESISTOR

COIL

2 3

1

5 4

HARNESS PLUG CONNECTOR

IGNITION SWITCH

5

lead. The reading should be within one volt of battery voltage.

5 If there is more than one-volt difference, repeat step 3 for the circuit shown.

6 Touch the positive voltmeter lead to cavity No. 3 and ground the negative lead. Again, the ignition switch must be on. The reading should be within one volt of battery voltage.

7 If the difference is more than one volt, repeat step 3 for the circuit illustrated.

8 To check the distributor pickup coil, turn off the ignition, and connect an ohmmeter between No. 4 and No. 5 cavities. The resistance should read

between 150 and 900 ohms. Note that the ignition switch must be off. Disconnect the dual lead connector if the reading is other than specified.

9 Now, with the ignition switch off, connect the ohmmeter leads to both terminals of the disconnected dual connector coming from the distributor. If the reading is not between 150 and 900 ohms, replace the pickup coil assembly in the distributor.

10 If the ohmmeter reading is within specs, check the wiring harness between the control unit and the dual lead connector with a volt/amp tester.

11 To check the electronic ground circuit, connect one ohmmeter lead to a good ground and the other lead to the control unit connector pin No. 5.

Make sure the ignition switch is off. The ohmmeter should show continuity (a full reading). If there is no continuity, loosen the control unit bolts and clean off any dirt around the bolts and the mounting area. Reinstall and tighten the bolts and retest. If there is still no continuity, replace the control unit. Reconnect the wiring harness at the control unit and distributor.

12 Check the air gap between the reluctor tooth and the pickup coil. To adjust the air gap, align one reluctor tooth with the pickup coil core. Loosen the pickup coil hold-down screw and place a .006-inch non-magnetic feeler gauge between the tooth and the core. Adjust the gap so contact is made between the tooth, feeler gauge, and core. Now tighten the hold-down screw.

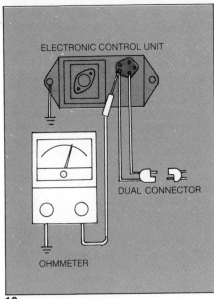

ELECTRONIC CONTROL UNIT

DUAL CONNECTOR

OHMMETER

10

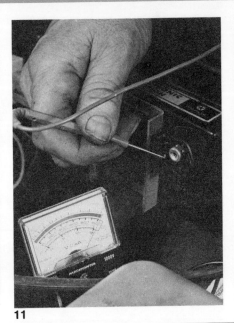

11

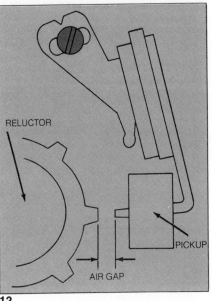

RELUCTOR

PICKUP

AIR GAP

12

Photosteps: HALL-EFFECT ELECTRONIC IGNITION SYSTEM

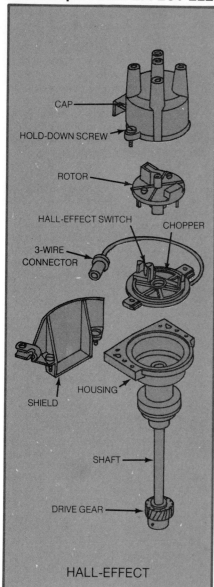

CAP

HOLD-DOWN SCREW

ROTOR

HALL-EFFECT SWITCH — CHOPPER

3-WIRE CONNECTOR

SHIELD — HOUSING

SHAFT

DRIVE GEAR

HALL-EFFECT

DISTRIBUTOR

COIL

1

3-WIRE CONNECTOR

2

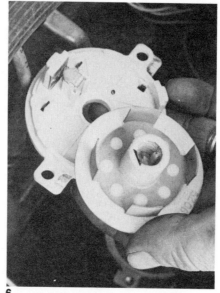

6

1 Overview of the crowded Plymouth Horizon engine compartment showing a transverse engine. Note the distance between the ignition coil and the distributor.

2 A 3-wire connector is mounted on the side of the distributor.

3 Remove the coil high-tension wire from the distributor cap and put it aside for later testing.

4 To lift off the distributor cap, remove the two hold-down screws with a Phillips-head screwdriver.

5 After removing the distributor cap, lift out the rotor for inspection. Check for cracks, excessive burning of the

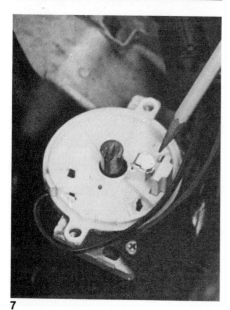

7

8

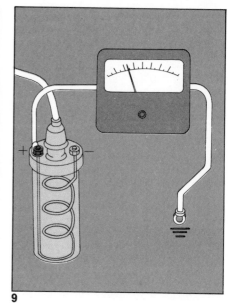

9

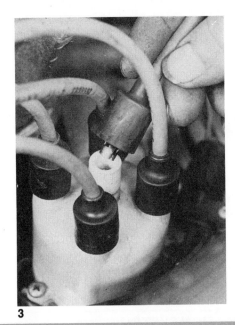

3

4

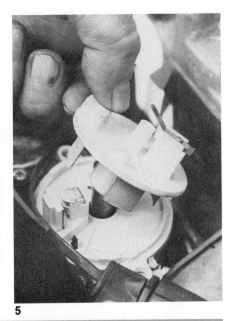

5

blade tip, and proper tension of the spring terminal. *Caution: Silicone grease on the metal part of the rotor is normal. Do not wipe it off. Light scaling on the tip can be removed with a sharp knife. If scaling is excessive, replace the rotor.*

6 Inspect the underside of the rotor for carbon tracking. Check the chopper and make sure the leading and trailing edges of the four vanes are square. Replace the chopper if it is defective.

7 The pencil points to the Hall-Effect switch (sensor). As the chopper turns, current to the coil is turned off and a high-voltage spark is induced and routed to a spark plug.

8 Disconnect the wire from the negative terminal of the ignition coil. With the ignition switch on, connect one end of a jumper wire to the negative terminal of the coil. Now touch the other end momentarily to an engine ground while holding the coil high-tension wire you disconnected in step 3 one-quarter of an inch from a good engine ground. A spark should occur.

9 If there is no spark when performing step 8, with the ignition switch on check for voltage at the positive terminal of the coil. If the voltmeter reads at least nine volts, the coil is defective and should be replaced. If voltage is below nine volts, check the ballast resistor, wiring, and connections.

10 If a spark occurred in step 8, reconnect the negative coil wire to its terminal and disconnect the 3-wire distributor connector. Turn the ignition switch on and measure the voltage between pin B and a good ground. It should be the same as battery voltage.

11 If the voltmeter reading in step 9 was not battery voltage, turn the ignition switch off and disconnect the 10-wire harness connector (arrow) going to the spark control computer.

12 Check for continuity between pin B of the 3-wire connector and pin 3 of the 10-wire connector.

Continued

10

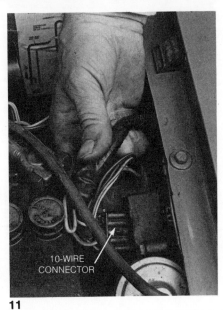

10-WIRE CONNECTOR

11

12

13 If there is no continuity, turn the ignition switch on and measure the voltage between pin 2 and pin 10 of the disconnected 10-wire connector. The reading should be battery voltage. If it is not, the wiring and connections of pin 2 and pin 10 should be checked. If battery voltage is obtained, the spark control computer is defective and should be replaced.

14 With the ignition switch on and the 10-wire connector reconnected, hold the center wire of the coil one-quarter inch from a good ground. Pass a feeler gauge (metal) through the pickup coil gap. A spark should occur. If there is no spark, disconnect the 3-wire connector going to the distributor and momentarily touch 10A to pin C with a jumper wire or a paper clip. If a spark occurs, the pickup assembly is defective and must be replaced.

15 To replace the pickup assembly (switch plate), remove the two lock springs. The pencil points to one of them. Lift out the pickup assembly, then remove the two screws holding the shield to the distributor. Reverse these procedures to install the new pickup assembly.

16 To set the ignition timing, you can use either a magnetic pulse timing light at the probe hole or an induction-type timing light at the timing marks.

13

Photosteps: AMERICAN MOTORS (PRESTOLITE) ELECTRONIC IGNITION SYSTEM

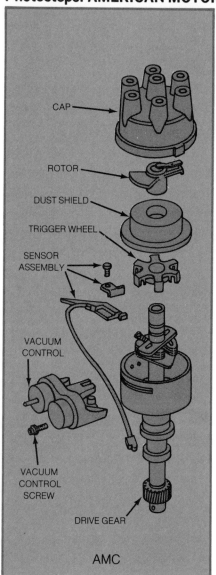

CAP
ROTOR
DUST SHIELD
TRIGGER WHEEL
SENSOR ASSEMBLY
VACUUM CONTROL
VACUUM CONTROL SCREW
DRIVE GEAR

AMC

CARBON TRACKING

WEAR

1

2

6

7

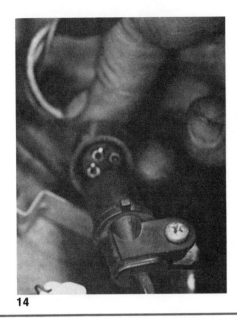

14

15

PROBE HOLE

TIMING MARKS

16

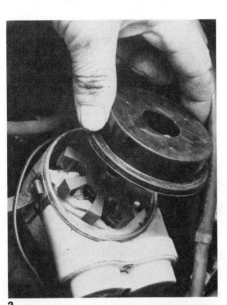

3

4

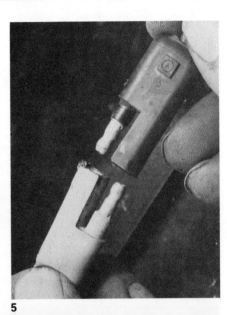

5

1 After removing the distributor cap, inspect the underside for wear or carbon tracking. Replace the cap if necessary. Inspect the carbon button in the center of the distributor cap. It should move down when pressure is put on it. When pressure is released, the button should move up due to spring action. If it does not, replace the cap.

2 Remove the rotor by lifting it off the distributor shaft. Inspect the rotor for worn blades and cracks, and replace it if necessary.

3 Remove the dust shield from the distributor to expose the vanes and trigger assembly for inspection.

4 The pen points to the small wires under the trigger wheel going to the sensor. Inspect these wires for chafing, breaks or shorting against the wheel. If the wires are damaged, the sensor unit must be replaced. A special tool, similar to a battery terminal puller, is necessary to remove the wheel.

5 Disconnect the dual-wire connector from the sensor. The connector is located on the side of the distributor.

6 To measure resistance in the sensor unit, use the distributor side of the disconnected dual-lead connector. Connect one ohmmeter lead to one terminal of the connector and the other

ohmmeter lead to the second terminal of the connector. Make sure the ignition switch is off. The reading should meet specs. If it does not, the sensor unit must be replaced. Wiggle the sensor wires while observing the ohmmeter reading. Any movement of the needle means trouble in that line, and you should replace the sensor unit.

7 To measure secondary resistance in the ignition coil, remove the coil wires. Touch one ohmmeter lead to the positive (primary) terminal of the coil and insert the other ohmmeter lead into the center (secondary) coil tower. The reading should meet specs. If it does not, replace the coil.

Continued

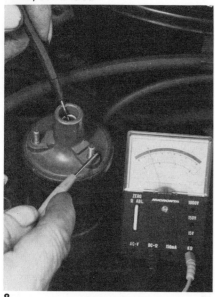

8

9

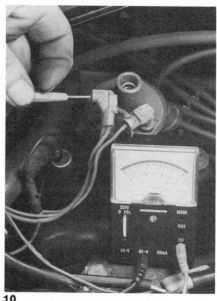

10

8 Now touch one ohmmeter lead to the negative (primary) terminal of the coil and insert the other ohmmeter lead into the center (secondary) coil tower. The reading should meet specs. If it does not, replace the coil.

9 To measure primary resistance in the ignition coil, remove the coil wires. Touch the ohmmeter leads to the positive and negative (primary) terminals of the coil. If the reading does not meet specs, replace the coil.

10 To test for voltage from the ignition switch to the coil, pull the positive coil lead off its terminal. Attach the positive voltmeter lead to the positive coil wire from the ignition switch. *Caution: To avoid a false reading, see that the positive voltmeter lead is not*

touching any other terminals. Attach the negative voltmeter lead to a good ground. Make sure the ignition switch is on. If the reading is not within specs, check the ignition switch and wiring going to the battery at each connecting point until the problem is found.

11 To check continuity through the coil primary circuit, reconnect the positive coil lead (from the ignition switch) to the ignition coil. With the ignition switch on, disconnect the negative coil lead (distributor side) and touch a voltmeter positive lead to the negative coil terminal and a negative voltmeter lead to a ground. If the reading is not within specs, replace the coil.

12 To inspect the connections between the control unit and the distributor, disconnect the 4-wire connector (shown on the fender well). Inspect it for corrosion and broken terminals. If the connector on the control-unit side is defective, the unit must be replaced.

13 To check the 4-way connector on the distributor side, hold the connector facing you so the two male terminals are on the left and the two female terminals on the right. With the ignition switch off, touch one ohmmeter probe to the top female terminal and the other probe to the top male terminal. The reading should indicate continuity. If it does not, replace the 4-way connector.

11

12

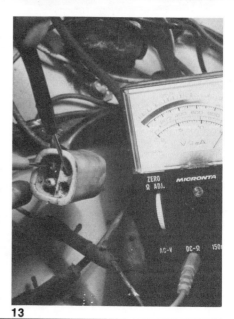

13

SPARK PLUG SERVICE

There are few parts of a car more closely identified with a tuneup than spark plugs. Ask even a motorist with limited mechanical knowledge of cars to name one tuneup operation and more times than not he will say, "Change the spark plugs!" Talk to your service station mechanic about tuning your car and see if he doesn't refer to the tuneup trinity of plugs, points, and condenser. And with electronic ignitions taking over, points and condenser may follow the running board into oblivion, leaving only plugs.

Exactly what is the function of spark plugs and why are they so important in the proper operation of a car? A spark plug might be called the match in the ignition system. When the high voltage from the coil jumps across the narrow gap of the plug, a spark occurs. This spark ignites the compressed mixture of air and fuel in the combustion chamber. If the plug is damaged, fouled with carbon or oil, or just worn out, it will not fire properly or not fire at all. The result will be an increase in fuel consumption and a poorly running engine. If your plugs are bad, you may have to crank the engine several times to fire it, and you stand a good chance of running down your battery and ruining your starter. So regular spark plug maintenance and replacement will make your engine start faster, run better, and burn less fuel.

Generally, plugs that have been in the car for 10,000 to 12,000 miles have served their purpose and should be retired. At least they should be checked. Learning to read spark plugs is one of the most valuable skills you can acquire to determine your engine's operating condition. Frequently, spark plugs are incorrectly blamed for poor engine performance. New plugs cannot permanently rectify poor performance caused by worn points, a weak coil, a faulty carburetor or worn rings or cylinders.

Too often spark plug cables, which have to bear the high voltage supplied by the coil, are ignored in maintenance schedules. If they're cracked, punctured, dirty or covered with oil or grease, the plugs can misfire, and even cause the car not to start at all. So be sure to put cables on your inspection list when doing a tuneup.

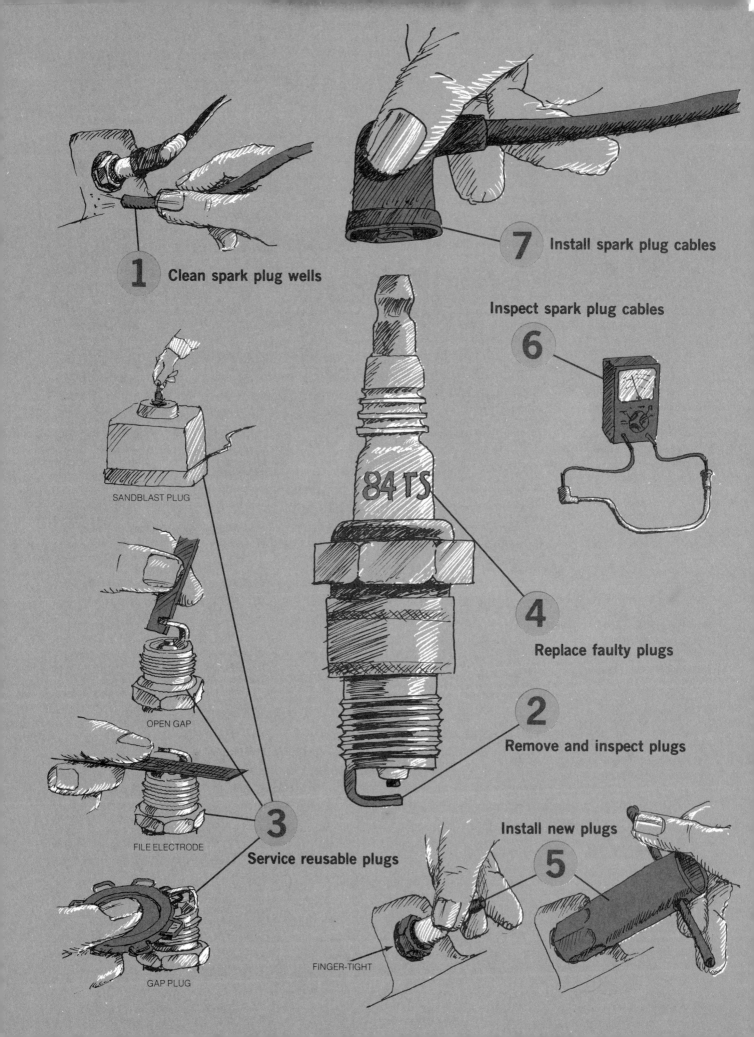

1 Clean spark plug wells

7 Install spark plug cables

Inspect spark plug cables

6

SANDBLAST PLUG

OPEN GAP

FILE ELECTRODE

GAP PLUG

84 TS

4 Replace faulty plugs

2 Remove and inspect plugs

3 Service reusable plugs

Install new plugs

5

FINGER-TIGHT

Spark Plug Service

1 Clean spark plug wells. See Step 2 of Compression Test, p. 90.

2 Remove and inspect plugs. Check the plugs for cracks, compression leaks, electrode wear, and oil or carbon deposits (p. 90).

3 Service reusable plugs. Clean them with a sandblaster. Open the plug gap and file the electrode square. Gap the plugs and reinstall them in the same spark plug holes (p. 90).

4 Replace faulty plugs. Make sure the new plugs have the same thread reach and seat design as the ones you removed. Also, be sure the new plugs meet your car's heat range and gap specs (p. 94).

5 Install new plugs. Screw in the plugs by hand until they are finger-tight. Then seat them to correct torque (p. 94).

6 Inspect spark plug cables. Check them for cuts, punctures, cracks, and age. Test them for resistance (p. 95). Damaged or old cables can mean poor engine performance and gas mileage, as well as hard starting in wet weather.

7 Install spark plug cables. Make sure the cables are of the correct length and are routed properly (p. 96).

Step 1 Clean Spark Plug Wells (See p. 54)

Step 2 Remove and Inspect Plugs

Essential. Basic tools (p. 20). Spark plug wrench, universal joint, extension • Spark plug cleaning solvent • Stiff brush • File • Wire feeler gauge • Towels or clean rags • Oil • Ohmmeter.
Handy. Masking tape and/or spring clothespin • Spark plug cable remover • Egg carton • Sandblaster (plug cleaner) • Electrode bending tool • Torque wrench.

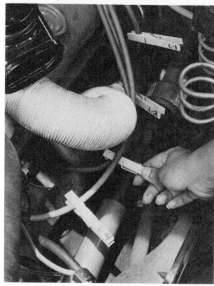

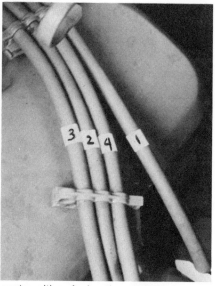

Identify all the spark plug wires. Before removing them, label each one, either with masking tape or a spring clothespin, so you will be able to connect the right cable to the right cylinder after you have serviced the plugs. A good way to mark the tape or clothespin if you're working on a V-type engine is to use code L-1, L-2, etc., for the plugs in the left cylinder bank and R-1, R-2, etc., for the plugs in the right bank. On in-line engines, all you have to do is number the plug wires from front to rear. Left and right cylinder banks are determined by the driver's seat position, facing the engine compartment. Keep in mind that cables routed through a bracket on the cylinder head cover or the engine are not always in the same sequence as they appear attached to the plugs. For example, L-1 cable may be positioned third in the bracket.

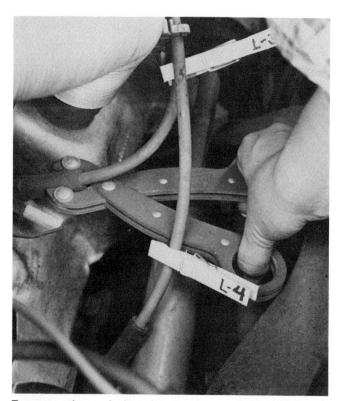

To remove the spark plug wires, grasp the boot—the heavy, rubbery part at the spark plug port—with a spark plug cable remover and twist the boot back and forth to free it from the plug. Then pull on the boot. If the engine is cold and you do not have a special wire remover, grasp the cable by its boot and carefully twist it back and forth to free it from the plug terminal. Then, still holding the boot, pull it carefully off the plug. Remove all the plug cables this way. *Caution: if you try to remove the cables by pulling on the wires, you stand a good chance of breaking the electrical conductor inside, so always grab the cables by their boots.*

To remove the spark plugs, use a spark plug wrench with a U-joint and, if necessary, an extension long enough to reach the plug you are removing. Place the socket over the plug and turn the wrench counterclockwise. Plug sockets usually come in three sizes: $\frac{13}{16}$-inch hex, $\frac{7}{8}$-inch hex, and $\frac{5}{8}$-inch hex. Generally, the $\frac{13}{16}$-inch hex is the one found on US-made cars and light trucks.

Reading Your Plugs

Next, inspect the spark plugs. Shown here and on the next page are 15 plugs taken from 15 different engines. They're printed in color on the back cover. Knowing how to "read" your plugs can help you do a better job tuning up your car. The 15 descriptions which follow should get you going:

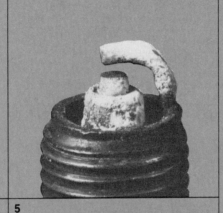

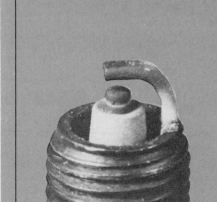

1 Almost white, fluffy gray deposits on the insulator tip and the side electrode: Normal for emission-controlled engines using lean mixtures and no-lead fuels. This plug has high mileage and should be replaced.

2 White with light tan tint: The soft deposits on the center electrode and the darker deposits on the side electrode indicate the proper heat range for the way this engine is being used—at moderate speeds and loads.

3 Light tan deposits on a well-used plug: Yellow deposits on the side electrode are normal and come from metallic additives.

4 Yellowish, soft white deposits on the center electrode and insulator: Normal for an engine using fuel containing certain metallic additives. Shell deposits are normal, not signs of wrong fuel mixtures.

5 A classic example of a normal plug with fluffy, chocolate brown deposits on the insulator: Note the slightly lighter color on the side electrode showing that it's running a bit hotter. Sooty, black deposits on the shell suggest a rich mixture, and perhaps a new air filter is needed.

6 Slightly oily deposits on the shell may be due to an engine not yet fully broken in. In an older engine, this might indicate the beginning of wear on piston rings, valve guides or seals.

7 Detonation damage: The firing end of the insulator is broken and metal has been transferred from the center electrode to the side electrode. Possible causes: a) Overadvanced ignition timing; b) Fuel too low in octane; c) Exhaust Gas Recirculation (EGR) system malfunctioning.

Reading Your Plugs

8 Preignition damage: White deposits on a blistered insulator, along with burned electrodes, reveal an extreme heat condition. Possible causes: a) Spark plug too hot; b) Over-advanced ignition timing; c) Glowing deposits in combustion chamber; d) Cooling system clogged; e) Exhaust system blocked.

9 Soot fouling: Fluffy, black soot deposits on the insulator and the electrodes. Possible causes: a) Excessively rich mixture due to sticking choke or defective carburetor; b) Faulty ignition primary circuit or defective spark plug wires; c) Excessively cold starting without engine warm-up.

10 Oil fouled: An oily, usually black, deposit covering the insulator and the electrodes. Possible causes: a) Excessive passage of engine oil into the combustion chamber due to piston ring or valve guide seal leakage; b) Defective Positive Crankcase Ventilation (PCV) system.

11 Carbon fouled: Hard, black carbon deposits on the insulator and the electrodes. Possible causes: a) Moderate amount of oil passing the rings or valves; b) Defective PCV system; c) Spark plug too cold; d) Spark plug not the correct type for engine.

12 Dirt fouling: Carbonized and sometimes granular deposits on and around the insulator and the electrodes. Possible causes: a) Air cleaner missing; b) Defective air-cleaner mountings.

13 Bridged gap: Carbon particles are lodged in the spark plug gap. Possible cause: Combustion chamber deposits accumulated during low-speed, light-load use break loose during demand for full power.

14 Glazed insulator: Glassy surface on the insulator as a result of deposits melting on the plug. Possible causes: a) Spark plug too hot; b) Local overheating due to cooling system blockage or a similar defect.

15 Splashed insulator: Splotches of black, almost paint-like deposits on the insulator. Possible cause: Delayed correction of an engine miss allows soft, oily deposits to accumulate in the cylinder. After tuneup, these deposits break loose and foul the plug.

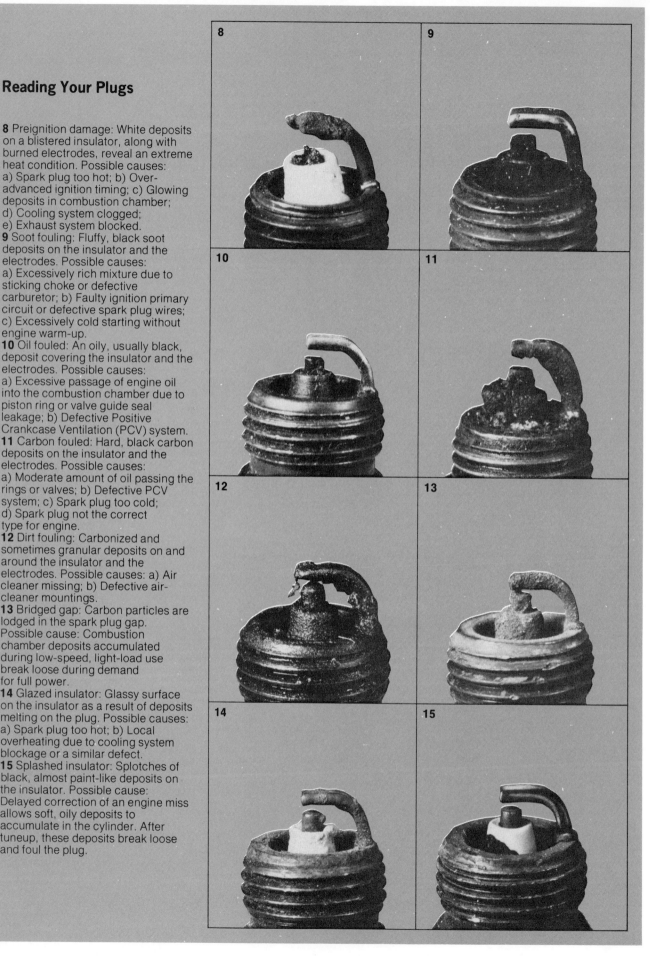

Step 3 Service Reusable Plugs

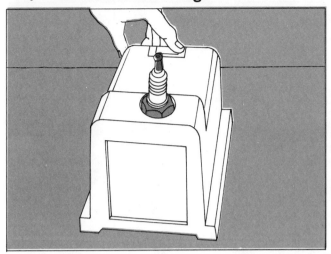

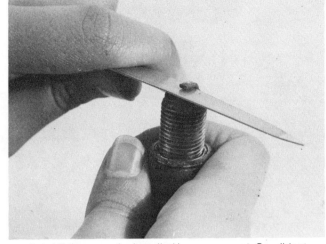

Cleaning spark plugs. If the plugs appear to be OK, and they have been in the car for less than 10,000 miles, you can clean, regap, and reinstall them. If they don't show too much wear, you can simply wash them with a solvent and a stiff brush. Never use a wire brush on the electrodes as this may "etch" them, allowing fresh deposits to adhere more easily. The best way to clean plugs is to sandblast them. If you don't have this kind of plug cleaner, for a small fee your local service shop will sandblast them like new. But don't think they're ready to be installed in your car yet. Sandblast cleaning not only removes the deposits but rounds off the electrodes as well, and it may remove certain essential alloys from the plug electrodes. The center electrode should always be filed so that its tip is flat.

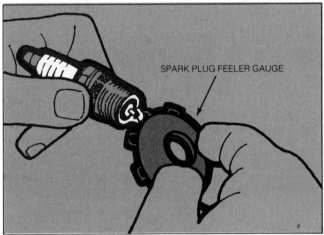

SPARK PLUG FEELER GAUGE

BENDING TOOL →

Setting the gap. Whether you are using cleaned plugs or new ones, always check their gap. Use a round feeler gauge to do this and set the gap to the specifications for your engine and year of car (see Appendix, Specifications by Make and Model) (p. 202). Push the wire gauge into the gap and then pull it out. If there is a slight drag or friction between the wire and the gap surfaces, the gap is correct. If the gauge goes in easily or "falls" through, then the side electrode must be bent down towards the center electrode to narrow the gap. A special bending tool is used for this. Recheck the gap and repeat the bending process until you get the correct one. If the gauge cannot be pushed into the gap, then it is too narrow and the side electrode must be bent up from the center electrode. Don't worry if you don't get it right the first time. Even the best pros have to bend the electrode several times before getting the correct gap.

A Handy Holder

You will need a spark plug holder. As you remove the plugs, store them in a safe place to prevent damage to the porcelain. An egg carton makes a handy holder. It's a good idea to keep the plugs in the same order as the cylinders from which they were removed. When you examine the plugs, knowing the cylinder each one came from will help you pinpoint any engine problems.

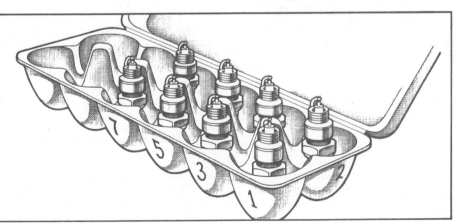

Step 4 Replace Faulty Plugs

18 MM   14 MM

TAPERED SEAT   GASKET STYLE

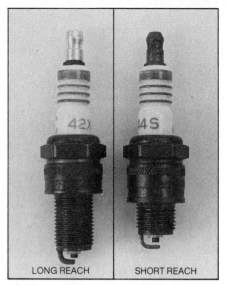

LONG REACH   SHORT REACH

When replacing spark plugs, make sure you buy the right ones. Know the thread diameter of the plugs used in your car. The two most popular in use today are 14mm and 18mm. Some plugs have a tapered seat design, while others must be used with a gasket. Depending on the cylinder head, engine builders have

manufactured spark plugs with different thread reaches. Thread reach is the distance from the shell seat to the end of the threaded section. Some plugs are designated long-reach, others short-reach. It is important for proper combustion to be sure that you install plugs that have the same thread reach

and the same seat design as the ones removed from your engine. When installing new plugs, never use short-reach plugs in a long-reach cylinder head. If you do, it will reduce combustion efficiency and increase your engine's fuel consumption, and it can severely damage the engine.

Step 5 Install New Plugs

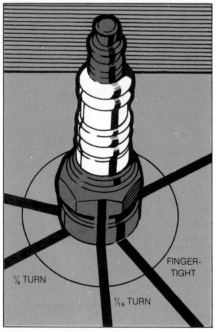

1/4 TURN   FINGER-TIGHT   1/16 TURN

With a clean cloth, wipe the threads and plug seat in the cylinder head. Run a thread chaser through the cylinder head threads to ease installation of the plugs. If you're reinstalling the original plugs, place new gaskets over the plug threads. Screw the plugs in by hand until they are finger-tight. If you're using tapered seat plugs (no gasket), tighten them an additional 1/16 turn with a wrench. Gasket-type plugs should be tightened one quarter turn more. If you have a torque wrench, tighten the plugs to the specifications in the torque chart opposite.

Go Chase a Thread

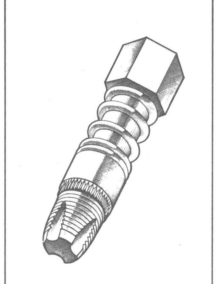

The object pictured above is a thread chaser and seat-cleaning tool, and you can and should buy one from your auto parts dealer if you do your own spark plug work. Its job is to thoroughly clean the threads and seats before the plugs are installed, and it's worth every cent you spend for it. If you fail just once to clean the seat of a spark plug port properly, a particle can lodge between the plug shell and the cylinder head. The outcome, at the least, could be a ruined plug. At the most, the cylinder head can be destroyed.

Spark Plug Heat Range

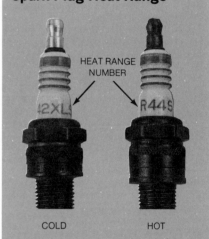

HEAT RANGE NUMBER

COLD   HOT

To achieve maximum engine performance under different driving conditions, spark plugs have various operating temperatures or heat ranges. The heat range is determined by the length of the insulator and how fast it can transfer heat from the insulator and electrodes into the cooling system and the atmosphere. The shorter the insulator tip, the colder the spark plug. The heat range is designated by a number on the porcelain. The lower the number, the colder the plug (except on foreign plugs, where the higher the number, the colder the plug). The heat range of a plug has nothing to do with its ability to fire the fuel-and-air mixture. It's simply a term that rates its heat-transferring qualities.

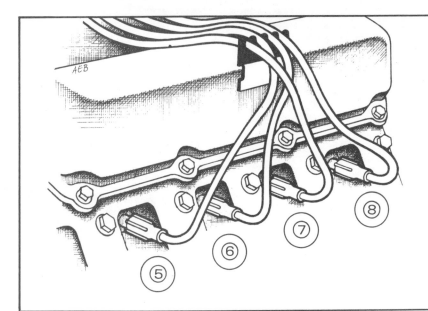

How to Avoid Getting Caught in the "Crossfire"

Crossfire is a word used to describe a condition that allows high voltage from one cable to induce electric current in an adjacent cable, thereby firing its spark plug out of turn. Crossfire is serious because it can damage the inside of a cylinder. The engine will run rough even though the ignition system, carburetion, and spark plugs are OK. If you think your car is suffering from this condition, check the firing order of the engine and find out if two cables serving cylinders that fire consecutively in the same cylinder bank are routed parallel to each other. For example, if cylinder eight fires right after cylinder seven, make sure the cables are separated in the cable bracket.

Step 6 Inspect Spark Plug Cables

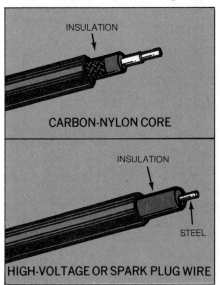

INSULATION

CARBON-NYLON CORE

INSULATION

STEEL

HIGH-VOLTAGE OR SPARK PLUG WIRE

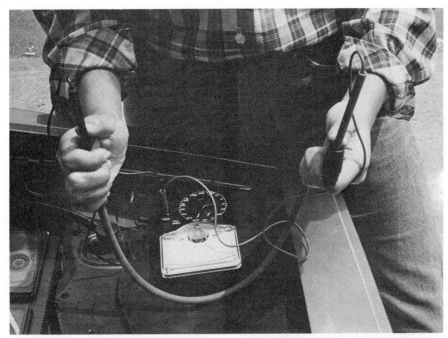

Suppression-type spark plug cables, known as TVRS (Television-Radio Suppressor), are the most popular today because they prevent radio and television interference. But you may find conductor wire (metal core) cables on older cars. If your car still has this kind of cable, replace it with the suppression-type. Inspect the cables for cracks, burns, oil, and grease. Bend them and check for brittleness or deterioration. Replace the entire set of cables, not just one or two.

Testing plug cable resistance. Remove one cable at a time from the spark plug and the distributor cap. Connect an ohmmeter between the ends of the cable. If the ohmmeter leads are probe types, you can insert the probes so they touch the terminals. Make sure they make good contact. If your ohmmeter has alligator clips, you can make contact with the spark plug end of the cable by inserting a screwdriver through the boot and attaching the alligator clip to the shank of the screwdriver. The other end of the cable will accept an alligator clip. If resistance is more than 30,000 ohms for cables up to 25 inches long and 50,000 ohms for cables longer than 25 inches, replace the cables.

RECOMMENDED INSTALLATION TORQUE				
SPARK PLUG THREAD SIZE	CAST IRON HEADS		ALUMINUM HEADS	
	with torque wrench	without torque wrench	with torque wrench	without torque wrench
GASKET TYPE	after seating	after seating		
10mm	8–12 lb./ft.	¼ turn	8–12 lb./ft.	¼ turn
12mm	10–18 lb./ft.	¼ turn	10–18 lb./ft.	¼ turn
14mm	26–30 lb./ft.	¼ to ⅜ turn	18–22 lb./ft.	¼ turn
18mm	32–38 lb./ft.	¼ turn	28–34 lb./ft.	¼ turn
TAPERED SEAT				
14mm	7–15 lb./ft.	1/16 turn (snug)	7–15 lb./ft.	1/16 turn (snug)
18mm	15–20 lb./ft.	1/16 turn (snug)	15–20 lb./ft.	1/16 turn (snug)

Testing cables for breaks. Sometimes spark plug cables have breaks that are not visible to the naked eye. To test for such breaks, attach one end of a jumper wire to a screwdriver blade and the other end to a good ground. Disconnect a cable from its plug. The engine should be running for this test. Hold the plug cable away from the engine and make sure it doesn't arc (ground). Now pass the screwdriver blade along the length of the cable. If arcing (sparking) occurs, it means there's a break in that cable and it should be replaced. Test the other plug cables in the same way. *Caution: When the screwdriver blade nears the exposed spark plug end of the cable, it may arc.*

Step 7 Install Spark Plug Cables

The trick here is to avoid cable mix-up. Start by removing the first cable at the right-hand side of the engine. Disconnect the cable from the distributor cap tower and lay it aside. Take a new cable about the same length as the one just removed (it can be slightly longer) and install it, first in the distributor cap and then to the spark plug. Do this for each of the cables. Make sure the cables are firmly attached. When removing the old cable from the distributor, see if there is any corrosion or damage in the cap. If there is, correct the problem before hooking up the rest of the cables.

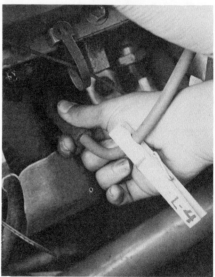

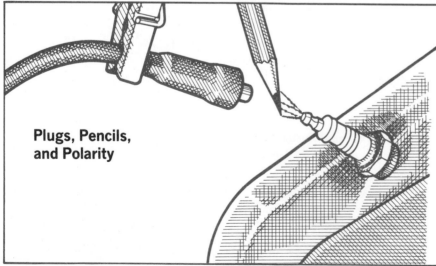

Plugs, Pencils, and Polarity

When you replace a coil, it is very important to make sure that the two primary leads are reconnected properly. A reverse connection reverses polarity, considerably decreasing the voltage available for ignition. An easy way to check polarity is to disconnect any cable at the spark plug and insert the tip of a soft lead pencil between the cable and the plug while the engine is running. The spark flare will be toward the plug terminal if the polarity is right. If not, reverse the leads at the coil.

FUEL SYSTEM SERVICE

The fuel system stores gasoline, mixes it with air, and distributes this mixture to the engine cylinders. Typical component parts include the fuel tank, the fuel pickup and gasoline gauge sending unit in the tank, fuel supply and return lines, the fuel pump, gasoline and air filters, a charcoal canister, the carburetor, and the intake manifold. The components of the system that require normal maintenance (the carburetor and filters) are treated in Chapter 9, on carburetor service. Because the fuel system handles gasoline, a potentially dangerous substance, you should inspect all its parts for cracks, leaks or other damage. Once a safety inspection of the system is performed, there is no need to go any further unless you suspect a problem. If the fuel pump doesn't deliver enough fuel to the carburetor, the engine will hesitate and stall or lose power at high speeds. In some cases, the car won't start. If the fuel pump delivers too much gasoline and the carburetor needle valve can't handle the high pressure, the car will burn too much gasoline. The engine will emit clouds of black smoke and stall. In extreme cases, the fuel will pour out of the carburetor onto the engine, creating a fire hazard. Fuel pumps in current use are not repairable and must be replaced if they are defective.

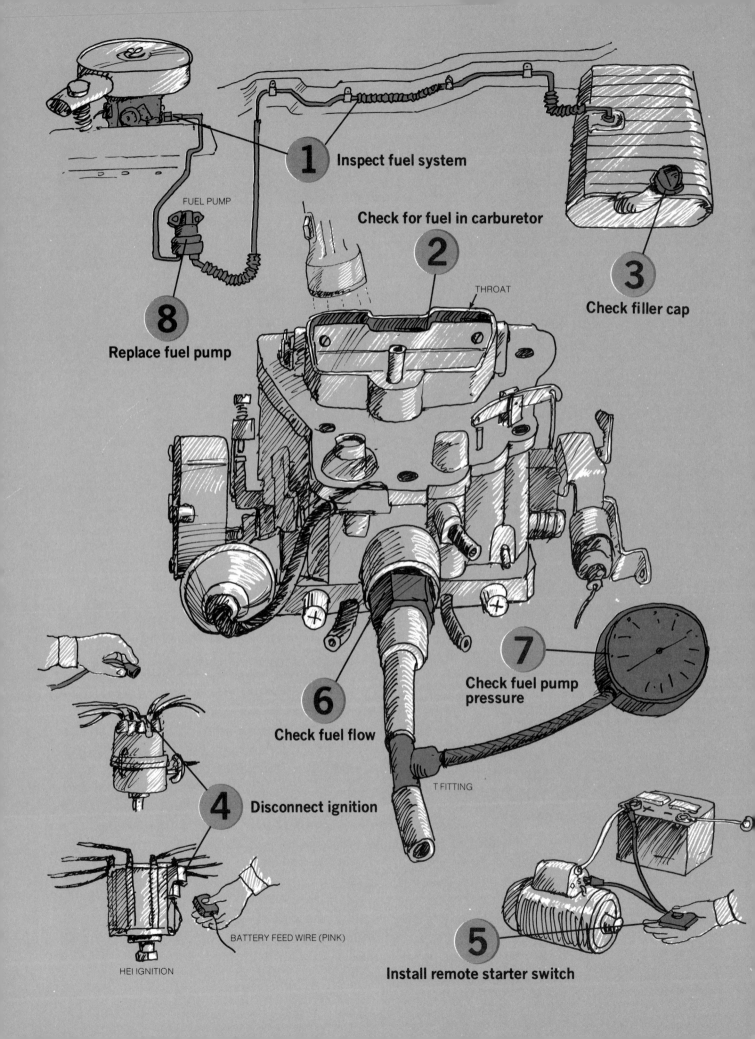

1 Inspect fuel system

2 Check for fuel in carburetor

THROAT

3 Check filler cap

FUEL PUMP

8 Replace fuel pump

7 Check fuel pump pressure

6 Check fuel flow

T FITTING

4 Disconnect ignition

BATTERY FEED WIRE (PINK)

HEI IGNITION

5 Install remote starter switch

Job Steps

Fuel System Service

Prep: Make sure there is enough gasoline in the tank to run the engine.

1 **Inspect fuel system.** Carefully check the system for leaks by starting at the carbure-tor inlet and tracing the fuel line all the way back to the fuel tank (p. 100). If there are any leaks or damaged lines, repair or replace them as necessary (p. 100).

2 **Check for fuel in carburetor.** Remove the top of the air cleaner (p. 100) and shine a flashlight into the carburetor while opening and closing the throttle. There should be a small stream of gasoline each time the throttle is opened (p. 100). Note: Make sure the accelerator pump is working (pp. 112–120).

3 **Check filler cap.** If the vent on the cap sticks, the engine can fail to start. Remove the cap and inspect it for damage (p. 101). On a no-start car, try starting with the cap removed. If the car starts, replace the cap (p. 101).

4 **Disconnect ignition.** To prevent the engine from starting during the test, remove the coil wire from the center of the distributor cap and ground with a jumper wire (p. 101). Most cars with HEI do not have a coil wire, so in these cases, disconnect the battery feed wire from the side of the distributor (p. 101).

5 **Install remote starter switch.** If you don't have a helper to crank the engine over from inside the car, you'll need a remote starter switch (p. 101).

6 **Check fuel flow.** This tells you if gasoline is flowing freely from the tank through the fuel pump to the carburetor. Disconnect the fuel line at the carburetor inlet and crank the engine (p. 101).

7 **Check fuel pump pressure.** This tells you if the fuel system is capable of providing enough fuel to the engine for all operating conditions (p. 101).

8 **Replace fuel pump.** If the flow or pressure tests indicate a defective pump, you should replace it (p. 102).

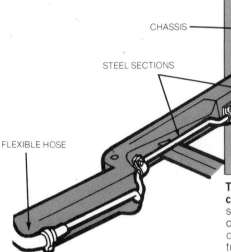

TOOLS

Essential. Basic tools (p. 20). Flashlight • Cutting pliers • Towels or clean rags • Test light • Vacuum/ pressure gauge.
Handy. Fender cover • Remote starter switch • Tubing flaring tool.

Step 1 Inspect Fuel System

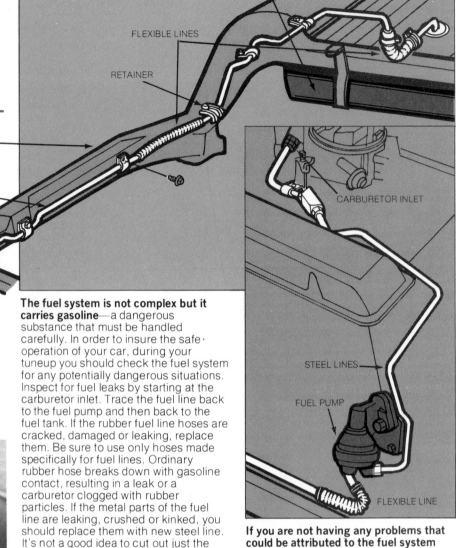

FUEL TANK

FLEXIBLE LINES

RETAINER

CHASSIS

STEEL SECTIONS

FLEXIBLE HOSE

CARBURETOR INLET

STEEL LINES

FUEL PUMP

FLEXIBLE LINE

The fuel system is not complex but it carries gasoline—a dangerous substance that must be handled carefully. In order to insure the safe operation of your car, during your tuneup you should check the fuel system for any potentially dangerous situations. Inspect for fuel leaks by starting at the carburetor inlet. Trace the fuel line back to the fuel pump and then back to the fuel tank. If the rubber fuel line hoses are cracked, damaged or leaking, replace them. Be sure to use only hoses made specifically for fuel lines. Ordinary rubber hose breaks down with gasoline contact, resulting in a leak or a carburetor clogged with rubber particles. If the metal parts of the fuel line are leaking, crushed or kinked, you should replace them with new steel line. It's not a good idea to cut out just the leaking section of a line with pinholes in it since the unrepaired sections will probably also start to leak in a short period of time.

Step 2 Check for Fuel in Carburetor

If you suspect a problem in your fuel system, make a quick check to make sure there is gasoline in the carburetor. Remove the air-cleaner cover (p. 107) and shine a flashlight into the throat of the carburetor. The choke should be open (p. 108) and the engine off. Open and close the throttle three times or have a helper pump the gas pedal. If there is a small squirt of gasoline each time the throttle is opened, then gasoline is reaching the carburetor. If you are troubleshooting a no-start condition, your problem is elsewhere, and further investigation of the fuel system is not required. If there isn't any gasoline squirt, proceed to the next step.

If you are not having any problems that could be attributed to the fuel system and you have completed the basic maintenance procedures described in the chapter on carburetors, there are no further steps after the safety inspection.

Replacing Fuel Lines
Some steel fuel lines are flared on the end for better sealing. Replacement

fuel line can be purchased from an auto supply store already flared or you can do the flaring yourself with a tubing flaring tool.

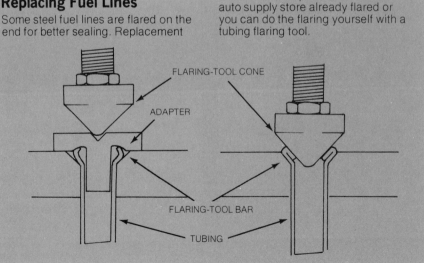

FLARING-TOOL CONE

ADAPTER

FLARING-TOOL BAR

TUBING

Step 3 Check Filler Cap

This cap is designed to keep gasoline in and dirt out of the fuel tank. Most cars built prior to 1970 use a vented filler cap. This means that air can pass in and out of the cap. If the vent fails, the engine won't start because of vacuum buildup in the tank. In some cases the engine will start but won't continue running. Remove the cap and try to start the engine. If it starts and runs, you should replace the cap. Cars built after 1970 no longer vent the gas tank to the air. Instead, fuel vapors are vented to the charcoal canister (p. 109) or to the

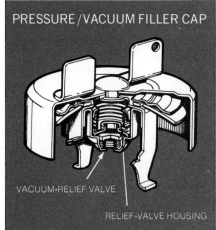

PRESSURE / VACUUM FILLER CAP

VACUUM-RELIEF VALVE

RELIEF-VALVE HOUSING

engine crankcase. These cars are equipped with a gasoline cap that is marked "pressure/vacuum." Such caps only open to the atmosphere when pressure exceeds ¾ to 1¼ psi (pounds per square inch) or vacuum exceeds approximately ½ inch of mercury (Hg). Check the pressure/vacuum cap by blowing into the relief valve housing. An instant leak with light blowing or no release with any amount of blowing indicates a defective cap. Make sure you replace the cap with one of the same type. Again, if the engine starts and runs with the cap removed, replace the cap. If the engine fails to start, proceed to the next step.

Step 4 Disconnect Ignition (See p. 44)

(See p. 44)

Step 5 Install Remote Starter Switch (See p. 44)

(See p. 44)

Step 6 Check Fuel Flow

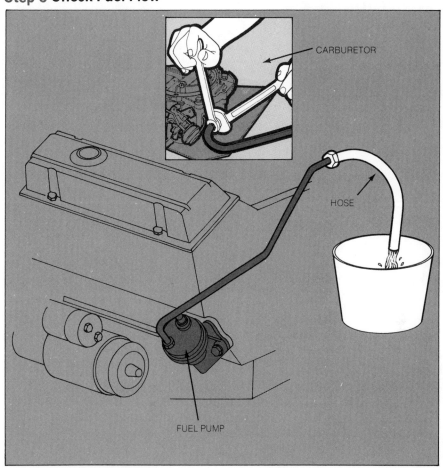

CARBURETOR

HOSE

FUEL PUMP

This will tell you if gasoline is flowing freely from the fuel tank to the carburetor. Disconnect the fuel line at the carburetor inlet and attach a rubber hose to the end of the line. Place the hose in a bucket or similar container and crank the engine for about ten seconds. A pulsing stream of fuel means that the fuel pump is supplying fuel to

the carburetor. A trickle of fuel or no fuel at all means that you have a defective fuel pump or a blocked line between the pump and the fuel tank. To isolate the pump as the defective component, reconnect the fuel line to the carburetor and proceed to the next step. Then reconnect the ignition system.

Step 7 Check Fuel Pump Pressure

This tells you if the fuel pump is capable of providing enough fuel for the engine. The test is performed with a vacuum/pressure gauge connected to the fuel line at the carburetor with the engine idling. To use the gauge, follow the manufacturer's directions. The typical hookup requires placing a T fitting between the carburetor inlet and the fuel line. The pressure tester is then connected to the T. Some gauge manufacturers recommend that you disconnect the fuel line at the carburetor and hook the gauge directly to the fuel line. In this method, the carburetor is not connected to the fuel system. The engine is then started and allowed to idle. The pressure should be greater

than two pounds. Some V8 engines produce pressure up to seven pounds. Manufacturers provide exact specifications. When the engine is shut off, the gauge should remain at the reading or slowly return to zero. An instant drop in pressure means that the check valve in the pump is bad. Any readings outside of specifications indicate a defective pump.

Pumps are not repairable. But before replacing yours, make sure the line between the pump and the fuel tank is open. The pump cannot draw gasoline from the tank if the line is blocked, crushed or kinked (p. 106).

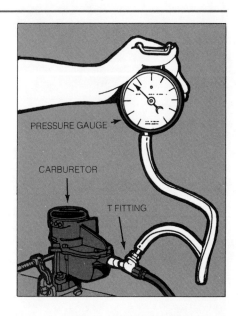

PRESSURE GAUGE

CARBURETOR

T FITTING

Step 8 Replace Fuel Pump

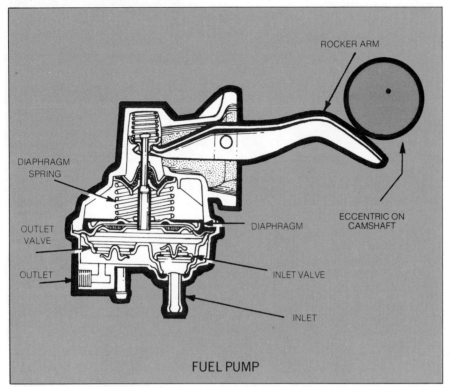

ROCKER ARM

DIAPHRAGM
SPRING

OUTLET
VALVE

OUTLET

DIAPHRAGM

ECCENTRIC ON
CAMSHAFT

INLET VALVE

INLET

FUEL PUMP

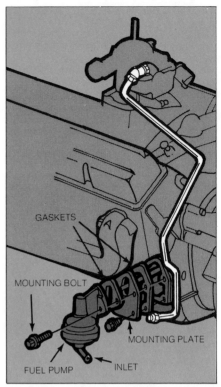

GASKETS

MOUNTING BOLT

MOUNTING PLATE

FUEL PUMP

INLET

There are two types of fuel pumps, mechanical and electrical. A mechanical pump is driven by an eccentric on the camshaft. As the engine turns, the rocker arm or plunger of the pump moves back and forth driving a diaphragm. The diaphragm draws in fuel from the tank on one stroke and forces fuel to the carburetor on the other stroke. Mechanical fuel pumps are bolted to the engine. To change a mechanical pump, disconnect the fuel inlet and outlet lines (and the vapor return line if your car has one). Plug the end of the inlet line to prevent unnecessary fuel leakage. Now take out the bolts holding the pump to the engine block (there are usually two). Remove the pump from the engine by tilting it up or down and pulling away from the block. Then remove the old gasket from the block. To install a new pump, reverse this procedure. Make sure the rocker arm is riding on the camshaft eccentric. The eccentric should be at the low spot before installing the new pump. On plunger-type pumps, hold the plunger in place by coating it with a small amount of grease before sticking it into the pump body. Always check for leaks after working on any part of the fuel system.

Finding the Filter

Most AMC and Chrysler and some Ford cars have an exposed fuel filter which is easily replaced. It is plugged into the fuel line and you should replace it every 12,000 to 15,000 miles. On other Ford cars and all GM's the fuel filter is inside the carburetor inlet. Although somewhat less accessible, this filter must be serviced just as frequently as the exposed filter. The filters may be made of bronze or paper. Replace either type when it shows signs of wear.

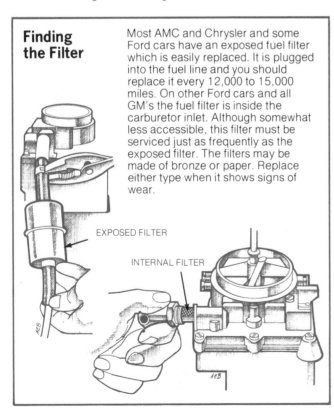

EXPOSED FILTER

INTERNAL FILTER

All About Electric Fuel Pumps

Electric fuel pumps are used on performance cars, cars with fuel injection, and some GM compacts. There are two locations for them, internal and external. An externally mounted pump may be installed anywhere along the fuel line between the fuel tank and the engine, though it is usually at the back of the car close to the tank. Internally mounted pumps are installed in the fuel tank as part of the fuel gauge sending unit and fuel pickup assembly. Most electric fuel pumps receive voltage through a safety circuit that shuts the pump off when the engine stops, even if the ignition key is not turned off. This safety circuit is usually routed through the oil pressure switch—when the oil pressure drops, the pump is shut off. Before replacing an electric fuel pump that has failed the pressure test (p. 101), first inspect the electrical supply circuit. Use a test light and check for ground and voltage at the pump. On cars with an oil pressure switch safety circuit, remove the wiring connector at the oil pressure switch and use a jumper wire to complete the circuit. With the ignition key in the "on" position, there should be voltage at the pump. If there is voltage, but the pump still does not work, the pump is defective and must be replaced. If there isn't voltage, the supply circuit is defective and must be repaired. Now retest the pump. Replacement of an internally mounted pump usually means that the fuel tank must be drained and removed from the car. In this case, you should see a professional mechanic.

CHAPTER

CARBURETOR SERVICE

The carburetor's function is simple—to combine gasoline with air into a burnable substance. This combination of fuel and air, called "the mixture," is then drawn through the intake manifold into the combustion chamber by the downward movement of the piston on the intake stroke. The ideal mixture, or the one that burns most efficiently, consists of approximately 15 parts air to one part gasoline. Because an engine operates over a range of speeds, loads, and temperatures, the carburetor adjusts the mixture to meet the variable demands. The amount of mixture and its exact proportions are constantly changing. All carburetors perform the same basic operations. First, the carburetor must receive gasoline. Second, it must meter or combine that gasoline with air. Third, it must adapt to variable demand and change the mixture. Most of the adjusting is done internally by the carburetor. However, there are several simple external adjustments you can perform to help make your car start easier, run smoother, and get better gas mileage. The two filters the carburetor uses, one for air and one for gasoline, must be changed at regular intervals. Otherwise, the engine will lose power and waste gasoline. The choke, which changes the mixture when the engine is cold, must be cleaned and checked for proper adjustment. The fast-idle speed, which works in conjunction with the choke, must be set so the engine doesn't stall when cold. It is a higher idle speed than the curb-idle speed to which the engine drops when it reaches normal operating temperature. Too slow and the engine stalls; too fast and it races and wastes gasoline.

Late-model engines also have emission controls which should be checked at the same time as the carburetor. The PCV valve vents gases in the engine crankcase back through the carburetor so they can be burned. If the valve isn't working properly, it can damage the mixture and cause a rough idle. Gasoline vapors from the fuel tank and carburetor are vented to a charcoal canister. Some cars have a filter in the canister that should be changed at the manufacturer's recommended intervals. Exhaust gases are recycled through the EGR valve back into the manifold. This valve should be cleaned with a wire brush about once a year.

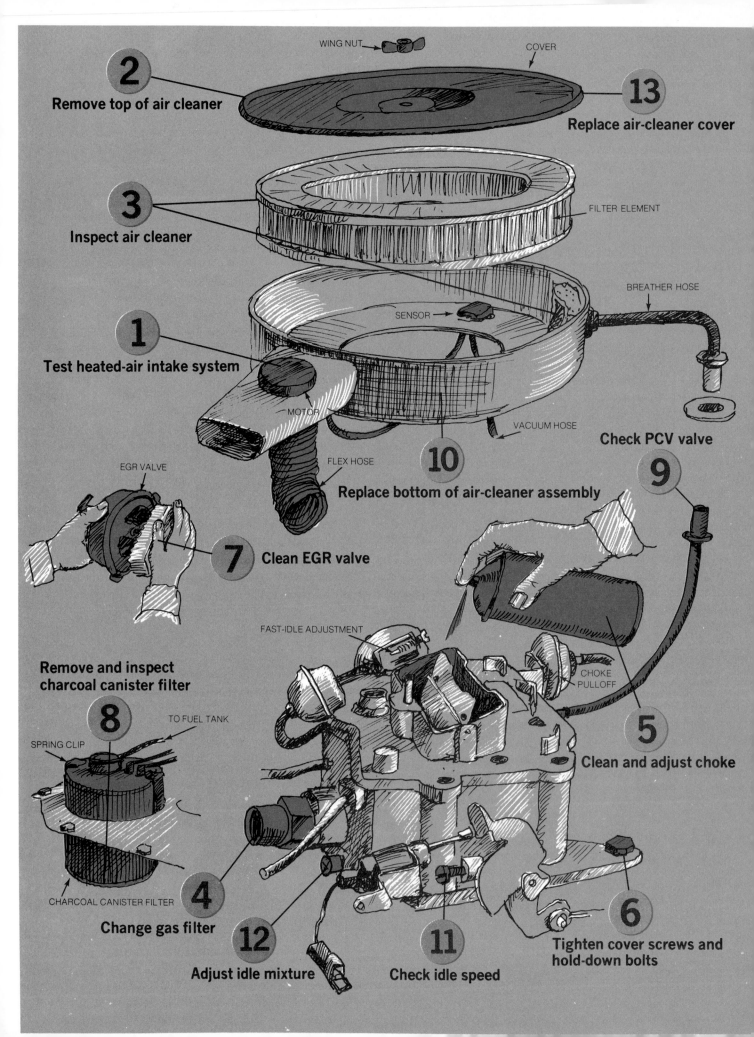

WING NUT →

COVER

2 Remove top of air cleaner

13 Replace air-cleaner cover

3 Inspect air cleaner

FILTER ELEMENT

BREATHER HOSE

SENSOR →

1 Test heated-air intake system

MOTOR

VACUUM HOSE

10 Replace bottom of air-cleaner assembly

FLEX HOSE

Check PCV valve

9

EGR VALVE

7 Clean EGR valve

FAST-IDLE ADJUSTMENT

CHOKE PULLOFF

5 Clean and adjust choke

Remove and inspect charcoal canister filter

8

SPRING CLIP

TO FUEL TANK

CHARCOAL CANISTER FILTER

4 Change gas filter

12 Adjust idle mixture

11 Check idle speed

6 Tighten cover screws and hold-down bolts

Job Steps

Carburetor Service

1 **Test heated-air intake system.** Make sure the heated-air intake system is working properly. Start the engine; the flapper valve should be closed on a cold engine, open on a warm engine. If it isn't, check for binding linkage (p. 106). Inspect the vacuum supply lines for cracks, leaks or restrictions (p. 106). Check the vacuum motor and the heat-sensing valve (p. 106). Shut the engine off.

2 **Remove top of air cleaner.** Air cleaners are held on by wing nuts, hold-down bolts, spring clips or nuts (p. 107). Inspect the breather element of the PCV (Positive Crankcase Ventilation) system and the hose; clean or replace if necessary (p. 107).

3 **Inspect air cleaner.** Disconnect the PCV hose from the side of the air cleaner (p. 107). Remove the flexible fresh-air duct attached to the snorkel if your car has such a duct. Remove the heat tube from the underside of the snorkel. Tag and remove the vacuum hose(s) (p. 107). Lift the air-cleaner off the carburetor, and clean it (p. 107).

4 **Change gas filter.** The gas filter is located in the carburetor inlet, or in the fuel line between the fuel pump and the carburetor (p. 108).

5 **Clean and adjust choke.** The choke should be closed when the engine is cold and open when it is warm (p. 108).

6 **Tighten cover screws and hold-down bolts.** The bolts should be snug (p. 109).

7 **Clean EGR valve.** Remove the EGR (Exhaust Gas Recirculation) valve from the carburetor base plate or intake manifold and brush off the exhaust deposits (p. 109).

8 **Remove and inspect charcoal canister filter.** Remove the filter from the bottom of the canister and clean or replace it as necessary (p. 109).

9 **Check PCV valve.** The PCV valve should be replaced according to the manufacturer's recommended intervals (p. 110).

10 **Replace bottom of air-cleaner assembly.** Reattach the vacuum lines (p. 110).

11 **Check idle speed.** Attach a tachometer to the engine. First set the curb-idle speed, then set the fast-idle speed (p. 110).

12 **Adjust idle mixture.** Late-model cars have limiter caps on the mixture-adjusting screw(s) to comply with emission laws. If adjusting the limiting screws does not do the job, the carburetor should be rebuilt or replaced (p. 111). If the mixture adjustment is changed, recheck the curb-idle speed (p. 110).

13 **Replace air-cleaner cover (p. 111).**

TOOLS

Essential. Basic tools (p. 20).
Adjustable wrench • Cutting pliers •
Tachometer • Flashlight.
Handy. Hose-clamp pliers • Flare
wrench • Wire brush • Fender cover •
Pen knife.

Servicing Carburetor Air Cleaners

You think you know everything you
need to know about the carburetor air
cleaner just because you change the
filter frequently? True, a dirty filter has
a choking effect on the engine that
consumes fuel and, in time, leads to
starting problems. But did you know
that the innocent-looking gasket
between the air-cleaner housing and
the carburetor air horn could damage
the engine? If this gasket is cracked
or missing, dirty air is drawn into the
engine. With some carburetors, a
gasket that isn't positioned squarely
on the air horn can interfere with
choke plate movement. So next time
you change the filter, check that
gasket!

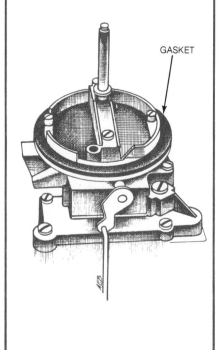

GASKET

Step 1 Test Heated-Air Intake System

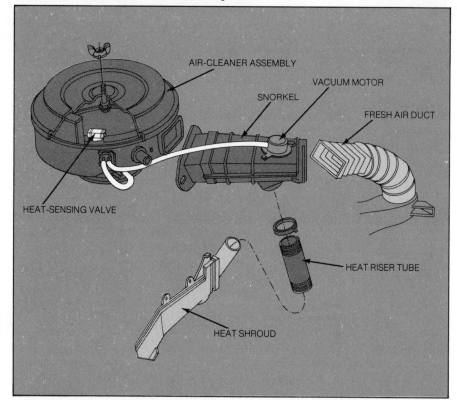

AIR-CLEANER ASSEMBLY
VACUUM MOTOR
SNORKEL
FRESH AIR DUCT
HEAT-SENSING VALVE
HEAT RISER TUBE
HEAT SHROUD

CLOSED

OPEN

**Most engines are equipped with some
type of heated-air intake system** to
provide preheated air to the carburetor
during cold running. Air is passed over
the exhaust manifold to warm it and then
into the air-cleaner snorkel. A flapper
valve in the snorkel controls the flow of
air. To test, start your engine and let it
idle. Shine a flashlight into the snorkel
and see if the valve is in the warm-air
position. On some engines, remove the
fresh-air duct from the end of the
snorkel. As the engine warms, the valve
will move to the fresh-air position so that
air is no longer drawn over the exhaust
manifold into the snorkel. If the flapper
valve isn't working, check to see if it is
binding in the air-cleaner housing.
Mechanical-type flapper valves, those
without vacuum lines, must be replaced
if they don't work. If you can see vacuum
lines coming from the snorkel, you have
a vacuum-activated flapper valve and
further testing is required.

On vacuum-type flapper valves, remove
the top of the air cleaner and check the
vacuum supply lines by starting at the
vacuum motor mounted on the snorkel
and working back to the source of
vacuum. Lines should be free of leaks,
cracks or restrictions. If the trouble still
isn't found, check the heat-sensing valve
(sensor) that is mounted in the base of
the air cleaner. This valve controls the
vacuum motor. There should be vacuum
to the valve on the carburetor side. If the
engine is warm, there should be no
vacuum through the heat-sensing valve
to the flapper valves. If the engine is
cold, there should be vacuum. If the
valve isn't operating properly, replace it.
If there is vacuum to the vacuum motor
and the flapper valve still doesn't work,
replace the vacuum motor. Note: A
stove (carburetor air heater) on the
exhaust manifold brings hot air from the
exhaust manifold to the carburetor.

Step 2 Remove Top of Air Cleaner

After you have tested the operation of the heated-air intake system, shut off the engine. The air cleaner is fastened to the top of the carburetor by wing nut(s) or bolt(s). To remove the top, turn the wing nut counterclockwise until the cleaner is free. Some air-cleaner tops are held in place by spring clips which snap off. Remove the top and inspect the breather element that is mounted on the wall of the air cleaner. If the breather element is clogged or dirty, replace it (see your owner's manual for replacement intervals). There are two types of breather elements. One kind slips into an open top holder. The other kind is attached to the side of the air cleaner with a C-clip. Check the hose that goes from the breather element to the valve cover. It should be free of kinks, cracks or restrictions.

Step 3 Inspect Air Cleaner

1 Gently lift the air filter from the housing, being careful not to drop any dust or dirt into the carburetor. Since the air filter keeps dirt out of the carburetor, the element gradually fills up with this dirt. If the filter isn't changed according to the manufacturer's recommended intervals, the carburetor will starve for air and hence waste gas.

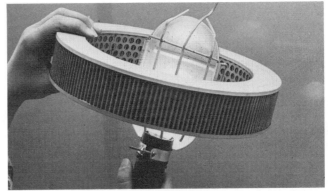

2 If you can see light through the filter when holding it up to the sky or by examining it with a droplight, and there aren't any holes or tears in the pleated-paper element, the filter can be reused. Clean it by blowing, from the inside out, with compressed air, if available, or gently tap the filter on a flat surface to dislodge the particles. If the filter is clogged with dirt, damaged, or wet with oil, replace it.

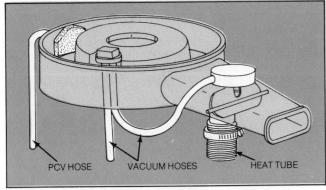

PCV HOSE   VACUUM HOSES   HEAT TUBE

3 Next take out the bottom part of the air-cleaner assembly: Remove the flexible fresh-air duct from the front of the snorkel, the PCV hose from the side of the assembly, and the heat tube from the underside of the snorkel. Gently lift the assembly up to see what vacuum lines are attached to the underside.

4 Tag the vacuum lines with masking tape and remove them from their source. Lift the air-cleaner housing off the carburetor, then wipe clean the inside of the housing to remove any dirt, dust or oil.

Step 4 Change Gas Filter

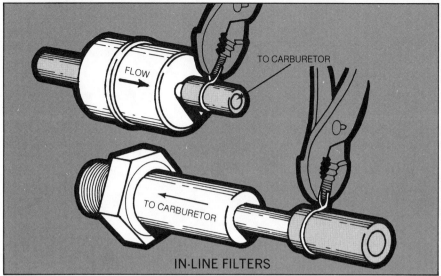

IN-LINE FILTERS

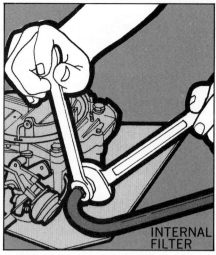

INTERNAL FILTER

American car manufacturers use two locations for gas filters. Most Ford and GM cars have a filter at the carburetor inlet. Chrysler cars have one in the fuel line between the fuel pump and the carburetor. The fuel filter traps any dirt before it reaches the carburetor. A plugged filter can cause engine stalling and hesitation. On cars equipped with an in-line filter, remove the spring clips from the rubber hose at each end of the filter. The clips can be expanded by squeezing the ends together with pliers. Slide the clips off the rubber hose. *Caution: Always replace the clips and hose.* Your new in-line filter will come

with replacement clips and hoses. Now remove the filter. When installing the new filter, observe the fuel direction arrow on the canister. The arrow should point toward the carburetor. Be certain the spring clips are behind the flange on the fuel line and filter.

Some Ford products use an in-line filter that is connected by a hose at one end to the fuel inlet line, while the other end screws into the carburetor. To change it, remove the spring clip from the hose and slide the hose off the filter. Then unscrew the filter from the carburetor. Reverse the procedure to install the new filter.

Most GM and some Ford cars have a filter inside the carburetor at the point where the fuel line attaches. Two wrenches are needed to change this gas filter; one for the large nut on the carburetor and one for the smaller fuel-line fitting. To remove the filter, hold the larger nut steady while turning the fuel-line fitting counterclockwise until the line is free of the carburetor. Next, turn the large nut counterclockwise until it is loose. Remove it from the carburetor slowly. There are three pieces inside, a gasket around the nut, a small paper or bronze filter, and a pressure relief spring behind it. Note the way the gas filter faces. To reinstall it, reverse the procedure. Be sure to reinstall the pressure relief spring and the gasket.

Step 5 Clean and Adjust Choke

The choke limits the amount of air entering the carburetor when the engine is cold. If it doesn't close, the engine will hesitate and stall when running, or, in extreme cases, the engine will fail to start altogether. Chokes are set at the factory and the only maintenance usually required is cleaning. The choke plate is the valve at the top of the carburetor. It is activated by a bimetal spring attached to the side of the carburetor or a bimetal spring mounted on the intake manifold. When the engine is cold, the choke should snap shut when the accelerator is opened. Check the valve to see if it moves freely back and forth. If in doubt, spray some carburetor cleaner on the pivot points at the side of the carburetor. The choke also activates a fast-idle cam. This increases the idle speed by holding the throttle open farther than it is when the engine is warm. While cleaning the choke, spray the carburetor around the fast-idle cam. The cam should now pivot freely. Chokes also have a vacuum assembly which opens the choke plate slightly when the engine is started. The vacuum pulloff is activated by engine vacuum and has a vacuum line running to the base of the carburetor. This line should be free of cracks and kinks.

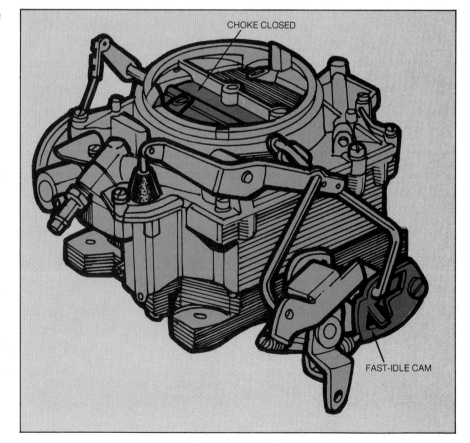

CHOKE CLOSED

FAST-IDLE CAM

Step 6 Tighten Cover Screws and Hold-down Bolts

Sometimes a carburetor can work its way loose due to the vibrations created by a running engine. Check the screws around the top of the carburetor and the bolts that hold the carburetor to the manifold. They should be snug.

Step 7 Clean EGR Valve

The EGR valve recycles exhaust gases back into the intake manifold. Most cars since 1973 are equipped with an EGR valve. It is located at the back of the carburetor or on the intake manifold. The valve should be wire-brushed about once a year to remove exhaust deposits. If these deposits build up, the valve can stick open, causing a rough engine idle. To clean the valve, remove the vacuum line from the top. Next, remove the bolts that hold it to the manifold or carburetor base. Turn the valve over and check the passageways for exhaust deposits. If deposits are found, wire-brush them clean. A pen knife can also be used to scrape the valve clean, but be careful not to damage the gasket. A damaged gasket must be replaced before the valve is reinstalled.

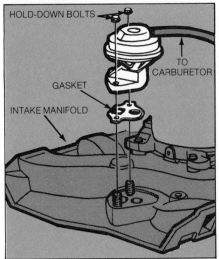

VACUUM LINE

VALVE STEM

HOLD-DOWN BOLTS

TO CARBURETOR

GASKET

INTAKE MANIFOLD

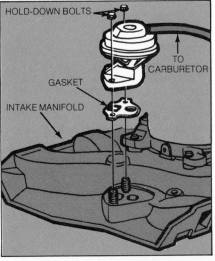

FIBERGLASS FILTER

Step 8 Remove and Inspect Charcoal Canister Filter

As part of the emission control system since 1970, the charcoal canister stores gasoline vapors that were vented to the atmosphere prior to the establishment of emission control standards. The vapors stored in the canister are drawn into the engine when it is running. The charcoal canister is usually located in the fender well opposite the side the battery is on. Most canisters have a filter on the bottom that should be checked. The filter can usually be slipped out of the canister bottom without removing the

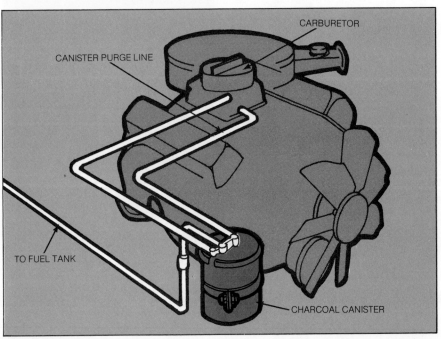

CARBURETOR

CANISTER PURGE LINE

TO FUEL TANK

CHARCOAL CANISTER

canister from the car. The filter should be replaced according to the manufacturer's recommendations. In between replacement intervals, the filter should be cleaned by shaking the dirt

out of it. It's also a good idea to check the rubber line between the charcoal canister and the carburetor for cracks or kinks. If the line(s) is damaged, you should replace it.

Step 9 Check PCV Valve

Step 10 Replace Bottom of Air-Cleaner Assembly

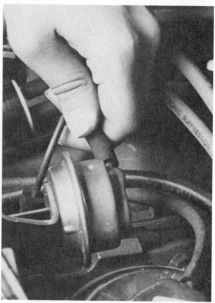

The PCV valve regulates the venting of engine crankcase gases back into the intake manifold so that they can be burned. If the valve doesn't function properly, engine stalling and a rough idle can result. The PCV valve should be changed according to the manufacturer's recommended intervals. Check the PCV valve by removing it from the intake manifold or valve cover and shaking it. The valve should rattle, indicating that the needle in the valve is moving back and forth. Replace a valve that doesn't rattle.

Place the air-cleaner assembly back on the top of the carburetor and reattach the vacuum lines and hoses that you removed in Step 3 (p. 107).

Step 11 Check Idle Speed

Connect a tachometer to the engine (p. 71), following the manufacturer's instructions. Start the engine and let it idle. Immediately inspect the fuel filter and attaching line(s) for gasoline leakage. If there aren't any leaks, set the curb-idle speed to the manufacturer's specifications (see Appendix, Specifications by Make and Model, p. 202). Refer to the underhood EPA sticker. The curb-idle speed is usually set with the engine warmed up and the choke valve fully opened. Set automatic transmissions in Drive and manual transmissions in Neutral. If the curb-idle speed is set in Drive, have a helper apply the brake. You can also put a brick in front of each wheel and apply the emergency brake to hold the car in Drive.

On carburetors with an idle-speed adjusting screw, turn the screw clockwise to increase the idle speed, counterclockwise to decrease it.

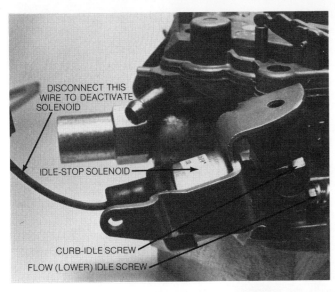

DISCONNECT THIS WIRE TO DEACTIVATE SOLENOID

IDLE-STOP SOLENOID

CURB-IDLE SCREW

FLOW (LOWER) IDLE SCREW

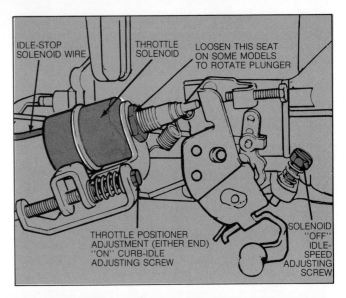

IDLE-STOP SOLENOID WIRE

THROTTLE SOLENOID

LOOSEN THIS SEAT ON SOME MODELS TO ROTATE PLUNGER

THROTTLE POSITIONER ADJUSTMENT (EITHER END) "ON" CURB-IDLE ADJUSTING SCREW

SOLENOID "OFF" IDLE-SPEED ADJUSTING SCREW

On carburetors equipped with an idle-stop solenoid, there are two adjustments, one with the solenoid activated, one with it off. With the solenoid activated, set to the curb-idle specifications by turning the solenoid plunger, by turning the solenoid in the mounting bracket or by turning the idle-stop solenoid wire adjusting screw. Then disconnect the idle-stop solenoid wire from the harness and set the lower (deactivated) idle speed to specifications by turning the idle-speed adjusting screw.

After the curb idle is set, put the transmission in Park and set the fast idle to specifications. The fast idle is set by opening the throttle and rotating the fast-idle cam until the fast-idle screw is in the specified position. Then the fast-idle screw is turned until the specified rpm is reached.

Step 12 Adjust Idle Mixture

Since 1968, cars have had limiter caps on the mixture-adjusting screw(s). For the best gas mileage, the mixture screw(s) should be turned in as much as possible. If the idle becomes rough, back the mixture screw(s) out (counterclockwise) until the engine smooths out. If adjusting the limiter caps does not do the job, the carburetor should be rebuilt—see a professional mechanic.

Step 13 Replace Air-Cleaner Cover

Install the air filter in the air-cleaner assembly and fasten the cover. Be sure the air-cleaner assembly is flat on top of the carburetor and all the hoses are attached.

General Carburetor Adjustment Procedures

Carburetor curb-idle adjustments are critical to your car's specific exhaust emission levels as required by law. The following adjustment procedures should be considered general guidelines and temporary adjustments in the absence of the infra-red meter, exhaust-emission analyzer, and propane-assist equipment necessary for the precise adjustment done by the professional mechanic.

1 Run the engine until it reaches normal operating temperature (about 1500°F.).

2 If the idle mixture screw(s) do not have limiter caps, turn the mixture screw(s) clockwise until they are lightly seated and then turn them counterclockwise about two turns. If the idle-mixture limiter caps are fitted, proceed directly to Step 7.

3 Turning the curb-idle speed screw or solenoid, set the curb-idle speed to about 50 rpm above the curb-idle speed indicated on the vehicle emission decal.

4 Slowly turn the idle-mixture screw(s) counterclock-wise, in $\frac{1}{16}$-turn increments, to set the engine to the specified curb-idle speed as indicated on the vehicle emission decal.

5 If the engine idle is rough, turn the mixture screw(s) clockwise or counterclockwise as necessary, in $\frac{1}{16}$-turn increments, until the idle smooths out.

6 Make the final curb-idle speed adjustment with the curb-idle speed screw or solenoid.

7 Where the idle-mixture screw limiter caps are fitted, adjust the mixture screw(s) for the best idle and make the final curb-idle speed adjustment with the curb-idle speed screw or solenoid.

Note: There are literally hundreds of carburetor variations in modern American cars. The carburetors shown on the following pages are representative of the more popular varieties from 1970 to 1980. Check your own carburetor to determine its similarities to the ones shown before making adjustments.

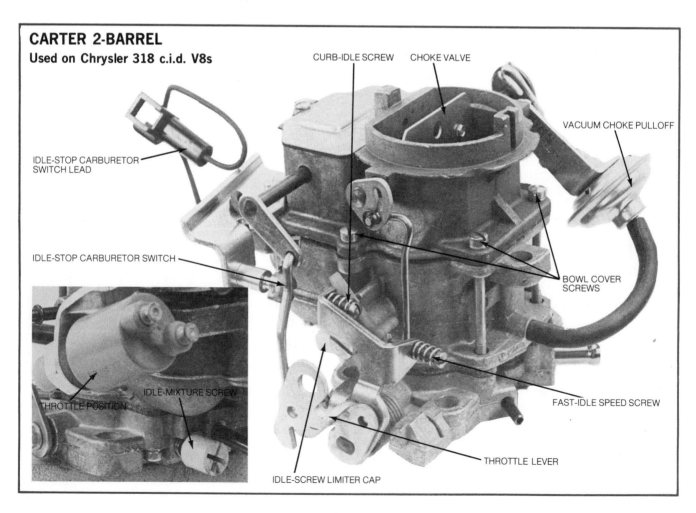

CARTER 2-BARREL
Used on Chrysler 318 c.i.d. V8s

CURB-IDLE SCREW   CHOKE VALVE

VACUUM CHOKE PULLOFF

IDLE-STOP CARBURETOR SWITCH LEAD

IDLE-STOP CARBURETOR SWITCH

BOWL COVER SCREWS

THROTTLE POSITION

IDLE-MIXTURE SCREW

FAST-IDLE SPEED SCREW

THROTTLE LEVER

IDLE-SCREW LIMITER CAP

CARTER THERMO-QUAD
Used on Chrysler 318, 360, 400, and 440 c.i.d. V8s 1978–79

CHOKE VALVE

ALTITUDE COMPENSATOR

BOWL VENT SOLENOID

IDLE-STOP CARBURETOR SWITCH

IDLE-STOP CARBURETOR SWITCH LEAD

THROTTLE POSITION TRANSDUCER

CURB-IDLE SPEED SCREW

CHOKE PULLOFF LINKAGE

CHOKE PULLOFF

CHOKE CONTROL LINKAGE

CHOKE VALVE

ALTITUDE COMPENSATOR

IDLE-ENRICHMENT VALVE

CHOKE CONTROL LINKAGE

THROTTLE POSITION TRANSDUCER

IDLE-MIXTURE SCREW LIMITER CAPS

FAST-IDLE ADJUSTMENT SCREW

CARTER THERMO-QUAD
Used on Chrysler V8s prior to 1978

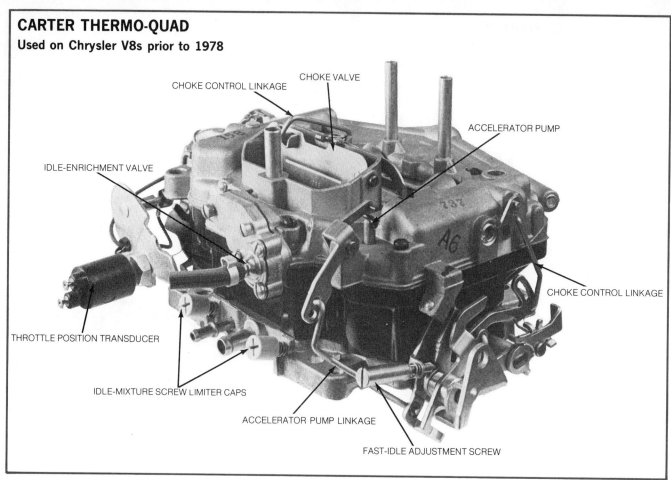

CHOKE CONTROL LINKAGE

CHOKE VALVE

ACCELERATOR PUMP

IDLE-ENRICHMENT VALVE

CHOKE CONTROL LINKAGE

THROTTLE POSITION TRANSDUCER

IDLE-MIXTURE SCREW LIMITER CAPS

ACCELERATOR PUMP LINKAGE

FAST-IDLE ADJUSTMENT SCREW

HOLLEY 1-BARREL
Used on Chrysler 6-cylinder engines

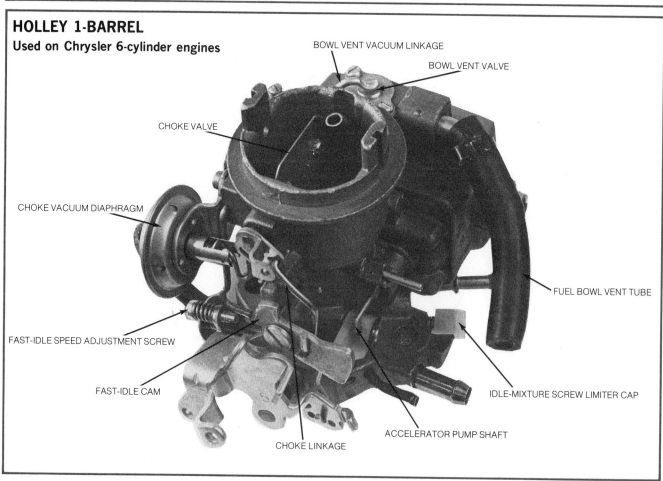

BOWL VENT VACUUM LINKAGE

BOWL VENT VALVE

CHOKE VALVE

CHOKE VACUUM DIAPHRAGM

FUEL BOWL VENT TUBE

FAST-IDLE SPEED ADJUSTMENT SCREW

FAST-IDLE CAM

IDLE-MIXTURE SCREW LIMITER CAP

CHOKE LINKAGE

ACCELERATOR PUMP SHAFT

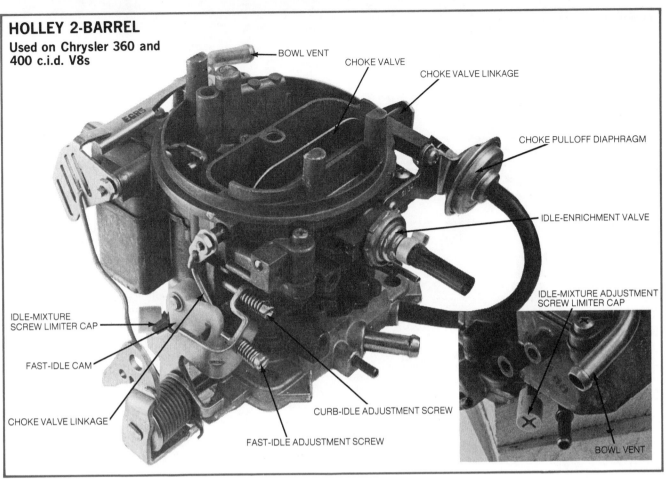

HOLLEY 2-BARREL
Used on Chrysler 360 and 400 c.i.d. V8s

BOWL VENT

CHOKE VALVE

CHOKE VALVE LINKAGE

CHOKE PULLOFF DIAPHRAGM

IDLE-ENRICHMENT VALVE

IDLE-MIXTURE ADJUSTMENT
SCREW LIMITER CAP

IDLE-MIXTURE
SCREW LIMITER CAP

FAST-IDLE CAM

CHOKE VALVE LINKAGE

CURB-IDLE ADJUSTMENT SCREW

FAST-IDLE ADJUSTMENT SCREW

BOWL VENT

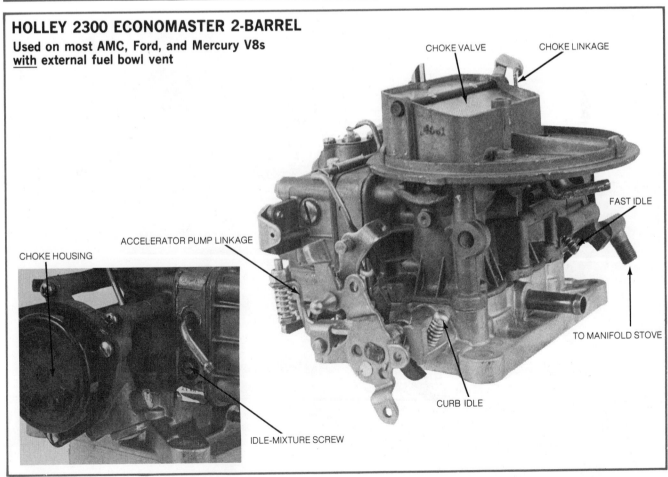

HOLLEY 2300 ECONOMASTER 2-BARREL
Used on most AMC, Ford, and Mercury V8s
<u>with</u> external fuel bowl vent

CHOKE VALVE

CHOKE LINKAGE

FAST IDLE

ACCELERATOR PUMP LINKAGE

CHOKE HOUSING

TO MANIFOLD STOVE

CURB IDLE

IDLE-MIXTURE SCREW

HOLLEY ECONOMASTER 2300
Used on most AMC, Ford, and
Mercury V8s <u>without</u> external fuel bowl vent

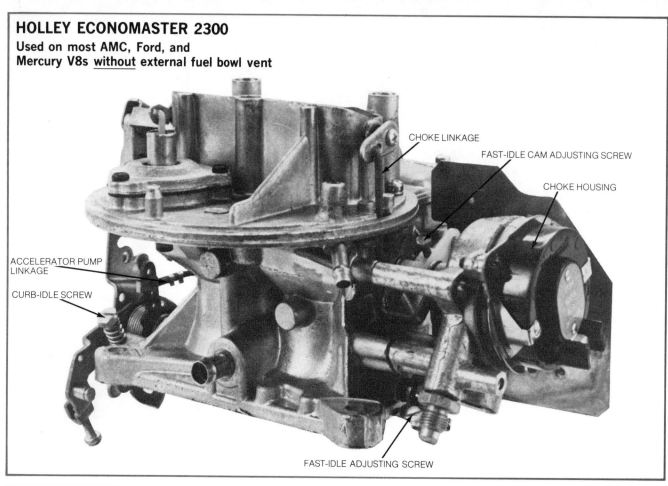

CHOKE LINKAGE

FAST-IDLE CAM ADJUSTING SCREW

CHOKE HOUSING

ACCELERATOR PUMP
LINKAGE

CURB-IDLE SCREW

FAST-IDLE ADJUSTING SCREW

HOLLEY 4360 ECONOMASTER 4-BARREL
Used on 1970–72 Chevrolet 350, 400, and
454 c.i.d. V8s

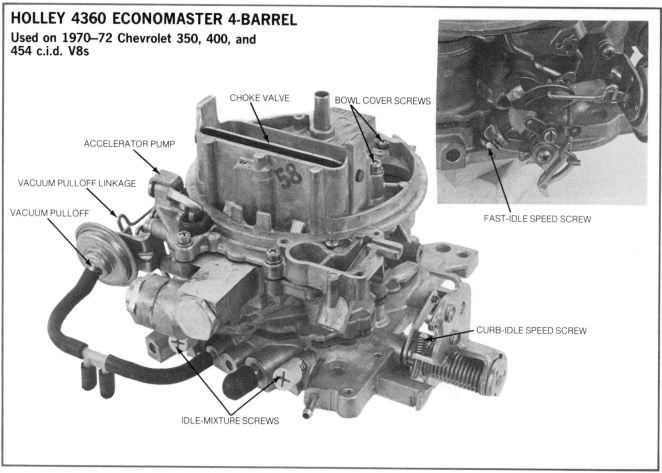

CHOKE VALVE

BOWL COVER SCREWS

ACCELERATOR PUMP

VACUUM PULLOFF LINKAGE

VACUUM PULLOFF

FAST-IDLE SPEED SCREW

CURB-IDLE SPEED SCREW

IDLE-MIXTURE SCREWS

HOLLEY 5200 C ECONOMASTER 2-BARREL
Used on 1971–74 Pinto, Mustang II, and GM 4-140 c.i.d. engines

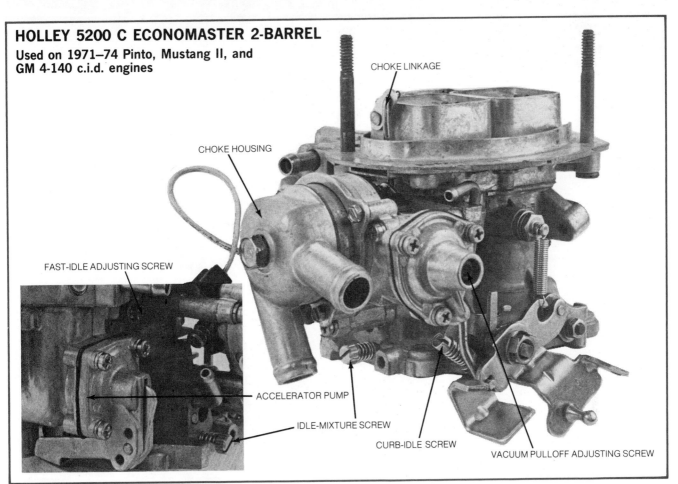

CHOKE LINKAGE

CHOKE HOUSING

FAST-IDLE ADJUSTING SCREW

ACCELERATOR PUMP

IDLE-MIXTURE SCREW

CURB-IDLE SCREW

VACUUM PULLOFF ADJUSTING SCREW

MOTORCRAFT 4-BARREL
Used on AMC, Ford, and Mercury V8s

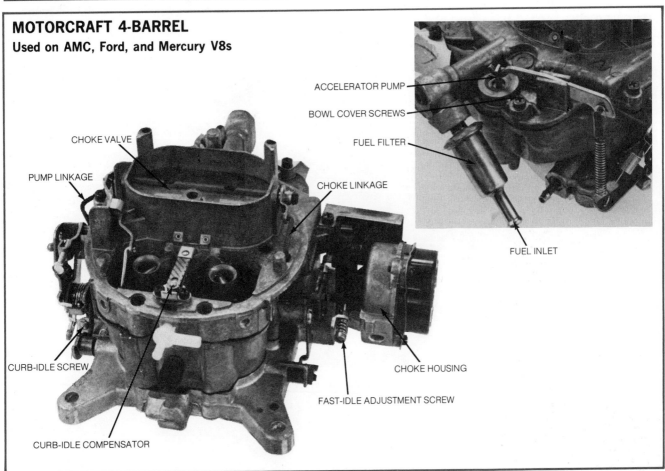

ACCELERATOR PUMP

BOWL COVER SCREWS

FUEL FILTER

FUEL INLET

CHOKE VALVE

PUMP LINKAGE

CHOKE LINKAGE

CURB-IDLE SCREW

CHOKE HOUSING

FAST-IDLE ADJUSTMENT SCREW

CURB-IDLE COMPENSATOR

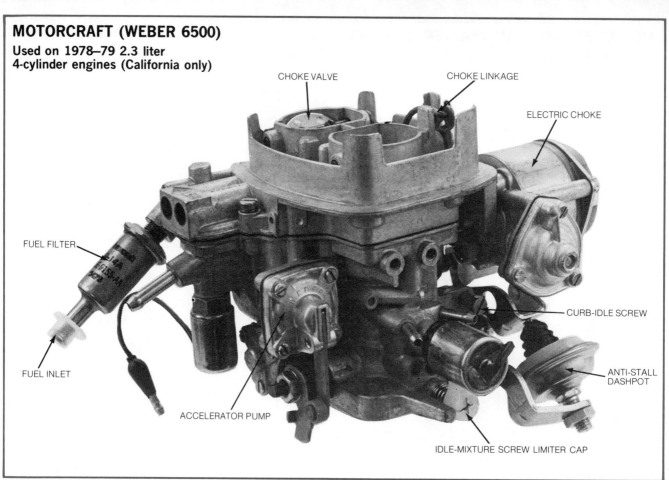

MOTORCRAFT (WEBER 6500)
Used on 1978–79 2.3 liter
4-cylinder engines (California only)

CHOKE VALVE

CHOKE LINKAGE

ELECTRIC CHOKE

FUEL FILTER

FUEL INLET

ACCELERATOR PUMP

CURB-IDLE SCREW

ANTI-STALL DASHPOT

IDLE-MIXTURE SCREW LIMITER CAP

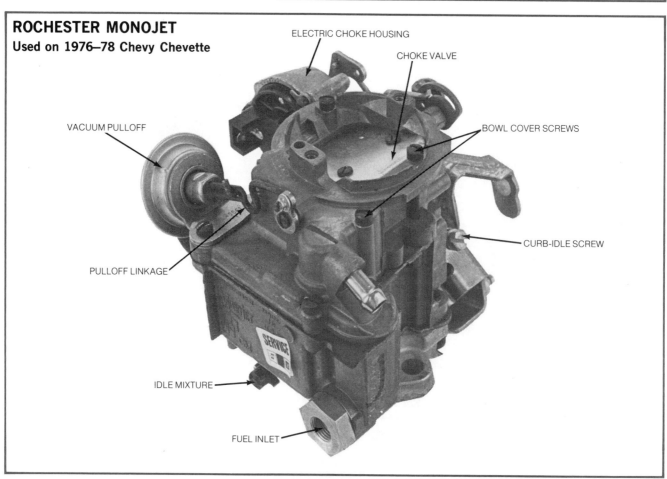

ROCHESTER MONOJET
Used on 1976–78 Chevy Chevette

ELECTRIC CHOKE HOUSING

CHOKE VALVE

VACUUM PULLOFF

BOWL COVER SCREWS

CURB-IDLE SCREW

PULLOFF LINKAGE

IDLE MIXTURE

FUEL INLET

ROCHESTER DUALJET
Used on GM 260 c.i.d. V8s

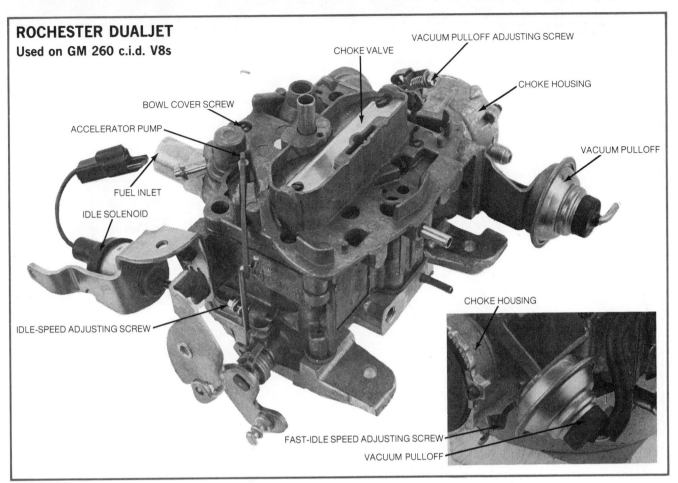

CHOKE VALVE

VACUUM PULLOFF ADJUSTING SCREW

CHOKE HOUSING

BOWL COVER SCREW

ACCELERATOR PUMP

VACUUM PULLOFF

FUEL INLET

IDLE SOLENOID

IDLE-SPEED ADJUSTING SCREW

CHOKE HOUSING

FAST-IDLE SPEED ADJUSTING SCREW

VACUUM PULLOFF

ROCHESTER 2-BARREL
Used on GM V8s except 260 c.i.d. engines

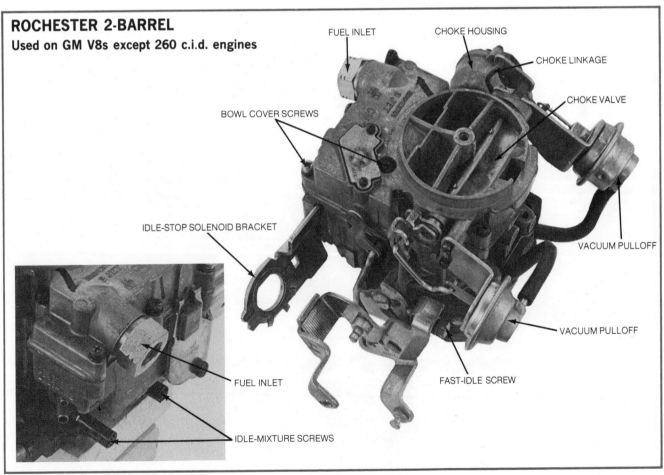

FUEL INLET

CHOKE HOUSING

CHOKE LINKAGE

CHOKE VALVE

BOWL COVER SCREWS

IDLE-STOP SOLENOID BRACKET

VACUUM PULLOFF

VACUUM PULLOFF

FUEL INLET

FAST-IDLE SCREW

IDLE-MIXTURE SCREWS

ROCHESTER VARAJET
Used on 1980 Chevy Citation, etc.

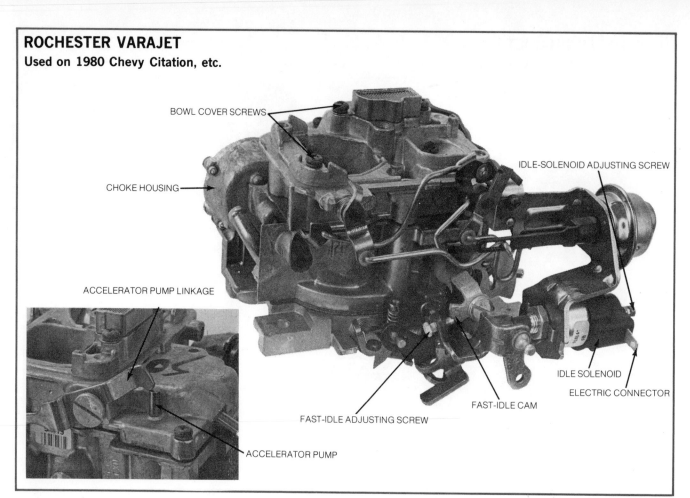

BOWL COVER SCREWS

CHOKE HOUSING

IDLE-SOLENOID ADJUSTING SCREW

ACCELERATOR PUMP LINKAGE

IDLE SOLENOID

ELECTRIC CONNECTOR

FAST-IDLE CAM

FAST-IDLE ADJUSTING SCREW

ACCELERATOR PUMP

ROCHESTER QUADRAJET
Used on GM V8s

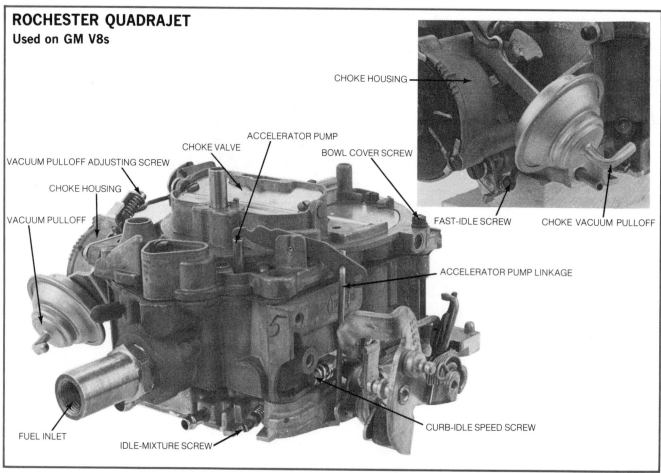

CHOKE HOUSING

VACUUM PULLOFF ADJUSTING SCREW

CHOKE HOUSING

VACUUM PULLOFF

CHOKE VALVE

ACCELERATOR PUMP

BOWL COVER SCREW

FAST-IDLE SCREW

CHOKE VACUUM PULLOFF

ACCELERATOR PUMP LINKAGE

CURB-IDLE SPEED SCREW

FUEL INLET

IDLE-MIXTURE SCREW

CHAPTER 10

OIL AND COOLING SYSTEMS SERVICE

Burdened with emission controls and a variety of convenience accessories, today's car engines are running hotter than ever. On top of this, they're smaller and work harder. Heat generated in the combustion chambers can sometimes exceed 4500° F. If this heat is not controlled, the moving parts of the engine will seize and stop working, and other parts under the hood will disintegrate.

The automobile has two systems to control excessive heat: a cooling system and a lubrication system. The cooling system dissipates heat with water/antifreeze; the lubrication system reduces friction with oil. For both systems to function properly, the do-it-yourselfer must service and inspect them periodically, and correct any problems before they get out of hand.

The cooling system must be protected against internal and external leaks, a clogged radiator, defective thermostat, radiator pressure cap or water pump, and worn or broken drive belts. The coolant must not only be maintained at the proper level, it must also be kept at the correct strength to protect against freezing and rust.

Lubricating oil must function well at all temperature extremes. There are a number of weights and types on the market to meet most driving conditions, so find out what motor oil is best for your car. Although the lubricating quality of engine oil does not diminish, the additives in the oil do get "used up" when the oil becomes contaminated with dirt, metal particles from engine wear, and byproducts of the combustion process. Then the oil must be replaced. As your car ages, it needs more frequent service. The engine that might need an oil and filter change at 6000 miles when it is relatively new, may require such service every 3000 miles when it gets older.

The home mechanic should inspect these two systems at regular intervals. This will keep them operating at maximum efficiency to assure a better working engine and keep repair bills to a minimum. A good rule of thumb is to check the cooling system twice a year and before long trips. Always keep an eye on your temperature and oil pressure gauges and suspect a problem if there is a sudden change in the engine's normal operating temperature or if the oil pressure light goes on.

OIL PAN
GASKET

1 Drain oil

2 Inspect oil pan

JACK STAND

Replace oil

4

3 Remove and replace filter

COAT NEW GASKET
WITH OIL

Job Steps

Oil System Service

Prep: Run the engine for about ten minutes to warm up the oil. Oil flows more easily when it's hot, so this way you stand a better chance of removing most of the dirt and contaminants when you drain the oil. Jack up the front of the car. For safety, support the front end on stands and chock the rear wheels.

1 Drain oil. Normally, you should change your engine oil every four to six months. For urban or severe driving, cut this interval in half. If you have any doubts about the interval for your car, check your owner's manual. After draining the old oil, be sure to replace the drain plug! (p. 124).

2 Inspect oil pan. A pan that is punctured must be replaced. If the gasket has deteriorated to the point where it is causing an oil leak, it must be replaced (p. 124). Note: Take off the oil pan only if its removal is not obstructed by a crossover pipe, a crossmember, the steering linkage, the flywheel cover, etc. If it is, let a professional mechanic do the job.

3 Remove and replace filter. Some car makers suggest replacing the oil filter after every *second* oil change. But if you're going to the expense of putting in clean oil, why contaminate it immediately with the dirty oil left in the old filter? (p. 125).

4 Replace oil. Make sure you're using the correct type, grade, and amount (p. 125).

TOOLS

Essential. Basic tools (p. 20).
Jack • Chocks • Stands • Drain pan •
Cloth or paper towels • Putty knife or
gasket scraper • Oil filter wrench •
Engine oil • Oil spout or funnel •
Fender cover.

Repairing the Drain Plug

Sometimes the threads in the oil pan
drain hole are stripped because a
faulty drain plug has been forced into
the drain hole. If you have this
problem, don't worry; you won't have
to replace the oil pan. You can repair
the drain hole with one of several
drain plug repair kits on the market.
One kit uses a self-tapping steel nut,
which is forced into the pan's drain
hole. A brass plug threads into the
steel nut and becomes the new drain
plug. Other kits use rubber stoppers,
but they don't hold up as well as the
steel nut.

Step 2 Inspect Oil Pan

Check around the lip of the pan. If the
gasket has deteriorated, there will be
leakage and you should replace the
gasket. Also, look for leakage as a result
of punctures or holes in the pan. If you
find them, replace the pan.

To replace the gasket, first drain the oil.
Remove the oil pan bolts and take down
the pan. Oil pans are usually sealed
against the block with a cork gasket.
However, some newer cars use a liquid
silicone sealant. Scrape the old gasket
or sealer from both the pan and the
engine with a putty knife or gasket
scraper. Apply a new gasket or sealer to
the pan. If liquid sealer is used, apply a
$3/16$-inch wide bead of heat-resistant
sealer evenly around the pan, inboard of
the bolt holes. If you're using a cork
gasket, apply a small amount of rubber
adhesive sealant to the four corners of
the gasket to hold it in place while you
tighten the bolts. Torque the bolts evenly
around the pan to avoid warping it.

Replacing the pan. First drain the oil.
Then remove the bolts and take down
the pan. When you replace the pan,
make sure that the new one is the same
size as the one you just removed and
that the bolt holes line up. Now scrape
the old gasket or sealer from the engine
and follow the instructions for replacing
the gasket.

Step 1 Drain Oil

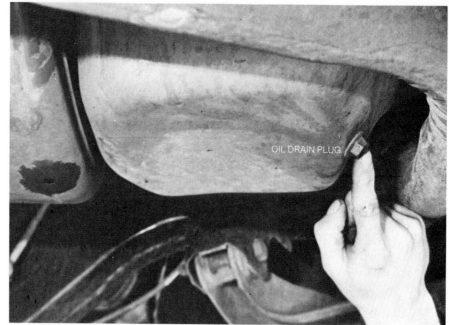

**With the engine warmed to operating
temperature** (at least 150° F) and the
front end of the car raised, place a pan
of at least the capacity to hold your car's
oil under the oil pan's drain plug. Loosen
the plug with a wrench and remove it
and its washer by hand. *Caution: The oil
is hot. To avoid burning your hand,
remove the plug and washer carefully
and quickly.* Allow the oil to drain out
completely into the pan. To do this,

lower the car until it is level with the
ground. This will allow all the oil to drain
out. If your car's plug is magnetized, it
will have attracted metal particles and
filings from the engine. Clean the drain
plug, especially the threads, with a rag
or paper towel. Clean the washer as
well. Reinstall them in the pan. If you
have trouble replacing the plug, check
the box on Repairing the Drain Plug.

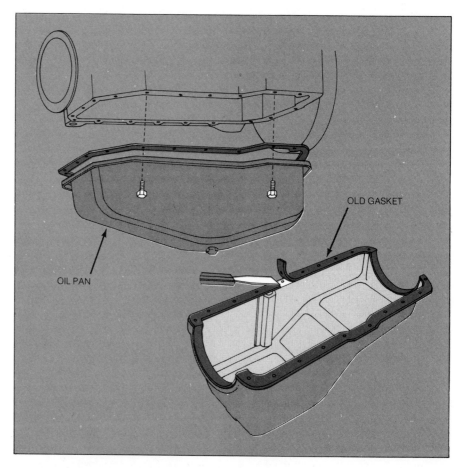

OLD GASKET

OIL PAN

Step 3 Remove and Replace Filter

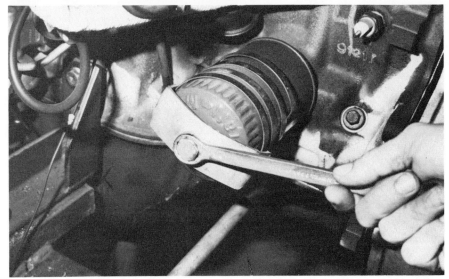

1 Removing the filter. First locate the oil filter. If your car is a V6 or V8, it's probably mounted on the bottom of the engine crankcase, near the oil pan. You will have to jack up the front of the car to get to it. On most in-line 4- or 6-cylinder cars, it's on the side of the engine and accessible by reaching into the engine compartment. Place a fender cover on the fender and put a drain pan below the filter. Using the correct oil filter wrench, loosen the filter by turning it counterclockwise two turns. When the oil from the filter has stopped draining into the pan, remove the filter by hand. *Caution: There will still be some oil in the filter, so remove it in an upright position to prevent spillage.*

2 Replacing the filter. With a cloth, clean the filter mating surface on the engine. Coat the filter gasket with a thin film of clean engine oil. Thread the new filter onto the engine and hand-tighten it. Do not use an oil filter wrench. Tightening instructions are printed on most filter cases or boxes.

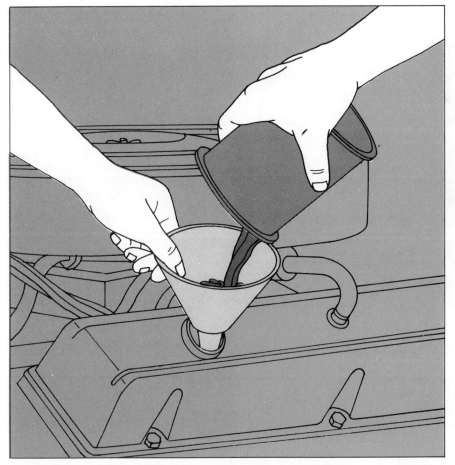

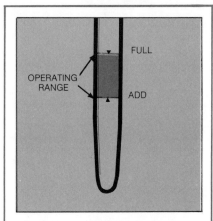

Checking the Oil Level

Engine oil should be kept at the FULL mark on the dipstick, although it is safe to wait until the level drops to the ADD mark before adding a quart. An engine should not be run if the oil level is one quart low, and old wives' tales that the engine runs best that way are wrong. The oil should be checked when the car is on level ground and only after the engine has been shut off for at least a few minutes. This allows the oil in various parts of the engine to drain down to the crankcase.

Locate the dipstick. Normally it can be found protruding out of one side of the engine or the other. The dipstick is a long metal rod, one end of which is curled into a loop so it can be conveniently pulled out of its tube by inserting a finger. When you remove the dipstick, wipe it clean with a cloth or paper towel. You should be able to see the markings ADD and FULL near the end of it. Insert the dipstick back into the tube, making sure to push it in as far as it will go. Now pull it straight out, keeping it in a vertical position, and read the oil level. If the oil is at the ADD mark, you need a quart. If it is on the FULL mark, the level is OK. Once in a while when the car is very low on oil, you may not get a reading at all. In this case, put in a quart of oil and take another reading. Continue to check the dipstick and add oil until the level is at FULL. *Caution: Do not overfill the engine with oil. This can cause the oil to foam when the engine is running and interfere with lubrication.*

Step 4 Replace Oil

Locate and remove the oil filler cap. It's usually on the cylinder head cover. Using an oil spout or funnel, add the correct amount of oil to the crankcase. For the correct grade, type, and amount of oil, see your owner's manual. Check the oil level and add more if necessary. Start the engine and inspect for leaks around the filter, then turn the engine off. Remove the drain pan and properly dispose of the waste oil and filter.

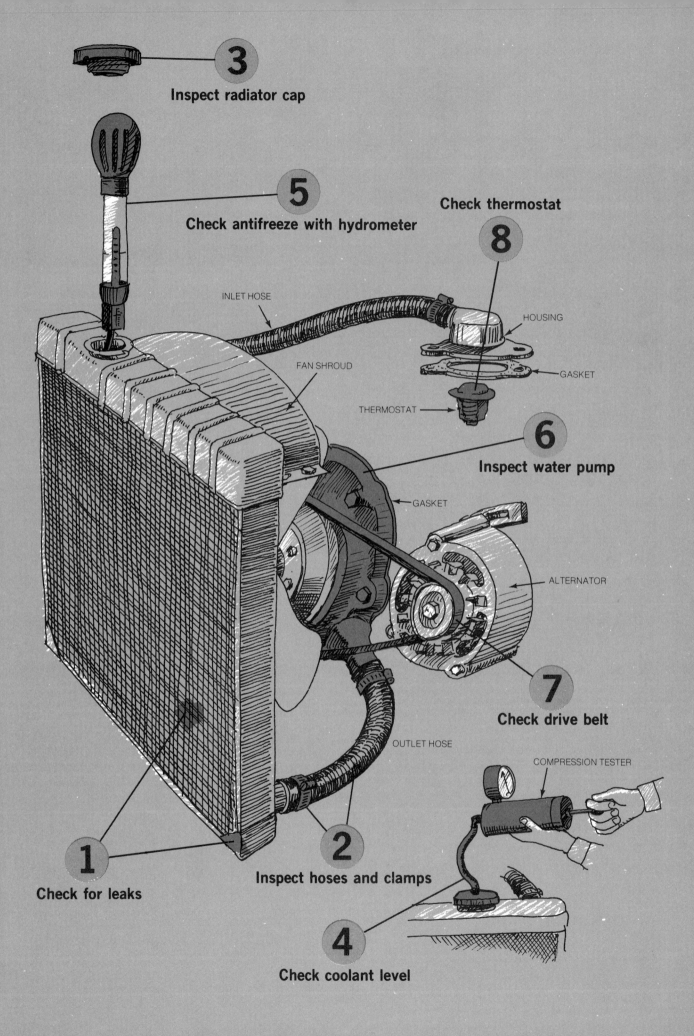

3 Inspect radiator cap

5 Check antifreeze with hydrometer

Check thermostat
8

INLET HOSE

HOUSING

FAN SHROUD

GASKET

THERMOSTAT

6 Inspect water pump

GASKET

ALTERNATOR

7 Check drive belt

OUTLET HOSE

COMPRESSION TESTER

2 Inspect hoses and clamps

1 Check for leaks

4 Check coolant level

Job Steps

Cooling System Service

1 **Check for leaks.** Inspect the radiator around seams, petcocks, automatic transmission oil cooler connections, hose connections, and block and drain plugs. Corrosion or antifreeze stains are a good indication there's a leak (p. 128).

2 **Inspect hoses and clamps.** Check the rubber for cracks, softness, brittleness, leaks, swelling, and chafing. Replace any hoses that show these conditions (p. 129).

3 **Inspect radiator cap.** If it's loose, replace it. Check the pressure relief valve for firm spring action (p. 129).

4 **Check coolant level.** Water should cover the tubes inside the upper tank or reach the "fill" level marked on the tank (p. 130). Suspect a leak if the level is low. If there are signs of oil, rust or scales inside the filler neck, you may have an internal leak. Take a compression test (p. 128). Clean and reverse-flush the system (p. 130).

5 **Check antifreeze with hydrometer.** For best protection, maintain the system to conform to the coldest weather in your area (p. 130).

6 **Inspect water pump.** With the belt removed, grasp the fan pulley with both hands, turning and moving it inward and outward. If it makes a noise when you spin it, the bearings are worn. If you see signs of coolant leakage, the seals are probably damaged. Leaks and/or bad bearings mean the pump should be replaced (p. 131).

7 **Check drive belt.** Turn the alternator pulley by hand. If it moves easily, the belt is slipping and should be adjusted (p. 132).

8 **Check thermostat.** Do this only if your engine is overheating. Replace a faulty thermostat, and always replace the gasket; never reuse the one you took off (p. 132).

TOOLS

Essential. Basic tools (p. 20). Garden hose • Hydrometer • Pressure tester and pressure cap adapter • Drain pan • Cloth or paper towels • Putty knife or gasket scraper.
Handy. Compression gauge • Flushing T • Filler neck deflector • Belt tensioner • Thermometer • .003-inch feeler gauge • Wire or string.

Testing for Leaks

1 With the engine cool, remove the radiator cap. Start the engine and allow it to heat up to normal operating temperature (at least 150° F). If necessary, add water to the cooling system. Then turn the engine off. Install the pressure tester on the radiator filler neck, following the manufacturer's instructions.

2 Operate the pump until the gauge's needle reaches the pressure prescribed for your engine. *Caution: Never exceed the prescribed pressure. If you do, you may damage the cooling system by rupturing the radiator or splitting the hoses.*

Step 1 Check for Leaks

Pressurized cooling system and coloring in the antifreeze make external leaks easy to locate visually. Inspect around the radiator seams, where the core is soldered to the upper and lower tanks, and around hose connections, petcocks, cylinder head gaskets, block plugs, drain plugs and, if your car has an automatic transmission, at the connections of the transmission oil cooler lines. If there is

3 With the pressure testing gauge at the prescribed pressure, look for leaks in the radiator hoses and connections, the heater itself, its hoses and connections, the thermostat housing gasket, the radiator tanks and core, and the water pump. If no leaks are detected, take a reading of the pressure gauge. It should maintain its reading for at least two minutes. If no visual leaks are detected, but the pressure gauge needle drops slowly, there may be an

an external leak, there could be telltale, whitish corrosion or antifreeze stains. Leaks must be corrected mechanically. The radiator should be removed and taken to a specialist. If there are no visible signs of leakage, but your engine has been overheating or you have been replacing coolant frequently, perform a pressure leak test.

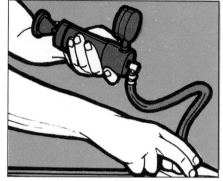

internal leak caused by a cracked block, cylinder head or water jacket. Have your car checked out by a professional mechanic in this case.

4 When the pressure test is completed, slowly release the pressure in the cooling system. Refer to the manufacturer's instructions for releasing pressure. Then remove the tester from the radiator.

Servicing the Radiator

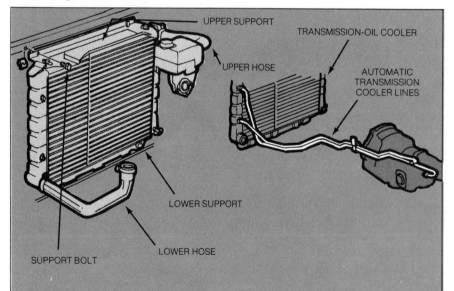

UPPER SUPPORT

TRANSMISSION-OIL COOLER

UPPER HOSE

AUTOMATIC TRANSMISSION COOLER LINES

LOWER SUPPORT

LOWER HOSE

SUPPORT BOLT

1 To remove the radiator, drain the cooling system, then remove the upper and lower radiator hoses. If the automatic transmission cooler lines are connected to the radiator tank, loosen the connections at the tank and disconnect the lines. Note: Place a clean pan under the cooler line connections to catch any transmission oil that may spill.

Caution: Do not start the engine. If you do, you will lose all your transmission oil. Locate the radiator supports and remove the support bolts. If your car is equipped with a radiator shroud, remove the bolts that hold it and move it away from the radiator (toward the engine). Lift the radiator out of the engine compartment. *Caution: When lifting the radiator out, be*

Check That Transmission Oil

You may lose some of the transmission fluid when you disconnect the automatic transmission oil cooler lines from the radiator. So when you button up the job, check the transmission fluid level and add oil if necessary.

careful not to rub it against any sharp objects, such as the fan or hood. If you do, you may damage it.

2 To install a repaired or new radiator, replace the supporting bolts. Bolt the shroud in place and connect the transmission cooler lines, if your car is equipped with them. Replace the upper and lower radiator hoses and fill the cooling system with coolant. Start the engine and allow it to reach normal operating temperature (at least 150° F). Then replace the radiator cap and check for leaks.

Step 2 Inspect Hoses and Clamps

A radiator cooling system has a minimum of four hoses—top and bottom hoses and two heater hoses. Sometimes there's a bypass hose between the water pump and the engine. The average life of a radiator hose is about two years or 25,000 miles. Check hoses when the engine is cold. When you squeeze them they should feel firm, and when you release them they should return to their shape immediately. Pay particular attention to the bottom hose. Sometimes there is a spring inside it, to prevent it from being drawn closed. If it gets extremely rough treatment from the water pump, the spring can collapse if the hose softens. If the hose is loose or cracked, air can get into the system, causing rust. Soft hoses are particularly dangerous because they can deteriorate from the inside and small pieces of rubber may break off and clog the radiator and heater core. Examine clamps and clamp areas, and replace broken or weak clamps. Look for white or rust-colored deposits around the clamps. These signify a leak. Try tightening the clamp to correct the leak. If this doesn't work, replace the clamp and/or the hose.

Step 3 Inspect Radiator Cap

Pressure caps are important to the cooling system. They increase the temperature at which the coolant boils, increase water pump efficiency, and eliminate coolant loss due to evaporation. Defective caps can cause overheating, which could ultimately result in engine damage. A radiator cap should fit tightly on the filler neck. Replace it if it's loose. Inspect the pressure relief valve. Its spring action should be firm when you press down on it.

Testing the Cap for Pressure

1 To make a more accurate check of relief pressure, connect a radiator pressure cap adapter, supplied with a pressure tester. Wet the cap's rubber seal with water and connect the cap to the adapter.

2 Read the markings on your pressure cap to determine the rated capacity in pounds per square inch (psi).

3 Pump the pressure tester until the gauge reads the rated capacity of the cap.

4 This pressure reading should hold for at least two minutes. If the pressure drops before that time, the radiator cap is defective and should be replaced.

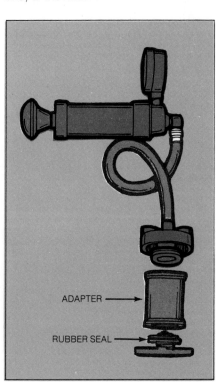

ADAPTER

RUBBER SEAL

Cleaning Debris From Radiator

Use a garden hose to clean leaves, insects, and other debris from the radiator. For the best results, apply water at high pressure from the engine side.

Replacing Hoses and Clamps

Remove hoses when the engine is cool. If only the upper hose is to be replaced, drain out about two quarts of coolant. If the lower hose is to be replaced, you must drain the radiator. If you want to reuse the coolant, drain it into a clean container. Loosen the clamps and slide them away from the ends of the hose you are replacing, then twist the hose off the connections. If the hose is fused to the metal, slit it lengthwise and pry it off with a screwdriver.

1 To install a new hose, first clean off all the old sealer from the connector, using either a wire brush or sandpaper.

2 Slide the clamps onto the new hose and position them about one quarter of an inch from the ends. Twist the new hose onto the connectors, making sure

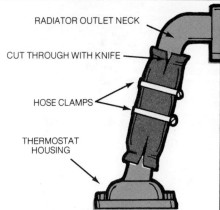

RADIATOR OUTLET NECK

CUT THROUGH WITH KNIFE

HOSE CLAMPS

THERMOSTAT HOUSING

the clamps are positioned past the raised beads. Tighten the clamps securely. Then close all petcocks, replace the coolant, and run the engine for at least 15 minutes to check for leaks.

Step 4 Check Coolant Level

Coolant should cover the tubes inside the upper tank or reach the "fill" mark stamped on the tank. If you have been replacing coolant frequently, suspect a leak. If signs of oil, rust or scales are found inside the upper tank, you may have an internal leak. While you may not be able to correct this kind of problem, you can take a compression test (p. 128) to confirm if and what kind of a leak may exist. If the test proves negative, clean and reverse-flush the system. If the test proves positive, let a professional mechanic check out your cooling system.

Reverse Flushing the Radiator

First, drain the cooling system by removing the radiator cap and opening the petcock. Remove the plug or disconnect the lower hose to drain the radiator. Disconnect the upper radiator hose from the thermostat housing and the lower hose from the water pump. Close the petcock and replace the pressure cap. Position the opening of the upper hose so it's pointing toward the ground, away from the engine. Insert a garden hose into the lower radiator hose opening and wrap a piece of cloth around the joint to seal it. Turn on the hose and allow water to flow into the lower section of the radiator, up through the radiator, and out through the upper radiator hose. Keep the water flowing until it is clear.

Reverse Flushing the Block

First, remove the thermostat and replace the thermostat housing gasket with a new one. Now's a good time to check the thermostat (p. 132). Disconnect the upper radiator hose at the radiator, but leave it connected to the thermostat housing. Disconnect the lower radiator hose at the radiator, but

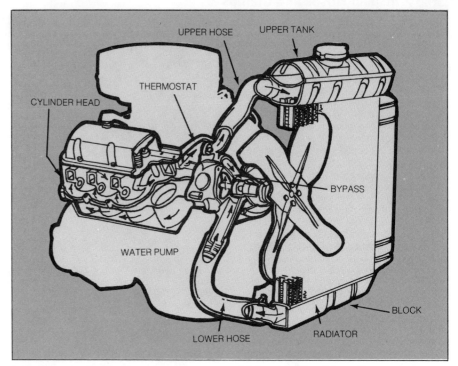

leave it connected to the water pump. Position the hose so the opening faces the ground, away from the engine. Insert a garden hose in the opening of the upper hose. Allow the water to flow through the engine block and out of the water pump through the lower hose to the ground until the water runs clear. Replace the thermostat, housing, and the gasket, and connect the upper and lower hoses. Add the proper amount of antifreeze, then fill the radiator with fresh water. Start the engine and allow it to reach the normal operating temperature (at least 150° F). Now check the coolant level, top off with fresh water if necessary, install the pressure cap, and check for leaks.

Step 5 Check Antifreeze With Hydrometer

Run the engine and allow the coolant to warm up. Draw off some coolant into a hydrometer. Now hold the hydrometer at eye level and read the scale. Some hydrometers use floating balls to indicate the freezing point; others use a floating degree scale. For best antifreeze protection, the cooling system should be maintained to conform to the coldest weather in your area. If additional antifreeze is necessary to maintain the desired degree of protection, add enough to reach a 60/40 mixture of antifreeze to water. To do this you first may have to drain some coolant from the radiator. If your car has an aluminum engine block, refer to the owner's manual for the right type of antifreeze to use.

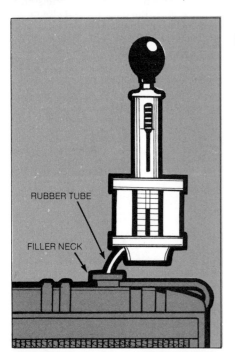

RUBBER TUBE

FILLER NECK

Using a Flushing T

First, attach a flushing T to the heater supply hose. That's the hose that goes to the engine or carburetor manifold. Don't mistake it for the hose that runs to the water pump. The T should be situated so that water pouring from it does not get on the alternator. If your radiator has an exceptional amount of grease buildup or corrosion, you may want to use a one-step, fast-flushing agent. After reverse-flushing the cooling system, replace the antifreeze. Remove the cap from the T when adding antifreeze.

Types of Clamps

1 A worm-drive clamp is tightened with an integral screw and a worm drive. It is compact and can be used in confined areas, but vibration can loosen it in time.
2 A wire-spring clamp is easily removed and installed with special pliers, but in time it may lose its spring action. Always replace this type of clamp. Never reuse one.
3 A twin-wire clamp uses a nut and bolt holding device. This type of clamp needs periodic tightening. Be careful, though, not to cut into the rubber by overtightening.
4 A banded or screw-tower clamp is not as commonly used as other types of clamps. It is hard to remove without damage, but it can be replaced with a worm-drive clamp.

Step 6 Inspect Water Pump

Most water pumps are lubricated and sealed at the factory and normally do not require periodic maintenance. But bearings, seals, and the impeller blades do wear out. One cause of bearing failure is excessive tightening of the fan belt. To check the pump, remove the fan belt and grasp the pulley in both hands. Turn and move it inward and outward. If there's a rough, grinding or loose feeling, the bearings are probably worn. Next check the ventilation hole below and behind the pulley by running your hand over it. If the seal is leaking, your hand will be wet from the coolant. Sand, rust, and other abrasive materials in the coolant will wear away the impeller blades. Corrosion of the impeller blades and housing may also result from using an antifreeze with inadequate corrosion and rust inhibitors. Replace a water pump that has a leak or worn bearings.

Servicing the Water Pump

1 Removing the water pump. Remove the radiator and shroud (p. 128). Loosen and remove the drive belts on the water pump pulley. If the front side of the fan is not marked, scribe a mark on the blade indicating the front for correct reinstallation. Remove the four fan mounting bolts and the fan and water pump pulley. Note: On some cars the fan is mounted with a spacer installed between the fan and the water pump hub. If your car has one, remove it. Apply a coating of gasket cement to the surface of the replacement pump and place the new gasket on the pump. Place the pump on a clean surface, gasket side down.

2 The position of the replacement pump should be identical to that of the old pump, which is still mounted on the engine. The water pump should always be installed with the vent hole at the bottom.

3 Water pump mounting bolts often differ in size and length. So to insure proper reinstallation, use the correct tool to remove one bolt at a time and insert it in the corresponding hole of the replacement pump. Remove the old water pump and scrape off the old gasket from the engine block. Clean the surface thoroughly with a cloth and apply a coating of gasket cement to it.

4 Replacing the pump. Taking care not to drop or remove the bolts in the replacement pump, lift and position it against the engine. Start all bolts by hand only. Push the pump in toward the engine until it is properly seated against the block and tighten the bolts evenly. Check the manufacturer's specifications for the correct torque. Replace the water pump pulley, spacer, and fan, and tighten the bolts securely. Install and adjust the drive belts to their proper tension. Then replace the radiator hoses and the transmission cooler lines.

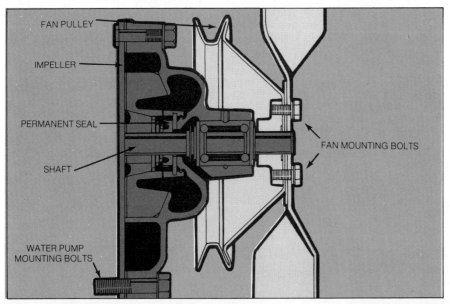

FAN PULLEY

IMPELLER

PERMANENT SEAL

SHAFT

WATER PUMP MOUNTING BOLTS

FAN MOUNTING BOLTS

How Not to Overheat Your Engine

There are a variety of reasons why an engine overheats. But these can usually be reduced to two basic causes: A mechanical problem either in the cooling system or in the engine, or a heat load—temporary or permanent—that is beyond the capacity of the cooling system to handle. To find out if your over-heating problem is mechanical, refer to the Troubleshooting chart on page 200. The tests and service procedures in this and other chapters will tell you how to find and correct such problems.

Two permanent causes of overheating by a load beyond the capacity of the cooling system are air conditioning and trailer towing. An air-conditioner condenser is located in front of the radiator, restricting air flow and giving off its own heat. If you've had an air conditioner installed in your car after it left the factory or you are planning to install one, make sure the radiator's capacity can handle the extra load. You may need a heavy-duty radiator. Towing makes an engine run harder and, therefore, hotter. So if you're planning to do any extensive towing, make sure your radiator is up to the additional load.

When there is temporarily too much heat for the cooling system to handle, the engine also overheats. For example, if you're stuck in traffic. In this case, try to bring the temperature down by shifting into Neutral and revving the engine. This will make the fan pull more air through the radiator and cool down the engine. At the same time, avoid getting too close to the car in front of you. Hot exhaust flowing into your car's radiator will not help the situation. If your air conditioner is on, turn it off. As a final resort, turn your heater to the high On position. Even though it may get uncomfortable in the passenger compartment, the heat, acting as a radiator, will cool off the engine a little. Of course, an overheated car moving at a moderate speed will, in most cases, keep the engine cooled down. So at the earliest opportunity, get out of traffic and find a road that will allow you to move at a higher speed. However, if steam and coolant is shooting out from under the hood, pull over and shut off the engine immediately. If it's safe, open the hood and let the engine cool a while. Slowly remove the radiator cap to relieve the pressure. *Caution: Don't attempt to remove the cap from a hot radiator. Sudden release of pressure can cause the coolant to turn to steam and forcefully blow out of the filler neck and overflow tube. Scalding steam can burn your face, hands, and legs.* To remove the cap, cover it with a thick cloth, such as a towel, and turn it slowly to the left (follow the arrows on the cap) to the safety stop. Step away from the car and allow any steam or pressure to blow off. Then press down and turn the cap to the left until it comes off. Now, with the engine running, very slowly add cold water. Before proceeding, check for leaks, broken hoses or fan belts, loose clamps or other visible mechanical problems, and correct these conditions if possible. In an emergency, you may be able to stop a small leak with a radiator sealant.

All About Fans

The fan and shroud do not require periodic maintenance. However, they should be inspected from time to time to see that they're operating properly. And there's no better time than when you're tuning up your engine. When inspecting the fan, look for bent blades, since these can cause the water pump bearings to wear abnormally. You can do this by first physically examining each blade, then, with the engine running, by sighting across the diameter of the fan from the side. Be careful not to let your clothing, hands or tools get too near the blades. If the blades are bent, the fan will not run "true" and you will see the blades shimmy from side to side. In this case, remove the fan and replace it with one of the same kind. Do not try to straighten a bent blade yourself.

Check the fan shroud to see if it's loose or damaged. A damaged shroud may make high-pitched noises. Since the shroud works like an air tunnel, your engine may overheat if the shroud is damaged. If it is loose, tighten the bolts. If it is damaged, replace it.

Beware of Flying Flex Fans!

The National Highway Traffic Safety Administration (NHTSA) has warned owners of 1970 through 1977 Ford passenger cars and light trucks that the blades on their engine cooling fans may break off. This could result not only in vehicle damage but possible personal injury. Ford says it has narrowed down the potentially dangerous flex fans to approximately 425,000 air-conditioned Lincolns, Montegos, and Torinos with 302-, 351-, and 400-cubic-inch engines. The problem of breaking fans is not limited to Ford cars, however. Fan breakage has been reported on American Motors and GM cars as well.

Home mechanics working under the hood of any make car should be extremely cautious about the fan. Fan blades become weakened and a potential hazard for a number of reasons. The problem with the Ford flex fan seems to be centered around the constant flexing of the blades as they flatten out when rpm increases. This leads to small cracks in the blades starting near the hub. It should be noted that not all flex fans have this problem. In the early stages when the crack is beginning, the only sure way to find it is to carefully examine the fan blade close to the hub. In later stages, flexing the blade by hand will cause a cracking sound. If your car happens to be one of those mentioned above, you should have the fan replaced.

Step 7 Check Drive Belts (See p. 36)

Step 8 Check Thermostat

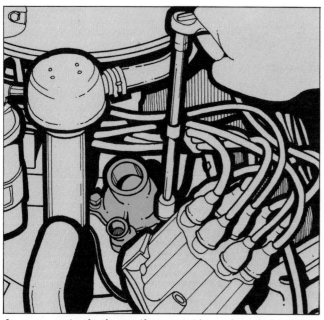

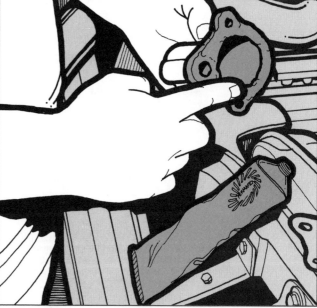

An easy way to check your thermostat is to remove the radiator cap and insert a thermometer in the radiator. After starting the engine, watch the thermometer. The thermostat should start opening when the coolant begins to flow. This can be checked by squeezing the upper radiator hose. You will be able to feel the coolant flowing as the engine warms.

A more complicated method, but a more accurate one, is to remove the thermostat and put it and a thermometer (which reads at least up to 250° F) in a pan of water. Heat the water and note when the thermostat starts to open. Continue to watch it until it is fully open. To check the opening temperature, attach a .003-inch feeler gauge to a wire or string and position the gauge between the valve and the housing. When the gauge can be pulled free, you know the thermostat has started to open. Two widely-used ratings are 185° F and 195° F. Thermostats are designed to *start* to open at the rated temperature and are *fully* open at about 20 degrees higher. If the thermostat doesn't meet specs, you should replace it.

Servicing the Thermostat

1 Drain the radiator and disconnect the upper radiator hose. If a coolant bypass hose is attached to the thermostat housing, disconnect it as well. Remove the bolts or nuts holding the thermostat housing to the engine, and lift out the housing. If it sticks, use a putty knife in the gasket joint to free it.

2 Scrape the old gasket from the housing and the engine with a putty knife. Do not use a screwdriver. After noting how the thermostat was installed, lift it out. Apply a thin film of non-hardening sealer to the thermostat housing and put the new gasket in place.

3 Install the new thermostat by reinstalling the housing and bolts or nuts, then reconnecting the coolant hose. Run the engine and check for leaks. If the housing leaks, stop the engine and remove the housing. Check the thermostat for correct alignment and the thermostat housing surface and gasket. Clean the surface again and replace the gasket. The thermostat mounting bolts must be torqued to the manufacturer's specifications.

WHEN YOUR CAR TALKS, LISTEN!

Although there are many excellent diagnostic tools you can buy that will help you track down a problem with your car, you already possess two that are very reliable and won't cost you a cent: your nose and your ears. If you learn how to use these well, they can be among the best diagnostic tools you own. But interpreting car noises and odors can be tricky. It requires not only a sharp sense of hearing and smell, but also a good deal of practice. Don't expect to zero in on a problem on the first try. However, once you learn how to use your nose and your ears well, they can alert you to a surprising number and variety of automotive problems.

Some engine noises indicate major problems, while others signal problems which are easily eliminated. The difficulty in trying to diagnose a noise problem in a book is making sure that the noise we're describing is the same noise you're hearing. There is a big difference, for example, between the noise of a piston slap and the noise from a sticking valve. The problem is recognizing the dif-

ference and identifying the part making the noise from the hundreds of other parts both inside and attached to the engine. The illustration on this page shows a cutaway of an engine, pinpointing some of the major problems that produce internal noises. The noises these and other malfunctions make are described by mechanics as slap, rap, rattle, click, whine, thump, and thud.

Keep in mind that we are now discussing sounds as symptomatic of *major* engine problems. We will cover "minor" problem sounds later. The word *minor* is encased in quotes because one of these noises—ping—may in fact be caused by a major problem. But we'll discuss that further on in this section. In determining which one of the noises applies to your engine, it's also important to ascertain under what conditions the sound occurs and, if possible, at what pitch. For example, is the noise loud, faint, sharp or dull? Does it occur regularly or intermittently? Does it happen when the engine is hot, cold or all the time? Is it noticeable during acceleration, deceleration, idling or at high speed?

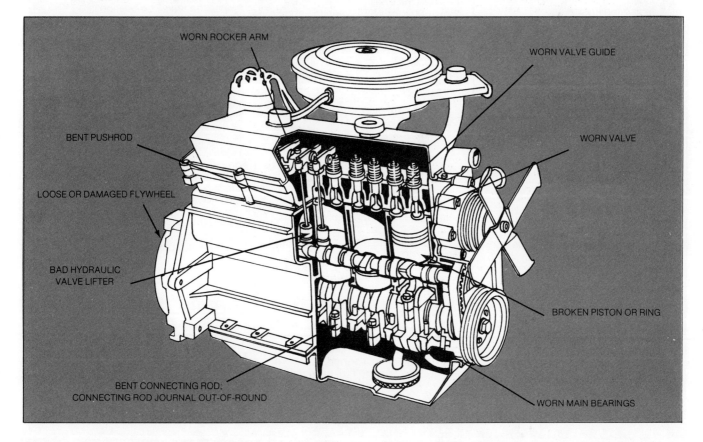

Noises Indicating Major Problems

Let's run down each of the various noises that are caused by major engine problems and define them:

Slap

This is described as a sound resembling a hammer striking a metal surface, but not sharply—it's a dull noise. The one part inside an engine that is most notorious for slapping is the piston. It happens when a piston loosens up.

Rap

A rap is similar to a slap—like a hammer hitting a metal surface—but it is much sharper in intensity. A primary cause of engine rap is putting a load on an engine or running it at high speed when it is low on oil. The noise is actually being made by connecting rods.

Rattle

A rattle sounds like a baby's rattle that is being furiously shaken. A loose piston may cause a rattle rather than a slap. Ignition timing which is too advanced can also cause a rattle.

Click

Run a stick along a picket fence and you have some idea of what is meant by engine click. A clicking sound that lasts for about 20 seconds when you start the engine in the morning and then disappears is frequently caused by a dry hydraulic valve lifter. As soon as the lifter gets pumped up with oil, the noise ceases.

A 20-second click (or less) produced by a dry lifter is no reason for ripping the engine apart. However, the longer the noise lasts, the more serious the problem. In time, the engine may have to be disassembled to reach and replace the bad lifter(s). Clicking can also be caused by excessive valve lash. This usually occurs in engines with mechanical lifters, and a valve adjustment may help. Or it may be caused by a piston that's lightly touching the head gasket or cylinder ridge or by a nick on a timing gear.

Whine

This one is in the gray area. It might indicate a major problem, but then again it might not. A whine is described as a high-pitched, continuous sound. It may be more pronounced at some speeds than at others. The noise may be caused by nothing more serious than a glazed fan belt. It might be the result of a malfunctioning rotor in the alternator, which again is not that serious. However, whine can also be caused by a loose or worn timing gear, and this means a major repair.

Thump

A thumping sound is a deep-throated noise that you seem to feel as well as hear. It indicates a serious condition, such as loose main bearings. A thump occurs intermittently—not on a regular rotational basis.

Thud

A thud is similar in pitch to a thump, but it occurs regularly—that is, every revolution. A loose flywheel or excessive crankshaft end play are two possible causes.

Old-timer's Test

Trying to analyze the cause of engine noise from sound alone is tough. However, there is an old-timer's test that we'll outline for you. Internal engine noise usually falls into one of these classifications:
• Noise that occurs once every revolution.
• Noise that occurs once every cycle (two revolutions).
• Noise that occurs intermittently, having no rhyme or reason.
Perform the test as follows:
1 Check the engine oil and replenish it if necessary.
2 Warm up the engine to normal operating temperature (at least 150°F).
3 Turn the engine off. Pull the boot off the plug (do not remove the cable) and place a neon-type spark plug tester on the plug. *Caution: Because of the high voltages involved, it is not advisable to perform this test if your car is equipped with an electronic ignition system.*
4 Restart the engine and let it idle at about 600 rpm. Note when the engine noise occurs in relation to the flashes of light. If the noise occurs twice for each flash (once every revolution), the cause of the sound is a part driven by or driving the crankshaft. Pistons, rings, pins, and main journals are in this category.

If the sound occurs once for each flash (once every cycle), anything driven by or with the camshaft could be causing the noise, since the camshaft makes a single revolution per cycle. Falling into this area are the valves, oil pump, distributor, fuel pump, and the camshaft itself.

If the noise occurs intermittently—neither once nor twice for every flash of light—the cause of the problem is some component that isn't tied directly into the camshaft or crankshaft. Consider excessive end play of one of the shafts or noise being made by some engine-driven component, such as the alternator, starter or distributor.

Noise can often be isolated by shorting out the spark plug of each cylinder in turn. If the noise stops when a cylinder is shorted, you have isolated the noise to that cylinder.

Pinging

The subject of engine ping deserves attention here, because while pinging usually indicates a minor condition, it may also tell you that your engine is in big trouble. It depends on whether ping is being produced by detonation of a mild sort, detonation of a serious nature or preignition. Detonation and preignition are very different and should not be confused.

Ping is a rapid, rattling knock coming from an engine. Ping caused by detonation occurs primarily when the engine is placed under a load, such as when the car is climbing a hill. It happens when gasoline isn't able to withstand the heat and pressure inside a cylinder. Instead of burning evenly and smoothly, as gasoline should, the unburned portion of the mixture ignites violently *after the mixture has been ignited by the spark plug.* This sudden premature bursting into flame of the unburned gasoline causes the engine's cylinder head to rattle. It is this noise that you hear as ping. Detonation can usually be eliminated or at least relieved greatly by seeing to it that the ignition timing is set to the manufacturer's specifications, that the engine isn't overheating, and that gasoline of the correct octane rating is being used. In checking timing, you should also check the condition of those parts affecting engine timing—the distributor and spark advance.

Ping caused by preignition occurs when there is combustion of gasoline in a cylinder *before the spark plug ignites the fuel.* Combustion is caused by a "hot spot" (red-hot carbon usually) in the cylinder. Preignition places moving parts under extraordinary stress and can cause the most serious damage. There is no such thing as harmless preignition, and at the first sign of the condition the engine should not be operated but should be disassembled for a carbon cleaning. But how can you tell the difference between ping caused by detonation and ping caused by preignition? It's very difficult to listen to the noise and distinguish between the two. So, if engine ping doesn't clear up at once by setting the timing, assuring the proper engine operating temperature, and changing to high-octane gasoline, watch out. You have a preignition problem.

Whistle

Bothered by a whistling sound coming from the engine compartment? Your dilemma could be a drive belt that is too tight or glazed. But many times a whistle

No Power?

Loose carburetor and manifold mounting bolts can also lead to another problem: lack of power on acceleration. If there is no vacuum leak to blame for the engine's

Dieseling

If your engine continues to run after you turn off the ignition, it's suffering from a condition known as dieseling, which is ignition in the absence of spark. It occurs when fuel in the combustion chambers is ignited by heat.

To help prevent dieseling, manufacturers have added a device called an idle-stop solenoid to the carburetors of most engines. The solenoid's job is to shut the throttle at once when the ignition is turned off, keeping excess fuel from entering the combustion chambers where it can be ignited by high temperatures. If your car has an idle-stop solenoid, dieseling will occur if the solenoid is not working. With the ignition on, the plunger in the base of the solenoid should be pressed against the throttle lever. As soon as the ignition is turned off, the plunger should retract at once, allowing the throttle valve to close.

Other causes of dieseling include the following:
• Improperly adjusted slow idling speed.
• An ignition malfunction, such as the wrong breaker-point dwell or misadjusted ignition timing.
• A carburetor linkage that is hanging up because of dirt or damage.
• A stuck manifold heat-control valve.
• An engine temperature that is exceeding the "normal" range.

How to Use Your Nose

Olfactory troubleshooting is more limited than auditory diagnosis. But there are several odors that are unmistakable and can help the home mechanic pinpoint a mechanical problem:
• Gas fumes, for example, tell you something is amiss in the fuel system. First check the carburetor for flooding, then check the fuel system back from the fuel inlet for leakage.
• The odor of burning oil signals a problem in the lubrication system. The odor is the result of leaking oil hitting a hot engine. Check for external leaks around the engine, especially the valve cover gasket. Also check the air cleaner. If engine blowby is the problem, there will usually be oil deposits in the cleaner housing.
• When checking the transmission fluid level, sniff the dipstick. If it has a burnt smell, suspect burned clutches in the transmission.
• A heavy acrid smell coming from under the hood could indicate smoldering electrical wiring about to burst into flames. Stop the car immediately and shut off the engine. A short circuit is probably the cause.

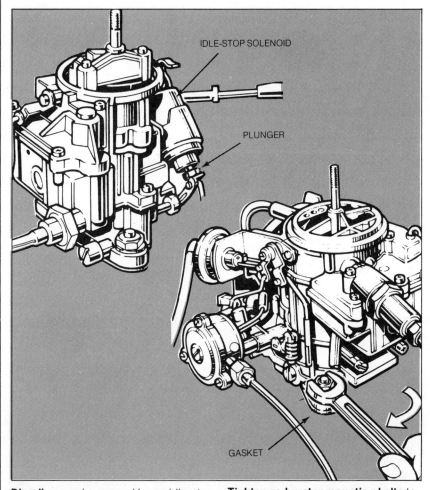

IDLE-STOP SOLENOID

PLUNGER

GASKET

Dieseling can be caused by an idle-stop solenoid that is not working properly.

Tighten carburetor mounting bolts to prevent air leaks and loss of power.

coming from under the hood is produced by a vacuum leak caused by loose intake manifold attaching screws, loose carburetor mounting bolts or a leaking gasket. To determine if one of these is causing the noise, start the engine and spread a mixture of oil and kerosene around the manifold and carburetor. If the whistle ceases or changes pitch, you have found the cause. Tighten up all bolts. If this doesn't help, the gasket should be replaced.

unresponsiveness, then the following should be checked out (consult the respective section in this book):
In the fuel system:
• Improper carburetor float level.
• Damaged needle valve-seat assembly.
• Restricted gas line or fuel filter.
• Weak fuel pump.
• Malfunctioning carburetor accelerator pump.
• Dirty carburetor.
In the ignition system:
• Weak coil.
• Incorrect ignition timing.
• Insufficient point dwell.
• Fouled or improperly gapped spark plugs.
• Damaged spark advance unit.
• Worn distributor cam.
• Excessive play in the distributor shaft.

WHAT'S DIFFERENT ABOUT DIESELS?

Many of the routine service procedures, tests, and common breakdown repairs on diesels are similar to those performed on cars with conventional gasoline engines. The *different* service procedures described in this chapter are still doable by a home mechanic.

The truck industry's experience with the diesel engine has been very good. Fuel mileage is superb, much routine maintenance (such as ignition) is eliminated and, while parts aren't inexpensive, their longevity almost makes up for their high price.

There are at least seven foreign and domestic carmakers with diesel-powered engines on the road in this country and more on the way. Although you will find something different on every one of these models, all diesels are different from gasoline engines in the design and/or function of the cylinder heads, combustion chambers, fuel distribution system, air-intake manifold, and method of ignition. This discussion will outline the

service procedures for two significantly different types of diesels with a head-start on the US market: the Oldsmobile 350 V8 and the VW Rabbit.

How They Work

The diesel engine requires little maintenance when compared with the gasoline engine, primarily because it doesn't have complicated ignition and carburetion systems as the gasoline engine has.

The intake stroke of the diesel is similar to the intake stroke of the gasoline engine, except that there is no carburetor to mix fuel with air and no throttle valve to restrict the amount of air entering the cylinder. Therefore, the cylinder fills with air only. When this air becomes compressed, its temperature rises above the ignition point of the fuel. As the piston nears the end of the compression stroke, fuel is injected into the combustion chamber by a fuel-injection system that meters, pressurizes, and distributes fuel to all cylinders. The fuel is ignited by the heat of the compressed air.

Since this type of ignition does not require an electrical-spark-ignition system, the diesel does not have a distributor, spark plug wires, spark plugs or high-voltage ignition. In very cold weather, tiny electrical heaters called glow plugs heat the precombustion chambers to assist in starting. They remain on a short time after the engine is started, then turn off when the air in the chamber reaches a high enough temperature to ignite the fuel when it is compressed.

1 Overview of the Oldsmobile 350 V8 diesel engine. Note the two 12-volt batteries in parallel up front.

2 Remove the hold-down bolts of the air-intake muffler attached to the air cleaner.

3 Air-intake manifold with air cleaner removed. Timing mark is on the injector, but the timing reference mark is on the engine.

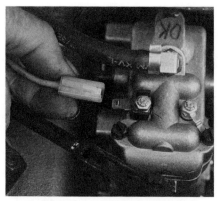

4 The power supply line must be disconnected from the diesel fuel heating unit prior to testing for continuity.

5 Adjust idle speed using the Mag-Tac, a pulse-actuated tachometer with digital readout. The unit is specially designed for diesel engines.

Servicing the Oldsmobile 350 V8 Diesel

The Oldsmobile diesel engine compares in size with the 350 V8 gasoline engine, which was the starting point in the engineering of the diesel version. However, the diesel's cylinder block, crankshaft, main bearings, rods, pistons, and pins are of heavier construction because of the higher compression ratio needed to ignite diesel fuel. Further, the Olds diesel does not have a catalytic converter or any emission control devices, except for a crankcase ventilation system.

Before attempting any Olds diesel engine maintenance service, read these two paragraphs:

1 Do not clean the engine until it has cooled to surrounding temperature. Spraying water or engine cleaning solvent on the diesel injection pump when it is warm or hot will damage the pump.

2 The Olds has many colored bolts, screws, etc. which are in metric measurement, but very close in dimension to fasteners in the current US system. So be careful when replacing the fasteners. Make sure the replacements have the same measurements and strengths as those removed.

The fuel-injection pump is mounted on top of the diesel engine. This pump provides the required timing advance under all operating conditions. Timing advance is preset at the factory.

The fuel filter is located between the mechanical fuel pump and the injection pump. The diaphragm-type mechanical fuel pump is mounted on the right side of the engine and is driven by a cam on the crankshaft. There is also a fuel filter in the fuel tank.

There are two types of electrical glow plug systems used in Olds diesels—both operate off of two 12-volt batteries. One system has *two* relays on the firewall near the wiper motor that activate the *12-volt* glow plugs; the other has *one* relay box on the right fender filler panel that activates the *6-volt* glow plugs. Note: The two plugs are not interchangeable, so make sure you know which type your car takes. *Caution: The single relay box system supplies a pulsing current to the glow plugs. Do not bypass or apply electrical current to the relay because you will instantly damage the plugs.*

To test the glow plugs, connect a positive voltmeter lead to the battery positive post and a negative voltmeter lead to the battery negative post. Now turn the ignition switch on. Note: The voltmeter should read battery voltage. You will have two to five minutes to perform this test before the ignition switch turns off automatically to prevent the batteries from running down if the ignition is accidentally left on. To reset the system, turn the ignition switch off and then on again. If the "wait" light comes on, proceed with the test. If it doesn't come on, it means the engine is too warm for glow plug operation and the thermistor must be disconnected before the test can be made. The thermistor is a heat-sensing device whose electrical resistance decreases as its temperature increases. If you are making the test with the thermistor disconnected, the voltmeter reading should drop off one or two volts below battery voltage. Replace any plugs that do not meet specs.

6 To replace the fuel filter, the fuel line must first be disconnected.

7 The power connector must be disconnected from the glow plug before the plug can be removed.

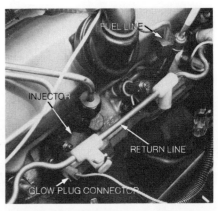

8 Each side of the engine has four fuel lines, four fuel injectors, four glow plugs, four plug connectors, and four fuel return T fittings.

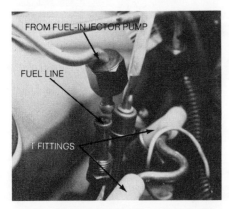

9 Remove the T fittings by pulling each one up a little at a time in sequence until they come off. Use two wrenches to uncouple the fuel line from the injector.

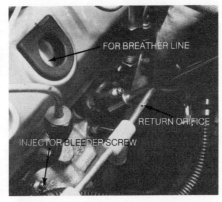

10 After the fuel line, return line, and glow plugs are disconnected, remove the injector retaining cap screw with a socket and extension ratchet.

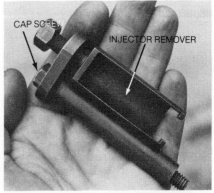

11 The special tool you will need to remove the fuel injector.

Continued

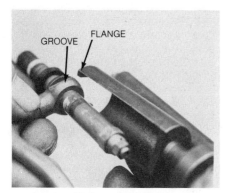

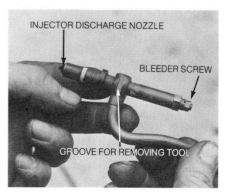

12 Install the injector removing tool so the flange of the tool enters the groove on the fuel injector. Lock the injector cap screw before beginning to pull out the injector.

13 Remove the injector from the engine with a $\frac{9}{16}$-inch closed-end wrench.

14 Identify different components of the injector nozzle assembly.

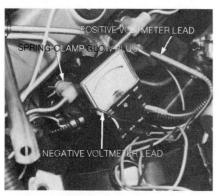

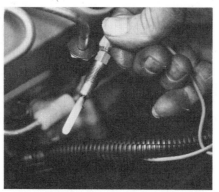

15 After attaching the voltmeter, turn the ignition key on and note the voltage reading.

16 With ignition switch on, connect the glow plug supply line to each plug and ground the plug. If it doesn't glow, check plug power circuit for continuity. If there's voltage, but no glow, replace the glow plug.

17 After all tests are completed, reassemble the system reversing the above procedures. A hammer handle will help you to seat the fuel return line.

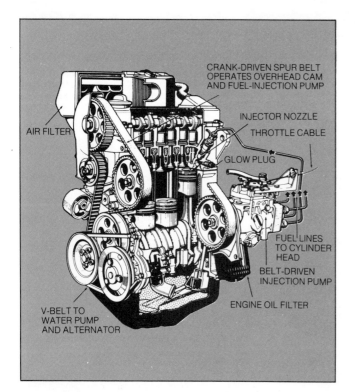

Servicing the VW Rabbit Diesel

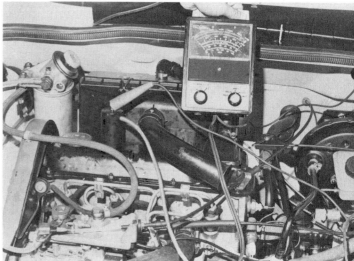

1 Engine rpm on the VW diesel is measured with a special vibration sensor to which a standard tachometer is connected.

18 Remove a glow plug and install a special high-pressure compression tester in the plug hole.

19 The finger points to the wires to be tested when checking a plug that does not glow.

20 Remove the fuel injector line. The fuel injector has as many injector lines as there are cylinders in the engine. Note the similarity to the ignition wires in a conventional gasoline engine.

21 Adjust the fast idle on the solenoid with an open-end wrench. Use a Mag-Tac tachometer to monitor engine rpm.

22 Make sure the throttle linkage is free and properly adjusted.

23 A magnetic pulse timing hole is designed to accept the Mag-Tac probe to measure engine speed.

The engine block, crankshaft, flywheel, and main bearings are straight out of the gasoline version. The cylinder head looks a lot like the one used on the VW gasoline engine, but it is modified to accommodate fuel injection directly into the cylinders.

The fuel-injection system is the major external difference between the VW diesel and the VW gasoline engine. The diesel has a mechanical pulley-and-belt system, and its injectors thread into tiny precombustion chambers leading directly to the main combustion chambers at the top of the cylinders.

2 Engine idle is adjusted at the fuel-injection pump. Slacken the lock nut with a wrench and turn the screw to get the desired engine rpm.

3 The fuel shutoff solenoid automatically cuts off fuel to the engine. To service it, first remove the nut, then disconnect the wire.

Idle Speed

The first new procedure you face is setting the idle speed to specifications. This is new because there is no electrical ignition system to connect a tachometer to. VW's solution is a vibration sensor with a magnet in the base. Place it on the valve cover and connect its two lead wires to the car battery. Engine vibration and 12-volt battery current create an electrical pulse that will operate a standard tachometer (Fig. 1). To set idle-speed adjustment, loosen the lock nut and turn the

Continued

screw on the accelerator linkage at the fuel injection pump (Fig. 2).

There is no fast idle and no choke. For cold starts, you pull a dashboard knob, and linkage from the knob to the fuel injection pump operates an internal pump mechanism that advances the fuel injection on the crankshaft by 5°.

The VW diesel engine has a maximum speed of 5450 rpm which is controlled by a governor inside the fuel pump. Check the governed maximum speed by flooring the accelerator pedal. To adjust the governor, slacken the lock nut and turn the governor screw—it's next to the one for idle speed.

Fuel Flow Solenoid

To turn off the VW diesel, the fuel supply must be shut off. Fuel flow is controlled by a solenoid valve on the pump. When the solenoid is energized, the fuel passes into the injection circuits; when the key is turned off, the solenoid de-energizes and fuel flow stops. Whenever you work on the engine, particularly if it is cranked, it's standard procedure to disconnect the wire from the solenoid (Fig. 3).

The solenoid is a potential trouble point. If it fails to energize, the VW diesel engine won't start. If it doesn't disengage, the engine won't turn off. To check the solenoid, place your fingers on it. You should be able to feel it click when the key is turned on.

Fuel Injection Pump

The fuel injection pump on the VW diesel must time its fuel delivery to the injectors as precisely as ignition is timed on the gasoline engine. As engine speed increases, the injection system must spray fuel earlier. The advance system is built into the pump, just as spark advance is automatic in the distributor in the gasoline engine. But the basic pump timing must be correct.

Check the basic timing setting with a dial indicator inserted into the pump. First, turn the crankshaft pulley with a wrench, until the flywheel top dead center mark is lined up at the bell-housing opening (the same setup used for ignition timing on the gasoline engine) (Fig. 4). Next, insert the dial indicator until its rod

causes the dial needle to move a few millimeters. The rod is now bearing against the pump injection plunger, the part that pushes fuel under pressure up to the injectors.

Turn the crank backward until the dial needle stops moving, set the dial to zero, and turn the crank forward until the top dead center mark lines up again. The dial needle should have moved forward a specified distance, which is equal to the pump plunger stroke (0.83mm). If the reading is too great or too little, slacken the four mounting bolts on the pump and turn it one way or the other to get the exact reading on the dial (Fig. 5). The bolts pass through elongated holes to permit adjustment. This adjustment, plus engine speed and replacement of a defective shutoff solenoid, are the only jobs that can be done on the fuel pump. If the pump fails, it must be replaced.

To help extend fuel pump life, use No. 2 diesel fuel, which has better lubricating qualities than the lighter No. 1. Fuel is the pump's only source of lubrication, so this is important. A quality No. 2 is seasonally blended for cold weather, so startability should be tolerable. Only in extremely cold weather, with no other choice, should No. 1 fuel be used to ease starting.

Compression

The VW diesel develops much higher compression than a gasoline engine. The typical gas engine will run satisfactorily with cranking compression as low as 90 to 100 psi (pounds per square inch). The VW diesel should produce pressures in the 400 to 500 psi range in order to raise the air temperatures high enough to ignite diesel fuel.

A conventional compression gauge, with its 250 to 300 psi limit, won't do. VW supplies a model that not only reads to 600 psi, but includes a roll of paper and an automatic marking pen (in place of the standard indicator needle), to provide a permanent record of compression readings.

Since there is no spark plug hole on the diesel, the special diesel compression gauge is threaded into a fuel-injector hole. To get the VW injectors out, remove the fuel lines at the pump and at the injectors. Then take out the injectors with a ratchet and deep socket. When reinstalling the injectors, tighten them to specs with a torque wrench.

Next, withdraw the heat shields, which look like plug gaskets and sit over the injector holes, narrow-side down (Fig. 6). Thread the hose fitting into the injector hole and tighten with a wrench. Now you're set to crank the engine and take your readings.

4 The outer plug should be removed so the top dead center mark on the flywheel can be aligned with the pointer inside the bell housing.

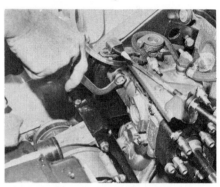

5 Injection pump bolts are loosened with a curved wrench. Turn the pump to adjust the timing. The indicator checks the plunger stroke.

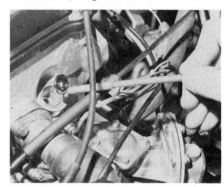

6 After the fuel injectors are removed, the heat shields are visible. Remove them with a magnet. Do not reuse the heat shields.

7 Drive belt replacement requires two simple tools. Here the camshaft is kept from turning with an L-shaped steel bar.

8 To change the drive belt, keep the injection pump pulley from turning with a simple locking plug.

9 This gauge measures belt tension. For adjustment, slacken the lock nut and turn the large hex nut on the idler pulley with a wrench.

10 In the VW system, the bus bar connects the glow plugs in a single circuit. Wire-brush the plugs' heating element tip as necessary.

11 A glow plug relay is a plug-in unit on the fuse box under the left side of the dash. It can be removed and replaced easily.

Drive Belt

The rubber drive belt on the VW diesel is reinforced with steel wire for longer life. If it breaks, serious engine damage could result, because there is very little clearance between the top of the piston and the closed valves when the piston is at the top of its stroke. If the belt snaps, the overhead camshaft stops and some valves are left open. The crank continues to rotate and when it brings the pistons up, they crash into the valves. This can also happen if the belt is loose and jumps a number of teeth on the pulley. There is no recommended replacement interval for the VW belt, but it is a good idea to pull the guard and check the belt periodically. If it is frayed or has stretched a bit, consider replacing it, although the belt can be retensioned.

You can change a drive belt with inexpensive but specialized tools. One holds the camshaft (Fig. 7); another locks the injection pump pulley (Fig. 8). Line up the flywheel timing marks so both tools can be inserted to prevent accidental turning of either pulley. Loosen the idler pulley lock nut, replace the belt, and tighten it. To measure tension accurately, a special gauge is used. The gauge, which measures belt deflection to the millimeter, is hooked onto the belt, the specified deflection is dialed in, and the idler pulley is tensioned with the wrench as shown (Fig. 9).

Valve Shims

The Rabbit engine—gasoline or diesel—has a shim-type valve clearance adjustment. The cam follower and valve must be pushed down to remove the old shim and install a replacement. Although this is normally a job for the dealer service department, which has a stock of replacement shims, note one problem area if you decide to do the job yourself: On the VW diesel, the limited clearance between the valve and the top of the piston means you can't push the valve down when the piston is at top dead center. Measure the clearance at this point, then rotate the crank 90° to bring the piston down. Now you can depress the cam follower and valve to replace the shim.

Glow Plugs

The VW diesel glow plugs are heated by battery current supplied by a key switch and a relay. The relay also turns off a dashboard indicator light when preheating is complete and the engine can be started. This second function is time-controlled according to engine temperature—the light may take anywhere from seconds to more than a minute to go off.

Failure of the glow plug circuit is a common cause of hard starting in cold weather. A simple check of the entire glow plug system begins with disconnecting the wire from the relay to the bus bar, which is the current supply bar connected to all the glow plugs. Then attach a test lamp to the wire and to a ground and have a helper turn the key to the glow position. The lamp should light. If it does not, listen for a click at the relay, which is a simple plug-in to the fuse box. If there is no click, the relay is probably bad (Fig. 10, 11).

Individual glow plugs can be tested by removing the bus bar, attaching a test lamp to the battery starter terminal, and touching the probe to each glow plug terminal. If the lamp lights, the plug is probably good. If the car has high mileage, remove each glow plug and inspect the heating element for carbon deposits. Wire-brush clean, if necessary.

Fuel System

As long as the diesel fuel is clean, the injectors should last indefinitely. The VW diesel manual calls for testing the injectors if the engine is misfiring and compression is normal. It takes an expensive pressure tester-pump device to pump fuel into the injector at operating pressure (1700 to 1850 psi), so you might consider giving this job to a pro. Since the price of an injector is less than two hours of a professional mechanic's labor charge, checking a suspect injector by substituting one you know is OK may be a cheaper way to make this test.

The VW diesel has a king-size spin-on fuel filter to protect the injectors and the pump. It should be changed every 15,000 miles. To replace the fuel filter, take it and the mounting adapter off the bracket, loosen the filter at the base with a wrench, then spin it off. Lube the new filter gasket with clean diesel fuel, then spin it on finger-tight and refit it to the bracket.

VW engine oil, which must be Service CC grade, should be changed at 7500-mile intervals. A good-quality gasoline oil may also qualify for CC, so check the markings on the can. Diesel oil blackens very quickly, sometimes in a few miles, so don't panic.

TROUBLESHOOTING BY THE NUMBERS

On the following 59 pages, you will find diagnostic charts covering all the common—and many not-so-common—symptoms of engine malfunction. By consulting these charts, you should be able, easily and quickly, to track down the cause of almost any engine problem to which your car might fall victim. Once you match your problem with the appropriate step-by-step charts, they will tell you what to check, what to repair, what to replace, and where in the tuneup chapters to go for detailed procedures. And in cases where advanced knowledge or ultrafancy tools or both are required, the charts will respectfully suggest that you go to a professional.

How to use the charts

These Troubleshooting by the Numbers charts are organized alphabetically by symptoms ("Dieseling" precedes "Poor Gas Mileage"). But since you might describe a problem in different words from those we use, you may want to read through the whole list in the table of contents, opposite, ticking off every heading that seems related to the symptom you're checking out.

Now, go to the page where the most likely symptom starts and begin at the panel next to the large 1. This will give you one or two instructions or visual checks. Next you will be referred to specific tests and adjustments in the tuneup chapters. Following the dotted lines, proceed until the problem is solved. The right-hand panel lets you know if the job is done and, if not, where to go from there. With luck, you'll finish the job in a step or two. Very complicated problems could require up to ten steps, maybe even more.

Remember that these Troubleshooting charts are diagnostic aids only. They tell you **what** to do, not how to do it. For the how-to side of the job, you must check out the page or pages in the tuneup section of the book that the chart directs you to.

Before beginning your troubleshooting, study the sample chart and read over the explanatory notes.

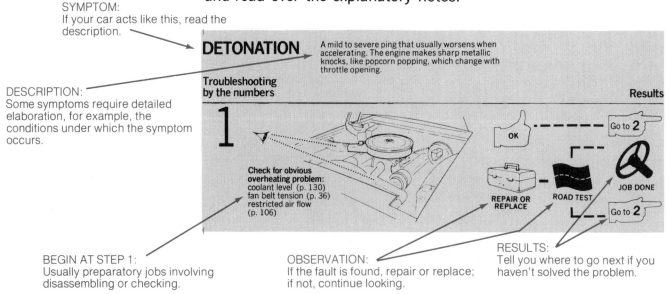

SYMPTOM:
If your car acts like this, read the description.

DESCRIPTION:
Some symptoms require detailed elaboration, for example, the conditions under which the symptom occurs.

BEGIN AT STEP 1:
Usually preparatory jobs involving disassembling or checking.

OBSERVATION:
If the fault is found, repair or replace; if not, continue looking.

RESULTS:
Tell you where to go next if you haven't solved the problem.

DETONATION A mild to severe ping that usually worsens when accelerating. The engine makes sharp metallic knocks, like popcorn popping, which change with throttle opening.

Troubleshooting by the numbers

Results

1

OK — Go to 2

Check for obvious overheating problem:
coolant level (p. 130)
fan belt tension (p. 36)
restricted air flow (p. 106)

REPAIR OR REPLACE — ROAD TEST — JOB DONE

Go to 2

CONTENTS: IDENTIFYING THE PROBLEM

ALTERNATOR LIGHT IS OFF/IGNITION IS ON/ENGINE IS NOT RUNNING

**Troubleshooting
by the numbers**

1

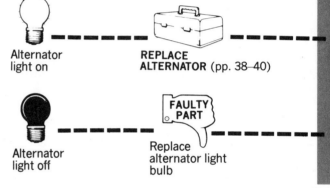

Ignition on

Make sure all indicator and courtesy lights show proper warning

Any other lights off → **FAULTY PART** Replace gauges or courtesy light fuse (p. 40) → Alternator light on → **JOB DONE**

Other lights on → **Go to 2**

2

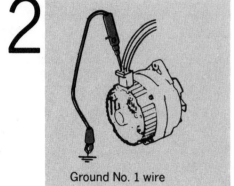

Ground No. 1 wire

Alternator light on → **REPLACE ALTERNATOR** (pp. 38–40) → **JOB DONE**

Alternator light off → **FAULTY PART** Replace alternator light bulb → **JOB DONE**

ALTERNATOR LIGHT ON, IGNITION OFF

1

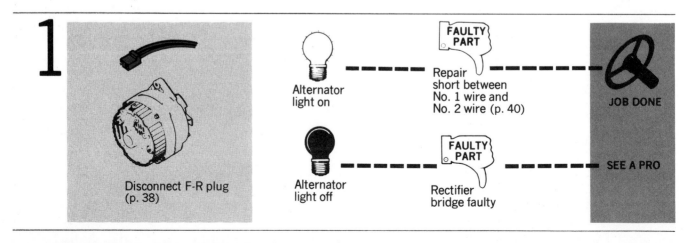

Disconnect F-R plug (p. 38)

Alternator light on → **FAULTY PART** Repair short between No. 1 wire and No. 2 wire (p. 40) → **JOB DONE**

Alternator light off → **FAULTY PART** Rectifier bridge faulty → **SEE A PRO**

ALTERNATOR LIGHT IS ON/ENGINE IS RUNNING

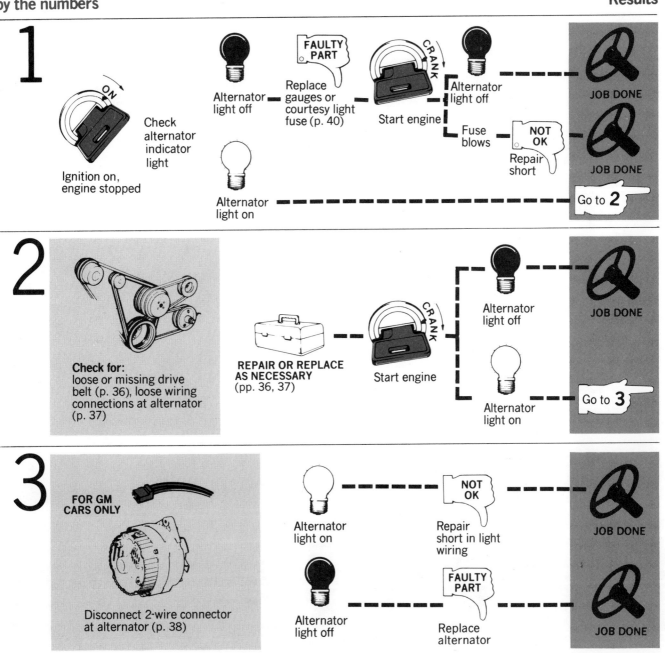

1 Ignition on, engine stopped — Check alternator indicator light

Alternator light off — FAULTY PART — Replace gauges or courtesy light fuse (p. 40) — Start engine (CRANK) — Alternator light off → JOB DONE

Fuse blows — NOT OK — Repair short → JOB DONE

Alternator light on — — — — — → Go to **2**

2 Check for: loose or missing drive belt (p. 36), loose wiring connections at alternator (p. 37)

REPAIR OR REPLACE AS NECESSARY (pp. 36, 37) — Start engine (CRANK) — Alternator light off → JOB DONE

Alternator light on → Go to **3**

3 FOR GM CARS ONLY — Disconnect 2-wire connector at alternator (p. 38)

Alternator light on — NOT OK — Repair short in light wiring → JOB DONE

Alternator light off — FAULTY PART — Replace alternator → JOB DONE

BATTERY LOSES ITS CHARGE (ALTERNATOR LIGHT IS WORKING)

Troubleshooting
by the numbers

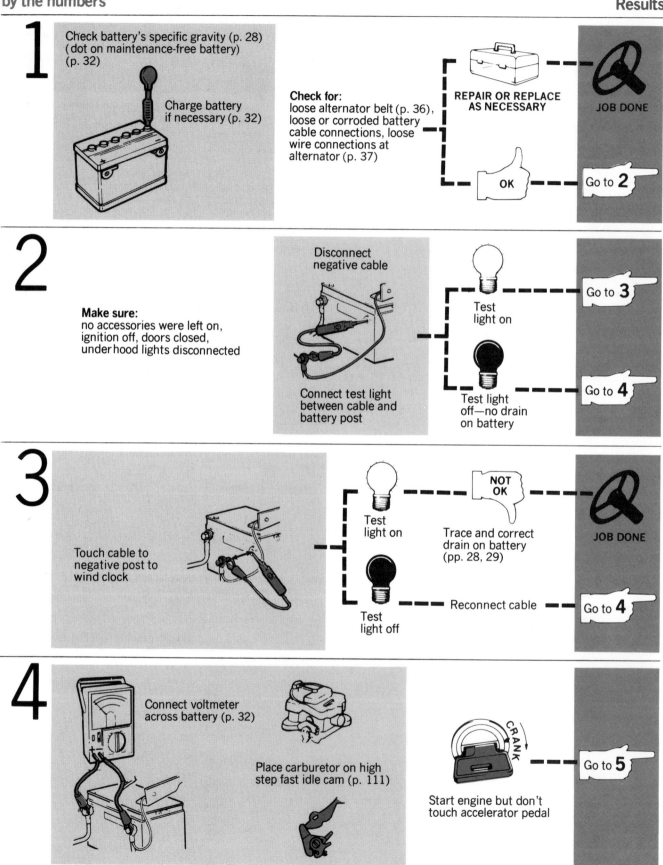

1 Check battery's specific gravity (p. 28) (dot on maintenance-free battery) (p. 32)

Charge battery if necessary (p. 32)

Check for: loose alternator belt (p. 36), loose or corroded battery cable connections, loose wire connections at alternator (p. 37)

REPAIR OR REPLACE AS NECESSARY

JOB DONE

OK — Go to **2**

2 **Make sure:** no accessories were left on, ignition off, doors closed, underhood lights disconnected

Disconnect negative cable

Connect test light between cable and battery post

Test light on — Go to **3**

Test light off—no drain on battery — Go to **4**

3 Touch cable to negative post to wind clock

Test light on

NOT OK — Trace and correct drain on battery (pp. 28, 29) — JOB DONE

Test light off — Reconnect cable — Go to **4**

4 Connect voltmeter across battery (p. 32)

Place carburetor on high step fast idle cam (p. 111)

CRANK

Start engine but don't touch accelerator pedal

Go to **5**

Troubleshooting by the numbers

5

Turn all accessories on: headlights on high, radio on, air conditioning on high, blower-type defogger on high

Check voltage reading after one minute

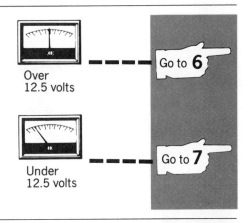

Over 12.5 volts → Go to **6**

Under 12.5 volts → Go to **7**

6

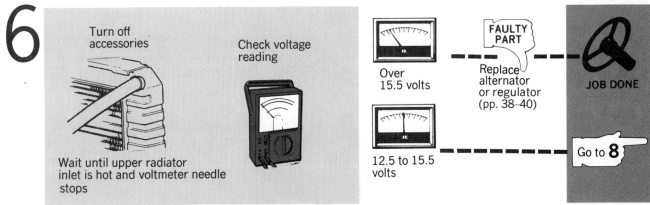

Turn off accessories

Check voltage reading

Wait until upper radiator inlet is hot and voltmeter needle stops

Over 15.5 volts → **FAULTY PART** Replace alternator or regulator (pp. 38–40) → **JOB DONE**

12.5 to 15.5 volts → Go to **8**

7

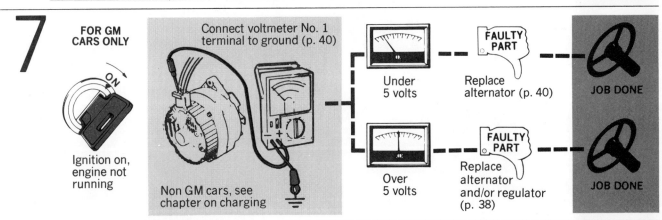

FOR GM CARS ONLY

Ignition on, engine not running

Connect voltmeter No. 1 terminal to ground (p. 40)

Non GM cars, see chapter on charging

Under 5 volts → **FAULTY PART** Replace alternator (p. 40) → **JOB DONE**

Over 5 volts → **FAULTY PART** Replace alternator and/or regulator (p. 38) → **JOB DONE**

8

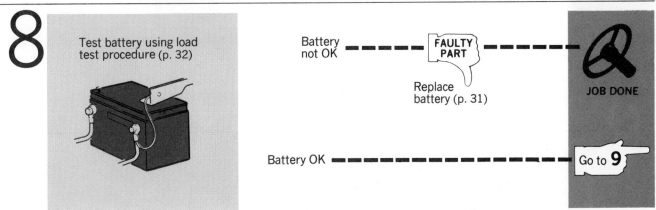

Test battery using load test procedure (p. 32)

Battery not OK → **FAULTY PART** Replace battery (p. 31) → **JOB DONE**

Battery OK → Go to **9**

Troubleshooting
by the numbers

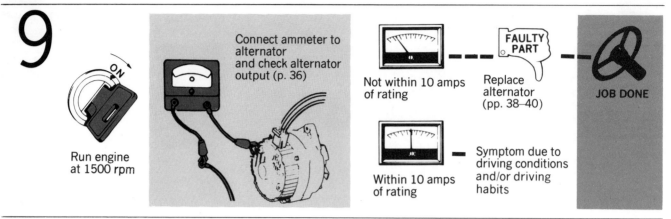

9

Run engine
at 1500 rpm

Connect ammeter to
alternator
and check alternator
output (p. 36)

Not within 10 amps
of rating

FAULTY
PART

Replace
alternator
(pp. 38–40)

JOB DONE

Within 10 amps
of rating

Symptom due to
driving conditions
and/or driving
habits

BATTERY IS LOW (ALTERNATOR LIGHT IS WORKING)

**Troubleshooting
by the numbers**

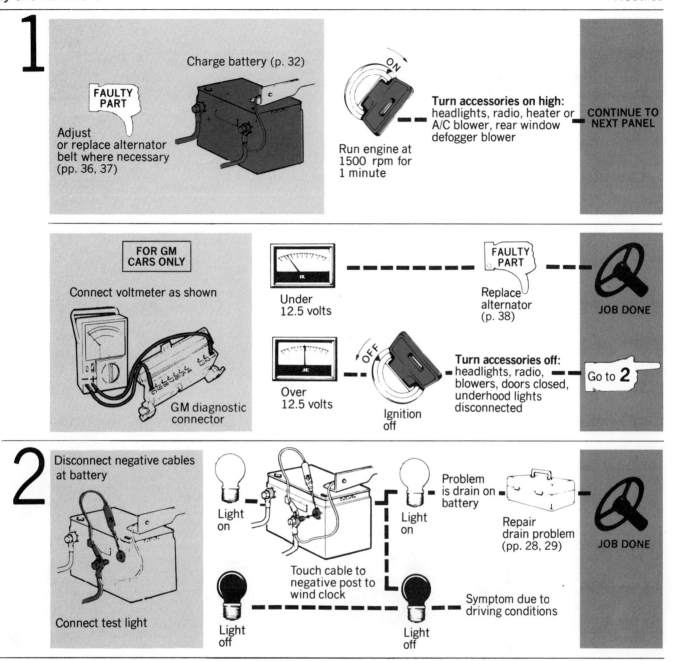

1

Charge battery (p. 32)

FAULTY PART

Adjust
or replace alternator
belt where necessary
(pp. 36, 37)

Turn accessories on high:
headlights, radio, heater or
A/C blower, rear window
defogger blower

Run engine at
1500 rpm for
1 minute

CONTINUE TO
NEXT PANEL

FOR GM
CARS ONLY

Connect voltmeter as shown

Under
12.5 volts

FAULTY
PART

Replace
alternator
(p. 38)

JOB DONE

GM diagnostic
connector

Over
12.5 volts

Ignition
off

Turn accessories off:
headlights, radio,
blowers, doors closed,
underhood lights
disconnected

Go to **2**

2

Disconnect negative cables
at battery

Light
on

Touch cable to
negative post to
wind clock

Light
on

Problem
is drain on
battery

Repair
drain problem
(pp. 28, 29)

JOB DONE

Connect test light

Light
off

Light
off

Symptom due to
driving conditions

BATTERY IS OVERCHARGED

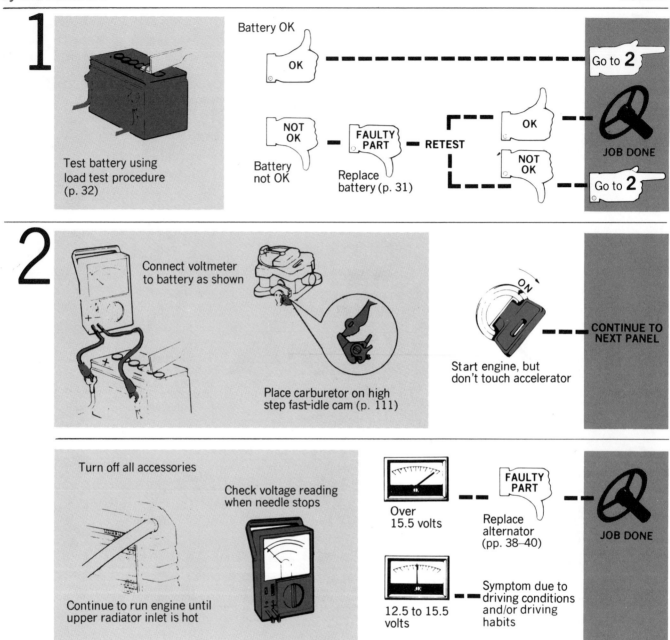

1 Test battery using load test procedure (p. 32)

Battery OK
OK
Go to **2**

NOT OK
Battery not OK
FAULTY PART
Replace battery (p. 31)
RETEST
OK
JOB DONE
NOT OK
Go to **2**

2 Connect voltmeter to battery as shown

Place carburetor on high step fast-idle cam (p. 111)

Start engine, but don't touch accelerator

CONTINUE TO NEXT PANEL

Turn off all accessories

Check voltage reading when needle stops

Continue to run engine until upper radiator inlet is hot

Over 15.5 volts

FAULTY PART
Replace alternator (pp. 38–40)

JOB DONE

12.5 to 15.5 volts

Symptom due to driving conditions and/or driving habits

BATTERY USES TOO MUCH WATER

Troubleshooting
by the numbers

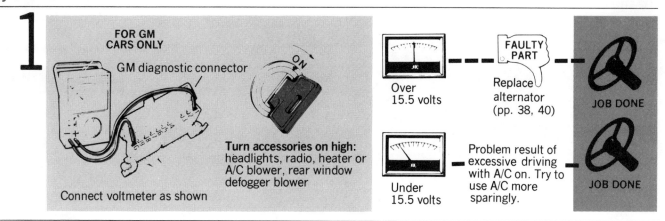

1

FOR GM
CARS ONLY

GM diagnostic connector

ON

Connect voltmeter as shown

Turn accessories on high:
headlights, radio, heater or
A/C blower, rear window
defogger blower

Over
15.5 volts

FAULTY
PART

Replace
alternator
(pp. 38, 40)

JOB DONE

Under
15.5 volts

Problem result of
excessive driving
with A/C on. Try to
use A/C more
sparingly.

JOB DONE

DETONATION

A mild to severe ping that usually worsens when accelerating. The engine makes sharp metallic knocks, like popcorn popping, which change with throttle opening.

Troubleshooting
by the numbers

Results

1

Check for obvious overheating problem:
coolant level (p. 130)
fan belt tension (p. 36)
restricted air flow (p. 106)

OK ----- Go to **2**

REPAIR OR REPLACE -- ROAD TEST

JOB DONE

Go to **2**

2

Disconnect and plug vacuum advance hose where applicable (p. 58)

Hook up tach/dwell meter and timing light (pp. 71, 72) then run engine at idle

Set dwell, timing and rpm to specs where applicable (pp. 71, 72)

ROAD TEST

JOB DONE

Unplug and reconnect vacuum advance hose.

Go to **3**

3

Aim timing light, then watch timing mark while opening throttle (p. 72)

Mark advances ----- OK ----- Go to **4**

Mark does not advance ----- REPLACE ADVANCE ----- SEE A PRO

4

If problem still exists, use an engine cleaner to remove carbon as follows:

Turn engine on

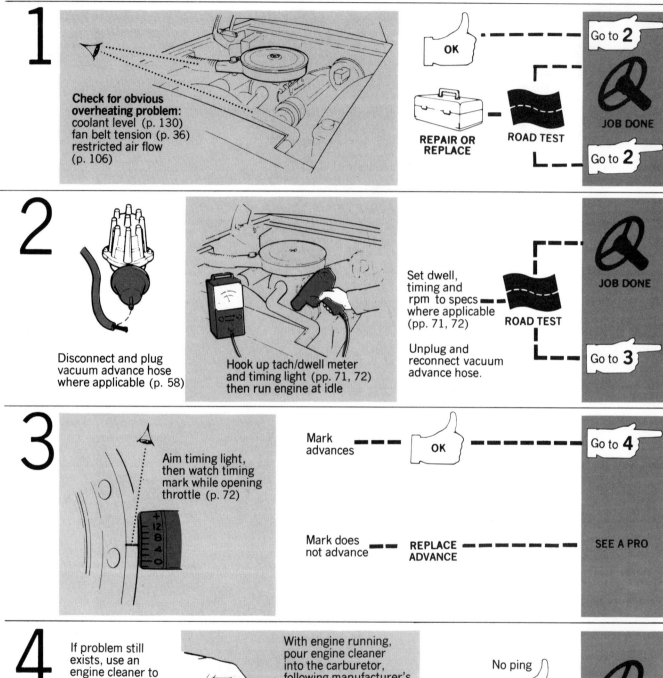

With engine running, pour engine cleaner into the carburetor, following manufacturer's instructions. This will remove carbon deposits.

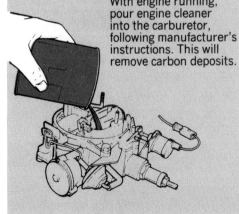

No ping

OK

ROAD TEST

JOB DONE

NOT OK

Condition still exists

TRY A DIFFERENT GASOLINE

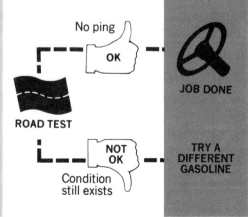

DIESELING

Engine continues to run after the ignition is turned off. It runs unevenly and may make knocking noises. The exhaust has a foul odor.

Troubleshooting by the numbers

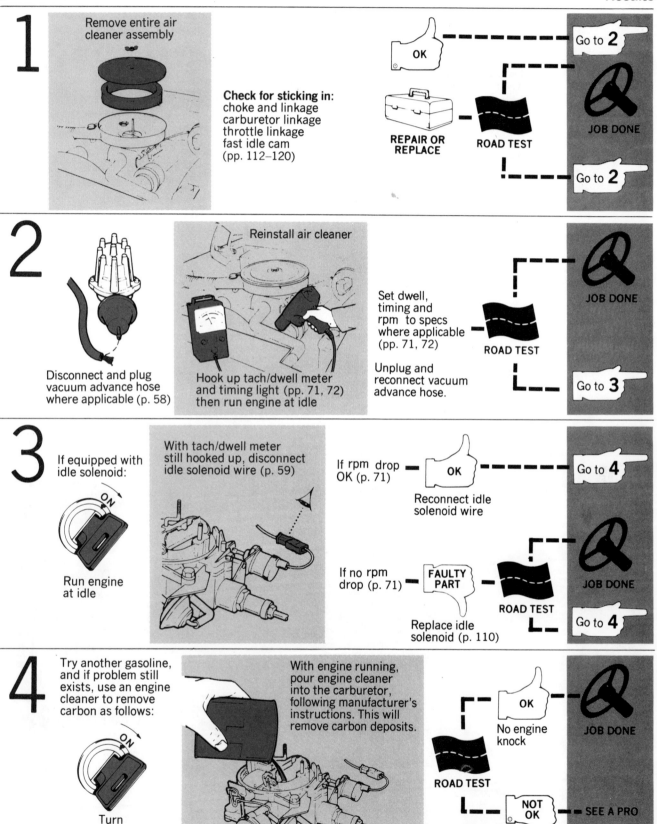

1 Remove entire air cleaner assembly

Check for sticking in: choke and linkage carburetor linkage throttle linkage fast idle cam (pp. 112–120)

OK → Go to **2**

REPAIR OR REPLACE → ROAD TEST → JOB DONE / Go to **2**

2 Disconnect and plug vacuum advance hose where applicable (p. 58)

Reinstall air cleaner

Hook up tach/dwell meter and timing light (pp. 71, 72) then run engine at idle

Set dwell, timing and rpm to specs where applicable (pp. 71, 72)

Unplug and reconnect vacuum advance hose.

ROAD TEST → JOB DONE / Go to **3**

3 If equipped with idle solenoid:

ON

Run engine at idle

With tach/dwell meter still hooked up, disconnect idle solenoid wire (p. 59)

If rpm drop OK (p. 71) → OK → Go to **4**

Reconnect idle solenoid wire

If no rpm drop (p. 71) → FAULTY PART

Replace idle solenoid (p. 110)

ROAD TEST → JOB DONE / Go to **4**

4 Try another gasoline, and if problem still exists, use an engine cleaner to remove carbon as follows:

ON

Turn engine on

With engine running, pour engine cleaner into the carburetor, following manufacturer's instructions. This will remove carbon deposits.

OK / No engine knock

ROAD TEST → JOB DONE

NOT OK → SEE A PRO

Engine needs carbon and valve job

ENGINE CRANKS SLOWLY, OR SOLENOID CLICKS

**Troubleshooting
by the numbers**

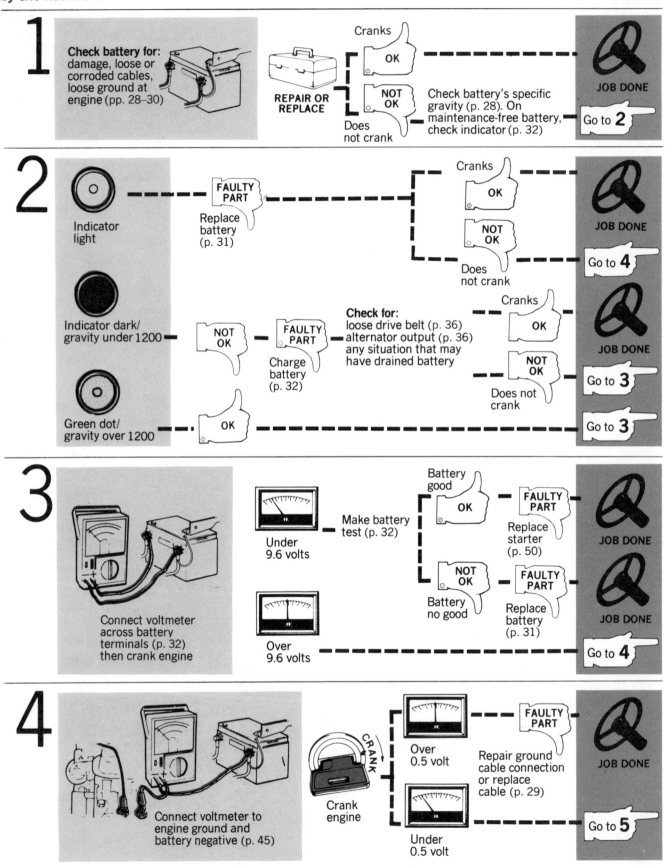

1 Check battery for: damage, loose or corroded cables, loose ground at engine (pp. 28–30)

REPAIR OR REPLACE

Cranks — OK — JOB DONE

NOT OK — Does not crank — Check battery's specific gravity (p. 28). On maintenance-free battery, check indicator (p. 32) — Go to **2**

2 Indicator light — FAULTY PART — Replace battery (p. 31)

Cranks — OK — JOB DONE

NOT OK — Does not crank — Go to **4**

Indicator dark/gravity under 1200 — NOT OK — FAULTY PART — Charge battery (p. 32)

Check for:
loose drive belt (p. 36)
alternator output (p. 36)
any situation that may
have drained battery

Cranks — OK — JOB DONE

NOT OK — Does not crank — Go to **3**

Green dot/gravity over 1200 — OK — Go to **3**

3 Connect voltmeter across battery terminals (p. 32) then crank engine

Under 9.6 volts — Make battery test (p. 32)

Battery good — OK — FAULTY PART — Replace starter (p. 50) — JOB DONE

NOT OK — Battery no good — FAULTY PART — Replace battery (p. 31) — JOB DONE

Over 9.6 volts — Go to **4**

4 Connect voltmeter to engine ground and battery negative (p. 45)

CRANK

Crank engine

Over 0.5 volt — FAULTY PART — Repair ground cable connection or replace cable (p. 29) — JOB DONE

Under 0.5 volt — Go to **5**

Troubleshooting
by the numbers

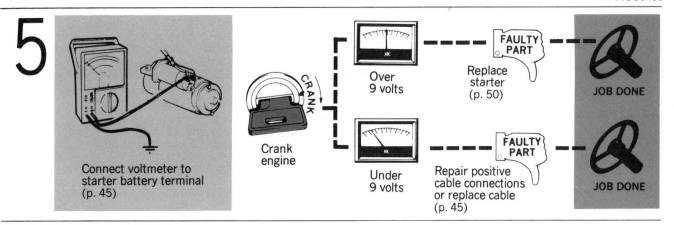

5

Connect voltmeter to
starter battery terminal
(p. 45)

CRANK

Crank
engine

Over
9 volts

Replace
starter
(p. 50)

FAULTY
PART

JOB DONE

Under
9 volts

Repair positive
cable connections
or replace cable
(p. 45)

FAULTY
PART

JOB DONE

ENGINE CRANKS BUT WON'T START, OR RUNS ROUGH THEN CUTS OUT (GM ELECTRONIC IGNITION-INTEGRAL COIL)

Troubleshooting by the numbers

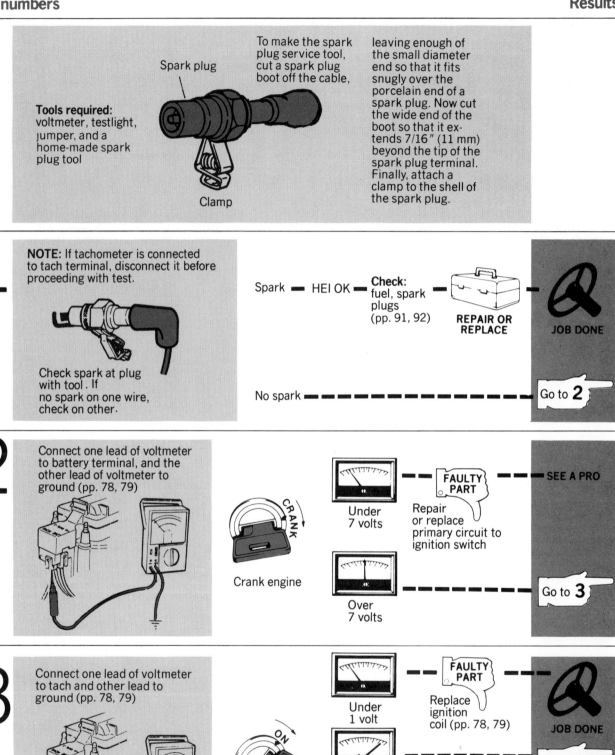

Tools required: voltmeter, testlight, jumper, and a home-made spark plug tool

Spark plug

Clamp

To make the spark plug service tool, cut a spark plug boot off the cable, leaving enough of the small diameter end so that it fits snugly over the porcelain end of a spark plug. Now cut the wide end of the boot so that it extends 7/16″ (11 mm) beyond the tip of the spark plug terminal. Finally, attach a clamp to the shell of the spark plug.

1

NOTE: If tachometer is connected to tach terminal, disconnect it before proceeding with test.

Check spark at plug with tool. If no spark on one wire, check on other.

Spark — HEI OK — **Check:** fuel, spark plugs (pp. 91, 92) **REPAIR OR REPLACE** — JOB DONE

No spark — Go to **2**

2

Connect one lead of voltmeter to battery terminal, and the other lead of voltmeter to ground (pp. 78, 79)

CRANK

Crank engine

Under 7 volts — **FAULTY PART** Repair or replace primary circuit to ignition switch — SEE A PRO

Over 7 volts — Go to **3**

3

Connect one lead of voltmeter to tach and other lead to ground (pp. 78, 79)

ON

Engine on

Under 1 volt — **FAULTY PART** Replace ignition coil (pp. 78, 79) — JOB DONE

Over 10 volts — Go to **4**

1 to 10 volts — **FAULTY PART** Replace module (pp. 78, 79) — JOB DONE

Troubleshooting
by the numbers

Results

4

Remove distributor cap, leaving connectors in place (pp. 78, 79)

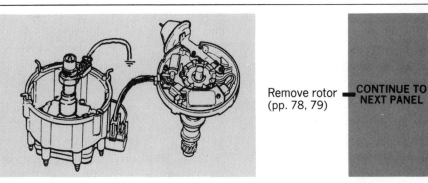

Connect tool to coil output terminal

Remove rotor (pp. 78, 79)

CONTINUE TO NEXT PANEL

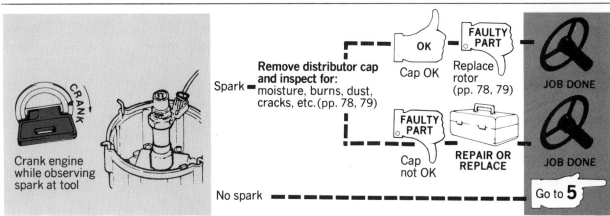

Crank engine while observing spark at tool

Spark ▬ **Remove distributor cap and inspect for:** moisture, burns, dust, cracks, etc. (pp. 78, 79)

OK Cap OK

FAULTY PART Replace rotor (pp. 78, 79)

JOB DONE

FAULTY PART Cap not OK

REPAIR OR REPLACE

JOB DONE

No spark ▬ ▬ ▬ ▬ ▬ ▬ ▬ ▬ ▬ ▬ ▬ ▬ ▬ ▬ ▬ ▬ ▬ Go to **5**

5

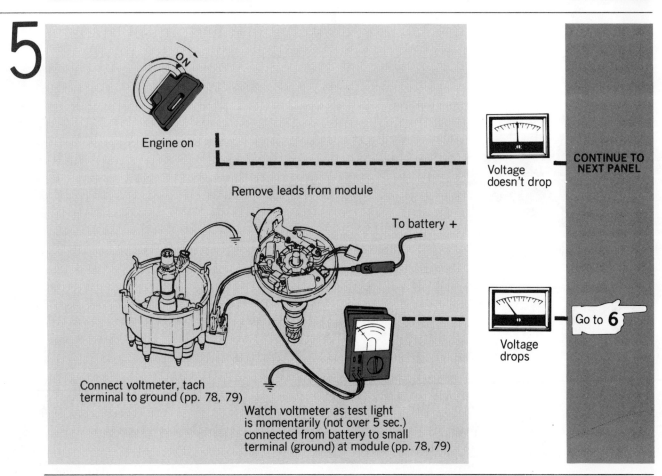

Engine on

Remove leads from module

To battery +

Connect voltmeter, tach terminal to ground (pp. 78, 79)

Watch voltmeter as test light is momentarily (not over 5 sec.) connected from battery to small terminal (ground) at module (pp. 78, 79)

Voltage doesn't drop

CONTINUE TO NEXT PANEL

Voltage drops

Go to **6**

Troubleshooting
by the numbers

Results

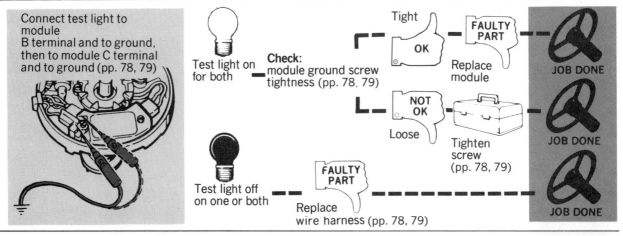

Connect test light to module B terminal and to ground, then to module C terminal and to ground (pp. 78, 79)

Test light on for both

Check: module ground screw tightness (pp. 78, 79)

Tight — OK — FAULTY PART — Replace module — JOB DONE

Loose — NOT OK — Tighten screw (pp. 78, 79) — JOB DONE

Test light off on one or both — FAULTY PART — Replace wire harness (pp. 78, 79) — JOB DONE

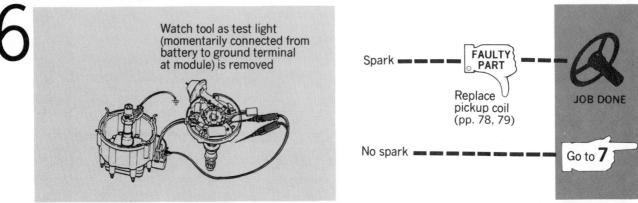

6

Watch tool as test light (momentarily connected from battery to ground terminal at module) is removed

Spark — FAULTY PART — Replace pickup coil (pp. 78, 79) — JOB DONE

No spark — Go to 7

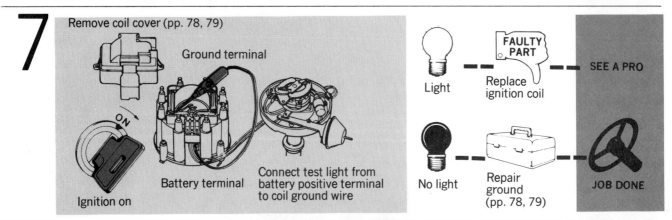

7

Remove coil cover (pp. 78, 79)

Ground terminal

Ignition on

Battery terminal

Connect test light from battery positive terminal to coil ground wire

Light — FAULTY PART — Replace ignition coil — SEE A PRO

No light — Repair ground (pp. 78, 79) — JOB DONE

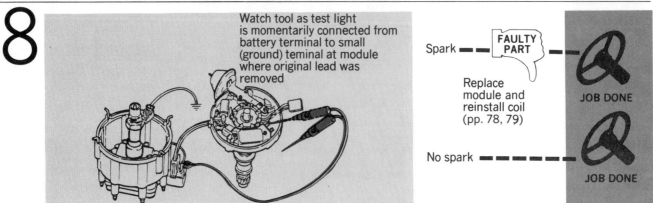

8

Watch tool as test light is momentarily connected from battery terminal to small (ground) teminal at module where original lead was removed

Spark — FAULTY PART — Replace module and reinstall coil (pp. 78, 79) — JOB DONE

No spark — JOB DONE

ENGINE CRANKS BUT WON'T START, OR RUNS ROUGH THEN CUTS OUT (ELECTRONIC IGNITION-SEPARATE COIL)

Troubleshooting by the numbers

1

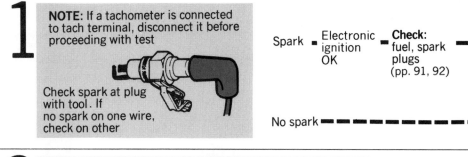

NOTE: If a tachometer is connected to tach terminal, disconnect it before proceeding with test

Check spark at plug with tool. If no spark on one wire, check on other

Spark ▪ Electronic ignition OK ▪ **Check:** fuel, spark plugs (pp. 91, 92) ▪ **REPAIR OR REPLACE** ▪ **JOB DONE**

No spark ---- Go to **2**

2

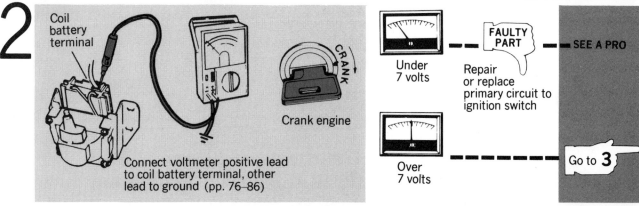

Coil battery terminal

Crank engine

Connect voltmeter positive lead to coil battery terminal, other lead to ground (pp. 76–86)

Under 7 volts ▪ **FAULTY PART** ▪ Repair or replace primary circuit to ignition switch ▪ **SEE A PRO**

Over 7 volts ---- Go to **3**

3

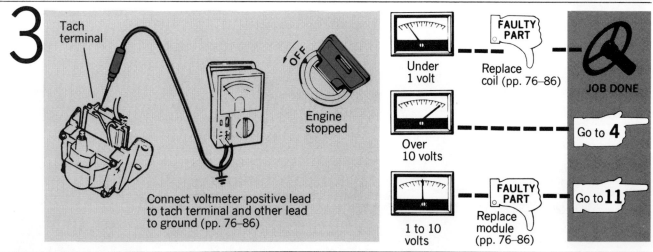

Tach terminal

Engine stopped

Connect voltmeter positive lead to tach terminal and other lead to ground (pp. 76–86)

Under 1 volt ▪ **FAULTY PART** ▪ Replace coil (pp. 76–86) ▪ **JOB DONE**

Over 10 volts ---- Go to **4**

1 to 10 volts ▪ **FAULTY PART** ▪ Replace module (pp. 76–86) ▪ Go to **11**

4

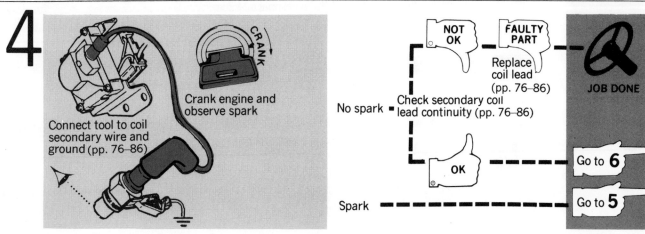

Crank engine and observe spark

Connect tool to coil secondary wire and ground (pp. 76–86)

No spark ▪ Check secondary coil lead continuity (pp. 76–86) — **NOT OK** ▪ **FAULTY PART** Replace coil lead (pp. 76–86) ▪ **JOB DONE**

OK ---- Go to **6**

Spark ---- Go to **5**

Troubleshooting by the numbers

Results

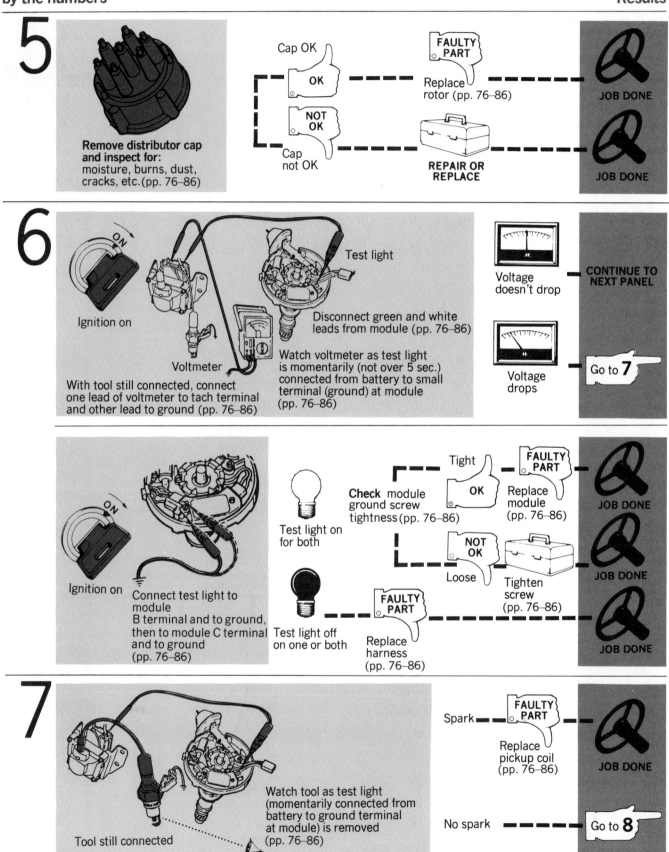

5

Remove distributor cap and inspect for: moisture, burns, dust, cracks, etc. (pp. 76–86)

Cap OK — OK — FAULTY PART Replace rotor (pp. 76–86) — JOB DONE

Cap not OK — NOT OK — REPAIR OR REPLACE — JOB DONE

6

ON Ignition on

Voltmeter

With tool still connected, connect one lead of voltmeter to tach terminal and other lead to ground (pp. 76–86)

Test light

Disconnect green and white leads from module (pp. 76–86)

Watch voltmeter as test light is momentarily (not over 5 sec.) connected from battery to small terminal (ground) at module (pp. 76–86)

Voltage doesn't drop — CONTINUE TO NEXT PANEL

Voltage drops — Go to **7**

ON Ignition on

Connect test light to module B terminal and to ground, then to module C terminal and to ground (pp. 76–86)

Test light on for both

Test light off on one or both

Check module ground screw tightness (pp. 76–86)

Tight — OK — FAULTY PART Replace module (pp. 76–86) — JOB DONE

Loose — NOT OK — Tighten screw (pp. 76–86) — JOB DONE

FAULTY PART Replace harness (pp. 76–86) — JOB DONE

7

Tool still connected

Watch tool as test light (momentarily connected from battery to ground terminal at module) is removed (pp. 76–86)

Spark — FAULTY PART Replace pickup coil (pp. 76–86) — JOB DONE

No spark — Go to **8**

Troubleshooting by the numbers

8

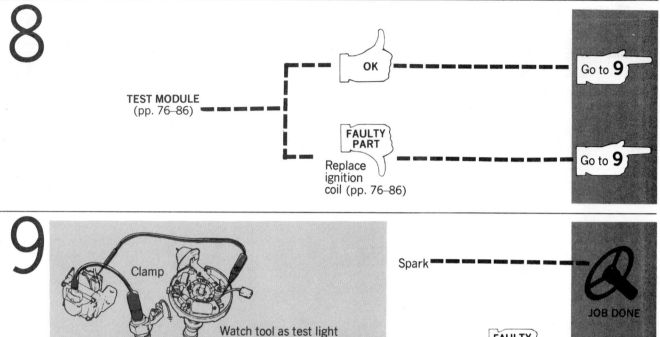

TEST MODULE
(pp. 76–86)

OK → Go to **9**

FAULTY PART
Replace ignition coil (pp. 76–86) → Go to **9**

9

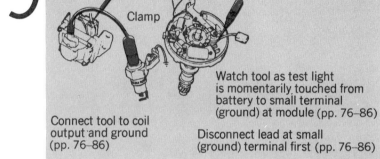

Clamp

Connect tool to coil output and ground (pp. 76–86)

Watch tool as test light is momentarily touched from battery to small terminal (ground) at module (pp. 76–86)

Disconnect lead at small (ground) terminal first (pp. 76–86)

Spark → JOB DONE

No spark — FAULTY PART
Replace module and reinstall original coil (pp. 76–86) → Go to **10**

10

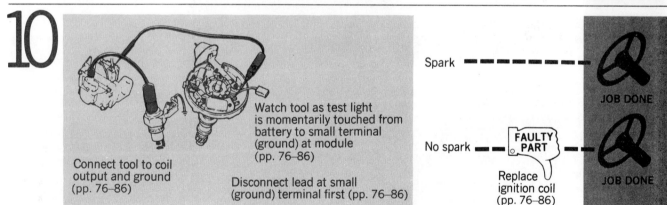

Connect tool to coil output and ground (pp. 76–86)

Watch tool as test light is momentarily touched from battery to small terminal (ground) at module (pp. 76–86)

Disconnect lead at small (ground) terminal first (pp. 76–86)

Spark → JOB DONE

No spark — FAULTY PART
Replace ignition coil (pp. 76–86) → JOB DONE

ENGINE CUTS OUT

Car loses power at times and sometimes stops completely. This condition gets worse when car is going uphill.

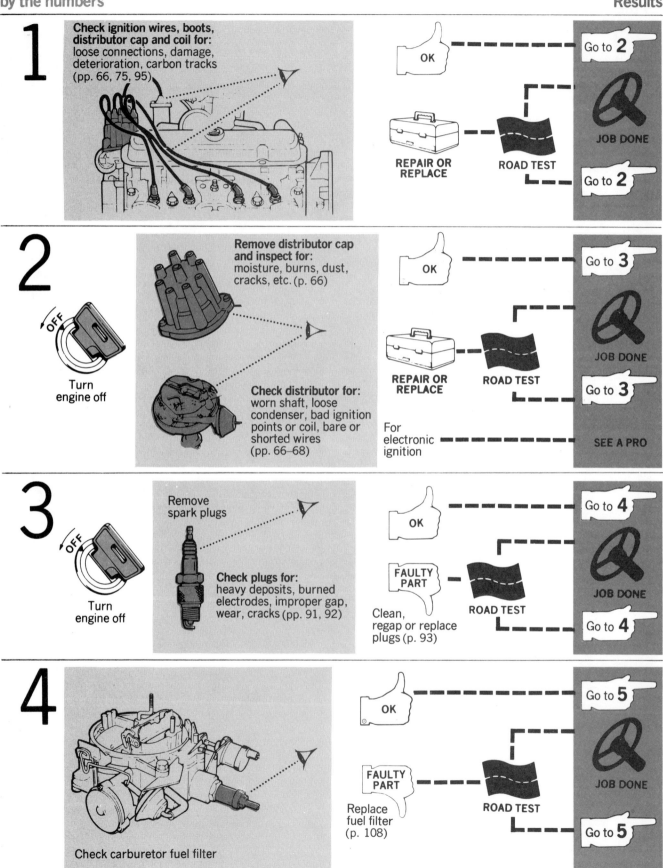

1 Check ignition wires, boots, distributor cap and coil for: loose connections, damage, deterioration, carbon tracks (pp. 66, 75, 95)

OK — — — Go to **2**

REPAIR OR REPLACE — — ROAD TEST — JOB DONE / Go to **2**

2 Turn engine off — Remove distributor cap and inspect for: moisture, burns, dust, cracks, etc. (p. 66)

Check distributor for: worn shaft, loose condenser, bad ignition points or coil, bare or shorted wires (pp. 66–68)

OK — — — Go to **3**

REPAIR OR REPLACE — — ROAD TEST — JOB DONE / Go to **3**

For electronic ignition — — — SEE A PRO

3 Turn engine off — Remove spark plugs

Check plugs for: heavy deposits, burned electrodes, improper gap, wear, cracks (pp. 91, 92)

OK — — — Go to **4**

FAULTY PART — — ROAD TEST — JOB DONE / Go to **4**

Clean, regap or replace plugs (p. 93)

4 Check carburetor fuel filter

OK — — — Go to **5**

FAULTY PART — — ROAD TEST — JOB DONE / Go to **5**

Replace fuel filter (p. 108)

Troubleshooting by the numbers

Results

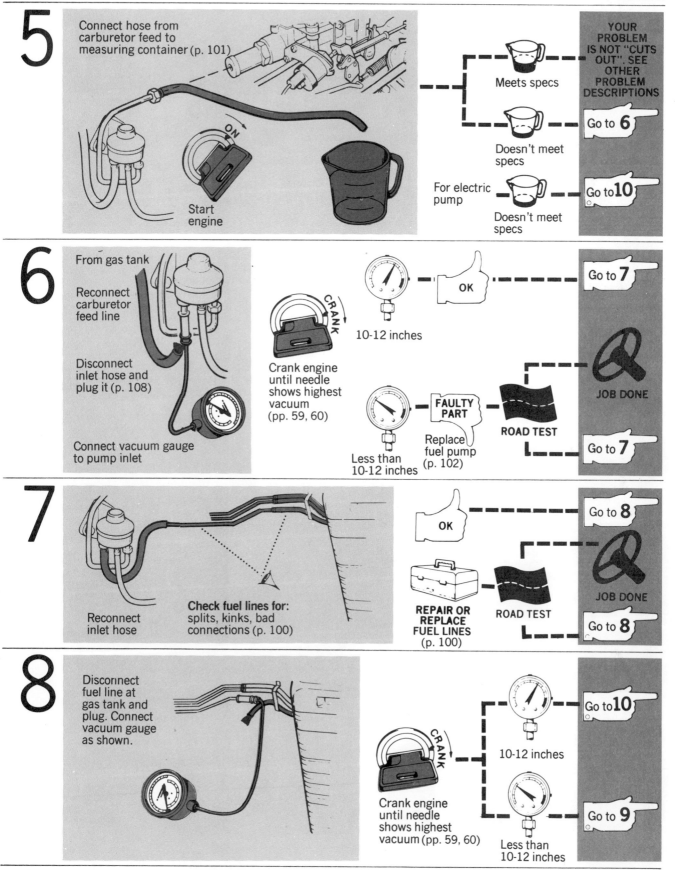

5 Connect hose from carburetor feed to measuring container (p. 101)

Start engine

Meets specs → YOUR PROBLEM IS NOT "CUTS OUT". SEE OTHER PROBLEM DESCRIPTIONS

Doesn't meet specs → Go to **6**

For electric pump / Doesn't meet specs → Go to **10**

6 From gas tank

Reconnect carburetor feed line

Disconnect inlet hose and plug it (p. 108)

Connect vacuum gauge to pump inlet

Crank engine until needle shows highest vacuum (pp. 59, 60)

10-12 inches / OK → Go to **7**

Less than 10-12 inches → FAULTY PART / Replace fuel pump (p. 102) → ROAD TEST → JOB DONE / Go to **7**

7 Reconnect inlet hose

Check fuel lines for: splits, kinks, bad connections (p. 100)

OK → Go to **8**

REPAIR OR REPLACE FUEL LINES (p. 100) → ROAD TEST → JOB DONE / Go to **8**

8 Disconnect fuel line at gas tank and plug. Connect vacuum gauge as shown.

Crank engine until needle shows highest vacuum (pp. 59, 60)

10-12 inches → Go to **10**

Less than 10-12 inches → Go to **9**

Troubleshooting by the numbers

9

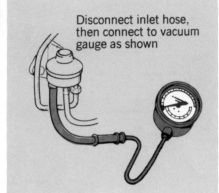

Disconnect inlet hose, then connect to vacuum gauge as shown

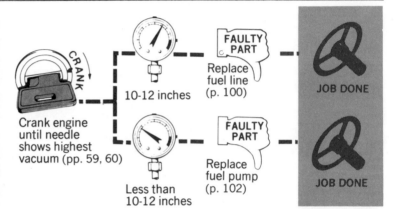

CRANK

Crank engine until needle shows highest vacuum (pp. 59, 60)

10-12 inches

FAULTY PART
Replace fuel line (p. 100)

JOB DONE

Less than 10-12 inches

FAULTY PART
Replace fuel pump (p. 102)

JOB DONE

10

For electric fuel pump:
Reconnect carburetor fuel line. Check fuel lines for kinks, good ground, and 10 volts minimum at pump while idling (p. 102)

Fuel pickup and sending units are located at gas tank

Possible problems include: defective fuel pickup and sending units

SEE A PRO

Possible problems include: dirt or water in gas tank

SEE A PRO

ENGINE IS HARD TO START OR WON'T START (EVEN THOUGH IT CRANKS OK)

Troubleshooting
by the numbers

1

Remove air-cleaner
cover and filter

- **Check choke for:**
  sticking, binding, hot
  and cold operation (p. 108)

- **Check vacuum hoses for:**
  splits, kinks, bad
  connections (p. 58)

- **Check carburetor for:**
  flooding

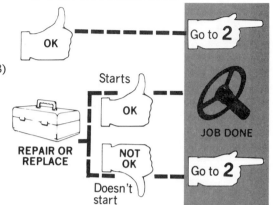

OK ---- Go to **2**

REPAIR OR REPLACE — Starts — **OK** ---- JOB DONE

NOT OK ---- Go to **2**

Doesn't start

2

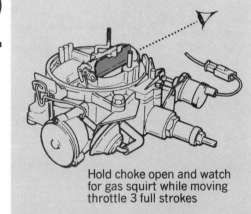

Hold choke open and watch
for gas squirt while moving
throttle 3 full strokes

3 full squirts — Check choke adjustment and adjust as needed (p. 108)

— **OK** — Starts ---- JOB DONE

— **NOT OK** — Doesn't start ---- Go to **8**

Less than 3 full squirts ---- Go to **3**

3

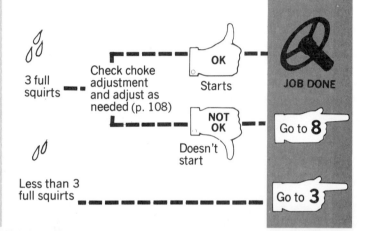

Connect hose from
carburetor feed to
a measuring container
(p. 101)

CRANK

Crank engine
for 15 seconds

Meets specs ---- Go to **8**

Doesn't meet specs ---- CONTINUE TO NEXT PANEL

For electric pump

Doesn't meet specs ---- Go to **7**

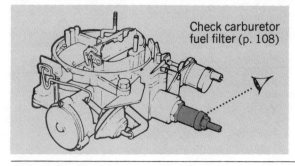

Check carburetor
fuel filter (p. 108)

FAULTY PART — Replace fuel filter (p. 108)

Starts — **OK** ---- JOB DONE

NOT OK — Does not start ---- Go to **4**

Troubleshooting by the numbers

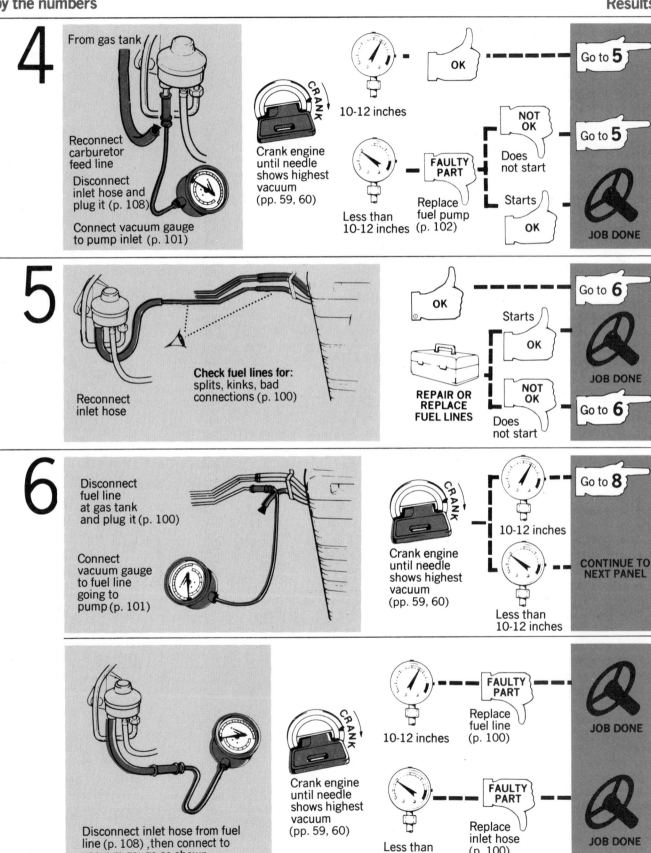

4

From gas tank

Reconnect carburetor feed line

Disconnect inlet hose and plug it (p. 108)

Connect vacuum gauge to pump inlet (p. 101)

Crank engine until needle shows highest vacuum (pp. 59, 60)

10-12 inches — OK ---- Go to **5**

Less than 10-12 inches — FAULTY PART Replace fuel pump (p. 102)

Does not start — NOT OK — Go to **5**

Starts — OK — JOB DONE

5

Reconnect inlet hose

Check fuel lines for: splits, kinks, bad connections (p. 100)

OK ---- Go to **6**

REPAIR OR REPLACE FUEL LINES

Starts — OK — JOB DONE

Does not start — NOT OK — Go to **6**

6

Disconnect fuel line at gas tank and plug it (p. 100)

Connect vacuum gauge to fuel line going to pump (p. 101)

Crank engine until needle shows highest vacuum (pp. 59, 60)

10-12 inches — Go to **8**

Less than 10-12 inches — CONTINUE TO NEXT PANEL

Disconnect inlet hose from fuel line (p. 108), then connect to vacuum gauge as shown

Crank engine until needle shows highest vacuum (pp. 59, 60)

10-12 inches — FAULTY PART Replace fuel line (p. 100) — JOB DONE

Less than 10-12 inches — FAULTY PART Replace inlet hose (p. 100) — JOB DONE

Troubleshooting by the numbers

Results

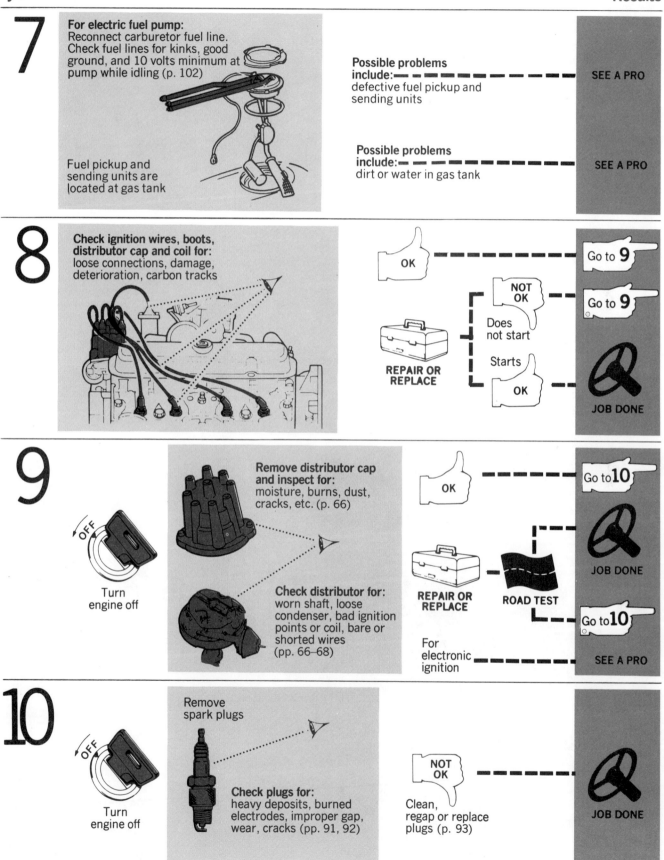

7

For electric fuel pump:
Reconnect carburetor fuel line.
Check fuel lines for kinks, good ground, and 10 volts minimum at pump while idling (p. 102)

Fuel pickup and sending units are located at gas tank

Possible problems include: defective fuel pickup and sending units — SEE A PRO

Possible problems include: dirt or water in gas tank — SEE A PRO

8

Check ignition wires, boots, distributor cap and coil for: loose connections, damage, deterioration, carbon tracks

OK — Go to **9**

REPAIR OR REPLACE — NOT OK — Does not start — Go to **9**

Starts — OK — JOB DONE

9

Turn engine off

Remove distributor cap and inspect for: moisture, burns, dust, cracks, etc. (p. 66)

Check distributor for: worn shaft, loose condenser, bad ignition points or coil, bare or shorted wires (pp. 66–68)

OK — Go to **10**

REPAIR OR REPLACE — ROAD TEST — JOB DONE

Go to **10**

For electronic ignition — SEE A PRO

10

Turn engine off

Remove spark plugs

Check plugs for: heavy deposits, burned electrodes, improper gap, wear, cracks (pp. 91, 92)

NOT OK — Clean, regap or replace plugs (p. 93) — JOB DONE

ENGINE STALLS
AND IDLES ROUGH (COLD ENGINE)

Troubleshooting
by the numbers

The engine quits running while idling or driving. At idle the engine runs unevenly, which may be bad enough to make the car shake.

Results

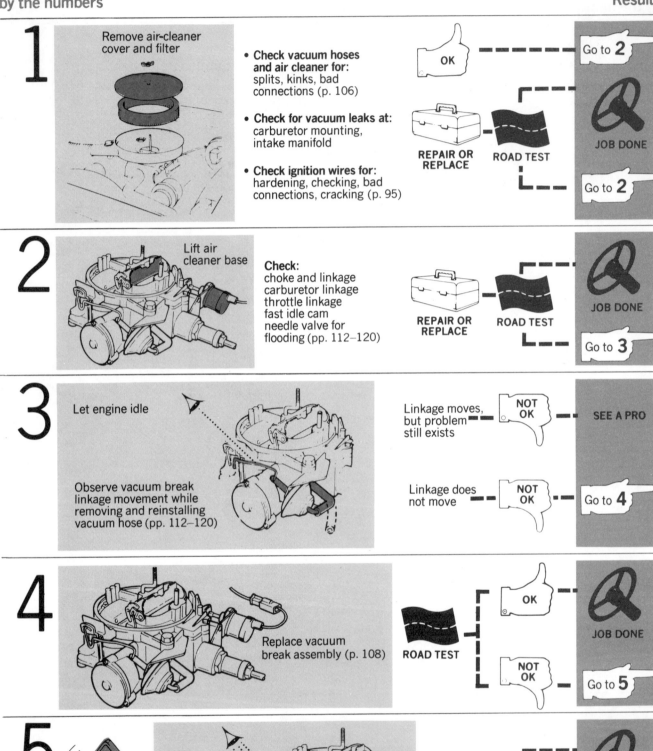

1 Remove air-cleaner cover and filter

- **Check vacuum hoses and air cleaner for:** splits, kinks, bad connections (p. 106)
- **Check for vacuum leaks at:** carburetor mounting, intake manifold
- **Check ignition wires for:** hardening, checking, bad connections, cracking (p. 95)

OK → Go to **2**

REPAIR OR REPLACE → ROAD TEST → JOB DONE

Go to **2**

2 Lift air cleaner base

Check: choke and linkage carburetor linkage throttle linkage fast idle cam needle valve for flooding (pp. 112–120)

REPAIR OR REPLACE → ROAD TEST → JOB DONE

Go to **3**

3 Let engine idle

Observe vacuum break linkage movement while removing and reinstalling vacuum hose (pp. 112–120)

Linkage moves, but problem still exists → NOT OK → SEE A PRO

Linkage does not move → NOT OK → Go to **4**

4 Replace vacuum break assembly (p. 108)

ROAD TEST → OK → JOB DONE

NOT OK → Go to **5**

5 Turn engine off

Recheck: choke, vacuum break, fast idle adjustment (pp. 112–120)

REPAIR OR REPLACE → ROAD TEST → JOB DONE

Go to **6**

Troubleshooting
by the numbers

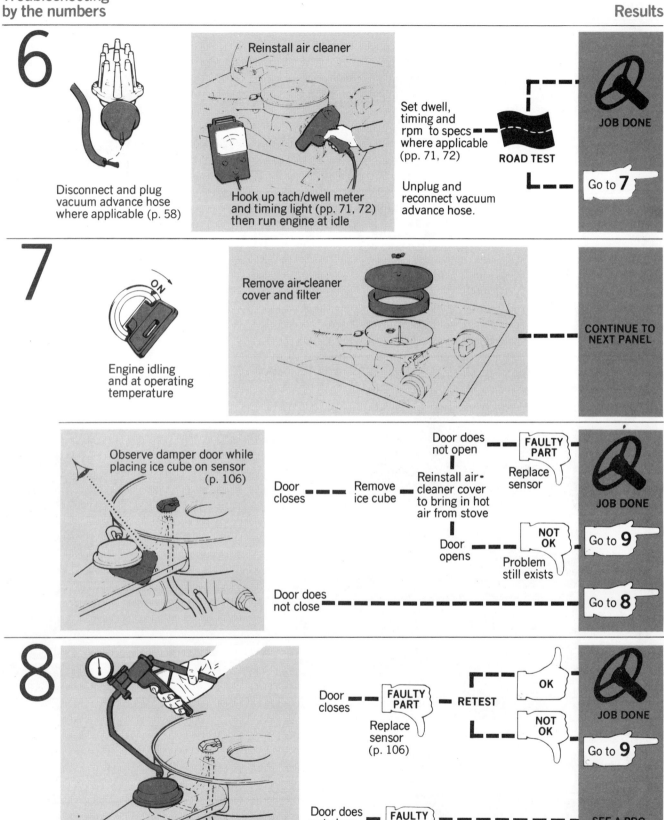

6

Disconnect and plug
vacuum advance hose
where applicable (p. 58)

Reinstall air cleaner

Hook up tach/dwell meter
and timing light (pp. 71, 72)
then run engine at idle

Set dwell,
timing and
rpm to specs
where applicable
(pp. 71, 72)

Unplug and
reconnect vacuum
advance hose.

ROAD TEST

JOB DONE

Go to **7**

7

Engine idling
and at operating
temperature

ON

Remove air-cleaner
cover and filter

CONTINUE TO
NEXT PANEL

Observe damper door while
placing ice cube on sensor
(p. 106)

Door
closes

Remove
ice cube

Door does
not open

Reinstall air-
cleaner cover
to bring in hot
air from stove

FAULTY
PART

Replace
sensor

JOB DONE

Door
opens

NOT
OK

Problem
still exists

Go to **9**

Door does
not close

Go to **8**

8

Hook up hand-vacuum pump
to vacuum motor

Door
closes

FAULTY
PART

Replace
sensor
(p. 106)

RETEST

OK

JOB DONE

NOT
OK

Go to **9**

Door does
not close

FAULTY
PART

Replace
vacuum motor

SEE A PRO

Troubleshooting by the numbers

Results

9

Engine idling
at 1400-1600 RPM

Transmission
in PARK

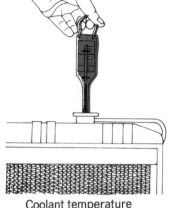

Coolant temperature
above 120° (49°C)

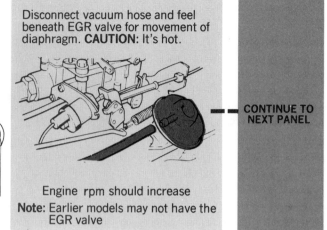

Disconnect vacuum hose and feel
beneath EGR valve for movement of
diaphragm. **CAUTION:** It's hot.

Engine rpm should increase

Note: Earlier models may not have the
EGR valve

CONTINUE TO
NEXT PANEL

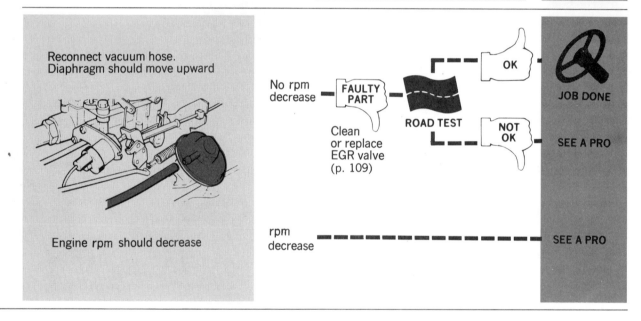

Reconnect vacuum hose.
Diaphragm should move upward

Engine rpm should decrease

No rpm
decrease — FAULTY PART

Clean
or replace
EGR valve
(p. 109)

ROAD TEST

OK → JOB DONE

NOT OK → SEE A PRO

rpm
decrease — SEE A PRO

ENGINE STALLS AND IDLES ROUGH (HOT ENGINE)

1

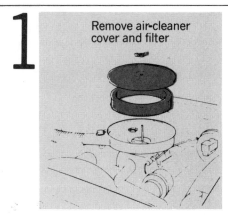

Remove air-cleaner
cover and filter

- **Check vacuum hoses for:**
  splits, kinks, bad
  connections (p. 106)

- **Check for vacuum leaks at:**
  carburetor mounting,
  intake manifold

- **Check ignition wires for:**
  hardening, checking, bad
  connections, cracking (p. 95)

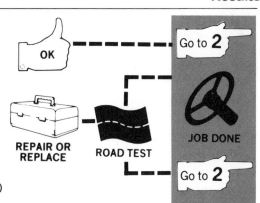

OK → Go to **2**

REPAIR OR REPLACE → ROAD TEST → JOB DONE

Go to **2**

2

Disconnect and
plug vacuum
advance hose
where applicable
(p. 58)

Reinstall air cleaner

Hook up tach/dwell meter
and timing light (pp. 71, 72)
then run engine at idle

Set dwell,
timing and
rpm to specs
where applicable
(pp. 71, 72)

Unplug and
reconnect vacuum
advance hose.

ROAD TEST → JOB DONE

Go to **3**

3

Engine
idling and
at operating
temperature

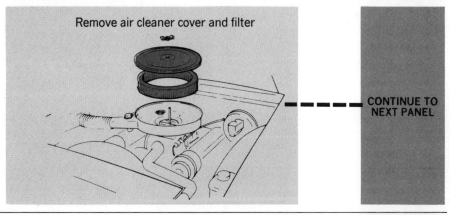

Remove air cleaner cover and filter

CONTINUE TO
NEXT PANEL

Observe damper door
while placing ice
cube over sensor
(p. 106)

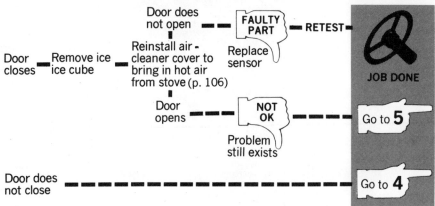

Door does
not open → FAULTY PART
Replace
sensor

Door
closes — Remove ice
ice cube

Reinstall air-
cleaner cover to
bring in hot air
from stove (p. 106)

Door
opens → NOT OK

Problem
still exists

RETEST → JOB DONE

Go to **5**

Door does
not close → Go to **4**

Troubleshooting
by the numbers

Results

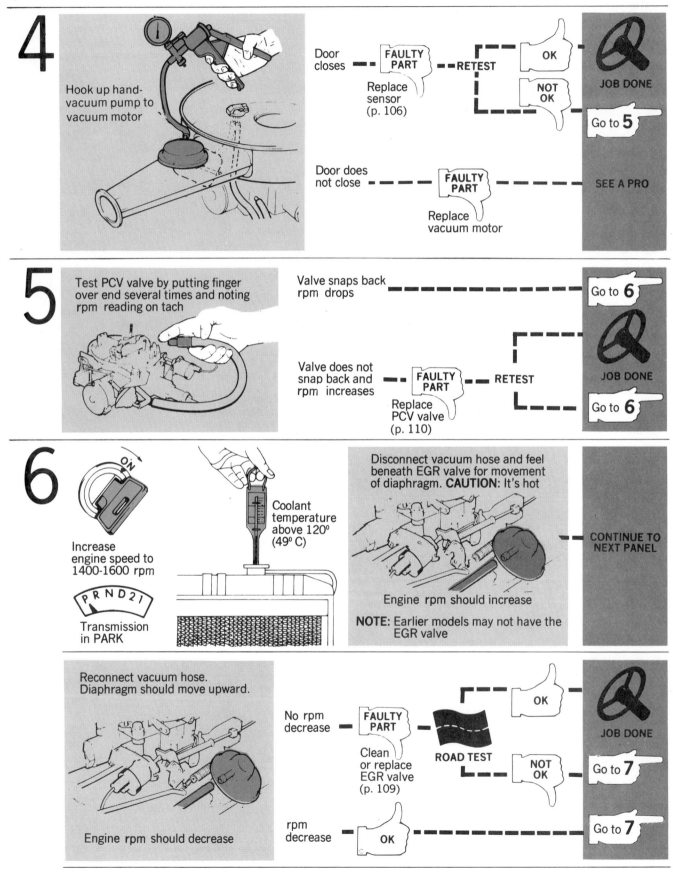

4 Hook up hand-vacuum pump to vacuum motor

Door closes — FAULTY PART — RETEST — OK → JOB DONE
Replace sensor (p. 106) — NOT OK → Go to **5**

Door does not close — FAULTY PART — Replace vacuum motor — SEE A PRO

5 Test PCV valve by putting finger over end several times and noting rpm reading on tach

Valve snaps back rpm drops → Go to **6**

Valve does not snap back and rpm increases — FAULTY PART — Replace PCV valve (p. 110) — RETEST — JOB DONE / Go to **6**

6 Increase engine speed to 1400-1600 rpm
PRND21
Transmission in PARK

Coolant temperature above 120° (49° C)

Disconnect vacuum hose and feel beneath EGR valve for movement of diaphragm. **CAUTION:** It's hot

Engine rpm should increase

NOTE: Earlier models may not have the EGR valve

CONTINUE TO NEXT PANEL

Reconnect vacuum hose. Diaphragm should move upward.

No rpm decrease — FAULTY PART — Clean or replace EGR valve (p. 109) — ROAD TEST — OK → JOB DONE / NOT OK → Go to **7**

Engine rpm should decrease

rpm decrease — OK → Go to **7**

Troubleshooting
by the numbers

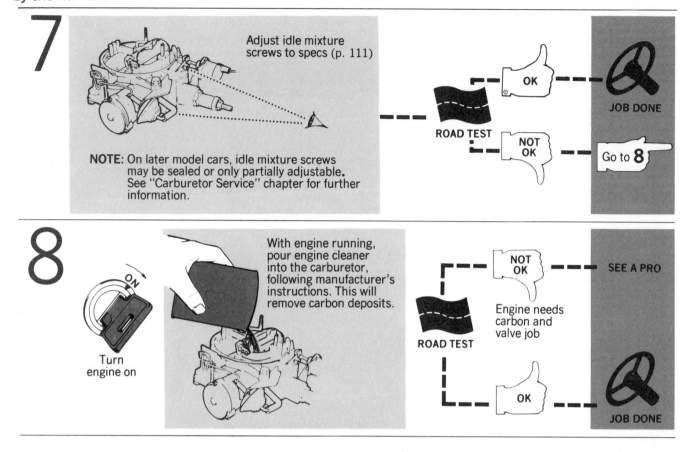

7 Adjust idle mixture screws to specs (p. 111)

ROAD TEST

OK — JOB DONE

NOT OK — Go to **8**

NOTE: On later model cars, idle mixture screws may be sealed or only partially adjustable. See "Carburetor Service" chapter for further information.

8 Turn engine on

With engine running, pour engine cleaner into the carburetor, following manufacturer's instructions. This will remove carbon deposits.

ROAD TEST

NOT OK — SEE A PRO

Engine needs carbon and valve job

OK — JOB DONE

ENGINE WON'T CRANK

When the ignition is turned on, there is no sound. Accessories may not work.

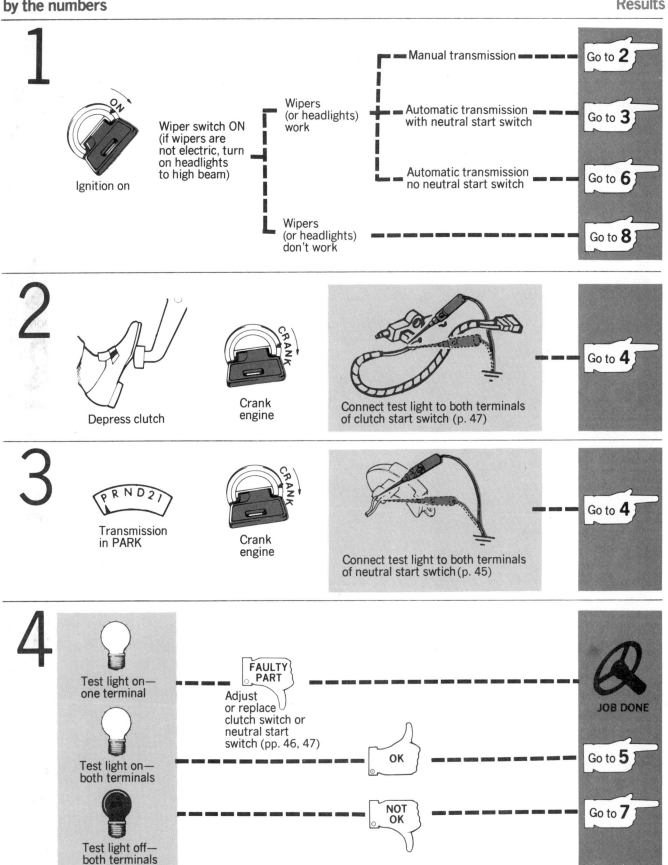

1 Ignition on

Wiper switch ON (if wipers are not electric, turn on headlights to high beam)

Wipers (or headlights) work

Manual transmission — Go to **2**

Automatic transmission with neutral start switch — Go to **3**

Automatic transmission no neutral start switch — Go to **6**

Wipers (or headlights) don't work — Go to **8**

2 Depress clutch — Crank engine — Connect test light to both terminals of clutch start switch (p. 47) — Go to **4**

3 Transmission in PARK — Crank engine — Connect test light to both terminals of neutral start swtich (p. 45) — Go to **4**

4

Test light on— one terminal — FAULTY PART Adjust or replace clutch switch or neutral start switch (pp. 46, 47) — JOB DONE

Test light on— both terminals — OK — Go to **5**

Test light off— both terminals — NOT OK — Go to **7**

Troubleshooting by the numbers

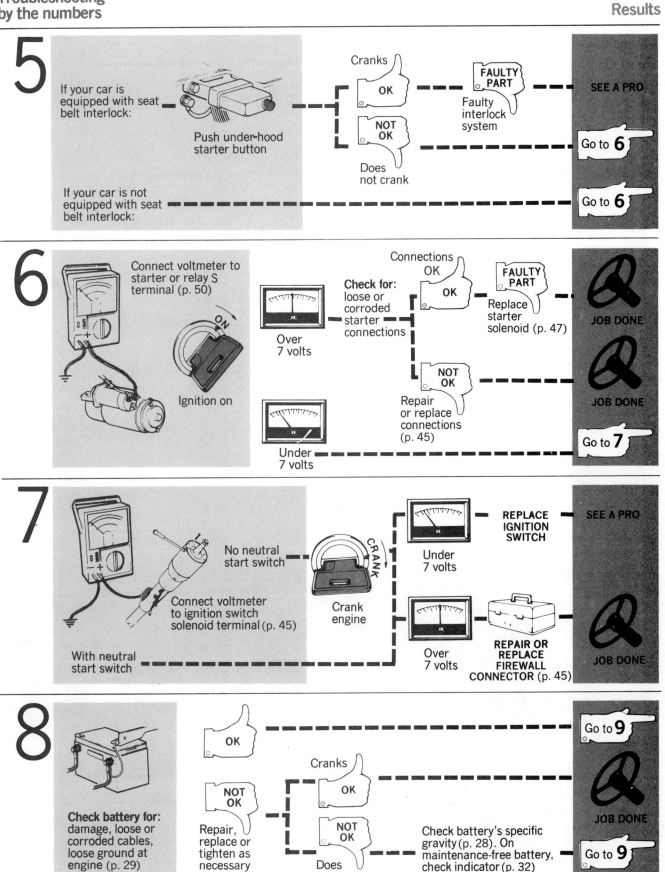

5

If your car is equipped with seat belt interlock:

Push under-hood starter button

Cranks — **OK** → Faulty interlock system → **FAULTY PART** → **SEE A PRO**

NOT OK — Does not crank → **Go to 6**

If your car is not equipped with seat belt interlock: → **Go to 6**

6

Connect voltmeter to starter or relay S terminal (p. 50)

Ignition on

Over 7 volts

Check for: loose or corroded starter connections

Connections OK — **OK** → Replace starter solenoid (p. 47) → **FAULTY PART** → **JOB DONE**

NOT OK → Repair or replace connections (p. 45) → **JOB DONE**

Under 7 volts → **Go to 7**

7

No neutral start switch

Connect voltmeter to ignition switch solenoid terminal (p. 45)

With neutral start switch

Crank engine

Under 7 volts → **REPLACE IGNITION SWITCH** → **SEE A PRO**

Over 7 volts → **REPAIR OR REPLACE FIREWALL CONNECTOR** (p. 45) → **JOB DONE**

8

Check battery for: damage, loose or corroded cables, loose ground at engine (p. 29)

OK → **Go to 9**

NOT OK → Repair, replace or tighten as necessary

Cranks — **OK** → **JOB DONE**

NOT OK — Does not crank → Check battery's specific gravity (p. 28). On maintenance-free battery, check indicator (p. 32) → **Go to 9**

Troubleshooting
by the numbers

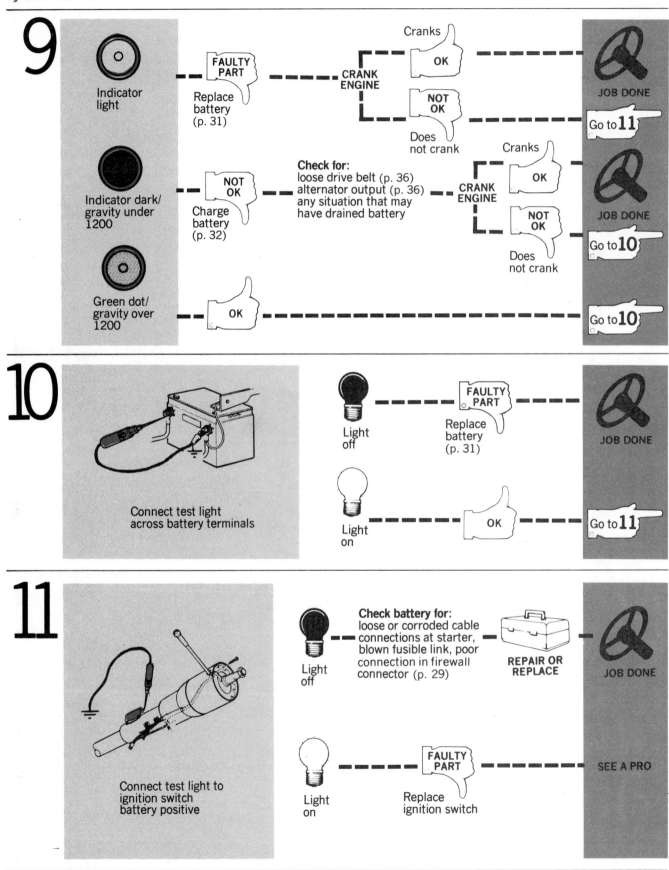

9

Indicator light

FAULTY PART
Replace battery (p. 31)

CRANK ENGINE

Cranks
OK

NOT OK
Does not crank

JOB DONE

Go to **11**

Indicator dark/gravity under 1200

NOT OK
Charge battery (p. 32)

Check for:
loose drive belt (p. 36)
alternator output (p. 36)
any situation that may
have drained battery

CRANK ENGINE

Cranks
OK

NOT OK
Does not crank

JOB DONE

Go to **10**

Green dot/gravity over 1200

OK

Go to **10**

10

Connect test light across battery terminals

Light off

FAULTY PART
Replace battery (p. 31)

JOB DONE

Light on

OK

Go to **11**

11

Connect test light to ignition switch battery positive

Light off

Check battery for:
loose or corroded cable connections at starter, blown fusible link, poor connection in firewall connector (p. 29)

REPAIR OR REPLACE

JOB DONE

Light on

FAULTY PART
Replace ignition switch

SEE A PRO

ENGINE WON'T START OR IGNITION MISSES/ENGINE CRANKS OK

Troubleshooting
by the numbers

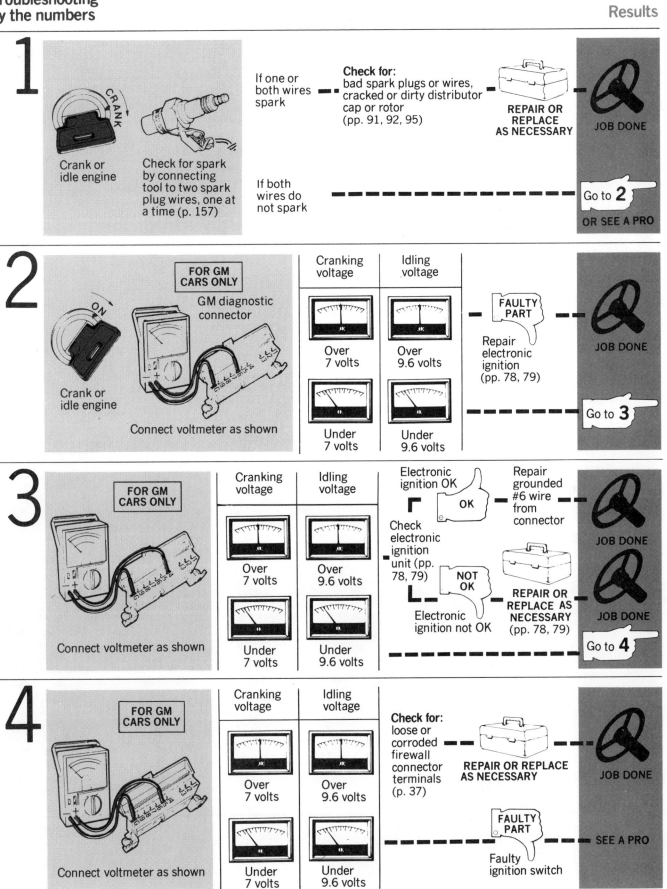

1

Crank or idle engine

Check for spark by connecting tool to two spark plug wires, one at a time (p. 157)

If one or both wires spark

Check for:
bad spark plugs or wires, cracked or dirty distributor cap or rotor (pp. 91, 92, 95)

REPAIR OR REPLACE AS NECESSARY

JOB DONE

If both wires do not spark

Go to **2**

OR SEE A PRO

2

FOR GM CARS ONLY

Crank or idle engine

GM diagnostic connector

Connect voltmeter as shown

Cranking voltage	Idling voltage
Over 7 volts	Over 9.6 volts
Under 7 volts	Under 9.6 volts

FAULTY PART

Repair electronic ignition (pp. 78, 79)

JOB DONE

Go to **3**

3

FOR GM CARS ONLY

Connect voltmeter as shown

Cranking voltage	Idling voltage
Over 7 volts	Over 9.6 volts
Under 7 volts	Under 9.6 volts

Check electronic ignition unit (pp. 78, 79)

OK Electronic ignition OK — Repair grounded #6 wire from connector — **JOB DONE**

NOT OK Electronic ignition not OK — **REPAIR OR REPLACE AS NECESSARY** (pp. 78, 79) — **JOB DONE**

Go to **4**

4

FOR GM CARS ONLY

Connect voltmeter as shown

Cranking voltage	Idling voltage
Over 7 volts	Over 9.6 volts
Under 7 volts	Under 9.6 volts

Check for:
loose or corroded firewall connector terminals (p. 37)

REPAIR OR REPLACE AS NECESSARY

JOB DONE

FAULTY PART

Faulty ignition switch

SEE A PRO

HESITATION

A pause before the car responds to the accelerator. This is most likely to happen when starting from a stopped position, but it can occur at any speed. The engine may even stall.

Troubleshooting by the numbers

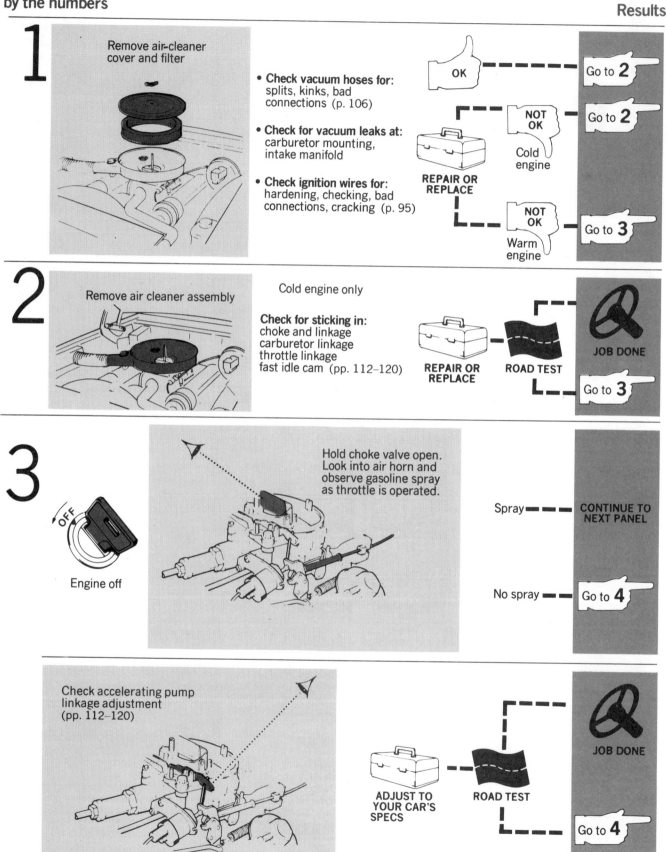

1 Remove air-cleaner cover and filter

- **Check vacuum hoses for:** splits, kinks, bad connections (p. 106)
- **Check for vacuum leaks at:** carburetor mounting, intake manifold
- **Check ignition wires for:** hardening, checking, bad connections, cracking (p. 95)

OK → Go to **2**

REPAIR OR REPLACE

NOT OK Cold engine → Go to **2**

NOT OK Warm engine → Go to **3**

2 Remove air cleaner assembly

Cold engine only

Check for sticking in: choke and linkage carburetor linkage throttle linkage fast idle cam (pp. 112–120)

REPAIR OR REPLACE → ROAD TEST → JOB DONE

Go to **3**

3 Engine off

Hold choke valve open. Look into air horn and observe gasoline spray as throttle is operated.

Spray - - - CONTINUE TO NEXT PANEL

No spray - - Go to **4**

Check accelerating pump linkage adjustment (pp. 112–120)

ADJUST TO YOUR CAR'S SPECS → ROAD TEST → JOB DONE

Go to **4**

Troubleshooting by the numbers

Results

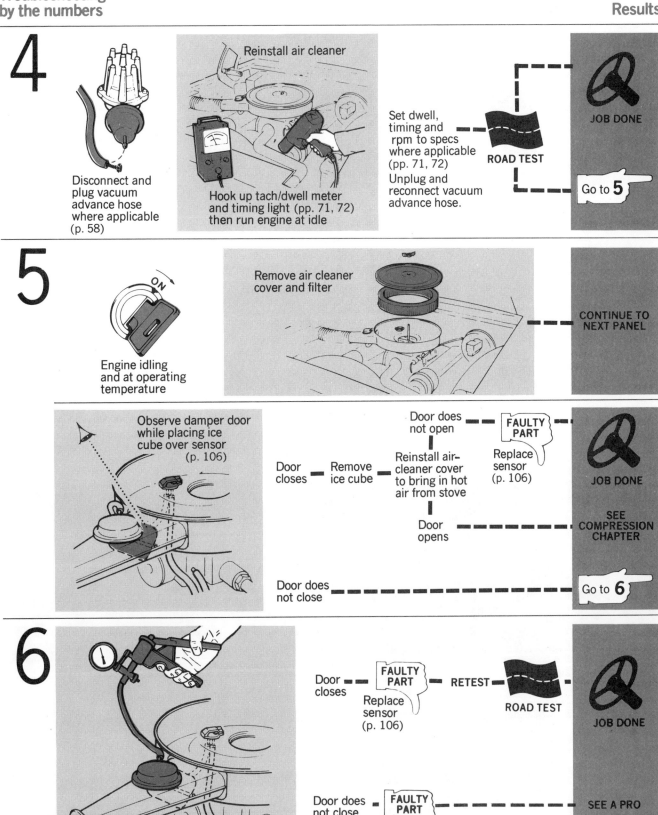

4

Disconnect and plug vacuum advance hose where applicable (p. 58)

Reinstall air cleaner

Hook up tach/dwell meter and timing light (pp. 71, 72) then run engine at idle

Set dwell, timing and rpm to specs where applicable (pp. 71, 72) Unplug and reconnect vacuum advance hose.

ROAD TEST

JOB DONE

Go to 5

5

Engine idling and at operating temperature

ON

Remove air cleaner cover and filter

CONTINUE TO NEXT PANEL

Observe damper door while placing ice cube over sensor (p. 106)

Door closes — Remove ice cube — Reinstall air-cleaner cover to bring in hot air from stove

Door does not open

FAULTY PART

Replace sensor (p. 106)

JOB DONE

Door opens

SEE COMPRESSION CHAPTER

Door does not close

Go to 6

6

Hook up hand-vacuum pump directly to vacuum motor

Door closes

FAULTY PART

Replace sensor (p. 106)

RETEST

ROAD TEST

JOB DONE

Door does not close

FAULTY PART

Replace vacuum motor

SEE A PRO

HIGH ENERGY IGNITION (GM): ENGINE CRANKS, BUT WON'T START

Troubleshooting
by the numbers

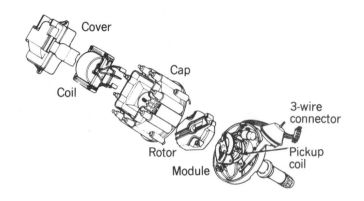

Cover

Cap

Coil

3-wire
connector

Rotor

Module

Pickup
coil

1

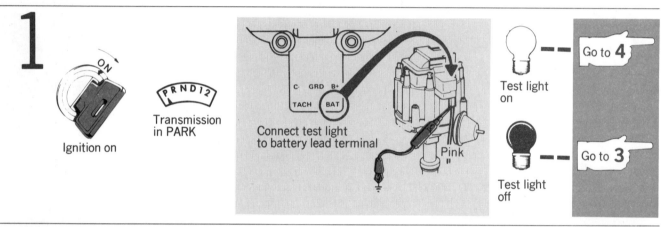

ON

Ignition on

PRND12

Transmission
in PARK

Connect test light
to battery lead terminal

C- GRD B+

TACH BAT

Pink

Test light
on → Go to 4

Test light
off → Go to 3

2

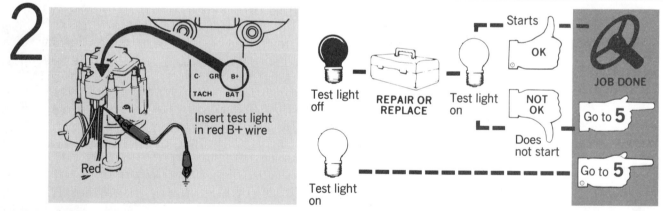

Insert test light
in red B+ wire

C- GR B+

TACH BAT

Red

Test light
off — REPAIR OR REPLACE — Test light on

Starts — OK

NOT OK — Does not start

JOB DONE

Go to 5

Test light
on

Go to 5

3

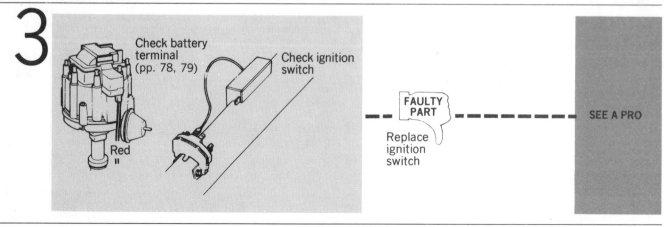

Check battery
terminal
(pp. 78, 79)

Check ignition
switch

Red

FAULTY PART

Replace
ignition
switch

SEE A PRO

Troubleshooting by the numbers

Results

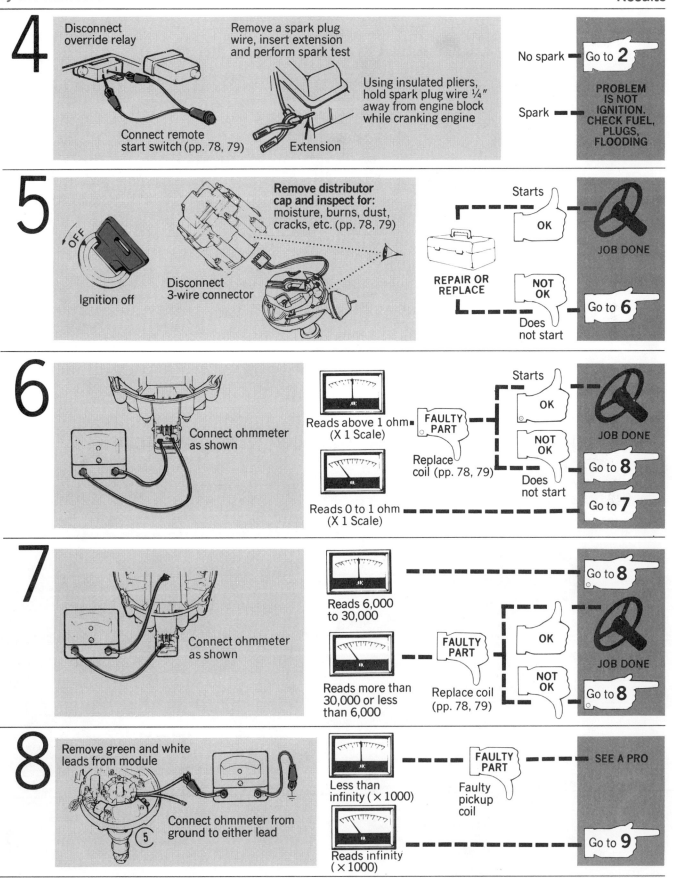

4 Disconnect override relay

Connect remote start switch (pp. 78, 79)

Remove a spark plug wire, insert extension and perform spark test

Using insulated pliers, hold spark plug wire ¼" away from engine block while cranking engine

Extension

No spark — Go to **2**

Spark — **PROBLEM IS NOT IGNITION. CHECK FUEL, PLUGS, FLOODING**

5 Ignition off

OFF

Disconnect 3-wire connector

Remove distributor cap and inspect for: moisture, burns, dust, cracks, etc. (pp. 78, 79)

Starts — OK — **JOB DONE**

REPAIR OR REPLACE

NOT OK — Does not start — Go to **6**

6 Connect ohmmeter as shown

Reads above 1 ohm (X 1 Scale) — **FAULTY PART** — Replace coil (pp. 78, 79)

Starts — OK — **JOB DONE**

NOT OK — Does not start — Go to **8**

Reads 0 to 1 ohm (X 1 Scale) — Go to **7**

7 Connect ohmmeter as shown

Reads 6,000 to 30,000 — Go to **8**

Reads more than 30,000 or less than 6,000 — **FAULTY PART** — Replace coil (pp. 78, 79)

OK — **JOB DONE**

NOT OK — Go to **8**

8 Remove green and white leads from module

Connect ohmmeter from ground to either lead

Less than infinity ($\times 1000$) — **FAULTY PART** — Faulty pickup coil — SEE A PRO

Reads infinity ($\times 1000$) — Go to **9**

**Troubleshooting
by the numbers**

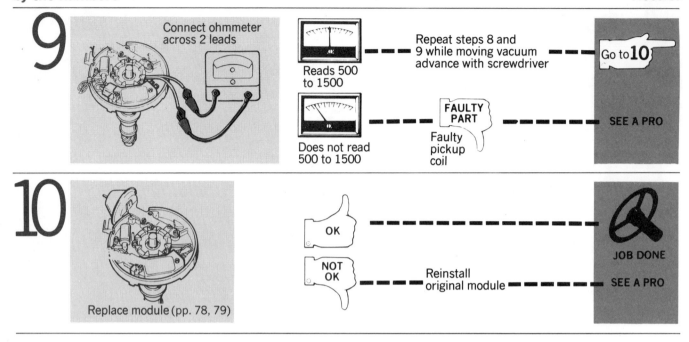

9 Connect ohmmeter across 2 leads

Reads 500 to 1500 — Repeat steps 8 and 9 while moving vacuum advance with screwdriver — Go to **10**

Does not read 500 to 1500 — **FAULTY PART** Faulty pickup coil — SEE A PRO

10 Replace module (pp. 78, 79)

OK — JOB DONE

NOT OK — Reinstall original module — SEE A PRO

HIGH ENERGY IGNITION (GM): ENGINE RUNS ROUGH OR CUTS OUT

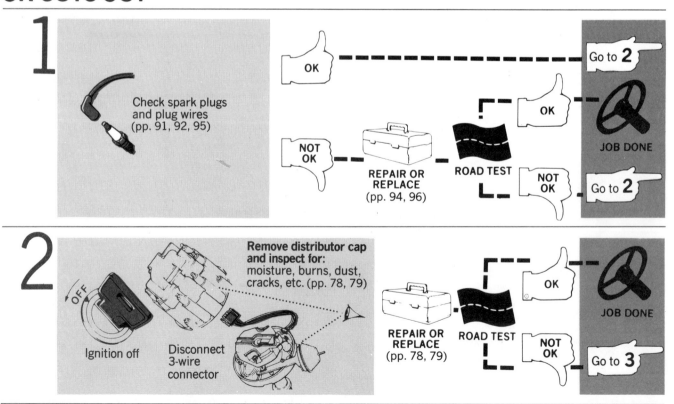

1 Check spark plugs and plug wires (pp. 91, 92, 95)

OK — Go to **2**

NOT OK — REPAIR OR REPLACE (pp. 94, 96) — ROAD TEST — OK — JOB DONE

ROAD TEST — NOT OK — Go to **2**

2 Ignition off   Disconnect 3-wire connector

Remove distributor cap and inspect for: moisture, burns, dust, cracks, etc. (pp. 78, 79)

REPAIR OR REPLACE (pp. 78, 79) — ROAD TEST — OK — JOB DONE

ROAD TEST — NOT OK — Go to **3**

Troubleshooting by the numbers

Results

3

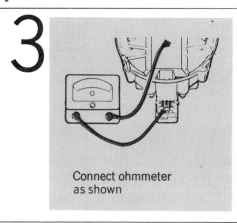

Connect ohmmeter as shown

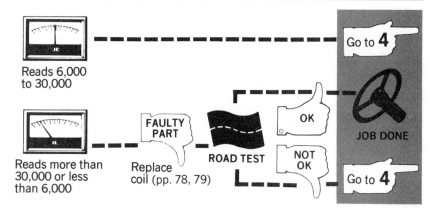

Reads 6,000 to 30,000

Reads more than 30,000 or less than 6,000

FAULTY PART
Replace coil (pp. 78, 79)

ROAD TEST

OK → **JOB DONE**

NOT OK → Go to **4**

Go to **4**

4

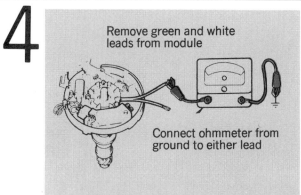

Remove green and white leads from module

Connect ohmmeter from ground to either lead

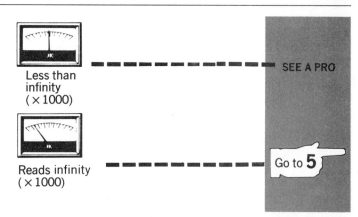

Less than infinity (× 1000)

SEE A PRO

Reads infinity (× 1000)

Go to **5**

5

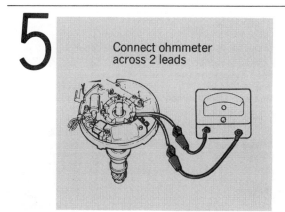

Connect ohmmeter across 2 leads

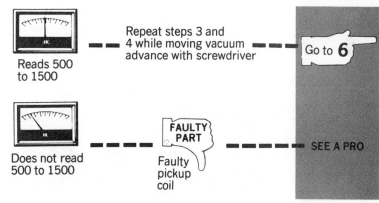

Reads 500 to 1500

Repeat steps 3 and 4 while moving vacuum advance with screwdriver

Go to **6**

Does not read 500 to 1500

FAULTY PART
Faulty pickup coil

SEE A PRO

6

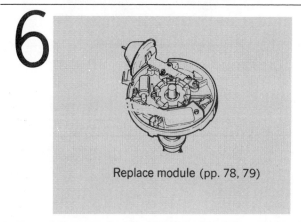

Replace module (pp. 78, 79)

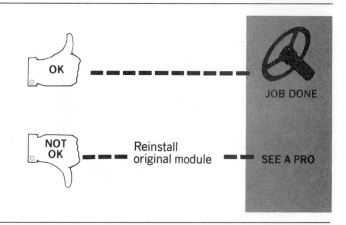

OK → **JOB DONE**

NOT OK → Reinstall original module → SEE A PRO

MISSES

A steady throbbing or misfire that occurs when the car is idling and can continue to 30 mph. The exhaust may have a putt-putt sound.

Troubleshooting by the numbers

1

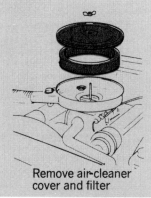

Remove air-cleaner cover and filter

- **Check vacuum hoses for:** splits, kinks, bad connections (p. 106)

- **Check for vacuum leaks at:** carburetor mounting, intake manifold

- **Check ignition wires for:** hardening, checking, bad connections, cracking (p. 95)

OK ----- Go to **2**

REPAIR OR REPLACE — ROAD TEST

JOB DONE

Go to **2**

2

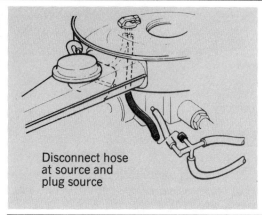

Disconnect hose at source and plug source

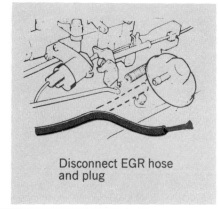

Disconnect EGR hose and plug

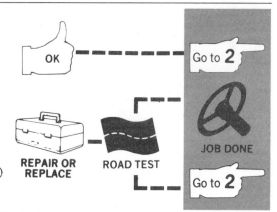

Start engine

Hook up tach/dwell meter (p. 71). Then remove one plug wire at a time with insulated spark plug pullers and ground (p. 90). Note rpm drop.

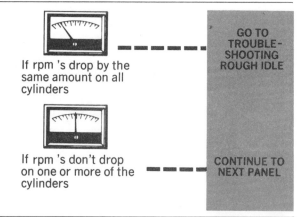

If rpm's drop by the same amount on all cylinders

GO TO TROUBLE-SHOOTING ROUGH IDLE

If rpm's don't drop on one or more of the cylinders

CONTINUE TO NEXT PANEL

Turn engine off

Remove the plug in question

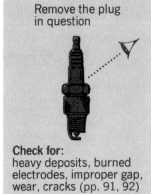

Check for: heavy deposits, burned electrodes, improper gap, wear, cracks (pp. 91, 92)

OK ----- Go to **3**

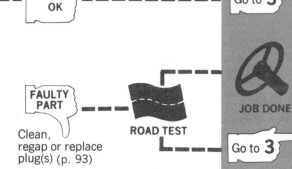

FAULTY PART

Clean, regap or replace plug(s) (p. 93)

ROAD TEST

JOB DONE

Go to **3**

Troubleshooting
by the numbers

3 Connect ohmmeter to questionable plug wire(s) (p. 95)

If ohmmeter reads under your car's specs (p. 95) → **Go to 4**

If ohmmeter reads over your car's specs (p. 95) → **FAULTY PART** Replace wires (p. 96) → **ROAD TEST** → JOB DONE / **Go to 4**

4 Turn engine off

Remove distributor cap and inspect for: moisture, burns, dust, cracks, etc. (p. 66)

Check distributor for: worn shaft, loose condenser, bad ignition points or coil, bare or shorted wires (pp. 66–68)

REPAIR OR REPLACE → **ROAD TEST** → JOB DONE / **Go to 5**

For electronic ignition → SEE A PRO

5 Make compression test on each cylinder

Compression OK → **Possible problems include:** bent push rods, worn rocker arms, broken valve springs, worn cam shaft lobe → SEE A PRO

Compression low → **Possible problems include:** burned valves, worn or broken piston rings → SEE A PRO

NO CRANKING OR SOLENOID SOUND/IGNITION IS ON

Troubleshooting by the numbers

Results

1

Check for:
battery damage, loose or corroded battery cables, loose ground at engine (pp. 28, 29)

REPAIR OR REPLACE AS NECESSARY (pp. 29–31)

Engine cranks — OK — **JOB DONE**

NOT OK — Engine doesn't crank — Check battery's specific gravity (p. 28). On maintenance-free battery, check indicator (p. 32) — Go to **2**

2

Indicator light

FAULTY PART
Replace battery (p. 31)

Engine cranks — OK — **JOB DONE**

NOT OK — Engine doesn't crank — Go to **3**

Indicator dark/ gravity under 1200

NOT OK
Charge battery (p. 32)

Check for:
loose drive belt (p. 36)
alternator output (p. 36)
any situation that may have drained battery

REPAIR OR REPLACE AS NECESSARY

Engine cranks — OK — **JOB DONE**

NOT OK — Engine doesn't crank — Go to **3**

Indicator green/ gravity over 1200

OK — Go to **3**

3

FOR GM CARS ONLY

GM diagnostic connector

Connect voltmeter as shown

Ignition in start — ON

Under 7 volts — FAULTY PART — Replace starter/solenoid (p. 48) — **JOB DONE**

Over 7 volts — Connect voltmeter as shown — CRANK

Over 9 volts — Go to **6**

Under 9 volts — Go to **4**

Troubleshooting by the numbers

Results

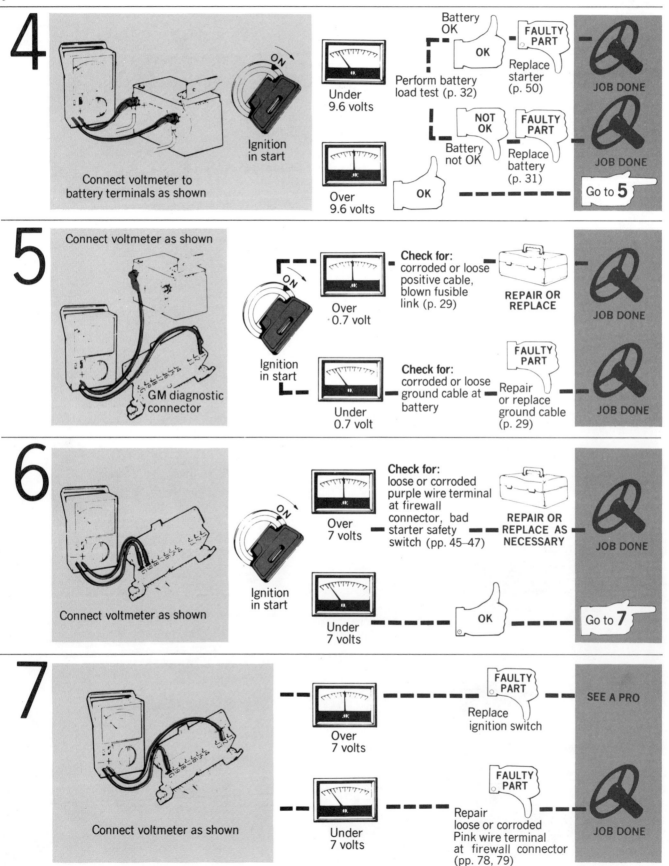

4 Connect voltmeter to battery terminals as shown

Ignition in start

Under 9.6 volts — Perform battery load test (p. 32) — Battery OK / OK — FAULTY PART Replace starter (p. 50) — JOB DONE

Battery not OK / NOT OK — FAULTY PART Replace battery (p. 31) — JOB DONE

Over 9.6 volts — OK — Go to **5**

5 Connect voltmeter as shown

GM diagnostic connector

Ignition in start

Over 0.7 volt — Check for: corroded or loose positive cable, blown fusible link (p. 29) — REPAIR OR REPLACE — JOB DONE

Under 0.7 volt — Check for: corroded or loose ground cable at battery — FAULTY PART Repair or replace ground cable (p. 29) — JOB DONE

6 Connect voltmeter as shown

Ignition in start

Over 7 volts — Check for: loose or corroded purple wire terminal at firewall connector, bad starter safety switch (pp. 45–47) — REPAIR OR REPLACE AS NECESSARY — JOB DONE

Under 7 volts — OK — Go to **7**

7 Connect voltmeter as shown

Over 7 volts — FAULTY PART Replace ignition switch — SEE A PRO

Under 7 volts — FAULTY PART Repair loose or corroded Pink wire terminal at firewall connector (pp. 78, 79) — JOB DONE

POOR GAS MILEAGE

Car's current mpg performance has fallen in comparison to its previous mpg history.

1

Remove and inspect air filter for obstructions

- **Check vacuum hoses and air cleaner for:** splits, kinks, bad connections (p. 106)

- **Check for vacuum leaks at:** carburetor mounting, intake manifold

- **Check ignition wires for:** hardening, checking, bad connections, cracking (p. 95)

- **Check for gas leaks at:** gas tank cap seal and check valve

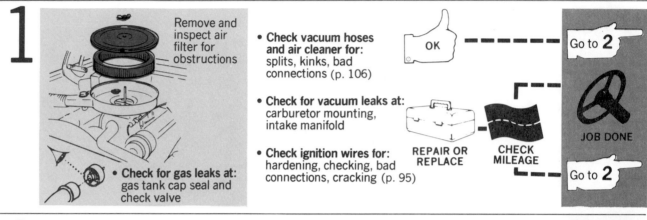

OK — Go to **2**

REPAIR OR REPLACE — CHECK MILEAGE — JOB DONE

Go to **2**

2

Engine idling and at operating temperature

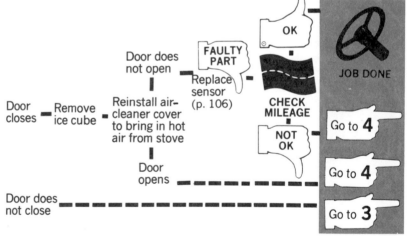

Remove air-cleaner cover and filter

CONTINUE TO NEXT PANEL

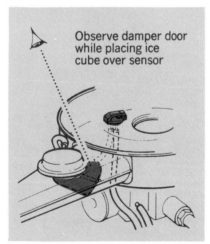

Observe damper door while placing ice cube over sensor

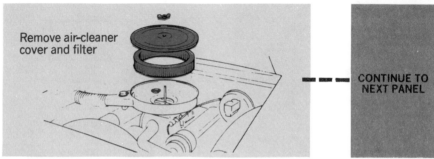

Door closes — Remove ice cube — Reinstall air-cleaner cover to bring in hot air from stove

Door does not open — **FAULTY PART** Replace sensor (p. 106)

Door opens

Door does not close

OK — CHECK MILEAGE — JOB DONE

NOT OK — Go to **4**

Go to **4**

Go to **3**

3

Hook up hand vacuum pump to vacuum motor

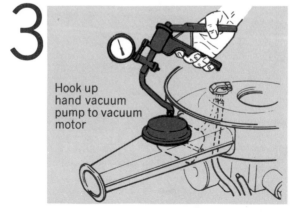

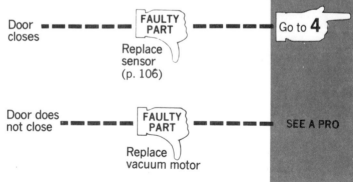

Door closes — **FAULTY PART** Replace sensor (p. 106) — Go to **4**

Door does not close — **FAULTY PART** Replace vacuum motor — SEE A PRO

Troubleshooting by the numbers

4

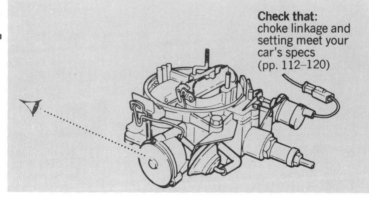

Check that: choke linkage and setting meet your car's specs (pp. 112–120)

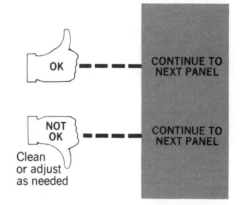

OK ——— CONTINUE TO NEXT PANEL

NOT OK ——— CONTINUE TO NEXT PANEL

Clean or adjust as needed

Disconnect and plug vacuum advance hose where applicable (p. 58)

Hook up tach/dwell meter and timing light (pp. 71, 72) then run engine at idle.

Set dwell, timing and rpm to specs where applicable (pp. 71, 72) Unplug and reconnect vacuum advance hose.

CONTINUE TO NEXT PANEL

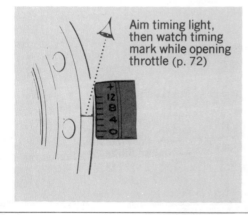

Aim timing light, then watch timing mark while opening throttle (p. 72)

Mark advances ——— OK ——— Go to **5**

Mark does not advance — **REPLACE ADVANCE** ——— SEE A PRO

5

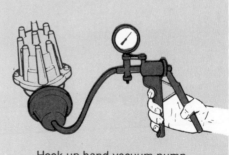

Engine off

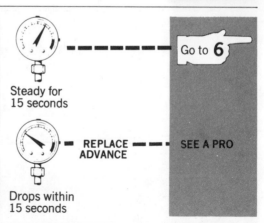

Hook up hand-vacuum pump to vacuum advance, and apply 15 inches of vacuum

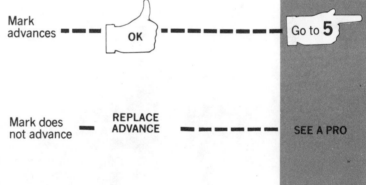

Steady for 15 seconds ——— Go to **6**

Drops within 15 seconds — **REPLACE ADVANCE** ——— SEE A PRO

Troubleshooting
by the numbers

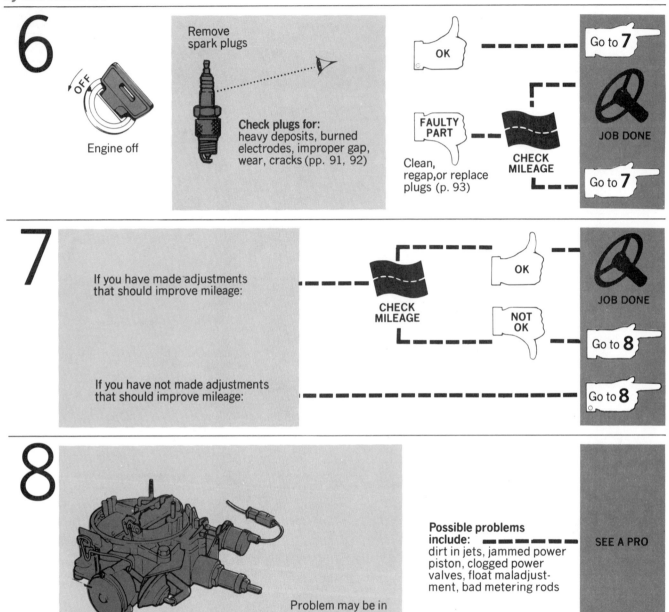

6 Engine off

Remove spark plugs

Check plugs for: heavy deposits, burned electrodes, improper gap, wear, cracks (pp. 91, 92)

OK — Go to **7**

FAULTY PART — CHECK MILEAGE — JOB DONE / Go to **7**

Clean, regap, or replace plugs (p. 93)

7 If you have made adjustments that should improve mileage:

CHECK MILEAGE — OK — JOB DONE / NOT OK — Go to **8**

If you have not made adjustments that should improve mileage: — Go to **8**

8 Problem may be in carburetor

Possible problems include: dirt in jets, jammed power piston, clogged power valves, float maladjustment, bad metering rods — SEE A PRO

SLUGGISH OR SPONGY

Engine doesn't deliver full power. Acceleration is poor or slower than usual. The engine may not respond to light acceleration. Only when the pedal is fully depressed is there a slight increase in speed.

Troubleshooting by the numbers

Results

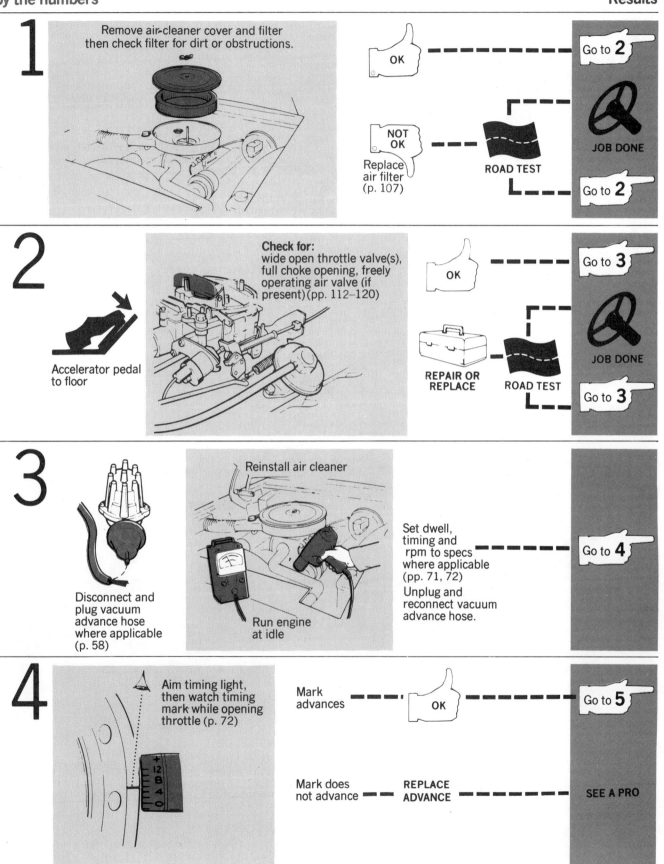

1 Remove air-cleaner cover and filter then check filter for dirt or obstructions.

OK — Go to **2**

NOT OK — Replace air filter (p. 107) — ROAD TEST — JOB DONE / Go to **2**

2 Accelerator pedal to floor

Check for: wide open throttle valve(s), full choke opening, freely operating air valve (if present) (pp. 112–120)

OK — Go to **3**

REPAIR OR REPLACE — ROAD TEST — JOB DONE / Go to **3**

3 Disconnect and plug vacuum advance hose where applicable (p. 58)

Reinstall air cleaner

Run engine at idle

Set dwell, timing and rpm to specs where applicable (pp. 71, 72) Unplug and reconnect vacuum advance hose. — Go to **4**

4 Aim timing light, then watch timing mark while opening throttle (p. 72)

Mark advances — OK — Go to **5**

Mark does not advance — REPLACE ADVANCE — SEE A PRO

Troubleshooting by the numbers

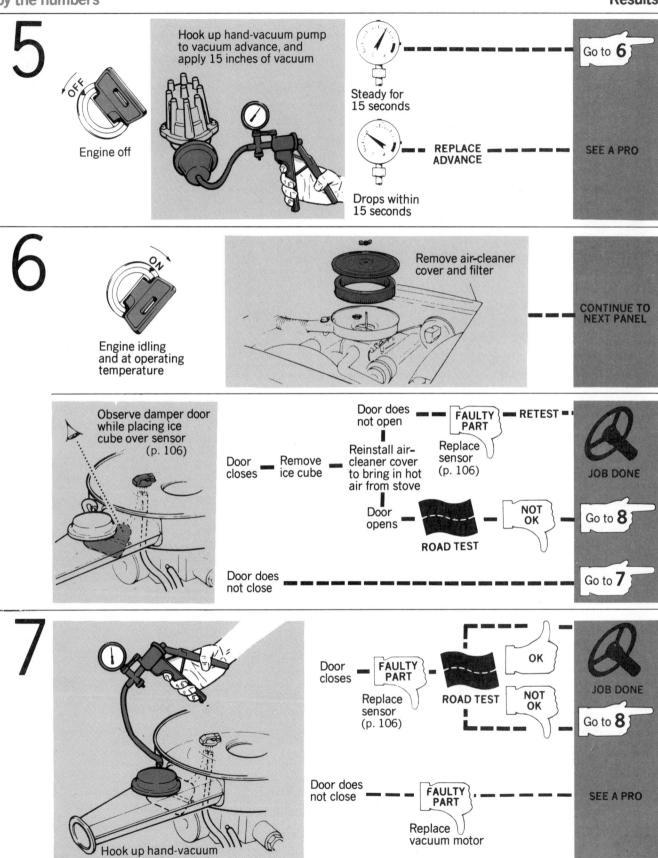

5

Engine off

Hook up hand-vacuum pump to vacuum advance, and apply 15 inches of vacuum

Steady for 15 seconds → Go to **6**

REPLACE ADVANCE → SEE A PRO

Drops within 15 seconds

6

Engine idling and at operating temperature

Remove air-cleaner cover and filter → CONTINUE TO NEXT PANEL

Observe damper door while placing ice cube over sensor (p. 106)

Door closes — Remove ice cube

Door does not open — FAULTY PART — RETEST → Replace sensor (p. 106)

Reinstall air-cleaner cover to bring in hot air from stove

Door opens — ROAD TEST — NOT OK → Go to **8**

JOB DONE

Door does not close → Go to **7**

7

Hook up hand-vacuum pump to vacuum motor

Door closes — FAULTY PART — ROAD TEST — OK → JOB DONE
Replace sensor (p. 106) — NOT OK → Go to **8**

Door does not close — FAULTY PART → SEE A PRO
Replace vacuum motor

Troubleshooting by the numbers

Results

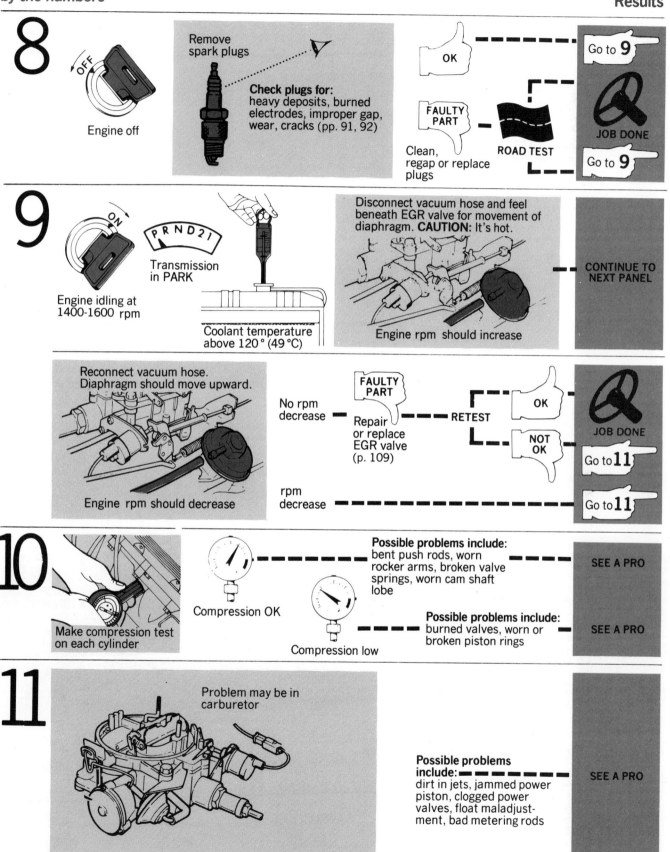

8 Engine off

Remove spark plugs

Check plugs for: heavy deposits, burned electrodes, improper gap, wear, cracks (pp. 91, 92)

OK — Go to **9**

FAULTY PART — Clean, regap or replace plugs — ROAD TEST — JOB DONE / Go to **9**

9 Engine idling at 1400-1600 rpm

Transmission in PARK

Coolant temperature above 120° (49°C)

Disconnect vacuum hose and feel beneath EGR valve for movement of diaphragm. **CAUTION:** It's hot.

Engine rpm should increase

CONTINUE TO NEXT PANEL

Reconnect vacuum hose. Diaphragm should move upward.

Engine rpm should decrease

No rpm decrease — FAULTY PART Repair or replace EGR valve (p. 109) — RETEST — OK — JOB DONE / NOT OK — Go to **11**

rpm decrease — Go to **11**

10 Make compression test on each cylinder

Compression OK — **Possible problems include:** bent push rods, worn rocker arms, broken valve springs, worn cam shaft lobe — SEE A PRO

Compression low — **Possible problems include:** burned valves, worn or broken piston rings — SEE A PRO

11 Problem may be in carburetor

Possible problems include: dirt in jets, jammed power piston, clogged power valves, float maladjustment, bad metering rods — SEE A PRO

SOLENOID CLICKS OR CHATTERS/ENGINE CRANKS SLOWLY

Troubleshooting
by the numbers

Results

1

Check for:
battery damage, loose
or corroded battery
cables, loose ground
at engine (pp. 28, 29)

REPAIR OR REPLACE
AS NECESSARY

Engine
cranks — OK — JOB DONE

Engine
doesn't crank

NOT
OK — Check battery's specific
gravity (p. 28). On
maintenance-free battery,
check indicator (p. 32) — Go to **2**

2

Indicator
light

Indicator dark/
gravity under
1200

Green dot/
gravity over
1200

FAULTY
PART
Replace
battery
(p. 31)

Engine
cranks — OK — JOB DONE

NOT
OK — Go to **3**

Engine
doesn't
crank

NOT
OK
Charge
battery
(p. 32)

Check for:
loose drive belt (p. 36)
alternator output (p. 36)
any situation that may
have drained battery

Engine
cranks — OK — JOB DONE

NOT
OK — Go to **3**

Engine
doesn't
crank

OK — Go to **3**

3

FOR GM
CARS ONLY

GM diagnostic
connector

Connect voltmeter as shown

Ignition
in start
ON

Over
9 volts

Connect voltmeter
ground to engine
(pp. 78, 79)

CONTINUE TO
NEXT PANEL

Under
9 volts

Go to **4**

194 TROUBLESHOOTING BY THE NUMBERS

Troubleshooting by the numbers

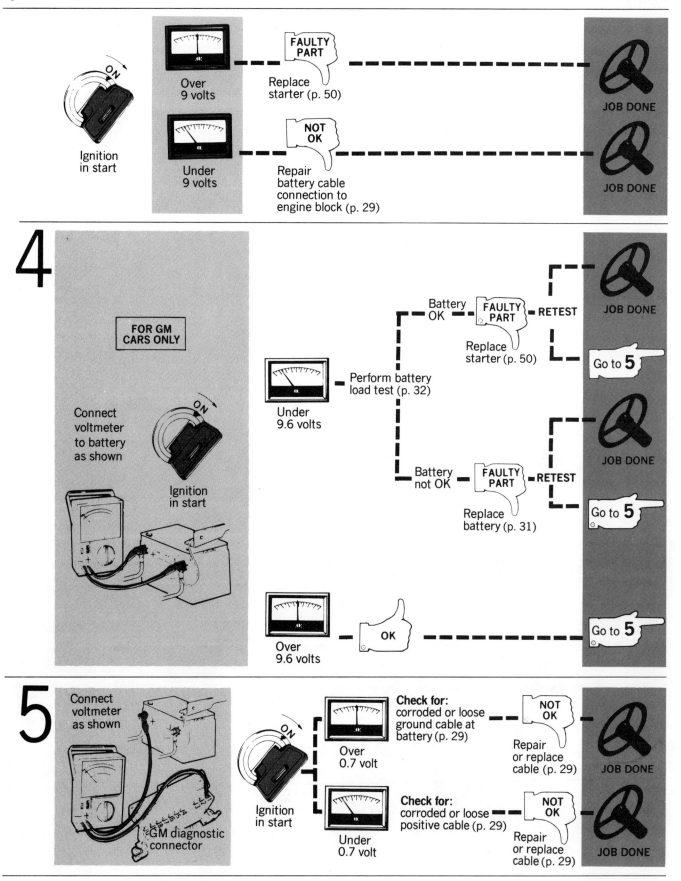

Ignition in start

Over 9 volts — **FAULTY PART** — Replace starter (p. 50) — JOB DONE

Under 9 volts — **NOT OK** — Repair battery cable connection to engine block (p. 29) — JOB DONE

4

FOR GM CARS ONLY

Connect voltmeter to battery as shown

Ignition in start

Under 9.6 volts — Perform battery load test (p. 32)

Battery OK — **FAULTY PART** — Replace starter (p. 50) — **RETEST** — JOB DONE / Go to **5**

Battery not OK — **FAULTY PART** — Replace battery (p. 31) — **RETEST** — JOB DONE / Go to **5**

Over 9.6 volts — **OK** — Go to **5**

5

Connect voltmeter as shown

GM diagnostic connector

Ignition in start

Over 0.7 volt — **Check for:** corroded or loose ground cable at battery (p. 29) — **NOT OK** — Repair or replace cable (p. 29) — JOB DONE

Under 0.7 volt — **Check for:** corroded or loose positive cable (p. 29) — **NOT OK** — Repair or replace cable (p. 29) — JOB DONE

SURGES

Car speeds up or slows down even though the accelerator is held in a steady position. This can occur at any speed.

Troubleshooting by the numbers

1

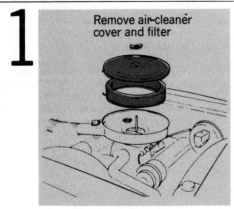

Remove air-cleaner cover and filter

- **Check vacuum hoses for:** splits, kinks, bad connections (p. 106)

- **Check for vacuum leaks at:** carburetor mounting, intake manifold

- **Check ignition wires for:** hardening, checking, bad connections, cracking (p. 95)

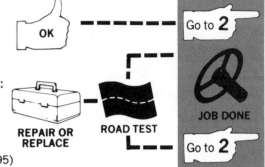

OK → Go to **2**

REPAIR OR REPLACE → ROAD TEST → JOB DONE / Go to **2**

2

ON

Engine idling and at operating temperature

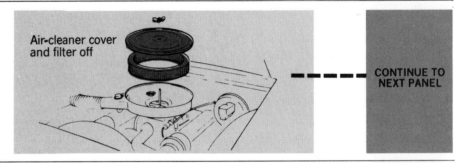

Air-cleaner cover and filter off

→ CONTINUE TO NEXT PANEL

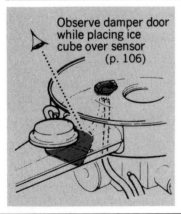

Observe damper door while placing ice cube over sensor (p. 106)

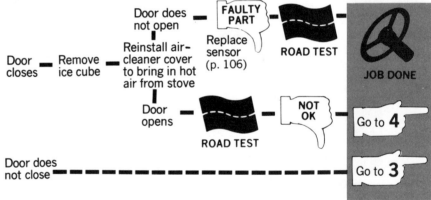

Door closes — Remove ice cube — Reinstall air-cleaner cover to bring in hot air from stove

Door does not open — **FAULTY PART** Replace sensor (p. 106) → ROAD TEST → JOB DONE

Door opens → ROAD TEST → **NOT OK** → Go to **4**

Door does not close → Go to **3**

3

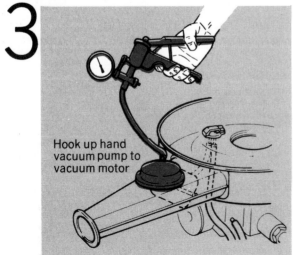

Hook up hand vacuum pump to vacuum motor

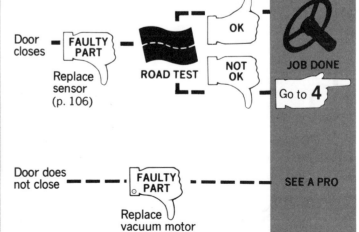

Door closes — **FAULTY PART** Replace sensor (p. 106) → ROAD TEST → **OK** → JOB DONE / **NOT OK** → Go to **4**

Door does not close — **FAULTY PART** Replace vacuum motor → SEE A PRO

Troubleshooting by the numbers

4

Disconnect and plug vacuum advance hose where applicable (p. 58)

Reinstall air cleaner

Hook up tach/dwell meter and timing light (pp. 71, 72) then run engine at idle

Set dwell, timing and rpm to specs where applicable (pp. 71, 72)

Unplug and reconnect vacuum advance hose.

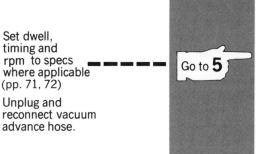 Go to **5**

5

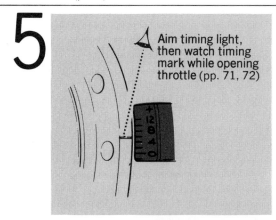

Aim timing light, then watch timing mark while opening throttle (pp. 71, 72)

Mark advances

Go to **6**

Mark does not advance — **REPLACE ADVANCE**

SEE A PRO

6

Engine off

Hook up hand-vacuum pump to vacuum advance, and apply 15 inches of vacuum

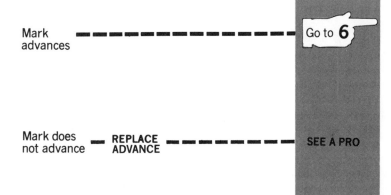

Steady for 15 seconds

Go to **7**

REPLACE ADVANCE

SEE A PRO

Drops within 15 seconds

7

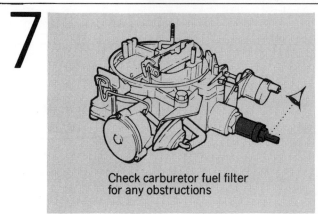

Check carburetor fuel filter for any obstructions

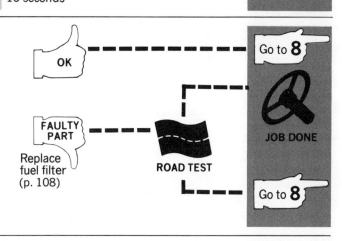

OK

Go to **8**

FAULTY PART

Replace fuel filter (p. 108)

ROAD TEST

JOB DONE

Go to **8**

Troubleshooting
by the numbers

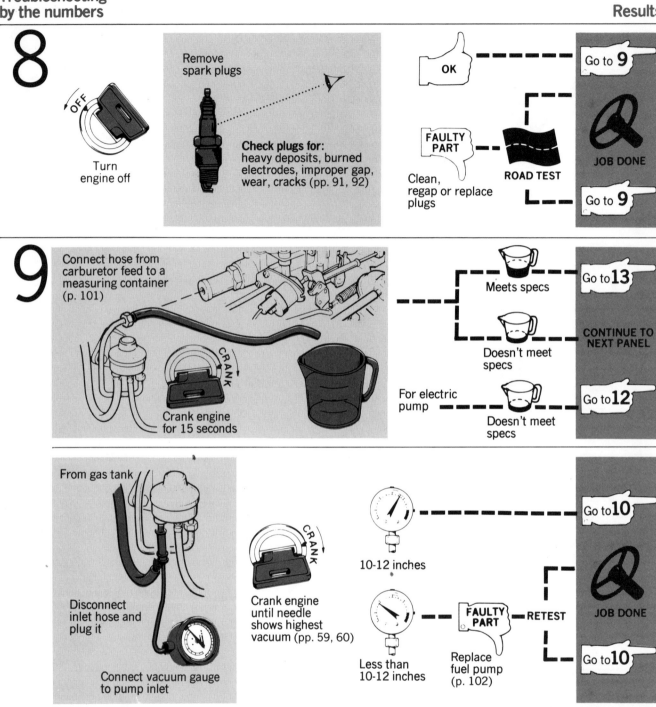

8

OFF

Turn
engine off

Remove
spark plugs

Check plugs for:
heavy deposits, burned
electrodes, improper gap,
wear, cracks (pp. 91, 92)

OK — Go to **9**

FAULTY
PART

Clean,
regap or replace
plugs

ROAD TEST

JOB DONE

Go to **9**

9

Connect hose from
carburetor feed to a
measuring container
(p. 101)

CRANK

Crank engine
for 15 seconds

Meets specs — Go to **13**

Doesn't meet
specs — CONTINUE TO
NEXT PANEL

For electric
pump — Go to **12**

Doesn't meet
specs

From gas tank

Disconnect
inlet hose and
plug it

Connect vacuum gauge
to pump inlet

CRANK

Crank engine
until needle
shows highest
vacuum (pp. 59, 60)

10-12 inches — Go to **10**

Less than
10-12 inches

FAULTY
PART

Replace
fuel pump
(p. 102)

RETEST

JOB DONE

Go to **10**

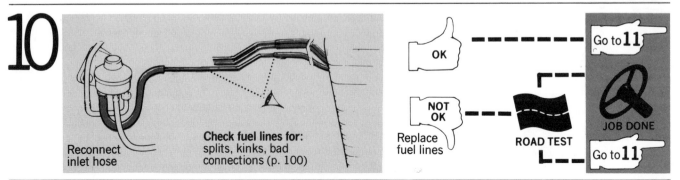

10

Reconnect
inlet hose

Check fuel lines for:
splits, kinks, bad
connections (p. 100)

OK — Go to **11**

NOT
OK

Replace
fuel lines

ROAD TEST

JOB DONE

Go to **11**

Troubleshooting by the numbers

11

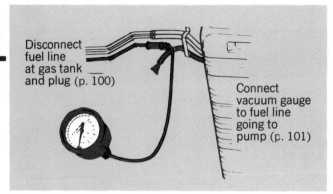

Disconnect fuel line at gas tank and plug (p. 100)

Connect vacuum gauge to fuel line going to pump (p. 101)

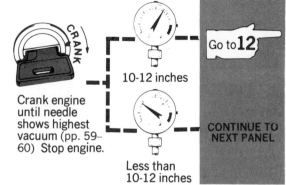

Crank engine until needle shows highest vacuum (pp. 59–60) Stop engine.

10-12 inches → Go to **12**

Less than 10-12 inches → CONTINUE TO NEXT PANEL

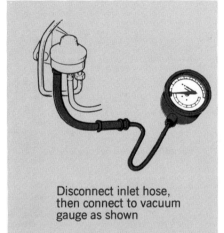

Disconnect inlet hose, then connect to vacuum gauge as shown

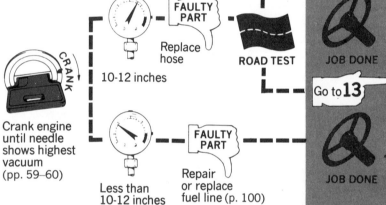

Crank engine until needle shows highest vacuum (pp. 59–60)

10-12 inches — **FAULTY PART** Replace hose — **ROAD TEST** → JOB DONE

Less than 10-12 inches — **FAULTY PART** Repair or replace fuel line (p. 100) → Go to **13** / JOB DONE

12

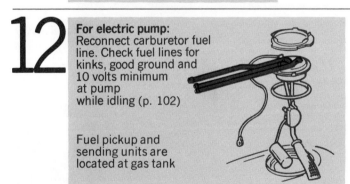

For electric pump: Reconnect carburetor fuel line. Check fuel lines for kinks, good ground and 10 volts minimum at pump while idling (p. 102)

Fuel pickup and sending units are located at gas tank

Possible problems include: defective fuel pickup and sending units → SEE A PRO

Possible problems include: dirt or water in gas tank → SEE A PRO

13

If you're feeling very ambitious, you may wish to adjust the carburetor in addition to what you've just done. Or, you may decide to replace it with either a new or reconditioned unit.

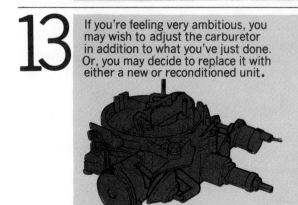

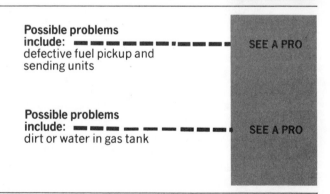

ROAD TEST — OK → JOB DONE

If you're not sure you wish to attempt this job but you still want the carburetor checked: → SEE A PRO

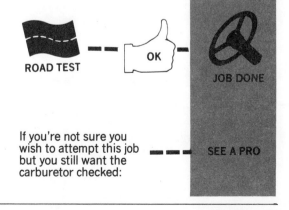

TEMPERATURE GAUGE SHOWS OVERHEATING

Troubleshooting
by the numbers

1

Tighten all hose clamps

Check for:
loose or missing fan belt, bugs etc.
on radiator/condenser, low engine
oil, coil spring in lower hose,
radiator low; leaks in thermostat
housing, water pump, hoses, head
gaskets, radiator, core plugs,
heater core, etc. (pp. 36, 121–132)

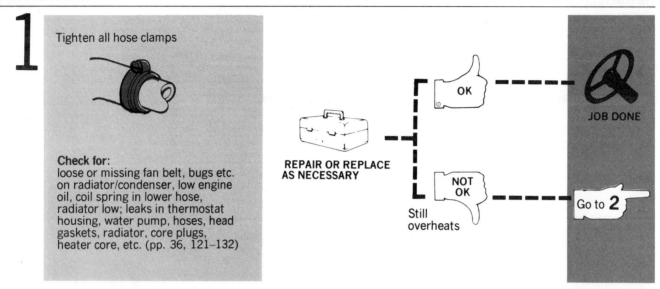

REPAIR OR REPLACE
AS NECESSARY

OK — JOB DONE

NOT OK
Still overheats — Go to **2**

2

For cars equipped
with clutch fan:

Spin fan
by hand

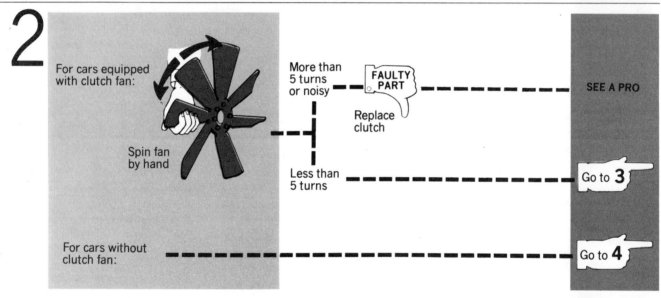

More than
5 turns
or noisy — **FAULTY PART**
Replace clutch — SEE A PRO

Less than
5 turns — Go to **3**

For cars without
clutch fan: — Go to **4**

3

Rotate shaft ½″

½″

Disconnect coil spring from front of clutch

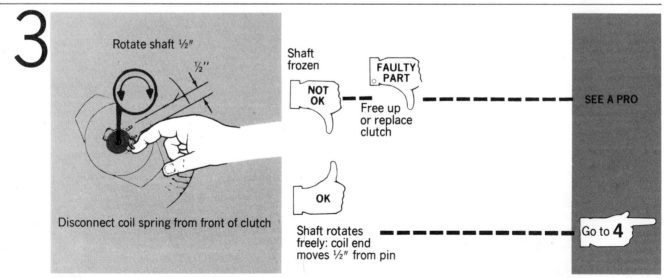

Shaft
frozen
NOT OK — **FAULTY PART**
Free up
or replace
clutch — SEE A PRO

OK
Shaft rotates
freely: coil end
moves ½″ from pin — Go to **4**

Troubleshooting
by the numbers

Results

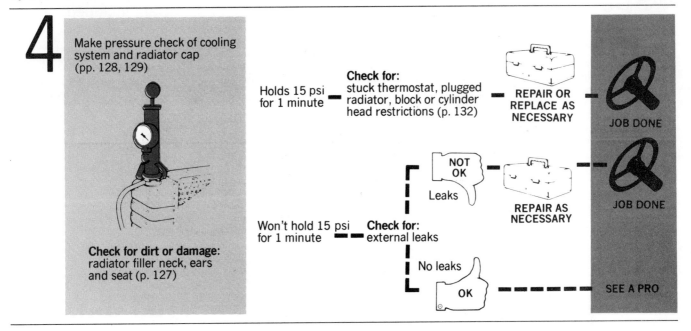

4 Make pressure check of cooling
system and radiator cap
(pp. 128, 129)

Holds 15 psi
for 1 minute

Check for:
stuck thermostat, plugged
radiator, block or cylinder
head restrictions (p. 132)

REPAIR OR
REPLACE AS
NECESSARY

JOB DONE

NOT
OK

Leaks

REPAIR AS
NECESSARY

JOB DONE

Won't hold 15 psi
for 1 minute

Check for:
external leaks

No leaks

OK

SEE A PRO

Check for dirt or damage:
radiator filler neck, ears
and seat (p. 127)

APPENDIX

Specifications

Vehicles in this section are arranged in consecutive groups of domestic cars starting on the next page, imported cars starting on page 269, and vans and trucks starting on page 282. This data will allow you to identify the exact engine in your vehicle and the manufac-turer's tune-up specifications for that engine. The contents list, below, covers all U.S. makes and models plus the three most popular imports manufactured between 1974 and 1979. Note too that these specs cover not only passenger cars but pickups, vans and 4-wheel drive vehicles. Occasionally you will find a footnote that refers you to the service section for another make. That means the same engine is also used in that make and you must turn to that section.

> ### Data included in this section
> Tune-up specifications
> * Spark plug type
> * Spark plug gap
> * Ignition point gap
> * Dwell angle
> * Firing order
> * Initial ignition timing
> * Idle speed

Contents By Make And Model

American Motors

ENGINE IDENTIFICATION

4-121 (1977-79): The engine code is located on a machined flange at the left rear of the cylinder block adjacent to the oil dipstick. The letter "G" denotes the 4-121 engine.

6-232 & 6-258 (1974-79): The engine code is located on a pad between number two and three cylinders. The letter "A" denotes the 258 engine with one barrel carburetor. The

letter "C" denotes the 258 engine with two barrel carburetor. The letter "E" denotes the 232 engine.

V8-304, 360, & 401 (1974-79): The engine code is located on a tag attached to the right bank rocker cover. The letter "H" denotes the 304 engine. The letter "N" denotes the 360 engine with 2 barrel carburetor while the letter "P" denotes the 360 engine with 4 barrel carburetor. The letter "Z" denotes the 401 engine.

TUNE UP SPECIFICATIONS

The following specifications are published from the latest information available. This data should be used only in the absence of a decal affixed in the engine compartment.

★When using a timing light, disconnect vacuum hose or tube at distributor and plug opening in hose or tube so idle speed will not be affected.

●When checking compression, lowest cylinder must be within 80 percent of highest.

▲Before removing wires from distributor cap, determine location of the No. 1 wire in cap, as distributor position may have been altered from that shown at the end of this chart.

Year/Engine	Spark Plug		Distributor		Ignition Timing★			Carb. Adjustments	
	Type	Gap Inch	Point Gap Inch	Dwell Angle Deg.	Firing Order Fig. ▲	Timing BTDC ①	Mark Fig.	Hot Idle Speed	
								Std. Trans.	Auto. Trans.②
1974									
6-232 L/EGR	N12Y	.035	.016	31–34	A	5°	D	700	600D
6-232 W/EGR	N12Y	.035	.016	31–34	A	5°	D	600	550D
6-232 Calif.	N12Y	.035	.016	31–34	A	5°	D	600	700D
6-258 L/EGR	N12Y	.035	.016	31–34	A	3°	D	550	700D
6-258 W/EGR	N12Y	.035	.016	31–34	A	3°	D	550	600D
6-258 Calif.	N12Y	.035	.016	31–34	A	3°	D	600	700D
V8-304	N12Y	.035	.016	29–31	B	⑩	C	750	700D
V8-360	N12Y	.035	.016	29–31	B	5°	C	750	700D
V8-401	N12Y	.035	.016	29–31	B	5°	C	750	700D
1975									
6-232	N12Y	.035	—	—	A	5°	E	600	⑥
6-258	N12Y	.035	—	—	A	3°③	E	600④	⑥
V8-304	N12Y	.035	—	—	B	5°	C	750	700D
V8-360	N12Y	.035	—	—	B	5°	C	—	700D
1976									
6-232	N12Y	.035	—	—	A	8°	E	850	⑥
6-258⑬	N12Y	.035	—	—	A	⑭	E	850	⑥
6-258⑮	N12Y	.035	—	—	A	⑭	E	600	700
V8-304	N12Y	.035	—	—	B	⑯	C	750	700D
V8-360	N12Y	.035	—	—	B	⑱	C	—	700D
V8-401⑰	N12Y	.035	—	—	B	⑱	C	—	700D

Continued

Year/Engine	Spark Plug		Distributor		Ignition Timing ★			Carb. Adjustments	
	Type	Gap Inch	Point Gap Inch	Dwell Angle Deg.	Firing Order Fig. ▲	Timing BTDC [1]	Mark Fig.	Hot Idle Speed	
								Std. Trans.	Auto. Trans. [2]
1977									
4-121	N8L	.035	.018	44–50	F	[25]	G	900	800D
6-232	N12Y	.035	—	—	A	[19]	E	[20]	[6]
6-258 Std. Tr. [13]	N12Y	.035	—	—	A	[21]	E	600	—
6-258 Auto. Tr. [13]	N12Y	.035	—	—	A	[22]	E	—	[6]
6-258 [15]	N12Y	.035	—	—	A	[14]	E	600	[23]
V8-304	RN12Y	.035	—	—	B	[18]	C	—	[7]
V8-360	RN12Y	.035	—	—	B	[18]	C	—	[24]
1978									
4-121	N8L	.035	.018	44–50	F	[25]	G	900	800D
6-232	N13L	.035	—	—	H	[26]	E	600	550D
6-258 [13]	N13	.035	—	—	H	[14]	E	850	700D
6-258 [15]	N13L [8]	.035	—	—	H	[14]	E	600	600D
V8-304	N12Y	.035	—	—	I	[18]	C	—	[24]
V8-360	N12Y	.035	—	—	I	10°	C	—	[35]
1979									
4-121	N8L	.035	.018	44–50	F	[25]	G	900	800D
6-232	N13L	.035	—	—	H	[26]	E	600	550D
6-258 [33]	N13L	.035	—	—	H	[36]	E	700	600D
6-258 [34]	N13L	.035	—	—	H	8°	E	—	700D
V8-304	N12Y	.035	—	—	I	[37]	C	800	600D

[1]—BTDC: Before top dead center.
[2]—D: Drive. N: Neutral.
[3]—Except distributor No. 3227331; distributor No. 3227331, Man. trans., 6° BTDC; auto. trans., 8° BTDC.
[4]—Set Matador sta. wag. with distributor No. 3227331 at 850 RPM.
[5]—Except Calif. models and vehicles with catalyic converter.
[6]—Exc. Calif., 550D; Calif., 700D.
[7]—Except early 1977 600D RPM; late 1977 700D RPM; Calif. all 700D RPM.
[8]—On models equipped with auto. trans. & 2.53 axle ratio use N12Y.
[9]—W/Air Guard 0.5–1.0%. W/O Air Guard 1.0–1.5%.
[10]—Exc. Calif. auto. trans., 5° BTDC; Calif. auto. trans., 2½° BTDC.
[11]—Exc. Calif. W/Air Guard, 0.8% maximum; Less Air Guard, 1.0% maximum.

[12]—With Air Guard–0.5%, with Air Guard disconnected on 1 bar. carb. models; less Air Guard–1.0%.
[13]—1 barrel carb.
[14]—Man. trans., 6° BTDC; auto. trans., 8° BTDC.
[15]—2 barrel carb.
[16]—Auto. trans. except Calif., 10° BTDC; man. trans. & Calif. auto. trans., 5° BTDC.
[17]—Police.
[18]—Except Calif., 10° BTDC; Calif., 5° BTDC.
[19]—Man. trans. except Calif. & high altitude, 8° BTDC; auto. trans., Calif. man. trans. & high altitude, 10° BTDC.
[20]—Except Calif., 600 RPM; Calif., 850 RPM.
[21]—Except high altitude, 6° BTDC; high altitude, 10° BTDC.
[22]—Matador except Calif., 6° BTDC; Gremlin Hornet & all Calif., models, 8° BTDC; high altitude all, 10° BTDC.
[23]—Except Calif., 600D RPM; Calif., 700D RPM

[24]—Except Calif. & high altitude, 600D RPM. Calif. & high altitude, 700D RPM.
[25]—Exc. Calif. auto. trans., 12° BTDC; Calif. auto; trans., 8° BTDC.
[26]—Manual trans., 8° BTDC; auto. trans., 10° BTDC.
[27]—California & altitude.
[28]—Calif., 6° BTDC; altitude, 10° BTDC.
[29]—Calif., 850 RPM; altitude, 600 RPM.
[30]—Calif., 8° BTDC; altitude, 10° BTDC.
[31]—Calif., 700D RPM; altitude, 550D RPM.
[32]—Except California & altitude.
[33]—Exc. Calif.
[34]—Calif.
[35]—Exc. Calif. & altitude, 600D RPM; Calif., 650D RPM; altitude, 700D RPM.
[36]—Manual trans., 4° BTDC; Auto. trans., 8° BTDC.
[37]—Manual trans., 5° BTDC; Auto. trans., 8° BTDC.

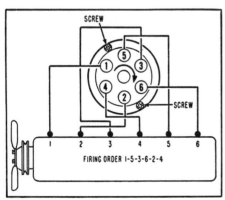

Fig. A

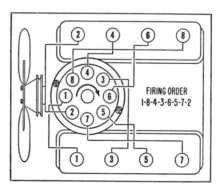

Fig. B

Fig. C

American Motors

TUNE UP NOTES—Continued

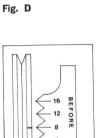
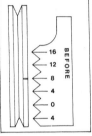

Fig. D

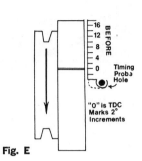

Fig. E

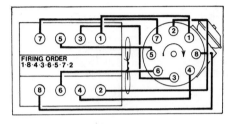

Fig. F

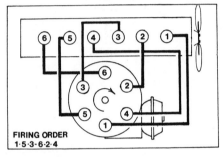

Fig. G

Fig. H

Fig. I

ENGINE IDENTIFICATION

Buick engines are stamped with two different sets of numbers. One is the engine production code which identifies the engine and its approximate production date. The other is the engine serial number which is the same number that is found on the vehicle identification plate. To identify an engine, look for the production code prefix letters, then refer to the following table for its identification.

On all Buick built engines except on 1975 models, the engine identification is located on the left bank cylinder head. On 1975 models the fifth digit in the VIN denotes the engine used.

On Chevrolet built 6-250 engines, the code is stamped on the cylinder block next to the distributor. On Chevrolet built V8 engines, the code is stamped on the engine case pad located below the cylinder head on the right hand side of the engine.

On all Oldsmobile built engines, the engine identification is located on the oil filler tube.

On all Pontiac built engines, the engine identification is located on the right front of the cylinder block.

Engine	Code Prefix
1974 6-250 Auto. Trans.[5]	CCW, CCX
6-250 Manual Trans.[5]	CCR
V8-350 2 Bar. Carb.	XC
V8-350 4 Bar. Carb.	XB
V8-455 4 Bar. Carb.	XF
V8-455 (Stage 1)	XS
V8-455 (Riviera G.S.)	XA

Engine	Code Prefix
1975 V6-231	C
6-250[5]	D
V8-260[4]	F
V8-350 2 Bar. Carb.	H
V8-350 4 Bar. Carb.	J
V8-400[3]	S
V8-455	T
1976 V6-231 Man. Trans.[1]	FA
V6-231 Auto. Trans.[1]	FB, FC
V6-231 Auto. Trans.[1]	FD, FE
V6-231 Auto. Trans.[2]	FF, FG
V6-231 Auto. Trans.[1]	FP, FR
V8-260 Man. Trans.[1][4]	QA, QD
V8-260 Auto. Trans.[1][4]	QB, QC
V8-260 Auto. Trans.[2][4]	TE, TJ
V8-350 2 Bar. Carb.[1]	PA, PB
V8-350 2 Bar. Carb.[1]	PC, PD
V8-350 4 Bar. Carb.[1]	PE, PF
V8-350 4 Bar. Carb.[2]	PK, PL
V8-350 4 Bar. Carb.[2]	PM, PN
V8-350 4 Bar. Carb.[2]	PR, PS
V8-350 4 Bar. Carb.[1]	PT, PU
V8-455 Auto. Trans.[1]	SA
V8-455 Auto. Trans.[2]	SB
1977 V6-231	RA, RB
V6-231	SG, SI, SJ, SK, SL
V6-231	SM, SN, ST, SU
V8-301[3]	YF, YJ, YW, YX
V8-305[5]	CPA, CPY
V8-350 2 Bar. Carb.	FA, FB, FK
V8-350 4 Bar. Carb.	FC, FD, FG
V8-350 4 Bar. Carb.	FH, FL
V8-350[4]	QK, QL

Engine	Code Prefix
V8-350[4]	QP, QQ, Q2, Q3, Q6, Q7
V8-350[4]	Q8, Q9, TK, TL, TN
V8-350[4]	TO, TQ, TX, TY
V8-350[5]	CKM, CKR
V8-403[4]	UA, UB, U2, U3
V8-403[4]	VA, VB, VJ, VK
1978 V6-196	PA, PB
V6-231 2 Bar. Carb.[6]	EA, EG, OH, OK
V6-231 2 Bar. Carb.[6]	EG, EI, EJ, EK, EL
V6-231 2 Bar. Carb.[7]	EO, OL
V6-231 4 Bar. Carb.[7]	EP, ER, ES
V8-301[3]	XA, XC
V8-305 2 Bar. Carb.[5]	CEK, CPZ, CRU, CRX
V8-305 2 Bar. Carb.[5]	CRY, CRZ, CTM, CTR
V8-305 2 Bar. Carb.[5]	CTW, CTX, C3P
V8-350 4 Bar. Carb.	MA, MB
V8-350 4 Bar. Carb.[4]	Q2, Q3, TO
V8-350 4 Bar. Carb.[4]	TP, TQ, TS
V8-350 4 Bar. Carb.[5]	CHM, CKM, CMC
V8-403[4]	UA, UB, U2
V8-403[4]	U3, VA, VB

[1]—Except California
[2]—California
[3]—Pontiac built engine.
[4]—Oldsmobile built engine.
[5]—Chevrolet built engine.
[6]—Except turbocharged engine.
[7]—Turbocharged engine.

TUNE UP SPECIFICATIONS

The following specifications are published from the latest information available. This data should be used only in the absence of a decal affixed in the engine compartment.

★When using a timing light, disconnect vacuum hose or tube at distributor and plug opening in tube or hose so idle speed will not be affected.

●When checking compression, lowest cylinder must be within 80 percent of highest.

▲Before removing wires from distributor cap, determine location of the No. 1 wire in cap, as distributor position may have been altered from that shown at the end of this chart.

Year/Engine	Spark Plug		Distributor		Ignition Timing ★			Carb. Adjustments	
	Type	Gap Inch	Point Gap Inch	Dwell Angle Deg.	Firing Order Fig. ▲	Timing BTDC ①	Mark Fig.	Hot Idle Speed ②	
								Std. Trans.	Auto. Trans.
1974									
6-250⑧	R46T	.035	.019	31–34	A	③	D	950	600
V8-350	R45TS	.040	.016	29–31	④	4°	F	—	650
V8-455	R45TS	.040	.016	29–31	④	⑤	F	—	650
1975									
6-250⑧	R46TX	.060	—	—	I	10°	D	800	⑥
V6-231	R44SX	.060	—	—	J	12°	K	800	700
V8-260⑫	R46SX	.080	—	—	L	16°⑭	M	—	650
V8-350	R45TSX	.060	—	—	H	12°	F	—	600
V8-400 4 B. Carb.⑬	R45TSX	.060	—	—	N	16°	C	—	650
V8-455	R45TSX	.060	—	—	H	12°	F	—	600

TUNE UP SPECIFICATIONS—Continued

The following specifications are published from the latest information available. This data should be used only in the absence of a decal affixed in the engine compartment.

★When using a timing light, disconnect vacuum hose or tube at distributor and plug opening in tube or hose so idle speed will not be affected.

●When checking compression, lowest cylinder must be within 80 percent of highest.

▲Before removing wires from distributor cap, determine location of the No. 1 wire in cap, as distributor position may have been altered from that shown at the end of this chart.

Year/Engine	Spark Plug		Distributor		Ignition Timing ★			Carb. Adjustments	
	Type	Gap Inch	Point Gap Inch	Dwell Angle Deg.	Firing Order Fig. ▲	Timing BTDC (1)	Mark Fig.	Hot Idle Speed (2)	
								Std. Trans.	Auto. Trans.
1976									
V6-231	R44SX	.060	—	—	J	12°	(26)	800	600
V8-260(12)	R46SX	.080	—	—	L	(9)	M	—	650(10)
V8-350	R45TSX	.060	—	—	H	12°	F	—	600
V8-455	R45TSX	.060	—	—	H	12°	F	—	600
1977									
V6-231	R46TS	.040	—	—	O	12°	P(27)	500/800(22)	600
V6-231	R46TSX	.060	—	—	Q	15°	R(27)	—	600/670
V8-301(13)	R46TSX	.060	—	—	N	12°	G	—	550/650
V8-305(6)	R45TS	.045	—	—	E	8°	D	—	500/650
V8-350(17)	R46TS	.040	—	—	H	12°	P(27)	—	(23)
V8-350(8)(18)	R45TS	.045	—	—	E	8°	D	—	500/650(21)
V8-350(12)(20)	R46SZ	.060	—	—	L	(24)(14)	M	—	550/650(21)
V8-403(12)	R46SZ	.060	—	—	L	(25)(14)	M	—	550/650(21)
1978									
V6-196	R46TSX	.060	—	—	Q	15°	R(27)	600/800	600
V6-231(7)	R46TSX	.060	—	—	Q	15°	R(27)	600/800	600/670
V6-231(11)	R44TSX	.060	—	—	Q	15°	R(27)	—	650
V8-301(13)	R46TSX	.060	—	—	N	12°	G	—	550/650
V8-305(8)(28)	R45TS	.045	—	—	E	(30)	D	—	(31)
V8-305(8)(29)	R45TS	.045	—	—	E	4°	D	—	500/600
V8-350(17)	R46TSX	.060	—	—	H	15°	R(27)	—	550
V8-350(8)(18)	R45TS	.045	—	—	E	8°	D	—	(32)
V8-350(12)(20)	R46SZ	.060	—	—	L	20°(14)	M	—	(33)
V8-403(12)	R46SZ	.060	—	—	L	20°(14)	M	—	(34)
1979									
V6-196	(35)	.060	—	—	Q	15°	R(27)	600/800	550/670D
V6-231(7)(36)	(35)	.060	—	—	Q	15°	R(27)	600/800	550/670D
V6-231(7)(37)	(35)	.060	—	—	Q	15°	R(27)	600/800	(38)
V6-231(11)	R44TSX	.060	—	—	Q	15°	R(27)	—	(39)
V8-301(13)	(40)	.060	—	—	N	12°	G	—	500/650D
V8-305(8)(28)	R45TS	.045	—	—	E	4°	D	—	(41)
V8-305(8)(29)	R45TS	.045	—	—	E	(42)	D	—	(43)
V8-350(17)	(35)	.060	—	—	H	15°	R(27)	—	550D
V8-350(8)(18)	R45TS	.045	—	—	E	8°	D	—	(43)
V8-350(12)(20)	R46SZ	.060	—	—	L	20°(14)	M	—	(44)
V8-403(12)	R46SZ	.060	—	—	L	20°(14)	M	—	(44)

Continued

TUNE UP NOTES

①—BTDC: Before top dead center.

②—Idle speed on manual trans. equipped vehicles is adjusted in Neutral and on auto. trans. equipped vehicle adjusted in Drive unless otherwise specified. Where two idle speeds are listed, the higher speed is with the A/C solenoid energized.

③—Manual trans., 8° BTDC; auto. trans., 6° BTDC.

④—Exc. H.E.I., Fig. B; H. E. I., Fig. H.

⑤—Exc. intermediate model Stage 1 eng., 4° BTDC; intermediate model Stage 1 eng., 10° BTDC.

⑥—Except California, 550D with A/C on & compressor clutch wires disconnected; California, 600D.

⑦—Exc. Turbocharged engine.

⑧—See Chevrolet chapter for service procedures on this engine.

⑨—Except California, 18° BTDC; California, 14° BTDC. At 1100 RPM.

⑩—California models with A/C on & compressor clutch wires disconnected.

㉕—R45TSX or R46TSX.

㉖—Except Calif. & high altitude.

㉗—California & high altitude.

㉘—California models less idle solenoid & high altitude, 600D R.P.M.; California models w/idle solenoid, 580/670D R.P.M.

㉙—Except Riviera, 650D R.P.M.; Riviera, 600/650D R.P.M.

⑪—Turbocharged engine.

⑫—See Oldsmobile chapter for service procedures on this engine.

⑬—See Pontiac chapter for service procedures on this engine.

⑭—At 1100 RPM.

⑮—Manual trans.

⑯—Auto. trans.

⑰—Distributor at front of engine.

⑱—Distributor at rear of engine, clockwise rotor rotation.

⑲—Exc. Calif. auto. trans., 8° BTDC; Calif. auto. trans. 6° BTDC.

⑳—Distributor at rear of engine, counter-clockwise rotor rotation.

㉑—High altitude, 600/650.

㉒—California, 600/800.

㉓—2 barrel carb., 600; 4 barrel carb., 550.

㉔—Exc. Calif., 20° BTDC; Calif.—exc. Sta. Wag., 18° BTDC; Sta. Wag., 20° BTDC.

㉕—Exc. Hi. Alt. & Calif., 24° BTDC; Hi. Alt. & Calif., 20° BTDC.

㉖—These engines use two different harmonic balancers. The harmonic balancer on late engines has two timing marks. The mark measuring 1/16 inch is used when setting timing with a hand held light. The mark measuring 1/8 inch is used when setting timing with magnetic timing equipment.

㉗—The harmonic balancer on these engines has two timing marks. The mark measuring 1/16 inch is used when setting timing with a hand held timing light. The mark measuring 1/8 inch is used when setting timing with magnetic timing equipment.

㉘—Two barrel carburetor.

㉙—Four barrel carburetor.

㉚—Exc. Calif. & high altitude, 4° BTDC; Calif., 6° BTDC; high altitude, 8° BTDC.

㉛—Exc. Calif. & high altitude, 600/500; Calif., 650/500; high altitude, 700/600.

㉜—Calif., 600/500; high altitude, 650/600.

㉝—Calif., 650/550; high altitude, 700/600.

㉞—Exc. high altitude, 650/550; high altitude, 700/600.

㊵—2 barrel carb., R46TSX; 4 barrel carb., R45TSX.

㊶—Less A/C, 500/600D R.P.M.; w/A/C, 550/600D R.P.M.

㊷—California, 4° BTDC; high altitude, 8° BTDC.

㊸—California, 500/600D R.P.M.; high altitude, 600/650D R.P.M.

㊹—Except Calif. & high altitude, 550/650D R.P.M.; California, 500/600D R.P.M.; high altitude, 600/700D R.P.M.

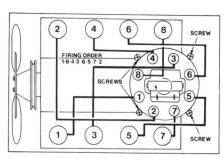

Fig. A

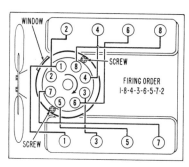

Fig. B

Fig. C

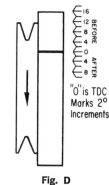

Fig. D

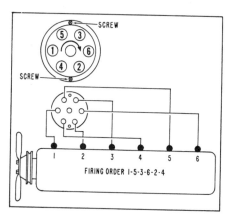

Fig. E

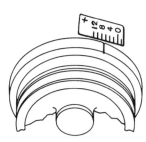

Fig. F

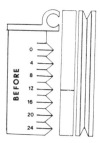

Fig. G

Buick—Except Skyhawk

TUNE UP NOTES—Continued

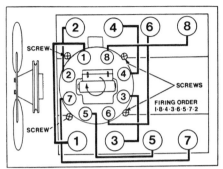

Fig. H

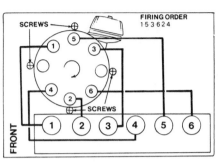

Fig. I

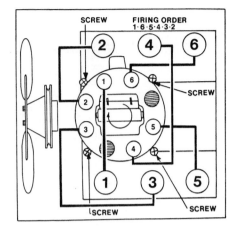

Fig. J

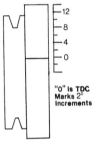

Fig. K

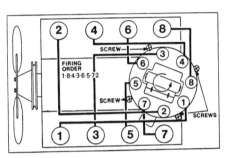

Fig. L

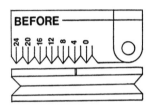

Fig. M

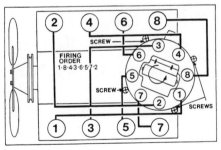

Fig. N

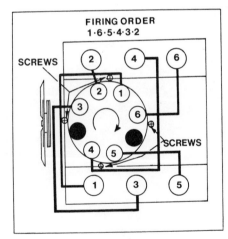

Fig. O

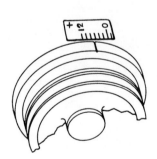

Fig. P

Continued

TUNE UP NOTES—Continued

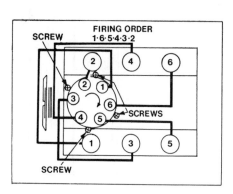

Fig. Q

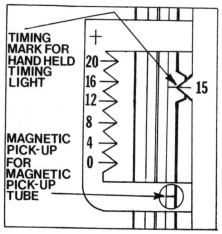

Fig. R

Cadillac

VEHICLE IDENTIFICATION NUMBER LOCATION: On 1974-79 models it is located on rear upper portion of cylinder block, behind intake manifold and on left side of transmission.

ENGINE UNIT NUMBER LOCATION: On 1974-79 except V8-350 at rear of cylinder block. 1976-79 V8-350 at front left hand side of cylinder block below cylinder head.

TUNE UP SPECIFICATIONS

The following specifications are published from the latest information available. This data should be used only in the absence of a decal affixed in the engine compartment.

★When using a timing light, disconnect vacuum hose or tube at distributor and plug opening in hose or tube so idle speed will not be affected.

●When checking compression, lowest cylinder must be within 80 percent of highest.

▲Before removing wires from distributor cap, determine location of No. 1 wire in cap, as distributor position may have been altered from that shown at the end of this chart.

Year/Engine	Spark Plug		Distributor		Ignition Timing ★			Carb. Adjustments	
	Type	Gap Inch	Point Gap Inch	Dwell Angle Deg.	Firing Order Fig. ▲	Timing BTDC ①	Mark Fig.	Hot Idle Speed	
								Std. Trans.	Auto. Trans. ②
1974	R45NS	.035	③	30	⑤	10°	D	—	600D④
1975–76 V8-500⑥	R45NSX	.060	—	—	E	6°	F	—	600D⑪
V8-500⑦	R45NSX	.060	—	—	E	12°	F	—	600D⑪
1976 V8-350	R47SX	.060	—	—	B	⑧	A	—	600D⑪
1977 V8-350	R47SX	.060	—	—	B	⑧	A	—	650D⑪
V8-425⑥	R45NSX	.060	—	—	E	18°⑩	F	—	600D⑪
V8-425⑦	R45NSX	.060	—	—	E	18°⑩	F	—	650D⑪
1978 V8-350	R47SX	.060	—	—	B	⑨	A	—	600D⑪
V8-350⑯	—	—	—	—	—	⑰	—		650D
V8-425⑥⑫	R45NSX	.060	—	—	E	⑬	F	—	600D⑪
V8-425⑥⑭	R45NSX	.060	—	—	E	⑮	F	—	600D⑪
V8-425⑦	R45NSX	.060	—	—	E	18°⑩	F	—	600D⑪
1979 V8-350	R47SX	.060	—	—	B	10°	A	—	600D
V8-350⑯	—	—	—	—	—	⑰	—		650D
V8-425⑥	R45NSX	.060	—	—	E	23°⑱	F	—	600N⑪
V8-425⑦	R45NSX	.060	—	—	E	18°⑩	F	—	650D

①—BTDC: Before top dead center.
②—D: Drive. N: Neutral.
③—Turn adjusting screw in (clockwise) until engine begins to misfire; then back screw out ½ turn.
④—When making adjustments, air conditioner must be turned off (if equipped). Also, hose must be disconnected at parking brake vacuum release cylinder. The hot idle compensator must be closed; this can be done by pressing finger or eraser end of pencil on compensator.

⑤—Exc. H.E.I., Fig. C; H.E.I., Fig. E.
⑥—Exc. Electronic Fuel Injection models.
⑦—Electronic Fuel Injection models.
⑧—Except Calif. 10° BTDC; Calif. 6° BTDC.
⑨—Except Calif. 10° BTDC; Calif. 8° BTDC before Eng. #180291 and 6° BTDC after.
⑩—At 1400 Rpm.
⑪—When making adjustments, A/C must be turned off. Disconnect parking brake hose at vacuum release cylinder and plug hose. If equipped, disconnect air leveling compressor hose at air cleaner and plug hose.

⑫—Except Eldorado.
⑬—Except high altitude, 21° BTDC at 1600 Rpm; high altitude, 23° BTDC at 1600 Rpm.
⑭—Eldorado.
⑮—Except Calif. & high altitude, 21° BTDC at 1600 Rpm; Calif., 18° BTDC at 1600 Rpm; high altitude, 23° BTDC at 1600 Rpm.
⑯—Diesel engine.
⑰—Refer to Oldsmobile chapter for service on this engine.
⑱—At 1600 RPM.

Continued

TUNE UP NOTES—Continued

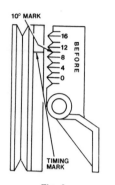

Fig. A

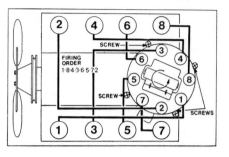

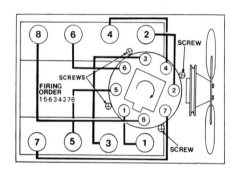

Fig. B

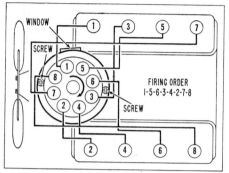

Fig. C

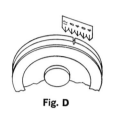

Fig. D

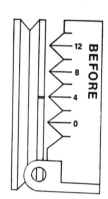

Fig. E

Fig. F

Checker Motors

SERIAL NUMBER LOCATION: Plate on left front door pillar, cowl left side above master cylinder or top of left side instrument panel

ENGINE NUMBER LOCATION

SIX CYL.: Pad at front righthand side of cylinder block at rear of distributor

V8 ENGINES: Pad at front righthand side of cylinder block

ENGINE IDENTIFICATION CODE

Engines are identified in the following table by the code letter or letters immediately following the engine serial number.

CODE	TRANS.	ENGINE
1974		
4SB	②	6-250
4SC	②	6-250⑤
4WD	②	V8-350
4WF	②	V8-350④
1975		
5SB	②	6-250
5SC	②	6-250⑤
5WD	②	V8-350

①—Std. trans.
②—Auto. trans.

CODE	TRANS.	ENGINE
1976		
6SB		6-250
6SC		6-250⑤
6WD		V8-350
6WF		V8-350④
1977		
7SB		6-250
7MK		V8-305

③—High performance.
④—Aerobus.
⑤—California.

CODE	TRANS.	ENGINE
7WD		V8-350⑤
7WF		V8-350④
1978		
8SB		6-250⑥⑦
8SC		6-250⑥
8SJ		6-250⑥⑧
8MK		V8-305⑥
8WD		V8-350⑤

⑥—Except Calif.
⑦—Less A/C.
⑧—With A/C.

TUNE UP SPECIFICATIONS

The following specifications are published from the latest information available. This data should be used only in the absence of a decal affixed in the engine compartment.

★When using a timing light, disconnect vacuum hose or tube at distributor and plug opening in hose or tube so idle speed will not be affected.

●When checking compression, lowest cylinder must be within 80 percent of highest.

▲Before removing wires from distributor cap, determine location of the No. 1 wire in cap, as distributor position may have been altered from that shown at the end of this chart.

Year/ Engine	Spark Plug		Distributor		Ignition Timing★			Carb. Adjustments	
								Hot Idle Speed	
	Type	Gap Inch	Point Gap Inch	Dwell Angle Deg.	Firing Order Fig. ▲	Timing BTDC ①	Mark Fig.	Std. Trans.	Auto. Trans.②
1974									
6-250	R46T	.035	⑧	31–34	A	6°	D	—	600D
V8-350	R44T	.035	⑧	29–31	B	8°	D	—	600D
1975									
6-250	R46TX	.060	—	—	E	10°	D	—	550D⑦
V8-350	R44TX	.060	—	—	C	6°	D	—	600D
1976									
6-250	R46TS	.035	—	—	E	10°	D	—	550D⑦
V8-350⑧	R45TS	.045	—	—	C	6°	D	—	600D
V8-350⑨	R44TX	.060	—	—	C	2°	D	—	700N

Continued

TUNE UP SPECIFICATIONS—Continued

Year/Engine	Spark Plug		Distributor		Ignition Timing ★			Carb. Adjustment	
	Type	Gap Inch	Point Gap Inch	Dwell Angle Deg.	Firing Order Fig. ▲	Timing BTDC ①	Mark Fig.	Hot Idle Speed	
								Std. Trans.	Auto. Trans. ②
1977									
6-250	R46TS	.035	—	—	E	⑩	D	—	550D③
V8-305	R45TS	.045	—	—	C	8°	D	—	500D④
V8-350⑥	R45TS	.045	—	—	C	8°	D	—	500D④
V8-350⑥⑧	R45TS	.045	—	—	C	8°	D	—	600D④
V8-350⑨	R45TS	.045	—	—	C	—	D	—	
1978									
6-250⑪	R46TS	.035	—	—	E	⑫	D	—	⑬
6-250⑭	R46TS	.035	—	—	E	6°	D	—	600D
V8-305⑪	R45TS	.045	—	—	C	4°	D	—	500D
V8-350⑭	R45TS	.045	—	—	C	8°	D	—	500D

①—BTDC: Before top dead center.
③—D: Drive. N: Neutral.
③—With A/C & High Altitude, 600D RPM.
④—On models with A/C, 650D RPM with A/C solenoid energized.
⑤—New points, .019", used, .016". On V8's,

turn adjusting screw in (clockwise) until engine misfires, then back off ½ turn.
⑥—High Altitude.
⑦—Calif. 600D RPM.
⑧—Marathon & Taxicab.
⑨—Aerobus.

⑩—Except high altitude, 8° BTDC; high altitude 10° BTDC.
⑪—Exc. Calif.
⑫—Less A/C, 10° BTDC; with A/C, 8° BTDC.
⑬—Less A/C, 550D RPM; with A/C, 600D RPM.
⑭—California.

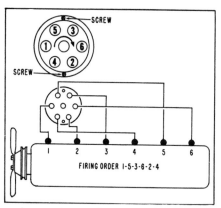

Fig. A

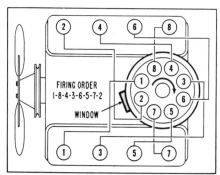

Fig. B

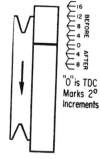

Fig. D

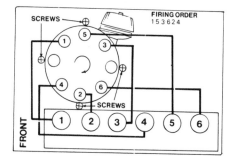

Fig. E

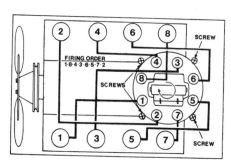

Fig. C

Chevrolet—Except Chevette, Monza & Vega

SERIAL NUMBER LOCATION: Plate on left front door pillar or top of left side instrument panel

ENGINE NUMBER LOCATION

4 & 6 CYL.: Pad at front righthand side of cylinder block at rear of distributor	V8 ENGINES: Pad at front righthand side of cylinder block

ENGINE IDENTIFICATION CODES

Engines are identified in the following table by the code letter
or letters immediately following the engine serial number.

CAMARO

CODE			CODE			CODE		
CCD	6-250	1977	CRC	8-350	1975	C3Y	6-250	1978
CCF	6-250	1977	CMF	8-350	1975	CTH	8-305	1978
CCR	6-250 with M/T	1974	CMH	8-350	1975	CTJ	8-305	1978
CCW	6-250 with T/H, E.E.C.	1974	CRX	8-350	1975	CTK	8-305	1978
CCW	6-250	1977	CHW	8-350	1975	C3N	8-305	1978
CCX	6-250 with T/H	1974	CHS	8-350	1975	CHF	8-350	1978
CJL	6-250	1975	CHT	8-350	1975	CHJ	8-350	1978
CJM	6-250	1975	CPA	8-305	1977	CHL	8-350	1978
CJR	6-250	1975	CPC	8-305	1977	CHR	8-350	1978
CJT	6-250	1975	CPY	8-305	1977	CHS	8-350	1978
CJU	6-250	1975	CCC	6-250	1976	CHT	8-350	1978
CJF	6-250	1975	CCD	6-250	1976	CHU	8-350	1978
CJY	6-250	1975	CCF	6-250	1976	C3T	8-350	1978
CJZ	6-250	1975	CHT	8-350	1976	DKA	6-250	1979
CKH	6-250	1977	CHU	8-350	1976	DKB	6-250	1979
CKM	8-350	1977	CML	8-350	1976	DKD	6-250	1979
CKR	8-350	1977	CPA	8-305	1976	DNF	8-305	1979
CKS	8-350	1977	CPB	8-305	1976	DNH	8-305	1979
CMA	8-350 with T/H	1974	CPJ	8-305	1976	DNK	8-305	1979
CMC	8-350 with M/T	1974	C2K	8-305	1977	DRC	8-350	1979
CKB	8-350 with M/T, 185 H.P.	1974	C2L	8-305	1977	DRD	8-350	1979
CKH	8-350 with 4 BC, M/T	1974	C8Y	6-250	1977	DRF	8-350	1979
CKH	8-350 with M/T, E.E.C., 185 H.P.	1974	9M	8-350	1976	DRH	8-350	1979
CLJ	8-350 with M/T, 245 H.P.	1974	9W	8-305	1976	DRL	8-350	1979
CKU	8-350 with T/H, 185 H.P.	1974	CCC	6-250	1977	DRY	8-350	1979
CKD	8-350 with 4BC, T/H	1974	CCH	6-250	1978	DTM	8-305	1979
CKD	8-350 with T/H, E.E.C., 185 H.P.	1974	CCJ	6-250	1978	DTR	8-305	1979
CLK	8-350 with 4BC, T/H	1974	CCK	6-250	1978	C8B	8-305	1979
CMU	8-350	1975				C8C	8-350	1979

CHEVROLET

CODE			CODE			CODE		
CCC	6-250	1977	CTC	8-400 with 4BC, E.E.C., 180 H.P.	1974	CXA	8-454	1974
CCF	6-250	1977	CTD	8-400 with 4BC, 180 H.P.	1974	CXX	8-454	1975
CCR	6-250	1977	CTK	8-400 with 4BC, E.E.C., 180 H.P., police	1974	CXY	8-454	1975
CCS	6-250	1977				CHS	8-350	1976
CKA	8-350	1977	CTJ	8-400 with 4BC, 180 H.P., police	1974	CMJ	8-350	1976
CKB	8-350	1977	CTA	8-400 with 150 H.P.	1974	CMM	8-350	1976
CKC	8-350	1977	CTB	8-400 with 150 H.P., police	1974	CSF	8-400	1976
CLL	8-350	1977	CPM	8-305	1977	CTL	8-400	1976
CMK	8-350 with 4BC, E.E.C., taxi & police	1974	CPR	8-305	1977	CXX	8-454	1976
			CTL	8-400	1975	CCA	6-250	1977
CMA	8-350 with E.E.C., taxi & police	1974	CTM	8-400	1975	CJA	6-250	1977
CMD	8-350 with taxi & police	1974	CTU	8-400	1975	CJB	6-250	1977
CMH	8-350 with 4BC, E.E.C., police	1974	CTW	8-400	1975	CJF	6-250	1977
CMJ	8-350 with 4BC, police	1974	CTY	8-400	1975	CCH	6-250	1978
CMJ	8-350	1975	CTZ	8-400	1975	CCK	6-250	1978
CMM	8-350	1977	CUB	8-350	1977	CCL	6-250	1978
CKD	8-350 with 4BC, E.E.C.	1974	CUC	8-350	1977	CCM	6-250	1978
CRU	8-350	1975	CUD	8-350	1977	CEJ	8-305	1978
CRW	8-350	1975	CWU	8-454 with police	1974	CEK	8-305	1978
CRY	8-350	1975	CWW	8-454 with E.E.C., police	1974	CTL	8-305	1978
CSA	8-400	1975	CWY	8-454 with E.E.C.	1974	CHF	8-350	1978

ENGINE IDENTIFICATION CODES—Continued

CHEVROLET—Continued

CODE		
CHH	8-350	1978
CHJ	8-350	1978
CHK	8-350	1978
CHL	8-350	1978
CHM	8-350	1978
CNT	8-350	1978
DCA	6-250	1979
DCB	6-250	1979
DCC	6-250	1979
DCD	6-250	1979

CODE		
DKB	6-250	1979
DKC	6-250	1979
DKD	6-250	1979
DKF	6-250	1979
DNL	8-305	1979
DNM	8-305	1979
DNR	8-305	1979
DRA	8-350	1979
DRB	8-350	1979
DRH	8-350	1979

CODE		
DRJ	8-350	1979
DRK	8-350	1979
DRL	8-350	1979
DRY	8-350	1979
DRZ	8-350	1979
DTC	8-305	1979
DTD	8-305	1979
DUB	8-350	1979
DUC	8-350	1979
DUD	8-350	1979

CHEVELLE, MALIBU & MONTE CARLO

CODE		
CCC	6-250	1977
CCD	6-250	1977
CCF	6-250	1977
CCR	6-250 with M/T	1974
CCW	6-250 with T/H, E.E.C.	1974
CCX	6-250 with T/H	1974
CCK	6-250	1974
CJL	6-250	1975
CLM	6-250	1975
CJR	6-250	1975
CJT	6-250	1975
CJU	6-250	1975
CJF	6-250	1975
CJZ	6-250	1975
CKH	8-350	1977
CKJ	8-350	1977
CKK	8-350	1977
CKM	8-350	1977
CKR	8-350	1977
CMC	8-350 with M/T	1974
CMA	8-350 with T/H	1974
CKH	8-350 with 4BC, M/T	1974
CKD	8-350 with 4BC, T/H	1974
CMF	8-350	1975
CMH	8-350	1975
CMJ	8-350	1975
CMU	8-350	1975
CTC	8-400 with T/H, E.E.C., 180 H.P.	1974
CTA	8-400 with T/H, 150 H.P.	1974
CPY	8-305	1977
CWA	8-454 with M/T	1974
CWX	8-454 with T/H	1974
CWD	8-454 with T/H, E.E.C.	1974
CRT	8-350	1975
CRU	8-350	1975

CODE		
CRX	8-350	1975
CSM	8-400	1975
CTL	8-400	1975
CTU	8-400	1975
CTX	8-400	1975
CXW	8-454	1975
CCC	6-250	1976
CCD	6-250	1976
CCF	6-250	1976
CPB	8-305	1976
CMH	8-350	1976
CMJ	8-350	1976
CMM	8-350	1976
CSB	8-400	1976
CSF	8-400	1976
CSX	8-400	1976
9R	8-350	1976
9W	8-305	1976
EA	6-231	1978
OH	6-231	1978
OK	6-231	1978
CWA	6-250	1978
CWB	6-250	1978
CWC	6-250	1978
CWD	6-250	1978
CER	8-305	1978
CPZ	8-305	1978
CRU	8-305	1978
CRW	8-305	1978
CRX	8-305	1978
CRY	8-305	1978
CRZ	8-305	1978
CMA	8-350	1978
CMB	8-350	1978
CMC	8-350	1978

CODE		
CMD	8-350	1978
NJ	V6-231	1979
RA	V6-231	1979
RB	V6-231	1979
RJ	V6-231	1979
RM	V6-231	1979
DHA	V6-200	1979
DHB	V6-200	1979
DHC	V6-200	1979
DMA	8-267	1979
DMB	8-267	1979
DMC	8-267	1979
DMD	8-267	1979
DMF	8-267	1979
DMH	8-267	1979
DNS	8-305	1979
DNT	8-305	1979
DNU	8-305	1979
DNW	8-305	1979
DNX	8-305	1979
DNY	8-305	1979
DRX	8-350	1979
DTA	8-305	1979
DTB	8-305	1979
DTF	8-305	1979
DTH	8-305	1979
DTJ	8-305	1979
DTS	8-305	1979
DTU	8-305	1979
DTW	8-305	1979
DTX	8-305	1979
DUF	8-350	1979
DUH	8-350	1979
DUJ	8-350	1979

CHEVY NOVA

CODE		
CCR	6-250 with M/T	1974
CCW	6-250 with T/H, E.E.C.	1974
CCX	6-250 with T/H	1974
CCK	6-250	1974
CCD	6-250	1977
CCF	6-250	1977
CCS	6-250	1975

CODE		
CCT	6-250	1975
CCT	6-250	1977
CCU	6-250	1977
CCU	6-250	1975
CCW	6-250	1975
CCW	6-250	1977
CGC	8-262	1975

CODE		
CGD	8-262	1975
CGF	8-262	1975
CGH	8-262	1975
CHW	8-350	1975
CJF	6-250	1975
CJL	6-250	1975
CJM	6-250	1975

ENGINE IDENTIFICATION CODE—Continued

CHEVY NOVA—Continued

CODE			CODE			CODE		
CJR	6-250	1975	CCC	6-250	1976	CCJ	6-250	1978
CJS	6-250	1975	CCD	6-250	1976	C2D	6-250	1978
CJT	6-250	1975	CCF	6-250	1976	CTH	8-305	1978
CJU	6-250	1975	CHT	8-350	1976	CTJ	8-305	1978
CJW	6-250	1975	CHU	8-350	1976	CTK	8-305	1978
CJX	6-250	1975	CML	8-350	1976	C2K	8-305	1978
CJZ	6-250	1975	CPA	8-305	1976	CHJ	8-350	1978
CKH	8-350	1977	CPB	8-305	1976	CHL	8-350	1978
CMC	8-350 with M/T	1974	CPJ	8-305	1976	NG	V6-231	1979
CMA	8-350 with T/H	1974	C2D	6-250	1977	NL	V6-231	1979
CKB	8-350 with M/T, 185 H.P.	1974	C2K	8-305	1977	NO	V6-231	1979
CKH	8-350 with 4BC, M/T	1974	C2L	8-305	1977	RF	V6-231	1979
CKH	8-350 with M/T, E.E.C., 185 H.P.	1974	C8Y	6-250	1977	RX	V6-231	1979
CKM	8-350	1977	9M	8-350	1976	RY	V6-231	1979
CKR	8-350	1977	9W	8-305	1976	SL	V6-231	1979
CKS	8-350	1977	CRX	8-350	1975	SR	V6-231	1979
CKU	8-350 with T/H, 185 H.P.	1974	CZF	8-262	1975	DKA	6-250	1979
CKD	8-350 with 4 BC, T/H, E.E.C.	1974	CZH	8-262	1975	DKB	6-250	1979
CMF	8-350	1975	CZJ	8-262	1975	DKD	6-250	1979
CMH	8-350	1975	CZK	8-262	1975	DNF	8-305	1979
CMU	8-350	1975	CZL	8-262	1975	DNJ	8-305	1979
CPA	8-305	1977	CZM	8-262	1975	DNK	8-305	1979
CPC	8-305	1977	CZY	8-262	1975	DRJ	8-350	1979
CPY	8-305	1977	CZZ	8-262	1975	DRY	8-350	1979
CRC	8-350	1975	CCH	6-250	1978	DTM	8-305	1979
CCB	6-250	1976	CCK	6-250	1978	C8B	8-305	1979

CORVETTE

CODE			CODE			CODE		
CHA	8-350	1975	CLB	8-350	1977	CKD	8-350	1977
CHB	8-350	1975	CLC	8-350	1977	CHW	8-350	1978
CHC	8-350	1975	CLD	8-350	1977	CLM	8-350	1978
CHR	8-350	1975	CLF	8-350	1977	CLR	8-350	1978
CHU	8-350	1975	CLH	8-350	1977	CLS	8-350	1978
CHZ	8-350	1975	CWM	8-454 with M/T	1974	CMR	8-350	1978
CKZ	8-350 with M/T	1974	CWR	8-454 with T/H	1974	CMS	8-350	1978
CLB	8-350 with M/T, E.E.C.	1974	CWS	8-454 with T/H, E.E.C.	1974	ZAA	8-350	1979
CLR	8-350 with M/T, 245 H.P.	1974	CLS	8-350	1976	ZAB	8-350	1979
CLA	8-350 with T/H	1974	CHC	8-350	1976	ZAC	8-350	1979
CLC	8-350 with T/H, E.E.C.	1974	CKC	8-350	1976	ZAD	8-350	1979
CLD	8-350 with T/H, 245 H.P.	1974	CKW	8-350	1976	ZBA	8-350	1979
CKZ	8-350	1977	CKX	8-350	1976	ZBB	8-350	1979
CLA	8-350	1977	CHD	8-350	1977			

NOTES

AIR: Air injection reactor
4BC: Four barrel carburetor

E.E.C.: Exhaust emission control.
HDC: Heavy duty clutch
M/T: Manual transmission

P/G: Powerglide
T/H: Turbo Hydramatic

Continued

TUNE UP SPECIFICATIONS

The following specifications are published from the latest information available. This data should be used only in the absence of a decal affixed in the engine compartment.

★When using a timing light, disconnect vacuum hose or tube at distributor and plug opening in hose or tube so idle speed will not be affected.

●When checking compression, lowest cylinder must be within 80 percent of highest.

▲Before removing wires from distributor cap, determine location of the No. 1 wire in cap, as distributor position may have been altered from that shown at the end of this chart.

Year/Engine	Spark Plug		Distributor		Ignition Timing★			Carb. Adjustments	
	Type	Gap Inch	Point Gap Inch	Dwell Angle Deg.	Firing Order Fig. ▲	Timing BTDC ①	Mark Fig.	Hot Idle Speed ②	
								Std. Trans.	Auto. Trans.
CAMARO									
1974									
6-250⑱	R46T	.035	④	31–34	D	8°	B	850	—
6-250⑲	R46T	.035	④	31–34	D	6°	B	—	600D
8-350, 145 H.P.⑱	R44T	.035	④	29–31	E	TDC	B	900	—
8-350, 145 H.P.⑲	R44T	.035	④	29–31	E	8°	B	—	600D
8-350, 160 H.P.⑱	R44T	.035	④	29–31	E	4°	B	900	—
8-350, 160 H.P.⑲	R44T	.035	④	29–31	E	8°	B	—	600D
8-350, 185 H.P.⑱	R44T	.035	④	29–31	E	8°⑥	B	900	—
8-350, 185 H.P.⑲	R44T	.035	④	29–31	E	8°	B	—	600D
8-350, 245 H.P.	R44T	.035	④	29–31	⑫	8°	B	900	700D
1975									
6-250	R46TX	.060	—	—	H	8°	B	850	600D
6-250⑦	R46TX	.060	—	—	H	10°	B	850	550D⑨
8-350 2 Bbl. Carb.	R44TX	.060	—	—	I	6°	B	800	600D
8-350⑱	R44TX	.060	—	—	I	6°⑥	B	800	—
8-350⑲	R44TX	.060	—	—	I	8°⑧	B	—	600D
1976									
6-250	R46TS	.035	—	—	H	6°	B	850	550D⑨
8-305⑱	R45TS	.045	—	—	I	6°	B	800	—
8-305⑲	R45TS	.045	—	—	I	8°⑬	B	—	600D
8-350 2 Bbl. Carb.	R45TS	.045	—	—	I	6°	B	—	600D
8-350 4 Bbl. Carb.	R45TS	.045	—	—	I	8°⑧	B	800	600D
1977									
6-250⑱	R46TS	.035	—	—	H	6°	B	③	—
6-250⑲	R46TS	.035	—	—	H	8°⑧	B	—	600
8-305	R45TS	.045	—	—	I	8°⑧	B	700	500/650
8-350⑱	R45TS	.045	—	—	I	8°	B	700	—
8-350⑲	R45TS	.045	—	—	I	8°	B	—	500/650
1978									
6-250⑱	R46TS	.035	—	—	H	6°	B	800	—
6-250⑲	R46TS	.035	—	—	H	10°⑧	B	—	550D⑨
8-305㉓	R45TS	.045	—	—	I	4°	B	600	500
8-305㉑	R45TS	.045	—	—	I	6°	B	—	500
8-350㉓	R45TS	.045	—	—	I	6°	B	700	500
8-350㉑	R45TS	.045	—	—	I	8°	B	—	500

TUNE UP SPECIFICATIONS—Continued

The following specifications are published from the latest information available. This data should be used only in the absence of a decal affixed in the engine compartment.

★When using a timing light, disconnect vacuum hose or tube at distributor and plug opening in hose or tube so idle speed will not be affected.

●When checking compression, lowest cylinder must be within 80 percent of highest.

▲Before removing wires from distributor cap, determine location of the No. 1 wire in cap, as distributor position may have been altered from that shown at the end of this chart.

Year/Engine	Spark Plug		Distributor		Ignition Timing★			Carb. Adjustments	
	Type	Gap Inch	Point Gap Inch	Dwell Angle Deg.	Firing Order Fig. ▲	Timing BTDC ①	Mark Fig.	Hot Idle Speed ②	
								Std. Trans.	Auto. Trans.
CAMARO—Continued									
1979									
6-250	R46TS	.035	—	—	H	㉘	B	—	—
V8-305	R45TS	.045	—	—	I	4°	B	—	—
V8-350	R45TS	.045	—	—	I	6°⑮	B	—	—
CHEVELLE, MALIBU & MONTE CARLO									
1974									
6-250⑱	R46T	.035	④	31-34	D	8°	B	850	—
6-250⑲	R46T	.035	④	31-34	D	6°	B	—	600D
8-350, 145 H.P.⑱	R44T	.035	④	29-31	E	TDC	B	900	—
8-350, 145 H.P.⑲	R44T	.035	④	29-31	E	8°	B	—	600D
8-350, 160 H.P.⑱	R44T	.035	④	29-31	E	4°	B	900	—
8-350, 160 H.P.⑲	R44T	.035	④	29-31	E	8°	B	—	600D
8-350, 185 H.P.⑱	R44T	.035	④	29-31	E	8°⑥	B	900	—
8-350, 185 H.P.⑲	R44T	.035	④	29-31	E	8°	B	—	600D
8-400	R44T	.035	④	29-31	E	8°	B	—	600D
8-454	R44T	.035	④	29-31	E	10°	B	800	600D
1975									
6-250	R46TX	.060	—	—	H	8°	B	850	600D
6-250⑦	R46TX	.060	—	—	H	10°	B	850	550D⑨
8-350 2 BBL. Carb.	R44TX	.060	—	—	I	6°	B	800	600D
8-350⑱	R44TX	.060	—	—	I	6°⑥	B	800	—
8-350⑲	R44TX	.060	—	—	I	8°⑧	B	—	600D
8-400	R44TX	.060	—	—	I	8°	B	—	600D
8-454	R44TX	.060	—	—	I	16°	B	—	600D
1976									
6-250	R46TS	.035	—	—	H	6°	B	850	550D⑨
8-305⑱	R45TS	.045	—	—	I	6°	B	800	—
8-305⑲	R45TS	.045	—	—	I	8°⑬	B	—	600D
8-350 2 Bbl. Carb.	R45TS	.045	—	—	I	6°	B	—	600
8-350 4 Bbl. Carb.	R45TS	.045	—	—	I	8°⑥	B	800	600D
8-400	R45TS	.045	—	—	I	8°	B	—	600D
1977									
6-250⑱	R46TS	.035	—	—	H	6°	B	③	—
6-250⑲	R46TS	.035	—	—	H	8°⑤	B	—	600⑤
8-305⑱	R45TS	.045	—	—	I	8°	B	700	—
8-350	R45TS	.045	—	—	I	8°	B	—	⑪

Continued

TUNE UP SPECIFICATIONS—Continued

The following specifications are published from the latest information available. This
data should be used only in the absence of a decal affixed in the engine compartment.

★When using a timing light, disconnect vacuum hose or tube at distributor and plug opening in hose or tube so idle speed will not be affected.

●When checking compression, lowest cylinder must be within 80 percent of highest.

▲Before removing wires from distributor cap, determine location of the No. 1 wire in cap, as distributor position may have been altered from that shown at the end of this chart.

| Year/Engine | Spark Plug | | Distributor | | Ignition Timing ★ | | | Carb. Adjustments | |
| | Type | Gap Inch | Point Gap Inch | Dwell Angle Deg. | Firing Order Fig. ▲ | Timing BTDC ① | Mark Fig. | Hot Idle Speed ② | |
								Std. Trans.	Auto. Trans.

CHEVELLE, MALIBU & MONTE CARLO—Continued

1978

Year/Engine	Type	Gap Inch	Point Gap	Dwell Angle	Firing Order	Timing BTDC	Mark	Std. Trans.	Auto. Trans.
6-200	R45TS	.045	—	—	F	8°	G	700	600
6-231 ㉔	R46TSX	.060	—	—	J	15°	K	—	600
8-305 ⑳	R45TS	.045	—	—	I	4°	B	600	500
8-305 ㉑	R45TS	.045	—	—	I	6°	B	—	500
8-305 ㉒	R45TS	.045	—	—	I	8°	B	—	600
8-350 ⑳	R45TS	.045	—	—	I	6°	B	700	500
8-350 ㉑㉒	R45TS	.045	—	—	I	8°	B	—	500

1979

Year/Engine	Type	Gap Inch	Point Gap	Dwell Angle	Firing Order	Timing BTDC	Mark	Std. Trans.	Auto. Trans.
V6-200 ⑱	R45TS	.045	—	—	F	8°	G	—	—
V6-200 ⑲	R45TS	.045	—	—	F	14°	G	—	—
V6-231 ㉔	R46TSX	.060	—	—	J	15°	K	—	—
V8-267 ⑱	R45TS	.045	—	—	I	4°	B	—	—
V8-267 ⑲	R45TS	.045	—	—	I	10°	B	—	—
V8-305	R43TS	.045	—	—	I	4°	B	—	—
V8-350	R43TS	.045	—	—	I	8°	B	—	—

CHEVY NOVA

1974

Year/Engine	Type	Gap Inch	Point Gap	Dwell Angle	Firing Order	Timing BTDC	Mark	Std. Trans.	Auto. Trans.
6-250 ⑱	R46T	.035	④	31–34	D	8°	B	850	—
6-250 ⑲	R46T	.035	④	31–34	D	6°	B	—	600D
8-350, 145 H.P. ⑱	R44T	.035	④	29–31	E	TDC	B	900	—
8-350, 145 H.P. ⑲	R44T	.035	④	29–31	E	8°	B	—	600D
8-350, 160 H.P. ⑱	R44T	.035	④	29–31	E	4°	B	900	—
8-350, 160 H.P. ⑲	R44T	.035	④	29–31	E	8°	B	—	600D
8-350, 185 H.P. ⑱	R44T	.035	④	29–31	E	8° ⑥	B	900	—
8-350, 185 H.P. ⑲	R44T	.035	④	29–31	E	8°	B	—	600D

1975

Year/Engine	Type	Gap Inch	Point Gap	Dwell Angle	Firing Order	Timing BTDC	Mark	Std. Trans.	Auto. Trans.
6-250	R46TX	.060	—	—	H	8°	B	850	600D
6-250 ⑦	R46TX	.060	—	—	H	10°	B	850	550D⑨
8-262	R44TX	.060	—	—	I	8°	A	800	600D
8-350 2 BBl. Carb.	R44TX	.060	—	—	I	6°	B	800	600D
8-350 ⑱	R44TX	.060	—	—	I	6° ⑥	B	800	—
8-350 ⑲	R44TX	.060	—	—	I	8° ⑧	B	—	600D

1976

Year/Engine	Type	Gap Inch	Point Gap	Dwell Angle	Firing Order	Timing BTDC	Mark	Std. Trans.	Auto. Trans.
6-250	R46TS	.035	—	—	H	6° ⑩	B	850	550D⑨
8-305 ⑱	R45TS	.045	—	—	I	6°	B	800	—
8-305 ⑲	R45TS	.045	—	—	I	8° ⑬	B	—	600D
8-350 2 Bbl. Carb.	R45TS	.045	—	—	I	6°	B	—	600D
8-350 4 Bbl. Carb.	R45TS	.045	—	—	I	8° ⑧	B	800	600D

Chevrolet—Except Chevette, Monza & Vega

TUNE UP SPECIFICATIONS—Continued

The following specifications are published from the latest information available. This data should be used only in the absence of a decal affixed in the engine compartment.

★When using a timing light, disconnect vacuum hose or tube at distributor and plug opening in hose or tube so idle speed will not be affected.

●When checking compression, lowest cylinder must be within 80 percent of highest.

▲Before removing wires from distributor cap, determine location of the No. 1 wire in cap, as distributor position may have been altered from that shown at the end of this chart.

Year/Engine	Spark Plug		Distributor		Ignition Timing★			Carb. Adjustments	
	Type	Gap Inch	Point Gap Inch	Dwell Angle Deg.	Firing Order Fig. ▲	Timing BTDC ①	Mark Fig.	Hot Idle Speed ②	
								Std. Trans.	Auto. Trans.

CHEVY NOVA—Continued

1977

6-250⑱	R46TS	.035	—	—	H	6°	B	③	—
6-250⑲	R46TS	.035	—	—	H	8°⑧	B	—	600⑥
8-305⑱	R45TS	.045	—	—	I	8°	B	700	—
8-305⑲	R45TS	.045	—	—	I	8°⑧	B	—	500/650
8-350	R45TS	.045	—	—	I	8°	B	700	⑪

1978

6-250㉖	R46TS	.035	—	—	H	6°	B	800	—
6-250⑲㉓	R46TS	.035	—	—	H	10°㉕	B	—	600D
8-305㉓	R45TS	.045	—	—	I	4°	B	600	500D
8-305㉑	R45TS	.045	—	—	I	6°	B	—	500D
V8-350	R45TS	.045	—	—	I	8°	B	—	650D⑨

1979

6-250	R46TS	.035	—	—	H	㉘	B	—	—
V8-305	R45TS	.045	—	—	I	4°	B	—	—
V8-350	R45TS	.045	—	—	I	8°	B	—	—

CHEVROLET

1974

8-350, 145 H.P.	R44T	.035	④	29–31	E	8°	B	—	600D
8-350, 160 H.P.	R44T	.035	④	29–31	E	8°	B	—	600D
8-400	R44T	.035	④	29–31	E	8°	B	—	600D
8-454	R44T	.035	④	29–31	⑫	10°	B	—	600D

1975

8-350 2 BBl. Carb.	R44TX	.060	—	—	I	6°	B	—	600D
8-350	R44TX	.060	—	—	I	8°⑧	B	—	600D
8-400	R44TX	.060	—	—	I	8°	B	—	600D
8-454	R44TX	.060	—	—	I	16°	B	—	600D

1976

8-350 2 Bbl. Carb.	R45TS	.045	—	—	I	6°	B	—	600D
8-350 4 Bbl. Carb.	R45TS	.045	—	—	I	8°⑧	B	—	600D
8-400	R45TS	.045	—	—	I	8°	B	—	600D
8-454	R45TSX	.060	—	—	I	12°	B	—	550D

Continued

TUNE UP SPECIFICATIONS—Continued

The following specifications are published from the latest information available. This data should be used only in the absence of a decal affixed in the engine compartment.

★When using a timing light, disconnect vacuum hose or tube at distributor and plug opening in hose or tube so idle speed will not be affected.

●When checking compression, lowest cylinder must be within 80 percent of highest.

▲Before removing wires from distributor cap, determine location of the No. 1 wire in cap, as distributor position may have been altered from that shown at the end of this chart.

Year/Engine	Spark Plug		Distributor		Ignition Timing★			Carb. Adjustments	
	Type	Gap Inch	Point Gap Inch	Dwell Angle Deg.	Firing Order Fig. ▲	Timing BTDC [1]	Mark Fig.	Hot Idle Speed [2]	
								Std. Trans.	Auto. Trans.
CHEVROLET—Continued									
1977									
6-250	R46TS	.035	—	—	H	8°[8]	B	—	600[5]
8-305	R45TS	.045	—	—	I	8°[8]	B	—	500/650
8-350	R45TS	.045	—	—	I	8°	B	—	[11]
1978									
6-250[23]	R46TS	.035	—	—	H	10°[26]	B	—	500D
6-250[21]	R46TS	.035	—	—	H	6°	B	—	600D
8-305[23]	R45TS	.045	—	—	I	4°	B	—	500D
8-305[21]	R45TS	.045	—	—	I	6°	B	—	500D
8-350[23]	R45TS	.045	—	—	I	6°	B	—	500D
8-350[21]	R45TS	.045	—	—	I	8°	B	—	500D
1979									
6-250	R46TS	.035	—	—	H	[8][29]	B	—	—
8-305	R45TS	.045	—	—	I	4°	B	—	—
8-350	R45TS	.045	—	—	I	[16][30]	B	—	—
CORVETTE									
1974									
8-350, 195 H.P.[18]	R44T	.035	[4]	29–31	C	8°[6]	B	900	—
8-350, 195 H.P.[19]	R44T	.035	[4]	29–31	C	8°	B	—	600D
8-350, 250 H.P.	R44T	.035	[4]	29–31	C	8°	B	900	700D
8-454	R44T	.035	[4]	29–31	E	10°	B	800	600D
1975									
8-350[18]	R44TX	.060	—	—	I	6°[6]	B	800	—
8-350[19]	R44TX	.060	—	—	I	6°	B	—	600D
1976									
8-350	R45TS	.045	—	—	I	8°[8]	B	1000	700D
8-350[14]	R45TS	.045	—	—	I	12°	B	1000	700D
1977									
8-350	R45TS	.045	—	—	I	8°	B	700	[11]
8-350[14]	R45TS	.045	—	—	I	12°	B	800	700/800
1978									
V8-350[16]	R45TS	.045	—	—	I	6°[16]	B	700	500[27]
V8-350[17]	R45TS	.045	—	—	I	12°	B	900	700

Chevrolet—Except Chevette, Monza & Vega

TUNE UP SPECIFICATIONS—Continued

The following specifications are published from the latest information available. This data should be used only in the absence of a decal affixed in the engine compartment.

★When using a timing light, disconnect vacuum hose or tube at distributor and plug opening in hose or tube so idle speed will not be affected.

●When checking compression, lowest cylinder must be within 80 percent of highest.

▲Before removing wires from distributor cap, determine location of the No. 1 wire in cap, as distributor position may have been altered from that shown at the end of this chart.

| Year/Engine | Spark Plug | | Distributor | | Ignition Timing★ | | | Carb. Adjustments | |
| | Type | Gap Inch | Point Gap Inch | Dwell Angle Deg. | Firing Order Fig. ▲ | Timing BTDC ① | Mark Fig. | Hot Idle Speed ② | |
								Std. Trans.	Auto. Trans.
CORVETTE—Continued									
1979									
8-350	R45TS	.045	—	—	I	6° ㉛	B	—	—
8-350	R45TS	.045	—	—	I	12°	B	—	—

①—BTDC: Before top dead center.
②—Idle speed on manual trans. equipped vehicles is adjusted in Neutral and on auto. trans. equipped vehicles is adjusted in Drive unless otherwise specified. Where two speeds are listed, the higher speed is with A/C solenoid energized.
③—Less A/C, 750 R.P.M.; with A/C, 800 R.P.M.
④—New points, .019", used .016". On V8s, turn adjusting screw in (clockwise) until engine misfires; then back off ½ turn.
⑤—California, 550 R.P.M.
⑥—For California set at 4° BTDC.
⑦—With integral intake manifold and all California models.

⑧—For California set at 6° BTDC.
⑨—For California 600 R.P.M.
⑩—With Distributor 1110662 set at 8° BTDC.
⑪—Exc. high altitude, 500/650; high altitude 600/650.
⑫—Exc. H.E.I., Fig. E; H.E.I., Fig. I.
⑬—For California set at TDC.
⑭—210 H.P.
⑮—For California, 8° BTDC.
⑯—Exc. high performance.
⑰—High performance.
⑱—With standard transmission.
⑲—With automatic transmission.
⑳—Exc. Calif. & high altitude.
㉑—Calif.

㉒—High altitude.
㉓—Exc. Calif.
㉔—For service on this engine, see Buick chapter.
㉕—With A/C, 8° BTDC.
㉖—With manual trans. exc. Calif.: with auto trans. Calif. only.
㉗—For high altitude, 600 R.P.M.
㉘—With manual trans., 8° BTDC; auto. trans. Exc. Calif., 10° BTDC; Calif. 6° BTDC.
㉙—Exc. Calif., 10° BTDC.
㉚—Exc. Calif., 6° BTDC.
㉛—For Calif. & high altitude, 8° BTDC.

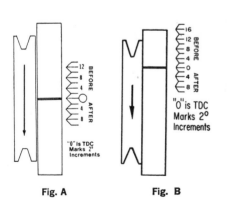

Fig. A   Fig. B

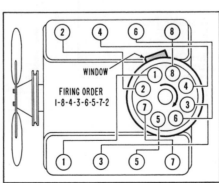

Fig. C

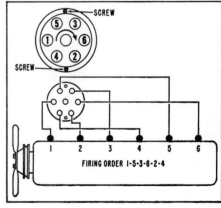

Fig. D

Continued

TUNE UP NOTES—Continued

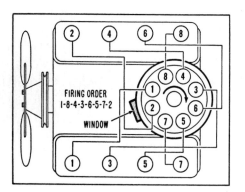

Fig. E

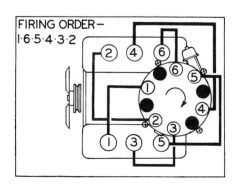

Fig. F

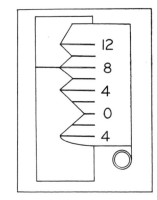

Fig. G

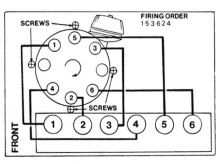

Fig. H

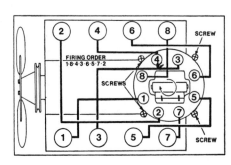

Fig. I

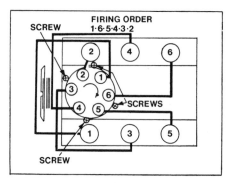

Fig. J

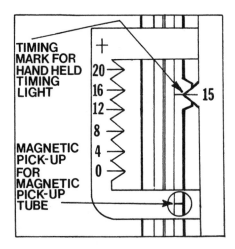

Fig. K

Chevrolet Chevette

SERIAL NUMBER LOCATION

On top of instrument panel, left front.

ENGINE NUMBER LOCATION

On pad at right side of cylinder block, below No. 1 spark plug.

ENGINE IDENTIFICATION CODE

Engines are identified in the following table by the code letter or letters immediately following the engine serial number.

Year	Engine	Code	Year	Engine	Code	Year	Engine	Code
1976	4-85	CDD, CDS, CDT		4-97	CNR, CNS, CNT		4-97	ZTT, ZTU, ZTW
	4-85	CDU, CVA, CVB		4-97	CNU		4-97	ZTX
	4-97	CNA, CNB, CYC		4-97	CYC, CYD, CYF	1979	4-97	DBA, DBB, DBC
	4-97	CYD, CYJ, CYK		4-97	CYH, CYY, CYZ		4-97	DBD, DBF, DBH
	4-97	CYW, CYX	1978	4-97	CYA, CYB, CYJ		4-97	DBJ, DBK, DBL
1977	4-85	CDS, CVA, CVB		4-97	CYK, CYL, CYM		4-97	DBM, DBR, DBS
	4-97	CNA, CNB, CNC		4-97	CYR, CYS, CYT		4-97	DBT, DBU, DBW
	4-97	CND, CNF, CNH		4-97	CYU, CYW, CYX		4-97	DBX, DBY, DBZ
							4-97	DSA, DSB

TUNE UP SPECIFICATIONS

The following specifications are published from the latest information available. This data should be used only in the absence of a decal affixed in the engine compartment.

★When using a timing light, disconnect vacuum hose or tube at distributor and plug opening in hose or tube so idle speed will not be affected.

●When checking compression, lowest cylinder must be within 80 percent of highest.

▲Before removing wires from distributor cap, determine location of the No. 1 wire in cap, as distributor position may have been altered from that shown at the end of this chart.

Year/Engine	Spark Plug		Distributor		Ignition Timing★			Carb. Adjustments	
	Type	Gap Inch	Point Gap Inch	Dwell Angle Deg.	Firing Order Fig. ▲	Timing BTDC ①	Mark Fig.	Hot Idle Speed	
								Std. Trans.	Auto. Trans.②
1976									
4-85	R43TS	.035 (.889 mm.)	—	—	A	10°	B	④	⑤
4-97.6	R43TS	.035 (.889 mm.)	—	—	A	③	B	④	⑥
1977									
4-85	R43TS	.035 (.889 mm.)	—	—	A	12°	B	800	800D
4-97.6	R43TS	.035 (.889 mm.)	—	—	A	8°⑦	B	800	⑧
1978									
4-97.6	R43TS	.035 (.889 mm.)	—	—	A	8°⑦	B	800	⑧
1979									
4-97.6		.035 (.889 mm.)	—	—	A		B		

Continued

TUNE UP NOTES

①—BTDC—Before top dead center.
②—D—Drive.
③—Man. trans., 8° BTDC; auto. trans., 10° BTDC.
④—All with solenoid energized—exc. Calif., 800 RPM; Calif., 1000 RPM. With solenoid de-energized—600 RPM.
⑤—All with solenoid energized—except Calif.: less A/C 800D RPM, with A/C 950D RPM; Calif.: 850D RPM. With solenoid de-energized —except Calif.: less A/C 700D RPM, with A/C 800D RPM; Calif.: 600D RPM.

⑥—All with solenoid energized—except Calif.: less A/C 800D RPM, with A/C 950D RPM; Calif.: less A/C 850D RPM, with A/C 950D RPM. With solenoid de-energized—except Calif.: less A/C 700D RPM, with A/C 800D RPM; Calif.: less A/C 600D RPM, with A/C 850D RPM.
⑦—At 800 RPM.
⑧—With A/C, 950D RPM; less A/C, 800D. RPM

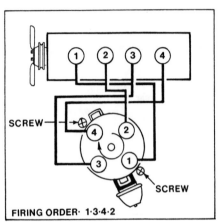

SCREW

SCREW

FIRING ORDER· 1·3·4·2

Fig. A

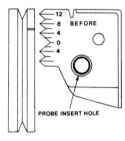

12
8
4
0
4

BEFORE

PROBE INSERT HOLE

Fig. B

Monza • Skyhawk • Starfire • Sunbird

SERIAL NUMBER LOCATION

On top of instrument panel, left front.

ENGINE NUMBER LOCATION

4-140 Cyl: On pad at right side of cylinder block, above starter.

4-151: On pad at right front side by distributor shaft hole. V6 & V8: Pad at front righthand side of cylinder block.

ENGINE IDENTIFICATION CODE

4-140 and Chevrolet V8 engines are identified by the code letters immediately following the engine number. 4-151 engines are identified by the code letters on the pad. V6-231 engines are identified by the code letters immediately preceding the engine number.

Monza

1975
4-140 . . . . CAM, CAR, CAS
4-140 . . . . CAT, CBB, CBC
V8-262 Std. Tr. . . . . CZA, CZB, CZC
V8-262 Std. Tr. . . . . . . CZD, CZT, CZU
V8-262 Auto. Tr. . . . . CZE, CZG
V8-262 Auto. Tr. . . . . . CGA, CGJ, CGK
V8-350 . . . . CHY
4-122 . . . . ZCA

1976
4-140 . . . . CAY, CAZ, CBK, CBL
4-140 . . . . CBS, CBT, CBU, CBW
4-140 . . . . CBX, CBY, CBZ
V8-262 . . . . . CGA, CGB, CGL, CZU, CZT
4-140 . . . . CAA, CAB

1977
4-140 . . . . CAY, CAZ, CBK, CBL
4-140 . . . . CBS, CBT, CBU, CBW
4-140 . . . . CBX, CBY, CBZ
V8-305 . . . . CPK, CPL, CPU, CPX
V8-305 . . . . CRC, CRD

1978
4-151 . . . . WB, WD, WH
4-151 . . . . XL, XN
4-151 . . . . AC, AD
4-151 . . . . ZA, ZB, ZC, ZD, ZF
4-151 . . . . ZH, ZJ, ZK, ZL, ZN
V6-196 . . . . PC, PD
V6-231 . . . . OC, OD, OE, OF
V8-305 . . . . . . CTA, CTB, CTC, CTD, CTF

1979
4-151 . . . . AB, AC, AD, AF, AM
4-151 . . . . WD, WJ, XJ, XK
4-151 . . . . ZA, ZB, ZP, ZR
V6-196 . . . . FC, FD
V6-231 . . . . NA, NB, NC, NF
V8-305 . . . . DNA, DNB, DNC, DND
V8-305 . . . . DTK, DTL

Skyhawk

1975
V6-231 . . . . AD

1976
V6-231 Std. Tr.① . . . . FH
V6-231 Std. Tr.② . . . . FO
V6-231 Auto. Tr.① . . . . FI
V6-231 Auto. Tr.② . . . . FJ

1977
V6-231 . . . . SA, SB, SD
V6-231 . . . . SO, SX, SY

1978
V6-231 . . . . OA, OB, OC
V6-231 . . . . OD, OE, OF
V6-231 . . . . OG

Starfire

1975
V6-231 Std. Tr.① . . . . FP
V6-231 Auto. Tr.① . . . . FR
V6-231 Auto. Tr.② . . . . FS

1976
4-140 Std. Tr.① . . . . BS
4-140 Std. Tr.② . . . . BK
4-140 Auto. Tr.① . . . . BT
4-140 Auto. Tr.② . . . . BL

1977
4-140 Std. Tr.① . . . . CAY, CBS
4-140 Std. Tr.② . . . . CAZ, CBK
4-140 Auto. Tr.① . . . . CBT
4-140 Auto. Tr.① . . . . CBL
4-140 Auto. Tr.③ . . . . CBS
4-140 Auto. Tr.③ . . . . CBT
V6-231 Std. Tr.① . . . . SA
V6-231 Std. Tr.② . . . . SB
V6-231 Auto. Tr.① . . . . SD, SW
V6-231 Auto. Tr.② . . . . SE, SY
V6-231 Auto. Tr.③ . . . . SF
V6-231 Std. Tr.① . . . . FH
V6-231 Std. Tr.② . . . . FO
V6-231 Auto. Tr.① . . . . FI
V6-231 Auto. Tr.② . . . . FJ
V6-231 . . . . SQ, SR
V8-305 Auto. Trans.① . . . . CRL
V8-305 Auto. Trans.② . . . . . . CRM, CRS
V8-305 Auto. Trans.③ . . . . CRT
V8-305 . . . . CPX, CPY

1978
4-151 Auto. Trans.① . . . . XL, XN
4-151 Man. Trans.① . . . . WD, WH
4-151 Auto. Trans.② . . . . ZK, ZJ
4-151 . . . . WB, ZA, ZB
V6-231 Man. Trans.① . . . . OA
V6-231 Auto. Trans.① . . . . ED, OB
V6-231 Man. Trans.② . . . . OD
V6-231 Man. Trans.③ . . . . OE
V6-231 Man. Trans.③ . . . . OF
V6-231 Auto. Trans.③ . . . . OC
V6-231 . . . . OH
V8-305 Man. Trans.① . . . . CTA
V8-305 Auto. Trans.① . . . . CTB
V8-305 Auto. Trans.② . . . . CTF
V8-305 Auto. Trans.③ . . . . CTD

1979
4-151 Auto. Trans.① . . . . XJ, XK
4-151 Man. Trans.① . . . . WJ, WM
4-151 Auto. Trans.② . . . . ZP, ZR
4-151 Man. Trans.② . . . . AF, AH
V6-231 Auto. Trans.① . . . . NB, NM
V6-231 Auto. Trans.① . . . . NH
V6-231 Man. Trans.① . . . . NA
V6-231 Man. Trans.② . . . . NC
V6-231 Auto. Trans.② . . . . NE
V8-305 Auto. Trans.① . . . . DTL
V8-305 Man. Trans.① . . . . DTK
V8-305 Auto. Trans.② . . . . DND

Sunbird

1976
4-140 Std. Tr.① . . . . AY, BH, BS
4-140 Std. Tr.① . . . . BW, BX, BZ
4-140 Std. Tr.② . . . . AZ, BK, BY

4-140 Auto. Tr.① . . . . BJ, BT, BU
4-140 Auto. Tr.② . . . . BL
V6-231 Std. Tr.① . . . . FH
V6-231 Std. Tr.② . . . . FC, FO
V6-231 Auto. Tr.① . . . . FI
V6-231 Auto. Tr.② . . . . FJ

1977
4-140 Std. Tr.① . . . . CAY, CBS, CBZ
4-140 Std. Tr.② . . . . CAZ, CBK, CBV
4-140 Std. Tr.③ . . . . CBS, CBZ
4-140 Auto. Tr.①③ . . . . CBT
4-140 . . . . CAK, CBL, CBU
4-140 . . . . CBW, CBX, CBY
4-151 Std. Tr.① . . . . WC, WD
4-151 Auto. Tr.① . . . . YL, YM
4-151 Auto. Tr.② . . . . ZH, ZJ
4-151 . . . . ZD, ZF, ZN, ZP
V6-231 Std. Tr.① . . . . SA
V6-231 Std. Tr.③ . . . . SB
V6-231 Auto. Tr.① . . . . SD
V6-231 Auto. Tr.② . . . . SY
V6-231 Auto. Tr.③ . . . . SX
V6-231 . . . . SO

1978
4-151 Man. Trans.① . . . . . WB, WD, WH
4-151 Auto. Trans.① . . . . XN, XL
4-151 Auto. Trans.② . . . . ZJ, ZK
4-151 . . . . AC, AD
4-151 . . . . ZA, ZB, ZC, ZD
4-151 . . . . ZH, ZF, ZL, ZN
V6-231 Auto. Trans.① . . . . ED
V6-231 Man. Trans.① . . . . OA
V6-231 Auto. Trans.② . . . . . . EK, EL, EE,
OE, EG
V6-231 Man. Trans.② . . . . OD
V6-231 Man. Trans.③ . . . . OC
V6-231 Man. Trans.③ . . . . OF
V6-231 . . . . OE, OB

1979
4-151 Man. Trans.④ . . . . WJ, WM
4-151 Man. Trans.④ . . . . AF, AH
4-151 Auto. Trans.④ . . . . XJ, XK
4-151 Auto. Trans.② . . . . ZP, ZR
V6-231 Man. Trans.④ . . . . . NA, NG, RA
V6-231 Man. Trans.② . . . . NC
V6-231 Auto. Trans.④ . . . NB, NJ, RB,
RC, RX
V6-231 Auto. Trans.② . . . . NH, RG,
RW, RY
V6-231 Auto. Trans.③ . . . . NE
V8-305 Man. Trans.④ . . . . . . DTK, DTM
V8-305 Auto. Trans.④ . . . . DNJ, DTL
V8-305 Auto. Trans.② . . . . DND

①—Except California.
②—California.
③—High altitude.
④—Exc. High altitude & Calif.

Continued

Monza • Skyhawk • Starfire • Sunbird

TUNE UP SPECIFICATIONS

The following specifications are published from the latest information available. This data should be used only in the absence of a decal affixed in the engine compartment.

★When using a timing light, disconnect vacuum hose or tube at distributor and plug opening in hose or tube so idle speed will not be affected.

●When checking compression, lowest cylinder must be within 80 percent of highest.

▲Before removing wires from distributor cap, determine location of No. 1 wire in cap, as distributor position may have been altered from that shown at the end of this chart.

| Year /Engine | Spark Plug | | Distributor | | Ignition Timing★ | | | Carb. Adjustments | |
| | Type | Gap Inch | Point Gap Inch | Dwell Angle Deg. | Firing Order Fig. ▲ | Timing BTDC ① | Mark Fig. | Hot Idle Speed ② | |
								Std. Trans.	Auto. Trans.
1975									
4-140	R43TSX④	.060	—	—	A	③	B	700	750
V6-231	R44SX	.060	—	—	C	12°	D	800	650
V8-262	R44TX	.060	—	—	E	8°	F	800	600
V8-350	R44TX	.060	—	—	E	6°	G	800	600
1976									
4-140 1 Bar. Carb.	R43TS	.035	—	—	A	⑦	B	⑧	750
4-140 2 Bar. Carb.⑤	R43TS	.035	—	—	A	⑨	B	700	750
4-140 2 Bar. Carb.⑥	R43TS	.035	—	—	A	⑨	B	⑩	750
V6-231	R44SX	.060	—	—	C	12°	D㉕	800	600
V8-262	R45TS	.045	—	—	E	8°	F	800	600
V8-305	R45TS	.045	—	—	E	⑪	G	—	600
1977									
4-140⑫	R43TS	.035	—	—	A	⑬	B	700/1250	650/850
4-140⑥	R43TS	.035	—	—	A	⑰	B	800/1250	650/850
4-140⑱	R43TS	.035	—	—	A	⑬	B	800/1250	700/850
4-151⑤	R44TSX	.060	—	—	H	14°	I	500/1200	650/850
4-151⑥	R44TSX	.060	—	—	H	12°	I	500/1000㉐	500/650㉐
V6-231⑭	R46TS	.040	—	—	J	12°	K㉕	800	600/670
V6-231⑯	R46TSX	.060	—	—	L	15°	M㉕	—	600/670
V8-305	R43TS	.035	—	—	E	㉒	G	700	500/650㉓
1978									
4-151	R44TSX	.060	—	—	H	㉔	I	1210/1000 ㉛	850/650
V6-196	R46TSX	.060	—	—	L	15°	M㉕	800	600
V6-231	R46TSX	.060	—	—	L	15°	M㉕	800	600
V8-305	R45TS	.045	—	—	E	⑱	G	700	⑲
1979									
4-151	R43TSX	.060	—	—	H	㉖	I	㉘㉙	㉗㉙
V6-196	—	—	—	—	L	—	M㉕	—	—
V6-231	R46TSX	.060	—	—	L	15°	M㉕	600/800㉐	㉙㉚
V8-305	R45TS	.045	—	—	E	4°	G	600	㉐㉑

Monza • Skyhawk • Starfire • Sunbird

TUNE UP NOTES

①—BTDC—Before Top Dead Center.
②—Idle speed on manual trans. equipped vehicles is adjusted in Neutral and on auto. trans. equipped vehicles is adjusted in Drive unless otherwise specified. Where two speeds are listed, the higher speed is with A/C solenoid energized.
③—Standard trans. 10°, Automatic trans. 12°.
④—If cold weather starting problems are encountered, use R43TS spark plug, gapped at .035 inch.
⑤—Exc. Calif.
⑥—California.
⑦—Man. trans., 10° BTDC; auto. trans., 8° BTDC.
⑧—Monza, 1200 RPM; Sunbird, 700 RPM.
⑨—Monza & Starfire man. trans., 10° BTDC; auto. trans. 12° BTDC. Sunbird man. trans., 8° BTDC; auto. trans., 10° BTDC.
⑩—Monza & Starfire; 1000 RPM; Sunbird, 700 RPM.
⑪—Except Calif., 8° BTDC; Calif., TDC.
⑫—Except high altitude & California engines.
⑬—Man. trans., TDC; auto. trans., 2° BTDC.
⑭—Exc. Even fire engine.
⑮—High altitude engine.
⑯—Even fire engine.

⑰—Man. trans., 2° ATDC; auto trans. TDC.
⑱—Exc. Calif. & High Altitude, 4°; Calif. 6°; High Altitude, 8°.
⑲—Manual trans., 600 R.P.M.; Auto. trans. Exc. High altitude, 500 RPM & High altitude, 600 RPM.
⑳—Higher speed is with idle solenoid energized.
㉑—Exc. Calif., Less A/C 500, with A/C 550/600. Calif. 600/650.
㉒—Except Calif., 8° BTDC; Calif., 6° BTDC.
㉓—High altitude, 600/700.
㉔—Auto. Trans. 12°; Man. trans. 14°.
㉕—The harmonic balancer on these engines has two timing marks. The mark measuring 1/16 inch is used when setting timing with a hand held timing light. The mark measuring 1/8 inch is used when setting timing with magnetic timing equipment.
㉖—Exc. Calif., 12° BTDC; Calif. 14° BTDC.
㉗—Less A/C, 500/650 see note ⑳; with A/C, 650/850.
㉘—Less A/C, 500/900 see note ⑳; with A/C, 950/1200.
㉙—A/C "on", clutch wires disconnected.
㉚—Exc. Calif. & High altitude, Less A/C 550, with A/C 550/670; Calif. & High altitude, 600 Drive.
㉛—California models less A/C 500/1000 see ⑳.

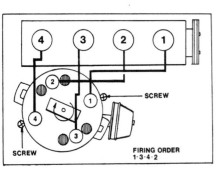

Fig. A

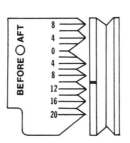

Fig. B

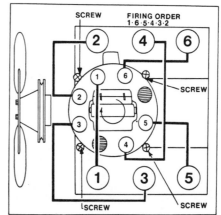

Fig. C

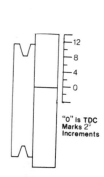

Fig. D

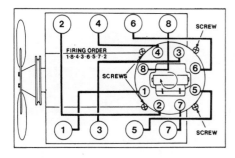

Fig. E

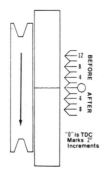

Fig. F

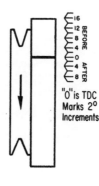

Fig. G

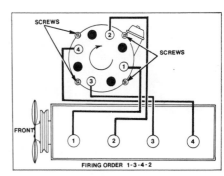

Fig. H

Continued

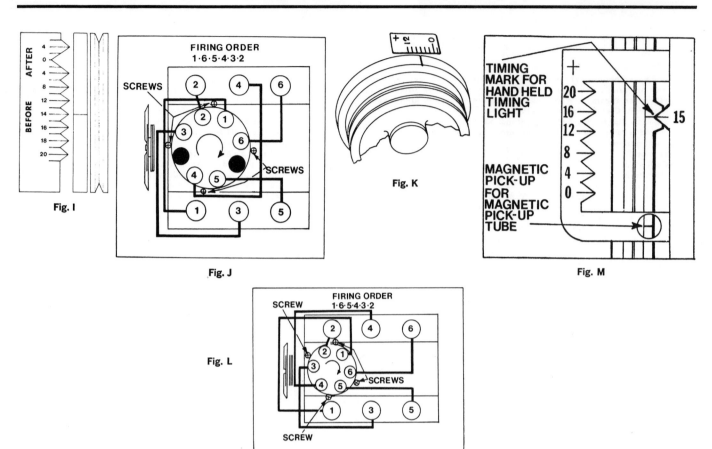

AFTER
BEFORE
4
0
4
8
12
14
16
18
20

Fig. I

FIRING ORDER
1·6·5·4·3·2
SCREWS
SCREWS

Fig. J

Fig. K

TIMING MARK FOR HAND HELD TIMING LIGHT
MAGNETIC PICK-UP FOR MAGNETIC PICK-UP TUBE
20
16
12
8
4
0
15

Fig. M

FIRING ORDER
1·6·5·4·3·2
SCREW
SCREWS
SCREW

Fig. L

Chevrolet Vega • Pontiac Astre

SERIAL NUMBER LOCATION

On top of instrument panel, left front.

ENGINE NUMBER LOCATION

4-140, On pad at right side of cylinder block below No. 3 spark plug at cylinder head parting line.
4-151, On distributor mounting pad.

ENGINE IDENTIFICATION CODE

Engines are identified in the following table by the code letter or letters immediately following the engine serial number.

Code		Code		Code	
CAB with T.H. 350, W/E.E.C.	1974	CAZ 4-140	1976	CBK 4-140	1977
CAA with M/T, W/E.E.C.	1974	CBK 4-140	1976	CBL 4-140	1977
CAH with T.H. 350, W/E.E.C.	1974	CBL 4-140	1976	CBS 4-140	1977
CAJ with M/T, W/E.E.C.	1974	CBS 4-140	1976	CBT 4-140	1977
CAC with T.H. 350, W/E.E.C.	1974	CBT 4-140	1976	CBU 4-140	1977
CAD with M/T, W/E.E.C.	1974	CBU 4-140	1976	CBV 4-140	1977
CAK with T.H. 350, W/E.E.C.	1974	CBW 4-140	1976	CBW 4-140	1977
CAL with M/T, W/E.E.C.	1974	CBX 4-140	1976	CBX 4-140	1977
CAM 4-140	1975	CBY 4-140	1976	CBY 4-140	1977
CAR 4-140	1975	CBZ 4-140	1976	CBZ 4-140	1977
CAS 4-140	1975	ZCB 4-122	1976	WC 4-151	1977
CAT 4-140	1975	CAA 4-140	1977	WD 4-151	1977
CBB 4-140	1975	CAB 4-140	1977	YL 4-151	1977
CBC 4-140	1975	CAC 4-140	1977	YM 4-151	1977
ZCA 4-122	1975	CAY 4-140	1977	ZH 4-151	1977
CAY 4-140	1976	CAZ 4-140	1977	ZJ 4-151	1977

M/T: Manual transmission
P/G: Powerglide
T/D: Torque drive

T/H: Turbo Hydramatic
L/E.E.C.: Less Exhaust Emission Control

W/E.E.C.: With Exhaust Emission Control

TUNE UP SPECIFICATIONS

The following specifications are published from the latest information available. This data should be used only in the absence of a decal affixed in the engine compartment.

★When using a timing light, disconnect vacuum hose or tube at distributor and plug opening in hose or tube so idle speed will not be affected.

●When checking compression, lowest cylinder must be within 80 percent of highest.

▲Before removing wires from distributor cap, determine location of the No. 1 wire in cap, as distributor position may have been altered from that shown at the end of this chart.

Year/ Engine	Spark Plug		Distributor		Ignition Timing★			Carb. Adjustments	
	Type	Gap Inch	Point Gap Inch	Dwell Angle Deg.	Firing Order Fig. ▲	Timing BTDC ①	Mark Fig.	Hot Idle Speed ②	
								Std. Trans.	Auto. Trans.
1974									
75 Horsepower	R42TS	.035	③	31–34	A	⑪	B	700/1000⑥	550/750⑥
85 Horsepower	R42TS	.035	③	31–34	A	⑪	B	700/1200⑥	500/750⑥
1975									
78 Horsepower	R43TSX	.060	—	—	C	⑬	D	700/1200⑥	550/750⑥
87 Horsepower	R43TSX⑭	.060	—	—	C	⑪	D	⑦	600/750⑥
Cosworth Vega	R43LTSX	.060	—	—	E	12°⑮	F	600	—

TUNE UP SPECIFICATIONS—Continued

Year /Engine	Spark Plug		Distributor		Ignition Timing★			Carb. Adjustments	
	Type	Gap Inch	Point Gap Inch	Dwell Angle Deg.	Firing Order Fig. ▲	Timing BTDC ①	Mark Fig.	Hot Idle Speed ②	
								Std. Trans.	Auto. Trans.
1976									
1 Bar. Carb.⑩	R43TS	.035	—	—	C	⑬	D	750/1200⑤	550/750⑤
2 Bar. Carb.⑩	R43TS	.035	—	—	C	⑰	D	700/1200⑤	600/750⑤
2 Bar. Carb.⑫	R43TS	.035	—	—	C	⑰	D	700/1000⑤	600/750⑤
Cosworth Vega	R43LTS	.035	—	—	E	12°⑮	F	600	—
1977									
4-140⑱	R43TS	.035	—	—	C	⑲	D	700/1250	650/850
4-140⑫	R43TS	.035	—	—	C	⑳	D	800/1250	650/850
4-140④	R43TS	.035	—	—	C	⑲	D	800/1250	700/850
4-151⑯	R44TSX	.060	—	—	G	⑧	H	500/1000⑤	500/650⑤
4-151⑥	R44TSX	.060	—	—	G	⑧	H	500/1200	650/850

①—BTDC—Before top dead center.
②—Idle speed on manual trans. equipped vehicles is adjusted in Neutral and on auto. trans. equipped vehicles is adjusted in Drive unless otherwise specified. Where two speeds are listed, the higher speed is with A/C solenoid energized.
③—New points .019", used .016".
④—High altitude.
⑤—Higher speed is with idle solenoid energized.
⑥—With air conditioning.
⑦—Exc. Calif., 700; Calif., 700/1200⑤.
⑧—Except Calif., 14° BTDC; Calif., 12° BTDC.
⑩—Exc. California.

⑪—Synchromesh trans. 10° BTDC; automatic trans. 12° BTDC.
⑫—California.
⑬—Synchromesh trans. 8° BTDC, automatic trans. 10° BTDC.
⑭—If cold weather starting problems are encountered, use R43TS spark plug, gapped at .035 inch.
⑮—At 1600 RPM.
⑯—Less air conditioning.
⑰—Astre man. trans., 8° BTDC; auto. trans., 10° BTDC. Vega man. trans., 10° BTDC; auto. trans., 12° BTDC.
⑱—Except California & high altitude.
⑲—Man. trans., TDC; auto. trans., 2° BTDC.
⑳—Man. trans., 2° ATDC; auto. trans., TDC.

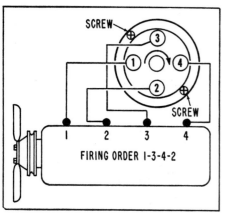

Fig. A

Fig. B

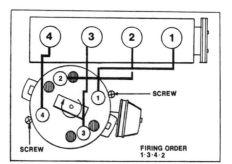

Fig. C

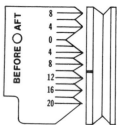

Fig. D

Chevrolet Vega · Pontiac Astre

TUNE UP NOTES—Continued

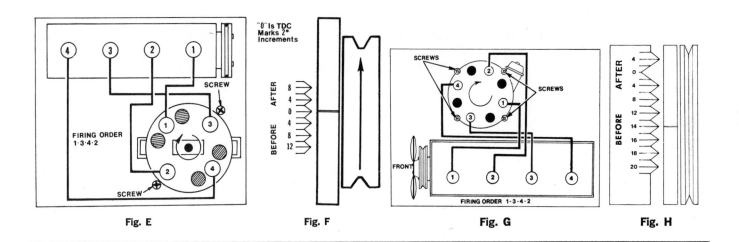

Fig. E   Fig. F   Fig. G   Fig. H

Chrysler • Dodge • Imperial • Plymouth

VEHICLE NUMBER LOCATION

1974-79: ON PLATE ATTACHED TO DASH PAD AND VISIBLE THROUGH WINDSHIELD.

ENGINE NUMBER LOCATION

1974-79 Six: Right front of block below cylinder head.
1974-78 318, 360: Left front of block below cylinder head.

1974-79 V8-400, 1974-75 V8-440: Upper right front of cylinder block.
1976-79 V8-440: Top of block left bank next to front tappet rail.

ENGINE IDENTIFICATION CODE

1974-79 engines are identified by the cubic inch displacement found within the engine number stamped on the pad.

TUNE UP SPECIFICATIONS

The following specifications are published from the latest information available. This
data should be used only in the absence of a decal affixed in the engine compartment.

★When using a timing light, disconnect vacuum hose or tube at distributor and plug opening in hose or tube so idle speed will not be affected.

●When checking compression, lowest cylinder must be within 80 percent of highest.

▲Before removing wires from distributor cap, determine location of the No. 1 wire in cap, as distributor position may have been altered from that shown at the end of this chart.

Year/Engine	Spark Plug		Distributor		Ignition Timing★			Carb. Adjustments	
	Type ⑦	Gap Inch	Point Gap Inch	Dwell Angle Deg.	Firing Order Fig. ▲	Timing BTDC ①	Mark Fig.	Hot Idle Speed	
								Std. Trans.	Auto. Trans. ②
CHRYSLER & IMPERIAL **1974**									
V8-400 ㉑	J13Y	.035	—	—	J	⑨	F	—	750
V8-400 ④ ㉔	J13Y	.035	—	—	J	5°	F	—	750
V8-400 ④ ㉖	J13Y	.035	—	—	J	5°	F	—	750
V8-440 ㉔	J11Y	.035	—	—	J	10°	F	—	750
V8-440 ㉖	J11Y	.035	—	—	J	5°	F	—	750
1975									
V8-318 ⑤	N13Y	.035	—	—	H	⑭	B	—	750N
V8-318 ⑧	N13Y	.035	—	—	H	2° ⑮	B	—	900N
V8-360	N12Y	.035	—	—	H	6°	B	—	750N
V8-400 ㉑	J13Y	.035	—	—	J	10°	F	—	750N
V8-400 ④	J13Y	.035	—	—	J	8°	F	—	750N
V8-400 ㉒	RJ87P	.035	—	—	J	6°	F	—	850N
V8-440	RJ87P	.040	—	—	J	6°	D	—	750N
1976									
V8-318 ⑤	RN12Y	.035	—	—	H	㊱	B	—	750
V8-318 ⑧	RN12Y	.035	—	—	H	2° ⑮	B	—	900
V8-360 ㉑	RN12Y	.035	—	—	H	6°	B	—	700
V8-360 ④	RN12Y	.035	—	—	H	6°	B	—	750
V8-400 ㉑	RJ13Y	.035	—	—	J	10°	F	—	700
V8-400 ④ ㉔	㊳	.035	—	—	J	6°	F	—	850
V8-400 ④ ㉖	RJ13Y	.035	—	—	J	8°	F	—	750
V8-440	RJ13Y	.035	—	—	J	8°	D	—	750

TUNE UP SPECIFICATIONS—Continued

The following specifications are published from the latest information available. This data should be used only in the absence of a decal affixed in the engine compartment.

★When using a timing light, disconnect vacuum hose or tube at distributor and plug opening in hose or tube so idle speed will not be affected.

●When checking compression, lowest cylinder must be within 80 percent of highest.

▲Before removing wires from distributor cap, determine location of the No. 1 wire in cap, as distributor position may have been altered from that shown at the end of this chart.

Year/Engine	Spark Plug Type (7)	Gap Inch	Point Gap Inch	Dwell Angle Deg.	Firing Order Fig. ▲	Timing BTDC (1)	Mark Fig.	Hot Idle Speed Std. Trans.	Auto. Trans. (2)
CHRYSLER & IMPERIAL—Continued									
1977									
V8-318	RN12Y	.035	—	—	H	(46)	B	(47)	(47)
V8-360 (21)	RN12Y	.035	—	—	H	10°	B	—	700
V8-360 (4)(48)	RN12Y	.035	—	—	H	6°	B	—	750
V8-360 (4)(49)	RJ13Y	.035	—	—	H	10°	B	—	750
V8-400 (49)	RJ13Y	.035	—	—	J	10°	F	—	750
V8-440 (48)	RJ13Y	.035	—	—	J	8°	D	—	750
V8-440 (49)	RJ13Y	.035	—	—	J	(50)	D	—	750
1978									
6-225 (42)	RBL16Y	.035	—	—	G	(50)	K	750	750
6-225 (21)	RBL16Y	.035	—	—	G	12°	K	750	750
V8-318 (21)	RN12Y	.035	—	—	H	16°	L	700	750
V8-318 (4)(25)	RN12Y	.035	—	—	H	10°	L	—	750
V8-360 (21)	RN12Y	.035	—	—	H	20°	L	—	750
V8-360 (4)(48)	RN12Y	.035	—	—	H	(6)	L	—	750
V8-360 (4)(49)	RN12Y	.035	—	—	H	16°	L	—	750
V8-400	(17)	.035	—	—	J	(26)	M	—	750
V8-440	(17)	.035	—	—	J	(27)	L	—	750
1979									
6-225 (42)	4091678	.035	—	—	G	(51)	K		(52)
6-225 (21)	4091678	.035	—	—	G	12°	K	—	725
V8-318 (21)	3874490	.035	—	—	H	16°	L	—	730
V8-318 (4)	3874490	.035	—	—	H	16°	L	—	750
V8-360 (21)	3874490	.035	—	—	H	12°	L	—	750
V8-360 (4)	3874490	.035	—	—	H	16°	L	—	750
DODGE									
1974									
6-198	N14Y	.035	—	—	G	2½°	C	800	750
6-225	N14Y	.035	—	—	G	TDC	C	800	750
V8-318	N13Y	.035	—	—	H	TDC	E	750	750
V8-360	N12Y	.035	—	—	H	5°(11)	E	850	850
V8-400 Auto. Trans. (21)	J13Y	.035	—	—	J	(9)	F	—	750
V8-400 Auto. Trans. (4)	J13Y	.035	—	—	J	5°	F	—	750
V8-400 Std. Trans. (22)	J11Y	.035	—	—	J	5°	F	900	—
V8-400 Auto. Trans. (16)	J11Y	.035	—	—	J	5°(13)	F	—	850
V8-440	J11Y	.035	—	—	J	(35)	F	—	850

Continued

TUNE UP SPECIFICATIONS—Continued

Year/Engine	Spark Plug		Distributor		Ignition Timing★			Carb. Adjustments	
	Type (7)	Gap Inch	Point Gap Inch	Dwell Angle Deg.	Firing Order Fig. ▲	Timing BTDC (1)	Mark Fig.	Hot Idle Speed	
								Std. Trans.	Auto. Trans. (2)
DODGE—Continued									
1975									
6-225	BL13Y	.035	—	—	G	TDC	A	800	750N
V8-318(5)	N13Y	.035	—	—	H	(14)	B	750	750N
V8-318	N13Y	.035	—	—	H	2°(15)	B	—	900N
V8-360	N12Y	.035	—	—	H	6°	B	—	750N
V8-360(22)	N12Y	.035	—	—	H	2°	B	—	850N
V8-400(21)	J13Y	.035	—	—	J	10°	F	—	750N
V8-400(4)	J13Y	.035	—	—	J	8°	F	—	750N
V8-400(22)	RJ87P	.035	—	—	J	6°	F	—	850N
V8-440	RJ87P	.040	—	—	J	6°	D	—	750N
V8-440(22)	J11Y	.035	—	—	J	10°	D	—	750N
1976									
6-225 Std. Tr.(23)	RBL13Y	.035	—	—	G	(39)	A	750(30)	—
6-225 Auto. Tr.(23)	RBL13Y	.035	—	—	G	2°	A	—	750
6-225(41)	RBL13Y	.035	—	—	G	12°	A	750(30)	750
V8-318(5)	RN12Y	.035	—	—	H	(36)	B	750	750
V8-318(6)	RN12Y	.035	—	—	H	2°(15)	B	—	900
V8-360(21)	RN12Y	.035	—	—	H	6°	B	—	700
V8-360(4)	RN12Y	.035	—	—	H	6°	B	—	750
V8-360(22)	RN12Y	.035	—	—	H	2°	B	—	850
V8-400(21)	RJ13Y	.035	—	—	J	10°	F	—	700
V8-400(4)(24)	(38)	.035	—	—	J	6°	F	—	850
V8-400(4)(25)	RJ13Y	.035	—	—	J	8°	F	—	750
V8-440	RJ13Y	.035	—	—	J	8°	D	—	750
V8-440(22)	RJ11Y	.035	—	—	J	(40)	D	—	750
1977									
6-225(42)(43)	RBL15Y	.035	—	—	G	(50)	A	(44)	(44)
6-225(42)(45)	RBL15Y	.035	—	—	G	(29)	A	(24)	(44)
6-225(21)	RBL15Y	.035	—	—	G	(30)	A	750(29)	750(29)
V8-318	RN12Y	.035	—	—	H	(46)	B	(47)	(47)
V8-360(21)	RN12Y	.035	—	—	H	10°	B	—	700
V8-360(4)(48)	RN12Y	.035	—	—	H	6°	B	—	750
V8-360(4)(49)	RJ13Y	.035	—	—	H	10°	B	—	750
V8-400(49)	RJ13Y	.035	—	—	J	10°	F	—	750
V8-440(48)	RJ13Y	.035	—	—	J	8°	D	—	750
V8-440(49)	RJ13Y	.035	—	—	J	(50)	D	—	750
V8-440(2)(49)	RJ11Y	.035	—	—	J	8°	D	—	750
1978									
6-225(42)	RBL16Y	.035	—	—	G	(50)	K	(44)	(44)
6-225(21)	RBL16Y	.035	—	—	G	12°	K	750	750
V8-318(21)	RN12Y	.035	—	—	H	16°	L	700	750
V8-318(4)(25)	RN12Y	.035	—	—	H	10°	L	—	750
V8-360(21)	RN12Y	.035	—	—	H	20°	L	—	750
V8-360(4)(48)	RN12Y	.035	—	—	H	(6)	L	—	750
V8-360(4)(49)	RN12Y	.035	—	—	H	16°	L	—	750
V8-400	(17)	.035	—	—	J	(26)	M	—	750
V8-440	(17)	.035	—	—	J	(28)	L	—	750

TUNE UP SPECIFICATIONS—Continued

The following specifications are published from the latest information available. This data should be used only in the absence of a decal affixed in the engine compartment.

★When using a timing light, disconnet vacuum hose or tube at distribtor and plug opening in hose or tube so idle speed will not be affected.

●When checking compression, lowest cylinder must be within 80 percent of highest.

▲Before removing wires from distributor cap, determine location of the No. 1 wire in cap, as distributor position may have been altered from that shown at the end of this chart.

| Year/Engine | Spark Plug | | Distributor | | Ignition Timing★ | | | Carb. Adjustments | |
| | Type ⑦ | Gap Inch | Point Gap Inch | Dwell Angle Deg. | Firing Order Fig. ▲ | Timing BTDC ① | Mark Fig. | Hot Idle Speed | |
								Std. Trans.	Auto. Trans. ②
DODGE—Continued									
1979									
6-225 ⑫	4091678	.035	—	—	G	⑤①	K	⑤②	⑤②
6-225 ㉑	4091678	.035	—	—	G	12°	K	—	725
V8-318 ㉑	3874490	.035	—	—	H	16°	L	—	730
V8-318 ④	3874490	.035	—	—	H	16°	L	—	750
V8-360 ㉑	3874490	.035	—	—	H	12°	L	—	750
V8-360 ④	3874490	.035	—	—	H	16°	L	—	750
PLYMOUTH									
1974									
6-198	N14Y	.035	—	—	G	2½°	C	800	750
6-225	N14Y	.035	—	—	G	TDC	C	800	750
V8-318	N13Y	.035	—	—	H	TDC	E	750	750
V8-360	N12Y	.035	—	—	H	5° ⑪	E	850	850
V8-400 Auto. Trans. ㉑	J13Y	.035	—	—	J	⑨	F	—	750
V8-400 Auto. Trans. ④	J13Y	.035	—	—	J	5°	F	—	750
V8-400 Std. Trans. ㉒	J11Y	.035	—	—	J	5°	F	900	—
V8-400 Auto. Trans. ⑯	J11Y	.035	—	—	J	5° ⑬	F	—	850
V8-440	J11Y	.035	—	—	J	㉟	F	—	850
1975									
6-225	BL13Y	.035	—	—	G	TDC	A	800	750N
V8-318 ⑤	N13Y	.035	—	—	H	⑭	B	750	750N
V8-318	N13Y	.035	—	—	H	2° ⑮	B	—	900N
V8-360	N12Y	.035	—	—	H	6°	B	—	750N
V8-360 ㉒	N12Y	.035	—	—	H	2°	B	—	850N
V8-400 ㉑	J13Y	.035	—	—	J	10°	F	—	750N
V8-400 ④	J13Y	.035	—	—	J	8°	F	—	750N
V8-400 ㉒	RJ87P	.035	—	—	J	6°	F	—	850N
V8-440	RJ87P	.040	—	—	J	6°	D	—	750N
V8-440 ㉒	J11Y	.035	—	—	J	10°	D	—	750N
1976									
6-225 Std. Tr. ㉓	RBL13Y	.035	—	—	G	㊴	A	750 ㉚	—
6-225 Auto. Tr. ㉓	RBL13Y	.035	—	—	G	2°	A	—	750
6-225 ㊶	RBL13Y	.035	—	—	G	12°	A	750 ㉚	750
V8-318 ⑤	RN12Y	.035	—	—	H	㊱	B	750	750
V8-318 ⑧	RN12Y	.035	—	—	H	2° ⑮	B	—	900
V8-360 ㉑	RN12Y	.035	—	—	H	6°	B	—	700
V8-360 ④	RN12Y	.035	—	—	H	6°	B	—	750
V8-360 ㉒	RN12Y	.035	—	—	H	2°	B	—	850
V8-400 ㉑	RJ13Y	.035	—	—	J	10°	F	—	700
V8-400 ④㉔	㉟	.035	—	—	J	6°	F	—	850
V8-400 ④㉕	RJ13Y	.035	—	—	J	8°	F	—	750
V8-440	RJ13Y	.035	—	—	J	8°	D	—	750
V8-440 ㉒	RJ11Y	.035	—	—	J	㊵	D	—	750

Continued

Chrysler • Dodge • Imperial • Plymouth

TUNE UP SPECIFICATIONS—Continued

Year/Engine	Spark Plug Type [7]	Gap Inch	Point Gap Inch	Dwell Angle Deg.	Firing Order Fig. ▲	Timing BTDC [1]	Mark Fig.	Hot Idle Speed Std. Trans.	Hot Idle Speed Auto. Trans. [2]
PLYMOUTH—Continued									
1977									
6-225 [42][43]	RBL15Y	.035	—	—	G	[50]	A	[44]	[44]
6-225 [42][45]	RBL15Y	.035	—	—	G	[29]	A	[44]	[44]
6-225 [21]	RBL15Y	.035	—	—	G	[30]	A	750 [29]	750 [29]
V8-318	RN12Y	.035	—	—	H	[46]	B	[47]	[47]
V8-360 [21]	RN12Y	.035	—	—	H	10°	B	—	700
V8-360 [4][48]	RN12Y	.035	—	—	H	6°	B	—	750
V8-360 [4][49]	RJ13Y	.035	—	—	H	10°	B	—	750
V8-400 [49]	RJ13Y	.035	—	—	J	10°	F	—	750
V8-440 [48]	RJ13Y	.035	—	—	J	8°	D	—	750
V8-440 [49]	RJ13Y	.035	—	—	J	[50]	D	—	750
V8-440 [22][49]	RJ11Y	.035	—	—	J	8°	D	—	750
1978									
6-225 [42]	RBL16Y	.035	—	—	G	[50]	K	[44]	[44]
6-225 [21]	RBL16Y	.035	—	—	G	12°	K	750	750
V8-318 [21]	RN12Y	.035	—	—	H	16°	L	700	750
V8-318 [4][25]	RN12Y	.035	—	—	H	10°	L	—	750
V8-360 [21]	RN12Y	.035	—	—	H	20°	L	—	750
V8-360 [4][48]	RN12Y	.035	—	—	H	[6]	L	—	750
V8-360 [4][49]	RN12Y	.035	—	—	H	16°	L	—	750
V8-400	[17]	.035	—	—	J	[26]	M	—	750
V8-440	[17]	.035	—	—	J	[28]	L	—	750
1979									
6-225 [42]	4091678	.035	—	—	G	[51]	K	[52]	[52]
6-225 [21]	4091678	.035	—	—	G	12°	K	—	725
V8-318 [21]	3874490	.035	—	—	H	16°	L	—	730
V8-318 [4]	3874490	.035	—	—	H	16°	L	—	750
V8-360 [21]	3874490	.035	—	—	H	12°	L	—	750
V8-360 [4]	3874490	.035	—	—	H	16°	L	—	750

[1]—BTDC: Before top dead center.
[2]—D: Drive. N: Neutral.
[3]—Before adjusting idle "CO", disconnect air pump outlet hose and plug tube leading to exhaust manifold, if equipped.
[4]—Four barrel carburetor.
[5]—With catalytic converter.
[6]—Dist. No. 3874115, 6° BTDC. Dist. No. 3874858, 8° BTDC.
[7]—Champion.
[8]—With air pump.
[9]—Early production—Exc. sta. wag., 7½° BTDC; sta. wag., 5° BTDC. Late production—Exc. sta. wag., 10° BTDC; sta. wag., 7½° BTDC.
[10]—Dist. No. 3656780, TDC. Dist. No. 3755336, 7½°. Dist. No. 3755337 & 3755365, 5°.
[11]—Calif. V8-360 Hi Perf. Manual Trans. 2½° BTDC.
[12]—Auto. trans.
[13]—Exc. Calif. auto. trans. & Police; Calif. auto. trans. & Police, 2½°.
[14]—Except Calif., 2° BTDC; Calif.: Early production, TDC, Late production, 2° ATDC.
[15]—ATDC: after top dead center.
[16]—High performance & Police.
[17]—Exc. high performance engine, OJ13Y; high performance engine, OJ11Y.
[18]—Exc. Calif. late production; Calif. late production, TDC.
[19]—Measured ahead of catalytic converter.
[20]—Measured in tailpipe.
[21]—Two barrel carburetor.
[22]—High performance engine.
[23]—Except "Dodge Lite" and "Feather Duster".
[24]—Exc. California.
[25]—California only.
[26]—Engine code E-64, 4500 lbs. vehicle curb weight, 24° BTDC; all others, 20° BTDC.
[27]—Calif. & high altitude, 8° BTDC; Exc. Calif. & high altitude—Chrysler, 12° BTDC, Cordoba, 16° BTDC.
[28]—Exc. Calif., 16° BTDC; Calif., 8° BTDC.
[29]—Exc. high altitude & Calif.—manual trans., 6° BTDC; auto trans., 2° BTDC; high altitude & Calif., 8° BTDC.
[30]—Exc. Calif., 12° BTDC; Calif. 4° BTDC.
[31]—Std. trans.
[32]—Exc. Calif., .3 (see note 19); Calif., .5 (see note 19).
[33]—Except Calif. .3 (see note 19), Calif. .5 (see note 20).
[34]—Except Calif. .3 (see note 19), Calif. 1.5 (see note 20).
[35]—Exc. Calif., 10° BTDC; Calif., 5° BTDC.
[36]—Exc. Calif., 2° BTDC; Calif., TDC.
[37]—Exc. Calif., .3 (see note 19); Calif., 1.0 (see note 19).
[38]—Exc. high performance engine, RJ13Y; high performance engine, RJ87P.
[39]—Exc. Calif., 6° BTDC; Calif., 4° BTDC.
[40]—Exc. Calif., 10° BTDC; Calif., 8° BTDC.
[41]—"Dodge Lite" and "Feather Duster".
[42]—One barrel carb.
[43]—Aspen & Volaré.
[44]—Except high altitude & Calif., 700 RPM; high altitude & Calif., 750 RPM.
[45]—Fury & Monaco.
[46]—Exc. high altitude & Calif. engines, 8° BTDC; high altitude & Calif., TDC.
[47]—Except high altitude & Calif., 700; High Altitude & Calif., 850.
[48]—Except Electronic Lean Burn engines.
[49]—Electronic Lean Burn engines.
[50]—Except high altitude & Calif., 12° BTDC; high altitude & Calif. 8° BTDC.
[51]—Except California, 12° BTDC; California, 8° BTDC.
[52]—Except Calif., 675 RPM; Calif., 750 RPM.

TUNE UP NOTES—Continued

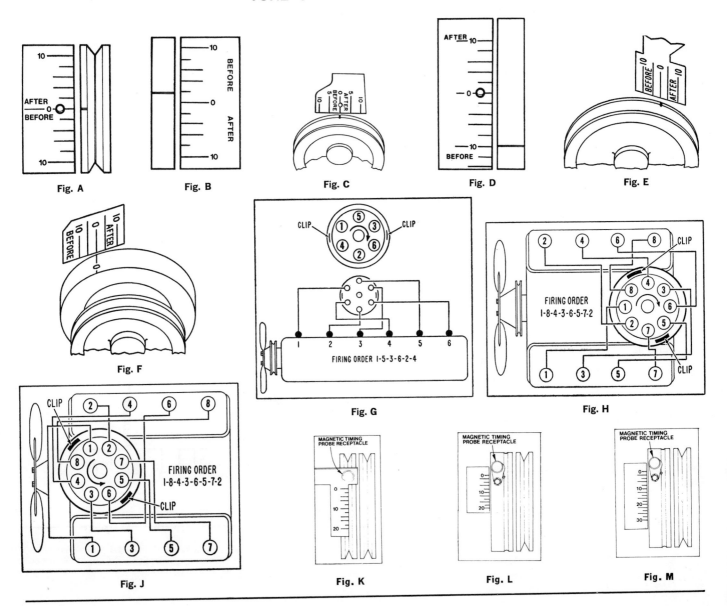

Fig. A   Fig. B   Fig. C   Fig. D   Fig. E

Fig. F   Fig. G   Fig. H

FIRING ORDER 1-5-3-6-2-4

FIRING ORDER 1-8-4-3-6-5-7-2

FIRING ORDER 1-8-4-3-6-5-7-2

Fig. J   Fig. K   Fig. L   Fig. M

MAGNETIC TIMING PROBE RECEPTACLE

Dodge Omni • Plymouth Horizon

TUNE UP SPECIFICATIONS

The following specifications are published from the latest information available. This data should be used only in the absence of a decal affixed in the engine compartment.

▲Before removing wires from distributor cap, determine location of the No. 1 wire in cap, as distributor position may have been altered from that shown at the end of this chart.

Year/Engine	Spark Plug		Distributor		Ignition Timing			Carb. Adjustments	
	Type	Gap Inch	Point Gap Inch	Dwell Angle Deg.	Firing Order Fig. ▲	Timing BTDC	Mark Fig.	Hot Idle Speed	
								Std. Trans.	Auto. Trans.
1978-79									
4-105 Man. trans.	RN-12Y	34-45	—	—	A	15°	B	900	—
4-105 Auto. trans.	RN-12Y	34-45	—	—	A	15°	C	—	900

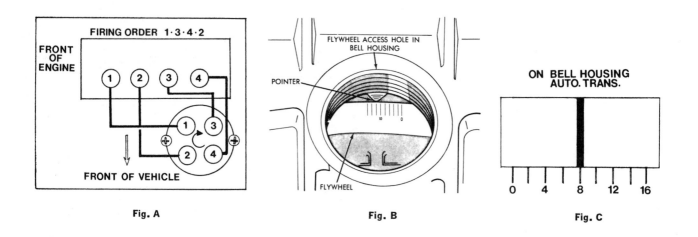

Fig. A   Fig. B   Fig. C

Ford & Mercury—Compact & Intermediate Models

ENGINE & SERIAL NUMBER LOCATION: Vehicle warranty plate on rear face of left front door.

ENGINE IDENTIFICATION: Engine code is last letter in serial number on vehicle warranty plate.

Year	Engine	Engine Code
1974	6-200	T
	6-250	L
	8-302	F
	8-351①	H
	8-351②	Q
	8-351③	R
	8-400	S
	8-460	A
	8-460④	C
1975–77	6-200	T
	6-250	L
	8-302	F

Year	Engine	Engine Code
	8-351	H
	8-400	S
	8-460	A
	8-460④	C
1978	8-400	S
1978–79	4-140	Y
	6-200	T
	6-250	L
	8-302	F
	8-351	H

①—Two barrel carburetor.
②—Four barrel carburetor.
③—High Performance.
④—Police Interceptor.

TUNE UP SPECIFICATIONS

The following specifications are published from the latest information available. This data should be used only in the absence of a decal affixed in the engine compartment.

★When using a timing light, disconnect vacuum hose or tube at distributor and plug opening in hose or tube so idle speed will not be affected.

●When checking compression, lowest cylinder must be within 75% of the highest.

▲Before removing wires from distributor cap, determine location of the No. 1 wire in cap, as distributor position may have been altered from that shown at the end of this chart.

Year/Engine	Spark Plug		Distributor		Ignition Timing ★			Carb. Adjustments	
								Hot Idle Speed	
	Type	Gap Inch	Point Gap Inch	Dwell Angle Deg.	Firing Order Fig. ▲	Timing BTDC ①	Mark Fig.	Std. Trans.	Auto. Trans.②

1974

Year/Engine	Type	Gap Inch	Point Gap Inch	Dwell Angle Deg.	Firing Order Fig.	Timing BTDC	Mark Fig.	Std. Trans.	Auto. Trans.
6-200	BRF-82	.034	.025	33	D	6°	A	750	550D
6-200⑭	BRF-82	.034	—	—	D	6°	A	750	550D
6-250	BRF-82	.034	.025	33	D	6°	A	600	600D
6-250⑭	BRF-82	.034	—	—	D	6°	A	600	600D
V8-302	BRF-42	.034	.017	26–30	E	6°	B	850	575D
V8-302⑭	BRF-42	.034	—	—	E	6°	B	850	575D
V8-351⑦㉓	BRF-42	.034	.017	26–30	F	6°	B	—	600D
V8-351⑦㉓⑭	BRF-42	.034	—	—	F	6°	B	—	600D
V8-351⑦㉒	ARF-42	.044	.017	26–30	F	10°	B	—	650D
V8-351⑦㉒⑭	ARF-42	.044	—	—	F	10°	B	—	650D
V8-351⑧	ARF-42	.034	㉑	26–31	F	⑳	B	900	800D
V8-351⑧⑭	ARF-42	.034	—	—	F	⑳	B	900	800D
V8-400⑭	ARF-42	.044	—	—	F	⑩	B	—	625D
V8-460⑭	ARF-52	.054	—	—	E	⑮	B	—	650D

Continued

TUNE UP SPECIFICATIONS—Continued

The following specifications are published from the latest information available. This data should be used only in the absence of a decal affixed in the engine compartment.

★When using a timing light, disconnect vacuum hose or tube at distributor and plug opening in tube or hose so idle speed will not be affected.

●When checking compression, lowest cylinder must be within 80 percent of highest.

▲Before removing wires from distributor cap, determine location of the No. 1 wire in cap, as distributor position may have been altered from that shown at the end of this chart.

Year/Engine	Spark Plug		Distributor		Ignition Timing★			Carb. Adjustments	
								Hot Idle Speed	
	Type	Gap Inch	Point Gap Inch	Dwell Angle Deg.	Firing Order Fig. ▲	Timing BTDC ①	Mark Fig.	Std. Trans.	Auto. Trans. ②
1975									
6-200 (14)	BRF-82	.044	—	—	D	6°	A	750	600D
6-250 (14)	BRF-82	.044	—	—	G	6°	A	750	600D
V8-302 (14)	ARF-42	.044	—	—	E	6°	B	900	650D
V8-351 (4)(14)	ARF-42	.044	—	—	F	12°	B	—	650D
V8-351 (14)(23)	ARF-42	.044	—	—	F	12°	B	—	650D
V8-400 (14)	ARF-42	.044	—	—	F	12°	B	—	650D
V8-460 (14)	ARF-52	.044	—	—	E	14°	B	—	650D
1976									
6-200 (14)	BRF-82	.044	—	—	D	6°	A	800	650D
6-250 (14)(30)	BRF-82	.044	—	—	G	(29)	A	850	600D
6-250 (14)(31)	BRF-82	.044	—	—	G	(32)	A	850	600D
V8-302 (14)(16)(33)	ARF-42	.044	—	—	E	4°	B	—	700D
V8-302 (14)(30)(33)	ARF-42	.044	—	—	E	(29)	B	750	650D
V8-302 (14)(17)(30)	ARF-42	.044	—	—	E	(18)	B	750	650D
V8-302 (14)(16)(17)(31)	ARF-42	.044	—	—	E	8°	B	—	700D
V8-351 (14)(23)	ARF-42	.044	—	—	F	10°	B	—	650D
V8-351 (4)(14)	ARF-42	.044	—	—	F	8°	B	—	650D
V8-400 (14)(30)	ARF-42	.044	—	—	F	(24)	B	—	650D
V8-400 (14)(25)(31)	ARF-42	.044	—	—	F	10°	B	—	625D
V8-400 (14)(26)(31)	ARF-42	.044	—	—	F	12°	B	—	625D
V8-460 (14)	ARF-52	.044	—	—	E	(27)(28)	B	—	650D
1977									
6-200	BRF-82	.050	—	—	L	6°	M	800	—
6-250 (5)(17)	BRF-82	.050	—	—	L	4°	A	850	—
6-250 (16)(30)	BRF-82	.050	—	—	L	6°	A	—	(6)
6-250 (16)(31)	BRF-82	.050	—	—	L	8°	A	—	600
6-250 (5)(33)	BRF-82	.050	—	—	L	(6)	A	(6)	—
V8-302 (31)	ARF-52-6	.060	—	—	J	12°	B	—	600
V8-302 (30)	(6)	(6)	—	—	J	(6)	B	(6)	(6)
V8-351 (33)	ARF-52	.050	—	—	K	4°	B	—	625
V8-351 (11)(23)	ARF-52	.050	—	—	K	(6)	B	—	625
V8-351 (4)	ARF-52	.050	—	—	K	(6)	B	—	650
V8-400 (31)	ARF-52-6	.060	—	—	K	(6)	B	—	(6)
V8-400 (30)	ARF-52	.050	—	—	K	(6)	B	—	(6)

Ford & Mercury—Compact & Intermediate Models

TUNE UP SPECIFICATIONS—Continued

The following specifications are published from the latest information available. This data should be used only in the absence of a decal affixed in the engine compartment.

★When using a timing light, disconnect vacuum hose or tube at distributor and plug opening in hose or tube so idle speed will not be affected.

●When checking compression, lowest cylinder must be within 75% of the highest.

▲Before removing wires from distributor cap, determine location of the No. 1 wire in cap, as distributor position may have been altered from that shown at the end of this chart.

Year /Engine	Spark Plug		Distributor		Ignition Timing★			Carb. Adjustments	
	Type	Gap Inch	Point Gap Inch	Dwell Angle Deg.	Firing Order Fig. ▲	Timing BTDC ①	Mark Fig.	Hot Idle Speed	
								Std. Trans.	Auto. Trans. ②
1978									
4-140 (14)(30)	AWSF-42	.034	—	—	H	6°	I	850	—
4-140 (14)(31)	AWSF-42	.034	—	—	H	(38)	I	850	800D
6-200 (14)(31)	BSF-82	.050	—	—	L	6°	M	600	650D
6-200 (14)(34)	BSF-82	.050	—	—	L	12°	M	600	650D
6-200 (13)(14)	BSF-82	.050	—	—	L	10°	M	700	650D
6-250 (14)(30)	BSF-82	.050	—	—	L	6°	A	—	600/700D (36)
6-250 (14)(31)	BSF-82	.050	—	—	L	(39)	A	800	600/700D (36)
V8-302 (14)(31)	ARF-52-6	.060	—	—	J	12°	B	—	600D
V8-302 (14)(34)	ARF-52	.050	—	—	J	14°	B	—	650/725D (36)
V8-302 (14)(30)(33)	ARF-52	.050	—	—	J	(40)	B	800	600/675D (36)
V8-302 (11)(14)	ARF-52	.050	—	—	J	14°	B	—	600D
V8-302 (12)(14)	ARF-52	.050	—	—	J	6°	B	—	600/675D (36)
V8-351 (14)(23)	ARF-52	.050	—	—	K	14°	B	—	600/650D (36)
V8-351 (4)(14)(31)	ASF-52	.050	—	—	K	16°	B	—	650D
V8-351 (4)(14)(34)	ASF-52	.050	—	—	K	12°	B	—	650D
V8-351 (4)(14)(30)(41)	ASF-52	.050	—	—	K	(9)	B	—	600/675D (36)
V8-351 (3)(4)(14)(30)	ASF-52	.050	—	—	K	14°	B	—	600/650D (36)
V8-400 (14)(34)	ASF-52	.050	—	—	K	8°	B	—	650D
V8-400 (14)(31)	ASF-52	.050	—	—	K	14°	B	—	600/675D (36)
V8-400 (14)(30)	ASF-52	.050	—	—	K	(19)	B	—	600/675D (36)
1979									
4-140 (14)	AWSF-42	.034	—	—	H	20°	I	—	800D
6-200 (12)(14)(16)	BSF-82	.050	—	—	L	10°	M	—	650D
6-200 (5)(12)(14)	BSF-82	.050	—	—	L	8°	M	700/850 (36)	—
6-250 (14)(16)(33)(37)	BSF-82	.050	—	—	L	10°	A	—	600D
6-250 (5)(14)(33)	BSF-82	.050	—	—	L	4°	A	800	—
V8-302 (14)	ASF-52	.050	—	—	J	8°	B	—	600/675 (36)
V8-351 (14)(23)	ASF-42	.050	—	—	K	15°	B	—	600/650 (36)
V8-351 (4)(14)	ASF-45	.050	—	—	K	12°	B	—	600/650 (36)

Continued

TUNE UP NOTES

①—BTDC: Before top dead center.
②—D: Drive.
③—Engineless air pump.
④—Modified Engine.
⑤—With manual trans.
⑥—Must refer to engine decal due to running production changes.
⑦—With two barrel carburetor.
⑧—With four barrel carburetor.
⑨—Early production models, 12° BTDC; mid production models, 9° BTDC; late production models, 14° BTDC.
⑩—Cougar 12°, all others 6°.
⑪—LTD II & Cougar.
⑫—Fairmont & Zephyr.
⑬—Exc. Calif. & high altitude.
⑭—Breakerless distributor.

⑮—Cougar 14°, all others 10°.
⑯—With auto. trans.
⑰—Comet and Maverick.
⑱—With auto. trans.; 8°. With manual trans.; 4°.
⑲—Early production models, 14° BTDC; late production models, 13° BTDC.
⑳—Manual trans. 16° BTDC, Auto. trans. 18° BTDC.
㉑—Manual trans. .020, Auto. trans. .017.
㉒—Cleveland engine.
㉓—Windsor engine.
㉔—Cougar; 10°. Elite, Montego, Torino; 12°.
㉕—Cougar.
㉖—Elite, Torino and Montego.
㉗—In drive with service and parking brake applied.
㉘—California and Police Interceptor; 14°. All

others; 10°.
㉙—With auto. trans.; 6°. With manual trans.; 4°.
㉚—Except Calif.
㉛—California.
㉜—With auto. trans.; 8°. With manual trans.; 6°.
㉝—Granada and Monarch.
㉞—High altitude.
㉟—LTD II.
㊱—High RPM is for A/C, A/C on.
㊲—Less A/C.
㊳—Manual trans., 6° BTDC; Auto. trans., 20° BTDC.
㊴—Manual trans., 4° BTDC; Auto. trans., 14° BTDC.
㊵—Manual trans., 12° BTDC; Auto. trans., 2° BTDC.
㊶—Engine with air pump.

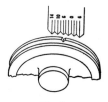

Fig. A

Fig. B

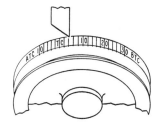

Fig. C

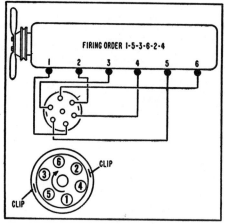

Fig. D

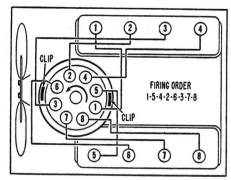

Fig. E

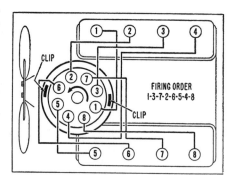

Fig. F

Ford & Mercury—Compact & Intermediate Models

TUNE UP NOTES—Continued

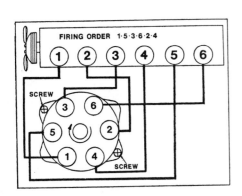

FIRING ORDER 1·5·3·6·2·4

Fig. G

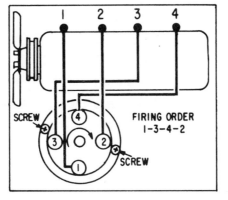

FIRING ORDER 1-3-4-2

Fig. H

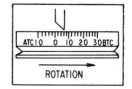

ATC 10 0 10 20 30 BTC

ROTATION

Fig. I

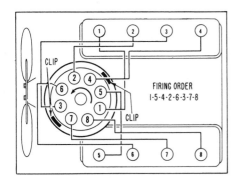

FIRING ORDER 1-5-4-2-6-3-7-8

Fig. J

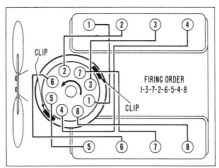

FIRING ORDER 1-3-7-2-6-5-4-8

Fig. K

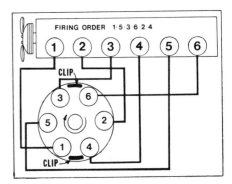

FIRING ORDER 1·5·3·6·2·4

Fig. L

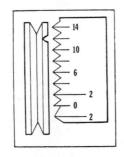

Fig. M

ENGINE & SERIAL NUMBER LOCATION
Plate On Left Front Door Pillar

ENGINE IDENTIFICATION
★Serial number on Vehicle Warranty Plate
Engine code for 1974-79 is the last letter in the serial number.

Year	Engine	Engine Code★	Year	Engine	Engine Code★	Year	Engine	Engine Code★
1974	V8-351	H		V8-400	S		V8-400	S
	V8-400	S		V8-460	A		V8-460	A
	V8-460	A	1979	V8-302	F	1979	V8-302	F
1975–77	V8-351②	Q		V8-351①	H		V8-351	H
				V8-351②	Q			

①—Windsor engine.
②—Modified engine.

TUNE UP SPECIFICATIONS
The following specifications are published from the latest information available. This data should be used only in the absence of a decal affixed in the engine compartment.

★When using a timing light, disconnect vacuum hose or tube at distributor and plug opening in tube or hose so idle speed will not be affected.

●When checking compression, lowest cylinder must be within 75% of the highest.

▲Before removing wires from distributor cap, determine location of the No. 1 wire in cap, as distributor position may have been altered from that shown at the end of this chart.

Year/Engine	Spark Plug		Distributor		Ignition Timing★			Carb. Adjustments	
	Type ⑤	Gap Inch	Point Gap Inch	Dwell Angle Deg.	Firing Order Fig. ▲	Timing BTDC ①	Mark Fig.	Hot Idle Speed	
								Std. Trans.	Auto. Trans.②
1974									
V8-351⑪	BRF-42	.034	.017	26–30	A	6°	E	—	600
V8-351⑪④	BRF-42	.044	—	—	A	6°	E	—	600
V8-351⑫	ARF-42	.044	.017	26–30	A	14°	E	—	650
V8-351⑫④	ARF-42	③	—	—	A	14°	E	—	650
V8-400④	ARF-42	.044	—	—	A	12°	E	—	625
V8-460④	ARF-52	.054	—	—	B	⑬	E	—	⑭
1975									
V8-351	ARF-42	.044	—	—	A	14°	E	—	700D
V8-400	ARF-42	.044	—	—	A	12°	E	—	625D
V8-460	ARF-52	.044	—	—	B	14°	E	—	650D
1976									
V8-351	ARF-42	.044	—	—	A	8°	E	—	650D
V8-400	ARF-42	.044	—	—	A	10°	E	—	⑩
V8-460	ARF-52	.044	—	—	B	10°	E	—	650D

Ford & Mercury—Full Size Models

TUNE UP SPECIFICATIONS—Continued

The following specifications are published from the latest information available. This data should be used only in the absence of a decal affixed in the engine compartment.

★When using a timing light, disconnect vacuum hose or tube at distributor and plug opening in hose or tube so idle speed will not be affected.

●When checking compression, lowest cylinder must be within 75% of the highest.

▲Before removing wires from distributor cap, determine location of the No. 1 wire in cap, as distributor position may have been altered from that shown at the end of this chart.

| Year/Engine | Spark Plug | | Distributor | | Ignition Timing★ | | | Carb. Adjustments | |
| | Type ⑤ | Gap Inch | Point Gap Inch | Dwell Angle Deg. | Firing Order Fig. ▲ | Timing BTDC ① | Mark Fig. | Hot Idle Speed | |
								Std. Trans.	Auto. Trans.②
1977									
V8-351	ARF-52	.050	—	—	F	⑧	E	—	⑧
V8-400⑥	ARF-52-6	.060	—	—	G	6°	E	—	600D
V8-400⑦	ARF-52	.050	—	—	G	⑧	E	—	⑧
V8-460⑮⑰	ARF-52	.050	—	—	G	⑧	E	—	⑧
V8-460⑯	ARF-52	.050	—	—	G	16°	E	—	700D
V8-460⑮⑱	ARF-52	.050	—	—	G	18°	E	—	600D
1978									
V8-302	ARF-52	.050	—	—	G	14°	E	—	650D
V8-351⑪	ARF-52	.050	—	—	F	14°	E	—	650D
V8-351⑲	ARF-52	.050	—	—	F	⑳⑧	E	—	600/675D㉑
V8-400⑥	ARF-52-6	.060	—	—	F	㉒⑧	E	—	㉓
V8-400⑦	ARF-52	.050	—	—	F	16°	E	—	650D
V8-460	ARF-52	.050	—	—	G	⑧⑨	E	—	580/650D㉑
1979									
V8-302	ASF-52	.050	—	—	G	6°	E	—	550/625㉑
V8-351	ASF-52	.050	—	—	F	—	E	—	550/640㉑

①—BTDC: Before top dead center.
②—D: Drive. N: Neutral.
③—Exc. Calif., .044; Calif., .054.
④—Breakerless distributor.
⑤—Autolite/Motorcraft.
⑥—Calif.
⑦—Exc. Calif.
⑧—Must refer to engine decal due to running production changes.

⑨—Early production models, 16° BTDC; Late production model, 10° BTDC.
⑩—Except Calif., 650D; Calif., 625D.
⑪—Windsor engine.
⑫—Cleveland engine.
⑬—Except Police Interceptor, 14° BTDC; Police Interceptor, 10° BTDC.
⑭—Except Police Interceptor, 650D; Police Interceptor, 700D.
⑮—Exc. Police Interceptor.

⑯—Police Interceptor.
⑰—Low altitude vehicles.
⑱—High altitude vehicles.
⑲—Modified engine.
⑳—Early production models, 9° BTDC; Late production models, 12° BTDC.
㉑—Higher RPM is for A/C, A/C on.
㉒—With A/C, 13° BTDC; Less A/C, 8° BTDC.
㉓—Less A/C, 650; With A/C A/C on, 650; A/C off, 575.

Continued

TUNE UP NOTES—Continued

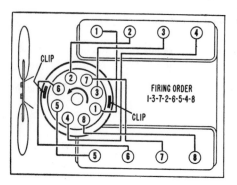

Fig. A

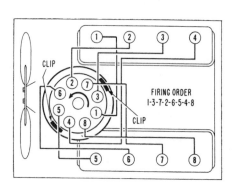

Fig. B

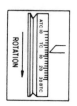

Fig. E

Fig. F

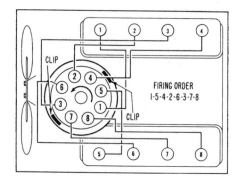

Fig. G

Ford Mustang II & Pinto • Mercury Bobcat

ENGINE & SERIAL NUMBER LOCATION: Vehicle warranty plate on rear face of left front door.

ENGINE IDENTIFICATION: Engine code is last letter in serial number on vehicle warranty plate.

Year	Engine	Engine Code
1974	4-122②	X
1974-79	4-140③⑤	Y
1979	4-140③⑥	W
1974-79	V6-171④	Z
1975-79	V8-302	F

①—1600 cc engine. ④—2800 cc engine.
②—2000 cc engine. ⑤—Non-turbocharged.
③—2300 cc engine. ⑥—Turbocharged.

TUNE UP SPECIFICATIONS

The following specifications are published from the latest information available. This data should be used only in the absence of a decal affixed in the engine compartment.

★When using a timing light, disconnect vacuum hose or tube at distributor and plug opening in hose or tube so idle speed will not be affected.

●When checking compression, lowest cylinder must be within 75 percent of highest.

▲Before removing wires from distributor cap, determine location of the No. 1 wire in cap, as distributor position may have been altered from that shown at the end of this chart.

Year/Engine	Spark Plug		Distributor		Ignition Timing★			Carb. Adjustments	
								Hot Idle Speed③	
	Type	Gap Inch	Point Gap Inch	Dwell Angle Deg.	Firing Order Fig. ▲	Timing BTDC ①	Mark Fig.	Std. Trans.	Auto. Trans.②
1974									
4-122, 2000 cc	BRF-42	.034	.025	35-41	⑩	6	D	750	650
4-140, 2300 cc	AGRF-52	.034	.027	35-41	G	6	E	850	750
V6-171, 2800 cc	AGR-42	.034	.027	35-41	H	12	F	750	650
1975									
4-140, 2300 cc	AGRF-52	.034	—	—	G	⑦	E	850	750D
V6-171, 2800 cc	AGR-42	.034	—	—	H	⑧	F	850	700D
V8-302⑨	ARF-42	.044	—	—	I	6°	J	—	700D
1976									
4-140, 2300 cc	AWRF-42	.034	—	—	G	⑦	E	750	650D
V6-171, 2800 cc	AWRF-42	.034	—	—	H	⑧	F	850	700D
V8-302⑨	ARF-42	.044	—	—	I	6°	J	—	700D
1977									
4-140, 2300 cc	AWRF-42	.034	—	—	G	⑪	E	850	⑫
V6-171, 2800 cc⑱	㉓	.034	—	—	H	⑬	F	—	⑭
V6-171, 2800 cc④⑳	⑲	.034	—	—	H	⑲	F	850	—
V6-171, 2800 cc④㉑	AWSF-42	.034	—	—	H	12°	F	—	㉒
V8-302⑨⑮	⑲	⑲	—	—	K	⑲	J	—	⑲
V8-302⑨⑯	ARF-52-6	.060	—	—	K	12°	J	—	700D
1978									
4-140, 2300 cc⑳	AWSF-42	.034	—	—	G	6°⑲	E	850	—
4-140, 2300 cc㉕㉑	AWSF-42	.034	—	—	G	20°⑲	E	—	800D
4-140, 2300 cc㉖	AWSF-42	.034	—	—	G	⑰⑲	E	—	750D
V6-171, 2800 cc⑳	AWSF-42	.034	—	—	H	10°	F	850	—
V6-171, 2800 cc㉑	AWSF-42	.034	—	—	H	⑬⑲	F	—	650/ 750D㉚
V8-302㉑	ARF-52	.050	—	—	K	㉛⑲	J	—	⑲
V8-302⑳	ARF-52	.050	—	—	K	10°	J	800/ 875D㉚	—

Continued

TUNE UP SPECIFICATIONS—Continued

Year/Engine	Spark Plug		Distributor		Ignition Timing★			Carb. Adjustments	
								Hot Idle Speed③	
	Type	Gap Inch	Point Gap Inch	Dwell Angle Deg.	Firing Order Fig. ▲	Timing BTDC ①	Mark Fig.	Std. Trans.	Auto. Trans.②
1979									
4-140, 2300 cc ㉑⑮	AWSF-42	.034	—	—	G	20°	E	—	800
4-140, 2300 cc ⑱⑳	AWSF-42	.034	—	—	G	6°	E	850	—
V6-171 2800 cc	AWSF-42	.034	—	—	H	9°	F	—	650/ 750D ㉚
V8-302 ⑳	ASF-52	.050	—	—	K	12°	J	—	800/875 ㉚

①—BTDC: Before top dead center.
②—D: Drive.
③—Headlamps on Hi Beam—Air Conditioner OFF. Where two speeds are listed, lower speed indicates solenoid disconnected.
④—Mustang.
⑤—Auto. trans., 9° BTDC; man. trans., 6° BTDC.
⑥—11.7:1 Except Calif.; 10:1 Calif.
⑦—Exc. Calif. Auto. Trans., 6° BTDC; Calif. Auto. Trans., 10° BTDC.
⑧—Manual Trans., 6° BTDC; Exc. Calif. Auto. Trans., 10° BTDC; Calif. Auto. Trans., 8° BTDC.
⑨—Refer to the Ford & Mercury—Compact & Intermediate Chapter for service procedures on this engine.
⑩—Since there are two alternate ignition wiring possibilities, be sure that the ignition wires are reinstalled in their proper locations referring to Fig. B.
⑪—Man. trans., 6° BTDC; auto. trans., 20° BTDC.
⑫—Except Calif. & high altitude, 800D RPM; Calif. & high altitude, 750D RPM.
⑬—Except Calif., 12° BTDC; Calif., 6° BTDC.

⑭—Except Calif. less A/C, 700D RPM; except Calif. with A/C & Calif. 750D RPM.
⑮—Except Calif.
⑯—Calif.
⑰—Early production, 20° BTDC; Late production Pinto & Bobcat, 17° BTDC; Mustang, 20° BTDC.
⑰—The distributor cap retaining clip locations have been changed in Fig. I. The new locations are between wire towers 3 & 7, 4 & 5.
⑱—Pinto and Bobcat.
⑲—Must refer to engine decal due to running production changes.
⑳—Manual trans.
㉑—Auto. trans.
㉒—With A/C, 750D RPM; less A/C, 700D RPM.
㉓—Exc. Calif., AWSF-42; Calif., AWRF-42.
㉔—Manual trans., 10° BTDC; Auto. trans. exc. Calif., 12° BTDC; Auto trans., Calif., 6° BTDC.
㉕—Exc. Calif.
㉖—Calif.
㉗—Exc. high altitude, 4° BTDC; High altitude, 16° BTDC.
㉘—Exc. Calif., 800 RPM; Calif., 750 RPM.
㉙—Exc. Calif., 650 RPM; Calif., 600 RPM.
㉚—High RPM is for A/C, A/C on.
㉛—Exc. High altitude, 10° BTDC; High altitude, 14° BTDC.

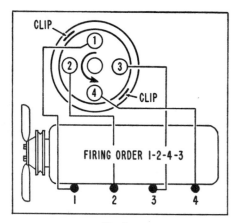

Fig. A

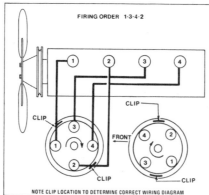

NOTE CLIP LOCATION TO DETERMINE CORRECT WIRING DIAGRAM

Fig. B

Fig. C

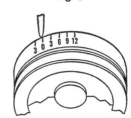

Fig. D

Ford Mustang II & Pinto • Mercury Bobcat

TUNE UP NOTES—Continued

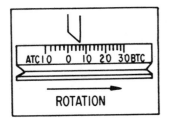

Fig. E

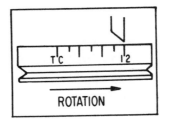

Fig. F

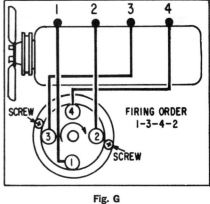

FIRING ORDER
1-3-4-2

Fig. G

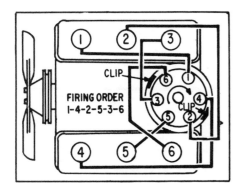

FIRING ORDER
1-4-2-5-3-6

Fig. H

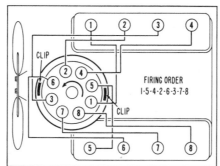

FIRING ORDER
1-5-4-2-6-3-7-8

Fig. I

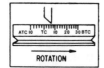

Fig. J

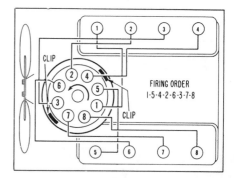

FIRING ORDER
1-5-4-2-6-3-7-8

Fig. K

Ford Thunderbird

ENGINE & SERIAL NUMBER LOCATION

Vehicle Warranty Plate On Left Front Door Pillar.

ENGINE IDENTIFICATION

*Serial number on vehicle
Warranty Plate.

Year	Engine	Engine Code
1974–76	V8-460	A
1977–78	V8-400	S
1977–79	V8-302	F
	V8-351	H

TUNE UP SPECIFICATIONS

The following specifications are published from the latest information available. This
data should be used only in the absence of a decal affixed in the engine compartment.

★When using a timing light, disconnect vacuum hose or tube at distributor and plug opening in hose or tube so idle speed will not be affected.
●When checking compression, lowest cylinder must be within 75 percent of highest.
▲Before removing wires from distributor cap, determine location of the No. 1 wire in cap, as distributor position may have been altered from that shown at the end of this chart.

Year/Engine	Spark Plug		Distributor		Ignition Timing★			Carb. Adjustments	
								Hot Idle Speed	
	Type	Gap Inch	Point Gap Inch	Dwell Angle Deg.	Firing Order Fig. ▲	Timing BTDC ①⑤	Mark Fig.	Std. Trans.	Auto. Trans.②⑤
1974									
8-460	ARF-52	③	⑧	—	A	14°	C	—	650D⑨
1975									
8-460	ARF-52	③	⑧	—	A	14°	C	—	650D
1976									
8-460⑪	ARF-52	.044	⑧	—	A	8°	C	—	650D⑬
8-460⑭	ARF-52	.044	⑧	—	A	14°	C	—	650D⑬
1977									
V8-302	ARF-52	.050	⑧	—	D	2°	C	—	600D
V8-351④⑪	ARF-52	.050	⑧	—	E	⑦	C	—	625D
V8-351⑪⑮	ARF-52	.050	⑧	—	E	⑦	C	—	650D
V8-351⑭⑮	ARF-52-6	.060	⑧	—	E	⑦	C	—	600D
V8-400⑪	ARF-52	.050	⑧	—	E	⑦	C	—	⑦
V8-400⑭	ARF-52-6	.060	⑧	—	E	6°	C	—	600D

Ford Thunderbird

TUNE UP SPECIFICATIONS—Continued

The following specifications are published from the latest information available. This data should be used only in the absence of a decal affixed in the engine compartment.

★When using a timing light, disconnect vacuum hose or tube at distributor and plug opening in hose or tube so idle speed will not be affected.

●When checking compression, lowest cylinder must be within 80 percent of highest.

▲Before removing wires from distributor cap, determine location of the No. 1 wire in cap, as distributor position may have been altered from that shown at the end of this chart.

| Year/Engine | Spark Plug | | Distributor | | Ignition Timing★ | | | Carb. Adjustments | |
| | Type | Gap Inch | Point Gap Inch | Dwell Angle Deg. | Firing Order Fig. ▲ | Timing BTDC ①⑤ | Mark Fig. | Hot Idle Speed | |
								Std. Trans.	Auto. Trans.②⑤
1978									
V8-302	ARF-52	.050	⑧	—	D	14°	C	—	600D
V8-351④	ARF-52	.050	⑧	—	E	14°	C	—	600/675D⑲
V8-351⑭⑮	ASF-52	.050	⑧	—	E	16°	C	—	600/650D⑲
V8-351⑨⑬	ASF-52	.050	⑧	—	E	12°	C	—	650D
V8-351⑩⑫⑮	ASF-52	.050	⑧	—	E	14°	C	—	600/650D⑲
V8-351⑩⑮⑯	ASF-52	.050	⑧	—	E	⑰	C	—	600/675D⑲
V8-400⑭	ASF-52	.050	⑧	—	E	14°	C	—	600/675D⑲
V8-400⑨	ASF-52	.050	⑧	—	E	8°	C	—	650D
V8-400⑩	ASF-52	.050	⑧	—	E	⑱	C	—	575/650D⑲
1979									
V8-302	ASF-52	.050	⑧	—	D	8°	C	—	600/675⑲
V8-351④	ASF-42	.050	⑧	—	E	15°	C	—	600/650⑲
V8-351⑮	ASF-52	.050	⑧	—	E	12°	C	—	600/650⑲

①—BTDC: Before top dead center.
②—D: Drive. N: Neutral.
③—Exc. Calif., .054 inch; Calif. .044 inch.
④—Windsor engine.
⑤—On models equipped w/vacuum release parking brake, whenever adjusting ignition timing or idle speed, vacuum line to brake release mechanism must be disconnected and plugged to prevent parking brake from releasing when selector is moved to Drive.
⑥—With lights and A/C off.
⑦—Must refer to engine decal due to running production changes.
⑧—Breakerless distributor.
⑨—High altitude.
⑩—Exc. Calif. & high altitude.
⑪—Exc. Calif.
⑫—Engines less air pump.
⑬—With A/C "On".
⑭—Calif.
⑮—Modified engine.
⑯—Engine with air pump.
⑰—Early production models, 12° BTDC; Mid production models, 9° BTDC; Late production Models, 14° BTDC.
⑱—Early production models, 14° BTDC; Late production models, 13° BTDC.
⑲—Higher RPM is for A/C, A/C on.

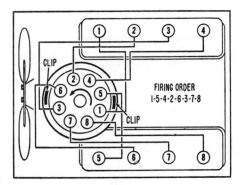

Fig. A

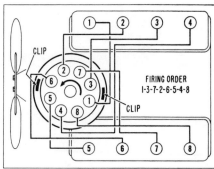

Fig. B

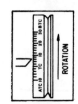

Fig. C

Continued

TUNE UP NOTES—Continued

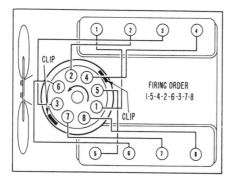

FIRING ORDER
1-5-4-2-6-3-7-8

Fig. D

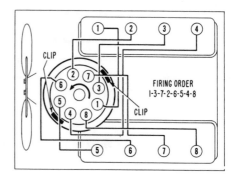

FIRING ORDER
1-3-7-2-6-5-4-8

Fig. E

Lincoln Continental & Versailles

SERIAL & ENGINE NUMBER LOCATION
Vehicle Warranty Plate on Left Front Door Pillar

ENGINE IDENTIFICATION

*Serial number on vehicle
Warranty Plate.

Engine code for 1974–79 is the last letter
in the serial number.

Year	Engine	Engine Code*
1974–78	V8-460	A
1974–79	V8-400	S
1977	V8-351W	H
1977–79	V8-302	F

TUNE UP SPECIFICATIONS
The following specifications are published from the latest information available. This
data should be used only in the absence of a decal affixed in the engine compartment.

★When using a timing light, disconnect vacuum hose or tube at distributor and plug opening in hose or tube so idle speed will not be affected.
●When checking compression, lowest cylinder must be within 75 percent of highest.
▲Before removing wires from distributor cap, determine location of No. 1 wire in cap, as distributor position may have been altered from that
shown at the end of this chart.

Year /Engine	Spark Plug		Distributor		Ignition Timing★			Carb. Adjustments	
								Hot Idle Speed	
	Type	Gap Inch	Point Gap Inch	Dwell Angle Deg.	Firing Order Fig. ▲	Timing BTDC ①	Mark Fig.	Std. Trans.	Auto. Trans.③
1974									
V8-460	ARF-52	.054	⑨	⑨	A	14°	B	—	650D
1975									
V8-460	ARF-52	.044	⑨	⑨	A	14°	B	—	650D
1976									
V8-460⑩	ARF-52	.044	⑨	⑨	A	8°③	B	—	650D⑤
V8-460④	ARF-52	.044	⑨	⑨	A	14°③	B	—	650D⑤
1977									
V8-302④	ARF-52	—	⑨	⑨	D	—	B	—	—
V8-302⑩	ARF-52	.050	⑨	⑨	D	12°	B	—	650
V8-351	ARF-52	.050	⑨	⑨	E	4°	B	—	625
V8-400⑩	ARF-52	.050	⑨	⑨	E	10°	B	—	600D
V8-460⑩	ARF-52	.050	⑨	⑨	D	10°	B	—	650D
1978									
V8-302⑦	ARF-52	.050	⑨	⑨	D	⑪⑫	B	—	⑬
V8-302④	ARF-52	.050	⑨	⑨	D	⑪⑮	B	—	600/625D⑭
V8-302⑧	ARF-52	.050	⑨	⑨	D	30°⑪⑰	B	—	625D
V8-400	ARF-52	.050	⑨	⑨	E	⑪⑯	B	—	⑱
V8-460	ARF-52	.050	⑨	⑨	D	⑪⑲	B	—	580/650D⑭
1979									
V8-302	ASF-52	.050	⑨	⑨	D	30°⑰	B	—	625D
V8-400	ASF-52	.050	⑨	⑨	E	14°	B	—	600/675D⑭

Continued

Lincoln Continental & Versailles

TUNE UP NOTES

①—BTDC-Before top dead center.
②—D-Drive. N-Neutral.
③—In Drive with service & parking brakes applied.
④—California.
⑤—With A/C "On".
⑥—Exc. high altitude.
⑦—High altitude.
⑧—Exc. Calif. & high altitude.

⑨—Breakerless distributor.
⑩—Exc. Calif.
⑪—Must refer to engine decal due to running production changes.
⑫—Early production, 14° BTDC; Late production, 15° BTDC set in drive.
⑬—Early production, 650/725D⑭; Late production, 625D with A/C on.
⑭—Higher RPM is for A/C, A/C on.

⑮—Early production, 12° BTDC; Late production, 15° BTDC set in drive.
⑯—Exc. Calif. & High altitude, 13° BTDC; Calif., 16° BTDC; High altitude, 8° BTDC.
⑰—Set in drive.
⑱—Exc. Calif. & High altitude, 575/650D⑭; Calif. 600/650D⑭; High altitude, 650D.
⑲—Early production 16° BTDC; Late production 10° BTDC.

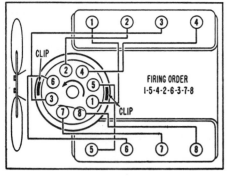

Fig. A

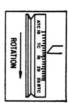

Fig. B

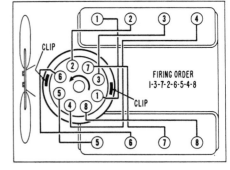

Fig. C

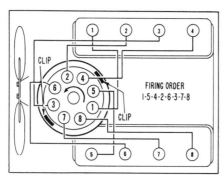

Fig. D

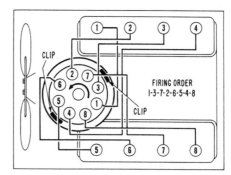

Fig. E

Oldsmobile—Except Starfire

Vehicle Identification Plate: 1974-79 on left upper dash.

ENGINE NUMBER LOCATION

1973–76 6-250: Right side of engine block directly to rear of distributor.
1974 V8s: Stamped on oil filler tube.
1975 V8-400, 1975–76 Omega V8-350, 1977–78 V6-231, V8-350 & Omega V8-350 with distributor located at rear of engine, clockwise distributor rotor rotation. Front right side of cylinder block.
1975–76 V8-455, 1975–78 V8-260, V8-350 Except Omega, 1977–78 Omega V8-350 with distributor located at rear of engine, counterclockwise distributor rotor rotation & V8-403: Stamped on engine oil filler tube

ENGINE IDENTIFICATION CODE

YEAR	ENGINE	ENGINE PREFIX
1974	6-250 Std. Tr.	CCC, CCD
	6-250 Auto. Tr.	CCA, CCB
	V8-350 2 Bar. Carb.	QS, QT
	V8-350 4 Bar. Carb.	QB, QC, QL
	V8-350 4 Bar. Carb.	QO, QU, QW
	V8-350 4 Bar. Carb.	TB, TC, TL, TO
	V8-455 2 Bar. Carb.	UU, UW
	V8-455 4 Bar. Carb.	UA, UB, UC
	V8-455 4 Bar. Carb.	UD, UL, UO
	V8-455 4 Bar. Carb.	UP, UN, UR
	V8-455 4 Bar. Carb.	UV, UX, VP
	V8-455 4 Bar. Carb.	VA, VB, VC
	V8-455 4 Bar. Carb.	VD, VL, VO
1975	6-250 Std. Tr. [1]	CJU
	6-250 Auto. Tr. [1]	CJT
	6-250 Auto. Tr. [2]	CJL
	V8-260 Std. Tr. [1]	QA, QK
	V8-260 Std. Tr. a/c [1]	QD, QN
	V8-260 Std. Tr. [2]	TA, TK
	V8-260 Std. Tr. a/c [2]	TD, TN
	V8-260 Auto. Tr. [1]	QE, QP
	V8-260 Auto. Tr. a/c [1]	QJ, QQ
	V8-260 Auto. Tr. [2]	TE, TP
	V8-260 Auto. Tr. a/c [2]	TJ, TQ
	V8-350 Auto. Tr. [1]	RW, QL
	V8-350 Auto Tr. a/c [1]	RX, QO, QX
	V8-350 Auto. Tr. [2]	RN, TL
	V8-350 Auto. Tr. a/c [2]	RO, TO, TX
	V8-400 Auto. Tr. [1]	YM, YT
	V8-455 Auto. Tr. [1]	UB, UE, UP
	V8-455 Auto. Tr. a/c [1]	UC, UD, UP
	V8-455 Auto. Tr. [2]	VB, VE, VP
	V8-455 Auto. Tr. a/c [2]	VC, VD, VP
1976	6-250 Std. [1]	CCD, CCJ
	6-250 Auto. Tr. [1]	CCF, CCH
	6-250 Auto. Tr. [2]	CCC
	V8-260 Std. Tr. [1]	QA, QK
	V8-260 Std. Tr. a/c [1]	QD, QN
	V8-260 Std. Tr. [2]	TA, TD, TK, TN
	V8-260 Auto. Tr. [1]	QB, QP, Q7, Q8
	V8-260 Auto. Tr. a/c [1]	QC, QT

YEAR	ENGINE	ENGINE PREFIX
	V8-260 Auto. Tr. [2]	TE, TP, T-2, T-3, T-4, T-5, T-7, T-8
	V8-350 2 Bar. Carb. Auto. Tr. [1]	PA
	V8-350 2 Bar. Carb. Auto. Tr. a/c [1]	PB
	V8-350 4 Bar. Carb. Auto. Tr. [1]	PE, Q2, Q4, Q6
	V8-350 4 Bar. Carb. Auto. Tr. a/c [1]	PF, Q3, Q5
	V8-350 4 Bar. Carb. Auto. Tr. [2]	PM, TL, TY
	V8-350 4 Bar. Carb. Auto. Tr. a/c [2]	PN, TO, TW, TX
	V8-455 Auto. Tr. [1]	UB, UE, U5, U6, U7, U8
	V8-455 Auto. Tr. a/c [1]	UC, UD, U3, U4
	V8-455 Auto. Tr. [2]	VB, VE, V5
	V8-455 Auto. Tr. a/c [2]	VD, V3, V4
1977	V6-231 Std. Tr. [1]	SG
	V6-231 Std. Tr. [2]	SU
	V6-231 Auto. Tr. [1]	SI
	V6-231 Auto. Tr. [2]	SK, SL
	V6-231 Auto. Tr. [3]	SM, SN
	V8-260 Std. Tr. [1]	QS, QT
	V8-260 Auto. Tr. [1]	QC, QD, QE, QJ, QU, QV
	V8-305 Std. Tr. [1]	CPA
	V8-305 Auto. Tr. [1]	CPY
	V8-350 4 Bar. Carb. Auto. Tr. [1]	QK, QL, QN, QO, QP, QQ
	V8-350 4 Bar. Carb. Auto. Tr. [2]	CKR, TK, TL, TN, TO, TP, TQ, TX, TY
	V8-350 4 Bar. Carb. Auto. Tr. [3]	Q2, Q3, Q6, Q7, Q8, Q9
	V8-403 Auto. Tr. [1]	UA, UB, UC, UD, UE
	V8-403 Auto. Tr. [2]	VA, VB, VE, VJ, VK
	V8-403 Auto. Tr. [3]	U2, U3, U6
1978	V6-231 Std. Tr. [4]	EA
	V6-231 Auto. Tr. [4]	EC, EK, EL, OH
	V6-231 Auto. Tr. [2]	EE, EK, EL, OK

YEAR	ENGINE	ENGINE PREFIX
	V6-231 Auto. Tr. [3]	EG
	V8-260 Std. Tr. [4]	QD, QE
	V8-260 Auto. Tr. [4]	QJ, QL, QK, QN, QT, QU
	V8-260 Auto. Tr. [2]	TK, TJ
	V8-305 Std. Tr. [4]	CTH, CRW
	V8-305 Auto. Tr. [4]	CPF, CTJ
	V8-305 Auto. Tr. [2]	CRY, CRZ
	V8-305 Auto. Tr. [3]	CPZ
	V8-350 Auto. Tr. [2]	TO, TP, TQ, TS, CHJ
	V8-350 Auto. Tr. [3]	Q2, Q3, CHL, CMC
	V8-350 Auto. Tr. [4]	QO, QP, QQ, QS, MA, MB
	V8-350 Diesel	QB, QC
	V8-403 Auto. Tr. [2]	VA, VB, VC
	V8-403 Auto. Tr. [3]	U2, U3, U4
	V8-403 Auto. Tr. [4]	UA, UB, UC, UD, UE
1979	V6-231 Auto. Tr. [2]	RG, RW, RY
	V6-231 Auto. Tr. [3]	RJ
	V6-231 Auto. Tr. [4]	NJ, NK, NL, RB, RC, RX
	V6-231 Std. Tr. [4]	NG, RA
	V8-260 Auto. Tr. [2]	VC
	V8-260 Auto. Tr. [3]	U5
	V8-260 Auto. Tr. [4]	UE, UJ, UK, UL, UN, UO
	V8-260 Std. Tr. [4]	UC, UD
	V8-260 Auto. Tr. [5]	UP, UQ
	V8-260 Std. Tr. [5]	UW, UX
	V8-301 Auto. Tr. [4]	XP, XR
	V8-305 Auto. Tr. [2]	DNX, DNY
	V8-305 Auto. Tr. [3]	DTA
	V8-305 Auto. Tr. [4]	DNJ, DNT, DNW, DTX
	V8-305 Std. Tr. [4]	DNS, DTM
	V8-350 Auto. Tr. [2]	VA, VK, DRJ
	V8-350 Auto. Tr. [3]	U2, U9, DRX, DRY
	V8-350 Auto. Tr. [4]	SA, SB, UA, US, UT, UU, UV
	V8-350 Diesel [3]	U3, V4, V6
	V8-350 Diesel [5]	UB, VN, VO, VP, VQ
	V8-403 Auto. Tr. [2]	TB
	V8-403 Auto. Tr. [3]	Q3
	V8-403 Auto. Tr. [4]	QB

[1]—Except California.
[2]—California.
[3]—High altitude.
[4]—Exc. Calif. & High altitude.
[5]—Exc. high altitude.

Continued

TUNE UP SPECIFICATIONS

The following specifications are published from the latest information available. This data should be used only in the absence of a decal affixed in the engine compartment.

★When using a timing light, disconnect vacuum hose or tube at distributor and plug opening in hose or tube so idle speed will not be affected.

●When checking compression, lowest cylinder must be within 80 percent of highest.

▲Before removing wires from distributor cap, determine location of the No. 1 wire in cap, as distributor position may have been altered from that shown at the end of this chart.

| Year/Engine | Spark Plug | | Distributor | | Ignition Timing ★ | | | Carb. Adjustments | |
| | Type | Gap Inch | Point Gap Inch | Dwell Angle Deg. | Firing Order Fig. ▲ | Timing BTDC ① | Mark Fig. | Hot Idle Speed | |
								Std. Trans.	Auto. Trans. ②
1974									
6-250(14)	R46TS	.035	.019	31–34	N	8°(7)	C	850	600D
8-350 4 Bar.	R46S	.040	.019	30	(20)	12°(16)	H	—	650D
8-455, 275 H.P.	R45S	.040	.019	30	(20)	14°(16)	H	—	650D
8-455 4 Bar.	R46S	.040	.019	30	(20)	8°(16)	H	—	650D
8-455 4 Bar.(8)	R46SX	.080	—	—	(20)	8°(16)	H	—	650D
8-455 4 Bar.(13)	R46S	.040	.019	30	(20)	10°(16)	H	—	650D
8-455 4 Bar.(8)(13)	R46SX	.080	—	—	(20)	10°(16)	H	—	650D
1975									
6-250(14)	R46TX	.060	—	—	I	10°	C	850	(19)
V8-260	R46SX	.080	—	—	J	(17)	G	750	650D
V8-350(10)	R45TSX	.060	—	—	K	12°	D	—	600D
V8-350	R46SX	.080	—	—	J	20°(16)	G	—	650D
V8-400(18)	R45TSX	.060	—	—	L	16°(16)	E	—	650D
V8-455	R46SX	.080	—	—	J	16°(16)	G	—	650D
V8-455(13)	R46SX	.080	—	—	J	12°(16)	G	—	650D
1976									
6-250(14)(21)	R46TS	.035	—	—	I	6°	C	850	—
6-250(14)(22)	R46TS	.035	—	—	I	10°	C	—	(19)
V8-260(23)	R46SZ	.060	—	—	J	(11)	G	750	650D(9)
V8-260(5)(24)	R46SZ	.060	—	—	J	(12)	G	—	650D(9)
V8-260(10)(24)	R46SZ	.060	—	—	J	(25)	G	—	650D(9)
V8-260(24)(26)	R46SZ	.060	—	—	J	14°(16)	G	750	—
V8-350	R46SZ	.060	—	—	J	20°(16)	G	—	(19)
V8-350(23)(27)	R46SZ	.060	—	—	J	22°(16)	G	—	650D(9)
V8-350(10)	R46TSX	.060	—	—	K	12°	D	—	600D
V8-455	R46SZ	.060	—	—	J	16°(16)	G	—	650D
V8-455	R46SZ	.060	—	—	J	18°(16)	G	—	650D(9)
V8-455(13)(23)	R46SZ	.060	—	—	J	14°(16)	G	—	650D(9)
V8-455(13)(24)	R46SZ	.060	—	—	J	12°(16)	G	—	650D(9)
1977									
V6-231(34)	R46TS	.040	—	—	(49)	12°	(50)	—	600N
V8-260	R46SZ	.060	—	—	J	(11)	G	750	650D(9)
V8-305(14)	R45TS	.045	—	—	O	8°(28)	C	700	650D
V8-350(14)(29)	R45TS	.045	—	—	O	(30)	C	—	650D
V8-350(35)	R46SZ	.060	—	—	J	20°(16)	G	—	650D(9)
V8-403	R46SZ	.060	—	—	J	(31)(32)	G	—	(9)(33)
1978									
V6-231(34)	R46TSX	.060	—	—	A	15°	P	800	670D(9)
V8-260	R46SZ	.060	—	—	J	(4)(16)	G	800	650D
V8-305(14)(36)	R45TS	.045	—	—	O	4°	C	700	600D
V8-305(14)(37)	R45TS	.045	—	—	O	8°	C	—	700D

TUNE UP SPECIFICATIONS—Continued

The following specifications are published from the latest information available. This data should be used only in the absence of a decal affixed in the engine compartment.

★ When using a timing light, disconnect vacuum hose or tube at distributor and plug opening in hose or tube so idle speed will not be affected.
● When checking compression, lowest cylinder must be within 70 percent of highest.
▲ Before removing wires from distributor cap, determine location of the No. 1 wire in cap, as distributor position may have been altered from that shown at the end of this chart.

Year/Engine	Spark Plug		Distributor		Ignition Timing ★			Carb. Adjustments — Hot Idle Speed	
	Type	Gap Inch	Point Gap Inch	Dwell Angle Deg.	Firing Order Fig. ▲	Timing BTDC ①	Mark Fig.	Std. Trans.	Auto. Trans. ②
1978—Continued									
V8-350 ⑭㉙	R45TS	.045	—	—	O	8°	C	—	650D
V8-350 ㉟	R46SZ	.060	—	—	J	20°⑯	G	—	650D
V8-350 ㊴	—	—	—	—	(51)	㊵	—	—	650D
V8-403 ㊱	R46SZ	.060	—	—	J	㊶⑯	G	—	650D
V8-403 ㊲	R46SZ	.060	—	—	J	20°⑯	G	—	650D㊸
V8-403 ⑬	R46SZ	.060	—	—	J	㉜㊷⑯	G	—	650D㊸
1979									
V6-231 ㉞	R46TSX	.060	—	—	A	15°	P	600/800㊺	㊹
V8-260 ㉑	R46SZ	.060	—	—	J	18°⑯	G	600/800N㊻	—
V8-260 ⑤㉒	R46SZ	.060	—	—	J	㊼⑯	G	—	㊽
V8-260 ⑥	R46SZ	.060	—	—	J	20°⑯	G	—	500/625㊻
V8-260 ㊴	—	—	—	—	(51)	㊵	—	—	640
V8-301 ⑱	R46TSX	.060	—	—	L	12°	Q	—	500/625㊻
V8-305 ⑮	R45TS	.045	—	—	O	4°	C	600/700N㊺	500/600㊻
V8-305 ③	R45TS	.045	—	—	O	8°	C	—	600/650㊻
V8-350 ㊱㉟	R46SZ	.060	—	—	J	20°⑯	G	—	550/650㊻
V8-350 ⑭㉔㉙	R45TS	.045	—	—	O	8°	C	—	500/600㊻
V8-350 ⑭㉙③	R45TS	.045	—	—	O	8°	C	—	600/650㊻
V8-350 ③㉟	R46SZ	.060	—	—	J	20°⑯	G	—	600/700㊻
V8-350 ㉔㉟	R46SZ	.060	—	—	J	20°⑯	G	—	500/600㊻
V8-350 ㊴	—	—	—	—	(51)	㊵	—	—	650
V8-403 ㊱	R46SZ	.060	—	—	J	20°⑯	G	—	550/650㊻
V8-403 ㉔	R46SZ	.060	—	—	J	20°⑯	G	—	500/600㊻
V8-403 ③	R46SZ	.060	—	—	J	20°⑯	G	—	600/700㊻

① BTDC: Before top dead center.
② D: Drive. N: Neutral. Add 50 R.P.M. to slow idle speed for air conditioned cars with A/C off.
③ High altitude
④ Exc. Calif. & Manual trans., 20° BTDC; Calif. & manual trans., 18° BTDC.
⑤ Cutlass.
⑥ Full size cars.
⑦ At 600 rpm with auto. trans. and 850 rpm with manual trans.
⑧ With High Energy Ignition system.
⑨ With A/C on and compressor clutch wires disconnected.
⑩ Omega only. See Buick Chapter for service procedures on this engine.
⑪ Manual trans., 16° BTDC; Auto. trans., 18° BTDC; at 1100 R.P.M.
⑫ Early production with EFE/EGR-TVS 16° BTDC, Late production less EFE/EGR-TVS 14° BTDC; at 1100 R.P.M.
⑬ Toronado.
⑭ See Chevrolet Chapter for service procedures on this engine.
⑮ Exc. High altitude.
⑯ At 1100 R.P.M.
⑰ Exc. Calif., 16° BTDC; Calif., 18° BTDC. At 1100 R.P.M.
⑱ See Pontiac Chapter for service procedures on this engine.
⑲ Exc. Calif., 550D; Calif., 600D.
⑳ Exc. H.E.I., Fig. F; H.E.I., Fig. J.
㉑ Manual trans.
㉒ Auto. trans.
㉓ Exc. California.
㉔ California.
㉕ Early production with EFE/EGR-TVS 14° BTDC, Late production less EFE/EGR-TVS 16° BTDC; at 1100 R.P.M.
㉖ 5 speed transmission.
㉗ With 2.41 axle ratio.
㉘ Manual trans., at 700D R.P.M.; auto. trans. at 500D R.P.M.
㉙ Distributor rotor rotation—clockwise.
㉚ Calif., 6° at 500D R.P.M.; high altitude, 8° at 600D R.P.M.
㉛ Except Calif. & high altitude, 24° BTDC; Calif. & high altitude, 20° BTDC. At 1100 R.P.M.
㉜ On models with EST, see text for procedure.
㉝ Except Toronado & high altitude, 650D; Toronado high altitude, 700D.
㉞ See Buick Chapter for service procedures on this engine.
㉟ Distributor rotor rotation—counter-clockwise.
㊱ Exc. Calif. and high altitude.
㊲ Calif. and high altitude.
㊳ Distributor at front of engine.
㊴ Diesel.
㊵ See text for procedure.
㊶ 98 & 88 Exc. wagon, 18° BTDC; 88 wagon, 20° BTDC.
㊷ Exc. Calif., 20° BTDC; Calif., 22° BTDC.
㊸ High altitude, 700 RPM.
㊹ Ex. Calif. & High altitude—Less A/C, 550D; with A/C 550/670D, see note ㊻. Calif. & Hi. Alt., 600D.
㊺ Where two idle speeds are listed, the higher speed is with idle solenoid energized.
㊻ Where two idle speeds are listed, the higher speed is with A/C solenoid energized & A/C "ON".
㊼ Exc. Calif.; 20° BTDC; Calif. 18° BTDC.
㊽ Exc. wagon & Calif.—Less A/C 500D; with A/C 550/625 see note ㊻. Wagon & Calif., 500/625D see note ㊻.
㊾ Exc. even fire, Fig. M; Even fire, Fig. A.
㊿ Exc. even fire, Fig. B; Even fire, Fig. P.
(51) Firing order, 1, 8, 4, 3, 6, 5, 7, 2.

Continued

TUNE UP NOTES—Continued

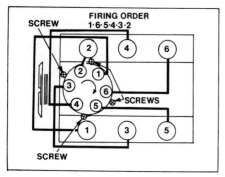

Fig. A

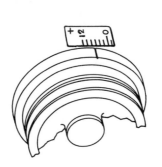

Fig. B

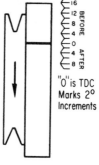

"O" is TDC
Marks 2°
Increments

Fig. C

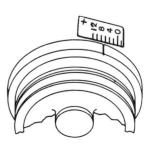

Fig. D

Fig. E

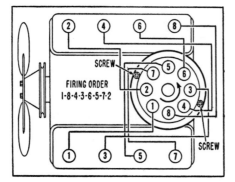

Fig. F

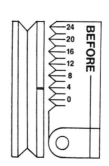

Fig. G

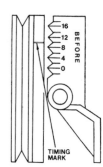

Fig. H

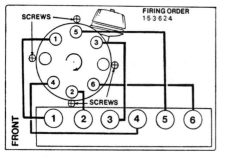

Fig. I

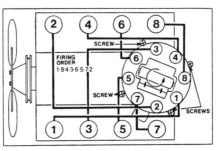

Fig. J

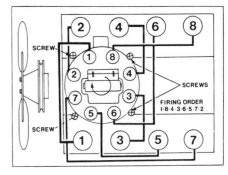

Fig. K

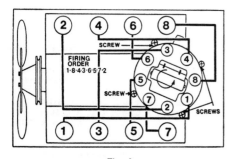

Fig. L

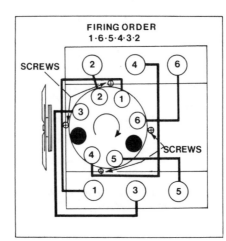

Fig. M

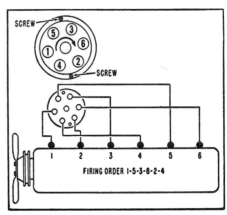

Fig. N

Oldsmobile—Except Starfire

TUNE UP NOTES—Continued

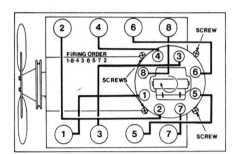

Fig. O

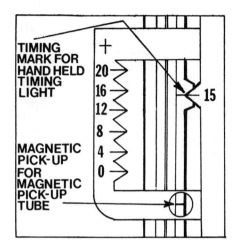

Fig. P

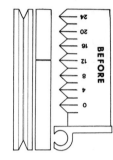

Fig. Q

SERIAL NUMBER LOCATION

1974-79: On plate fastened to upper left instrument panel area, visible through windshield.

ENGINE IDENTIFICATION

The V8 Pontiac manufactured engine code is located beneath the production engine number on a machined pad on the right-hand bank of the engine block.

The V8-260, 350 and 403 Oldsmobile manufactured engine code is located on the oil filler tube.

The V6-231 and 1975-76 Ventura V8 engine codes are located on the front right hand of cylinder block.

The 6-250 engine code is stamped on the pad at front right-hand side of cylinder block at rear of distributor.

1974

CODE	TRANS.	ENGINE
CCR	[4]	6-250[9]
CCX	[6]	6-250[9]
CCW	[6]	6-250[9]
AA	[6][13]	V8-350[1][10]
WB	[4]	V8-350[1]
WA	[6]	V8-350[1]
YB	[6]	V8-350[1]
YA	[6]	V8-350[1]
YC	[6]	V8-350[1]
YS	[6]	V8-350[2]
AD	[6]	V8-400[1][10]
ZB	[6]	V8-350[1]
ZA	[6]	V8-350[1]
WP	[6]	V8-350[1]
WN	[4]	V8-350[1]
YP	[6]	V8-350[2]
YN	[6]	V8-350[2]
ZP	[6]	V8-350[2]
AH	[6]	V8-400[1][10]
AT	[6]	V8-400[2][10]
A3	[6]	V8-400[2][10]
YH	[6]	V8-400[1]
YJ	[6]	V8-400[1]
ZH	[6]	V8-400[1]
WR	[4]	V8-400[2][10]
WT	[4]	V8-400[2][10]
YF	[6]	V8-400[2]
YK	[6]	V8-400[1][10]
YL	[6]	V8-400[2][10]
YM	[6]	V8-400[2][10]
YZ	[6]	V8-400[2]
Y3	[4]	V8-400[2][10]
YT	[6]	V8-400[2]
ZD	[6]	V8-400[1][10]
ZJ	[6]	V8-400[1][10]
ZK	[6]	V8-400[1][10]
ZS	[6]	V8-400[2][10]
ZT	[6]	V8-400[2]
AW	[6]	V8-455[2][10]
A4	[6]	V8-455[2][10]
YR	[6]	V8-455[2][10]
YW	[6]	V8-455[2][10]
YX	[6]	V8-455[2][10]
YY	[6]	V8-455[2][10]
Y4	[6]	V8-455[2][10]
Y6	[6]	V8-455[2][10]
Y9	[6]	V8-455[2][10]
YU	[6]	V8-455[2]
ZU	[6]	V8-455[2]
ZW	[6]	V8-455[2][10]
ZX	[6]	V8-455[2][10]
Z4	[6]	V8-455[2][10]
Z6	[6]	V8-455[2][10]
W8	[4]	V8-455[8]
Y8	[6]	V8-455[8]
JU	[4]	6-250[9]

1975

CODE	TRANS.	ENGINE
JT	[6]	6-250[9]
JL	[6]	6-250[9]
QA	[4]	V8-260[1]
QD	[4]	V8-260[1]
QE	[6]	V8-260[1]
QJ	[6]	V8-260[1]
TE	[6]	V8-260[1]
TJ	[6]	V8-260[1]
RS	[6]	V8-350[13]
RI	[6]	V8-350[13]
YA	[6]	V8-350[1]
YB	[6]	V8-350[1]
RW	[6]	V8-350[13]
RX	[6]	V8-350[13]
RN	[6]	V8-350[13]
RO	[6]	V8-350[13]
WN	[4]	V8-350[2]
ZP	[6]	V8-350[2]
YH	[6]	V8-400[1]
YT	[6]	V8-400[2]
ZT	[6]	V8-400[2]
YM	[6]	V8-400[2]
WT	[4]	V8-400[2]
YS	[6]	V8-400[2]
YW	[6]	V8-455[2]
ZU	[6]	V8-455[2]
ZW	[6]	V8-455[2]
WX	[5]	V8-455[2]

1976

CODE	TRANS.	ENGINE
CC	[6]	6-250[9][14]
CD	[4]	6-250[9][14]
CF	[6]	6-250[9][14]
CH	[6]	6-250[9][14]
CJ	[4]	6-250[9][14]
QA	[7]	V8-260[1][12]
QB	[6]	V8-260[1][12]
QC	[7]	V8-260[1][12]
QD	[7]	V8-260[1][12]
QK	[6]	V8-260[1][12]
QN	[7]	V8-260[1][12]
QP	[6]	V8-260[1][12]
QT	[6]	V8-260[1][12]
TA	[7]	V8-260[1][12]
TD	[7]	V8-260[1][12]
TE	[6]	V8-260[1][12]
TJ	[6]	V8-260[1][12]
TK	[7]	V8-260[1][12]
TN	[7]	V8-260[1][12]
TP	[6]	V8-260[1][12]
TT	[6]	V8-260[1][12]
T2	[6]	V8-260[1][12]
T3	[6]	V8-260[1][12]

1976 (Cont'd)

CODE	TRANS.	ENGINE
T4	[6]	V8-260[1][12]
T5	[6]	V8-260[1][12]
PA	[6]	V8-350[1][13]
PB	[6]	V8-350[1][13]
PO	[6]	V8-350[1][13]
XH	[6]	V8-350[1]
XN	[6]	V8-350[1]
YA	[6]	V8-350[1]
YB	[6]	V8-350[1]
YK	[6]	V8-350[1]
YL	[6]	V8-350[1]
YP	[6]	V8-350[1]
YR	[6]	V8-350[1]
PE	[6]	V8-350[2][13]
PF	[6]	V8-350[2][13]
PM	[6]	V8-350[2][13]
PN	[6]	V8-350[2][13]
PP	[6]	V8-350[2]
X3	[6]	V8-350[2]
YD	[6]	V8-350[2]
ZC	[6]	V8-350[2]
ZX	[6]	V8-350[2]
X3	[6]	V8-350[11]
XM	[6]	V8-350[11]
XP	[6]	V8-350[11]
XR	[6]	V8-350[11]
XU	[6]	V8-350[11]
XW	[6]	V8-350[11]
XX	[6]	V8-350[11]
ZF	[6]	V8-350[11]
ZH	[6]	V8-350[11]
XA	[6]	V8-400[1]
XB	[6]	V8-400[1]
XC	[6]	V8-400[1]
XJ	[6]	V8-400[1]
YC	[6]	V8-400[1]
YJ	[6]	V8-400[1]
Z8	[6]	V8-400[1]
WT	[5]	V8-400[2]
YS	[6]	V8-400[2]
YT	[6]	V8-400[2]
YY	[6]	V8-400[2]
YZ	[6]	V8-400[2]
Y6	[6]	V8-400[2]
Y7	[6]	V8-400[2]
ZA	[6]	V8-400[2]
ZK	[6]	V8-400[2]
X4	[6]	V8-400[11]
X6	[6]	V8-400[11]
X7	[6]	V8-400[11]
X9	[6]	V8-400[11]
X8	[6]	V8-400[11]
XS	[6]	V8-400[11]
XT	[6]	V8-400[11]
XY	[6]	V8-400[11]
XZ	[6]	V8-400[11]

ENGINE IDENTIFICATION—Continued

CODE	TRANS.	ENGINE
ZJ	[6]	V8-400[11]
ZL	[6]	V8-400[11]
WX	[5]	V8-455[2]
Y3	[6]	V8-455[2]
Y4	[6]	V8-455[2]
Y8	[6]	V8-455[2]
ZB	[6]	V8-455[2]
Z3	[6]	V8-455[2]
Z4	[5]	V8-455[2]
Z6	[6]	V8-455[2]

1977

CODE	TRANS.	ENGINE
WF	[7]	4-151[1]
WH	[7]	4-151[1]
YR	[6]	4-151[1]
YS	[6]	4-151[1]
SG	[4]	V6-231[1][13]
SI	[6]	V6-231[1][13]
SJ	[6]	V6-231[1][13]
SK	[6]	V6-231[1][13]
SL	[6]	V6-231[1][13]
SM	[6]	V6-231[1][13]
SN	[6]	V6-231[1][13]
SU	[4]	V6-231[1][13]
HK	[6]	V8-301[1]
WB	[5]	V8-301[1]
YH	[6]	V8-301[1]
YW	[6]	V8-301[1]
YX	[5]	V8-301[1]
Q2	[6]	V8-350[2][12]
Q3	[6]	V8-350[2][12]
Q6	[6]	V8-350[2][12]
Q7	[6]	V8-350[2][12]
Q8	[6]	V8-350[2][12]
Q9	[6]	V8-350[2][12]
QP	[6]	V8-350[2][12]
QQ	[6]	V8-350[2][12]
TK	[6]	V8-350[2][12]
TL	[6]	V8-350[2][12]
TN	[6]	V8-350[2][12]
TO	[6]	V8-350[2][12]
TX	[6]	V8-350[2][12]
TY	[6]	V8-350[2][12]
Y9	[6]	V8-350[2]

CODE	TRANS.	ENGINE
YA	[6]	V8-350[2]
YB	[6]	V8-350[2]
WA	[5]	V8-400[2]
XA	[6]	V8-400[2]
Y4	[6]	V8-400[2]
Y6	[6]	V8-400[2]
Y7	[6]	V8-400[2]
YC	[6]	V8-400[2]
YD	[6]	V8-400[2]
YU	[6]	V8-400[2]
U2	[6]	V8-403[2][12]
U3	[6]	V8-403[2][12]
UA	[6]	V8-403[2][12]
UB	[6]	V8-403[2][12]
VA	[6]	V8-403[2][12]
VB	[6]	V8-403[2][12]
VJ	[6]	V8-403[2][12]
VK	[6]	V8-403[2][12]

1978

CODE	TRANS.	ENGINE
YB	[6]	4-151[1]
YC	[6]	4-151[1]
EA	[4]	V6-231[1][13]
EC	[6]	V6-231[1][13]
EE	[6]	V6-231[1][13]
EI	[6]	V6-231[1][13]
EJ	[6]	V6-231[1][13]
EK	[6]	V6-231[1][13]
EL	[6]	V6-231[1][13]
OE	[6]	V6-231[1][13]
OH	[6]	V6-231[1][13]
OK	[6]	V6-231[1][13]
OR	[6]	V6-231[1][13]
XA	[6]	V8-301[1]
XB	[6]	V8-301[1]
XC	[6]	V8-301[1]
XD	[6]	V8-301[1]
XF	[6]	V8-301[2]
XH	[6]	V8-301[2]
XU	[6]	V8-301[2]
XW	[6]	V8-301[2]
CPF	[6]	V8-305[1][14]
CPH	[6]	V8-305[1][14]

CODE	TRANS.	ENGINE
CPZ	[6]	V8-305[1][14]
CRU	[6]	V8-305[1][14]
CRY	[6]	V8-305[1][14]
CRZ	[6]	V8-305[1][14]
CTH	[4]	V8-305[1][14]
CTJ	[6]	V8-305[1][14]
CTK	[6]	V8-305[1][14]
CTM	[6]	V8-305[1][14]
CTS	[6]	V8-305[1][14]
CTT	[6]	V8-305[1][14]
CTU	[6]	V8-305[1][14]
CTW	[6]	V8-305[1][14]
CTX	[6]	V8-305[1][14]
CTY	[6]	V8-305[1][14]
CTZ	[6]	V8-305[1][14]
MA	[6]	V8-350[2][13]
MB	[6]	V8-350[2][13]
TO	[6]	V8-350[2][12]
TP	[6]	V8-350[2][12]
TQ	[6]	V8-350[2][12]
TS	[6]	V8-350[2][12]
Q2	[6]	V8-350[2][12]
Q3	[6]	V8-350[2][12]
CHJ	[6]	V8-350[2][14]
CHL	[6]	V8-350[2][14]
CHR	[6]	V8-350[2][14]
CMC	[6]	V8-350[2][14]
WC	[4]	V8-400[2]
XJ	[6]	V8-400[2]
XK	[6]	V8-400[2]
X7	[6]	V8-400[2]
X9	[6]	V8-400[2]
Y	[6]	V8-400[2]
YA	[6]	V8-400[2]
YH	[6]	V8-400[2]
YJ	[6]	V8-400[2]
YK	[6]	V8-400[2]
U2	[6]	V8-403[2][12]
U3	[6]	V8-403[2][12]
U5	[6]	V8-403[2][12]
U6	[6]	V8-403[2][12]
VA	[6]	V8-403[2][12]
VB	[6]	V8-403[2][12]
VD	[6]	V8-403[2][12]
VE	[6]	V8-403[2][12]

[1]—Two barrel carburetor.
[2]—Four barrel carburetor.
[4]—Manual trans.
[5]—Four speed manual trans.
[6]—Automatic trans.
[7]—Five speed manual trans.
[8]—Super Duty engine.
[9]—One barrel carburetor.
[10]—High Energy Ignition System (H.E.I.).
[11]—Does not use harmonic balancer.
[12]—See Oldsmobile chapter for service procedures.
[13]—See Buick chapter for service procedures.
[14]—See Chevrolet chapter for service procedures.

Continued

TUNE UP SPECIFICATIONS

The following specifications are published from the latest information available. This
data should be used only in the absence of a decal affixed in the engine compartment.

★When using a timing light, disconnect vacuum hose or tube at distributor and plug opening in hose or tube so idle speed will not be affected.

●When checking compression, lowest cylinder must be within 80% of the highest.

▲Before removing wires from distributor cap, determine location of the No. 1 wire in cap, as distributor position may have been altered from that shown at the end of this chart.

Year/Engine	Spark Plug		Distributor		Ignition Timing ★			Carb. Adjustments	
								Hot Idle Speed②	
	Type	Gap Inch	Point Gap Inch	Dwell Angle Deg.	Firing Order Fig. ▲	Timing BTDC ①	Mark Fig.	Std. Trans.	Auto. Trans.
1974									
6-250⑭	R46T	.035	⑮	32½	E	6°	H	850	600
V8-350 2 Bar. Carb.	R46TS	.040	⑮	30	D	⑯	I	900	650
V8-350 2 Bar. Carb.④	R46TS	.040	⑮	30	D	10°	I	—	625
V8-350 4 Bar. Carb.	R46TS	.040	⑮	30	D	⑯	I	1000	650
V8-350 4 Bar. Carb.④	R46TS	.040	⑮	30	D	10°	I	—	625
V8-400 2 Bar. Carb.	R46TS	.040	⑮	30	⑩	⑯	I	—	650
V8-400 2 Bar. Carb.④	R46TS	.040	⑮	30	⑩	10°	I	—	625
V8-400 4 Bar. Carb.	R45TS	.040	⑮	30	⑩	⑯	I	1000	650
V8-400 4 Bar. Carb.④	R45TS	.040	⑮	30	⑩	10°	I	—	625
V8-455	R45TS	.040	⑮	30	⑩	⑯	I	—	650
V8-455④	R45TS	.040	⑮	30	⑩	10°	I	—	625
V8-455 S.D.	R44TS	.040	⑮	30	⑩	12°	I	1000	750
1975									
6-250⑭	R46TX	.060	—	—	L	10°	H	850	⑳
V8-260⑤㉑	R46SX	.080	—	—	M	16°⑨	J	750	650
V8-260⑤㉒	R46SX	.080	—	—	M	18°⑨	J	750	650
V8-350⑥	R45TSX	.060	—	—	N	12°	K	800	600
V8-350㉑	R46TSX	.060	—	—	O	12°	I	775	㉓
V8-350㉒	R46TSX	.060	—	—	O	16°	I	775	㉓
V8-400㉑	㉔	.060	—	—	O	12°	I	775	㉖
V8-400㉒	㉔	.060	—	—	O	16°	I	775	㉖
V8-455㉘	R45TSX	.060	—	—	O	16°	I	775	650D
V8-455④	R45TSX	.060	—	—	O	10°	I	—	675D
1976									
6-250⑭	R46T	.035	—	—	L	㉗	H	850	⑳
V8-260⑤㉖	R46SX	.080	—	—	M	⑬	J	750	550
V8-260⑤④	R46SX	.080	—	—	M	⑰	J	—	600
V8-350⑥	R45TSX	.060	—	—	N	12°	K	—	600D
V8-350	R46TSX	.060	—	—	O	16°	I	—	550D
V8-400 2 Bar. Carb.	R46TSX	.060	—	—	O	16°	I	—	550D
V8-400 4 Bar. Carb.	R45TSX	.060	—	—	O	⑧	I	775	575D
V8-455④	R45TSX	.060	—	—	O	12°	I	—	600D
V8-455㉘	R45TSX	.060	—	—	O	16°	I	775	550D
1977									
4-151⑱㉖	R44TSX	.060	—	—	F	14°	Q	500/1000③	500/650③
4-151⑲㉖	R44TSX	.060	—	—	F	14°	Q	500/1200③	650/850③
4-151④	R44TSX	.060	—	—	F	12°	Q		650/850㉘
V6-231㉛	R44TS	.040	—	—	G	12°	R㊼	600/800㉘	600/670㉘
V6-231㊺	R46TSX	.060	—	—	S	15°	T㊼	500/1000③	500/650D③
V8-301	R46TSX	.060	—	—	O	㉜	A	750/875㉘	550/650㉘
V8-305⑭	R45TS	.045	—	—	P	8°	H	700	500/650㉘

Pontiac—Except Astre & Sunbird

TUNE UP SPECIFICATIONS—Continued

The following specifications are published from the latest information available. This data should be used only in the absence of a decal affixed in the engine compartment.

★When using a timing light, disconnect vacuum hose or tube at distributor and plug opening in tube or hose so idle speed will not be affected.

●When checking compression, lowest cylinder must be within 80% of the highest.

▲Before removing wires from distributor cap, determine location of the No. 1 wire in cap, as distributor position may have been altered from that shown at the end of this chart.

Year/Engine	Spark Plug		Distributor		Ignition Timing★			Carb. Adjustments	
								Hot Idle Speed [2]	
	Type	Gap Inch	Point Gap Inch	Dwell Angle Deg.	Firing Order Fig. ▲	Timing BTDC [1]	Mark Fig.	Std. Trans.	Auto. Trans.
1977—Continued									
V8-350 [39][14]	R45TS	.045	—	—	P	8°	H	700	500/650[28]
V8-350 [33][35][40]	R45TSX	.060	—	—	O	16°	I	—	575/650[28]
V8-350 [5][34][41]	R46SZ	.060	—	—	M	20°[9]	J	—	550/650[28]
V8-350 [36][5][41]	R46SZ	.060	—	—	M	20°[9]	J	—	600/700[28]
V8-400 [29]	R45TSX	.060	—	—	O	18°	I	775	—
V8-400 [30][37]	R45TSX	.060	—	—	O	16°	I	—	575/650[28]
V8-400 [38]	R45TSX	.060	—	—	O	18°	I	—	600/700[28]
V8-403 [35][5]	R46SZ	.060	—	—	M	22°[9]	J	—	550/650[28]
V8-403 [4][5]	R46SZ	.060	—	—	M	20°[9]	J	—	550/650[28]
V8-403 [36][5]	R46SZ	.060	—	—	M	20°[9]	J	—	600/700[28]
1978									
4-151	R43TSX	.060	—	—	F	14°[9]	Q	—	650/850[28]
V6-231 [48]	R46TSX	.060	—	—	S	15°	T[47]	800	600/670[28]
V8-301	R45TSX	.060	—	—	O	12°	A	—	550/650[28]
V8-305 [14][35]	R45TS	.045	—	—	P	4°	H	600/700[28]	500/600[28]
V8-305 [14][4]	R45TS	.045	—	—	P	6°	H	—	500/650[28]
V8-305 [14][36]	R45TS	.045	—	—	P	8°	H	—	600/700[28]
V8-350 [14][39]	R45TS	.045	—	—	P	[42]	H	700	[43][28]
V8-350 [5][7]	R46SZ	.060	—	—	M	20°[9]	J	—	550/650[28]
V8-350 [11][12]	R46TSX	.060	—	—	N	15°	T[47]	—	550D
V8-400 [44]	R45TSX	.060	—	—	O	16°	I	—	575/650[28]
V8-400 [45]	R45TSX	.060	—	—	O	18°	I	775	600/700[28]
V8-403	R46SZ	.060	—	—	M	20°[9]	J	—	[46][28]
1979									
V6-231 [48]	[49]	.060	—	—	—	15°	T[47]	800	600
V8-301	[24]	.060	—	—	O	12°	A	—	550
V8-305 [14][35]	R45TS	.045	—	—	P	4°	H	700	500
V8-305 [14][4]	R45TS	.045	—	—	P	6°	H	—	600
V8-305 [14][36]	R45TS	.045	—	—	P	8	H	—	600

[1]—BTDC: Before top dead center.
[2]—Idle speed on manual trans. equipped vehicles is adjusted in neutral. Idle speed on auto. trans., equipped vehicles is adjusted in drive.
[3]—Where two idle speeds are listed, the higher speed is with idle solenoid energized.
[4]—California.
[5]—See Oldsmobile Chapter for service procedure.
[6]—Ventura only. See Buick Chapter for service procedures.
[7]—Distributor rotor rotation counter-clockwise.
[8]—Std. Trans. 12°, Auto. Trans. 16°.
[9]—At 1100 RPM.
[10]—Exc. H.E.I., Fig. D; H.E.I., Fig. O.
[11]—For service on this engine see Buick chapter.
[12]—Distributor at front of engine.

[13]—Manual trans., 16° BTDC; auto. trans., 18° BTDC.
[14]—For service on this engine, see Chevrolet Chapter.
[15]—New points .019″, used points .016″.
[16]—Std. trans. 10° BTDC. Auto trans. 12° BTDC.
[17]—Engine codes TE, TJ, T4, T5, TK, TN, TA, & TD, 14° BTDC. Engine codes TP, TT, T2 & T3, 16° BTDC.
[18]—Less A/C.
[19]—With A/C.
[20]—Exc. Calif., 550 RPM; Calif., 600 RPM.
[21]—Std. trans. & all California models.
[22]—Auto. trans. exc. California.
[23]—2 bbl. carb., 600 RPM; 4 bbl. carb.—Exc. Calif., 650 RPM; Calif., 625 RPM.
[24]—2 bbl. carb., R46TSX; 4 bbl. carb., R45TSX.
[25]—2 bbl. carb., 650 RPM; 4 bbl. carb.—Exc.

Calif. & Grand Safari sta. wag., 650 RPM; Grand Safari sta. wag. exc. Calif., 625 RPM; All Calif. models, 600 RPM.
[26]—Exc. California.
[27]—Std. trans., 6° BTDC; auto. trans., 10° BTDC.
[28]—Where two idle speeds are listed, the higher speed is with A/C solenoid energized & A/C "On".
[29]—Std. trans.
[30]—Auto. trans.
[31]—Exc. even fire engine.
[32]—Auto. trans., 12° BTDC @ 550 RPM. Manual trans., 16° BTDC @ 850 RPM.
[33]—Firebird, LeMans & Grand Prix.
[34]—Exc. High Altitude.
[35]—Exc. Calif. & high altitude.

Continued

TUNE UP NOTES—Continued

㊱—High altitude vehicles.
㊲—Exc. Firebird engine code Y6.
㊳—Firebird engine code Y6.
㊴—Distributor rotor rotation, clockwise.
㊵—Distributor rotor rotation, counter-clockwise. Fuel pump located at left side of engine.
㊶—Distributor rotor rotation, counter-clockwise. Fuel pump located at right side of engine.

㊷—Auto. trans., 8 BTDC; Manual trans., 6 BTDC.
㊸—Calif. 500/600; High altitude, 600/650.
㊹—Exc. high performance engine.
㊺—High performance engine.
㊻—Calif. 550/650; High altitude, 600/700.
㊼—The harmonic balancer on these engines has two timing marks. The mark measuring 1/16

inch is used when setting timing with a hand held timing light. The mark measuring 1/8 inch is used when setting timing with magnetic timing equipment.
㊽—Even fire engine.
㊾—Exc. Calif. & High altitude, R46TSX; Calif. & High altitude, R45TSX.

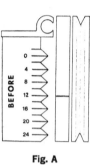

Fig. A

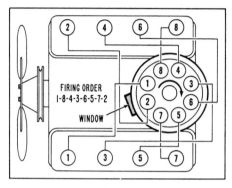

Fig. B

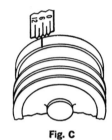

Fig. C

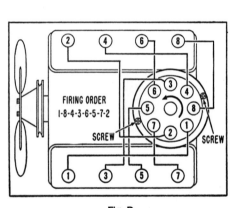

Fig. D

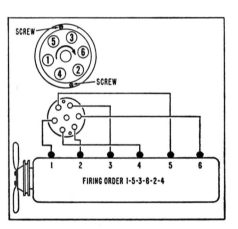

Fig. E

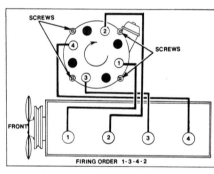

Fig. F

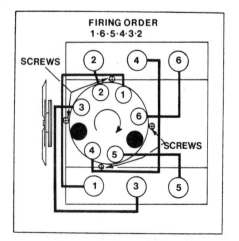

Fig. G

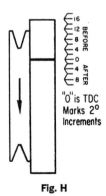

Fig. H

Fig. I

Pontiac—Except Astre & Sunbird

TUNE UP NOTES—Continued

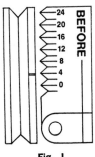

Fig. J

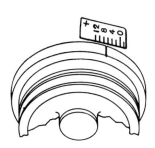

Fig. K

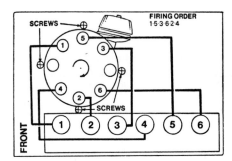

Fig. L

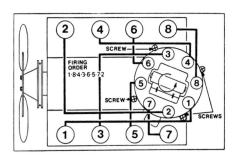

Fig. M

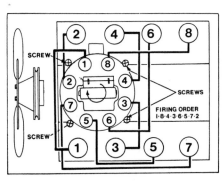

Fig. N

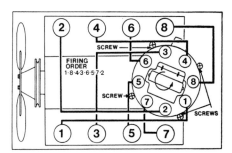

Fig. O

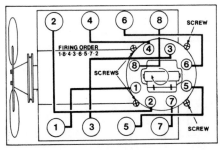

Fig. P

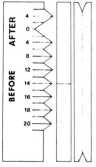

Fig. Q

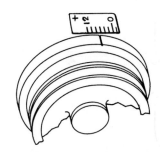

Fig. R

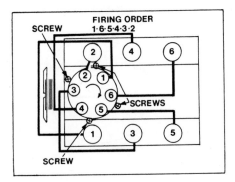

Fig. S

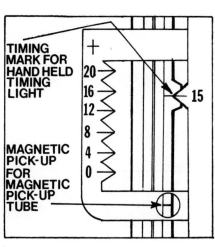

Fig. T

Chevrolet LUV

TUNE UP SPECIFICATIONS

The following specifications are published from the latest information available. This data should be used only in the absence of a decal affixed in the engine compartment.

★When using a timing light, disconnect vacuum hose or tube at distributor and plug opening in tube or hose so idle speed will not be affected.

▲Before removing wires from distributor cap, determine location of the No. 1 wire in cap, as distributor position may have been altered from that shown at the end of this chart.

Year/Engine	Spark Plug		Distributor		Ignition Timing★			Carb. Adjustment	
	Type	Gap Inch	Point Gap Inch	Dwell Angle Deg.	Firing Order Fig. ▲	Timing BTDC ②	Mark Fig.	Hot Idle Speed	
								Std. Trans.	Auto. Trans.
1974									
All	BP6ES	.035	.020	49–55	A	12°	C	700	—
1975									
All	BP6ES	.030	.020	49–55	A	12°	C	700	—
1976–78									
All	BPR6ES	.030	.018	47–57	B	6°	D	900	900N
1979									
All	BPR6ES	.030	.018	47–57	B	6°	D	①	900N

①—Except Calif. 800; Calif. 900.
②—BTDC: Before Top Dead Center.

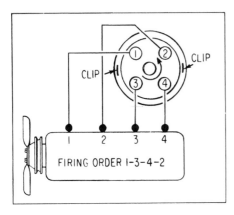

Fig. A

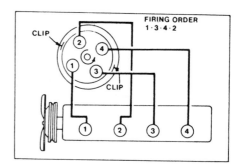

Fig. B

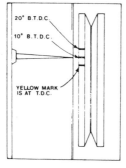

Fig. C

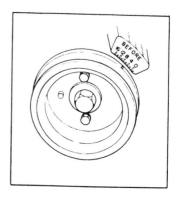

Fig. D

Datsun

ENGINE IDENTIFICATION

The engine number is stamped on the right side of the cylinder block. The prefix to the engine number designates the type engine.

Engine	Model
A13	1974 B210
A14	1975–79 B210 1976–78 F10 1979 310
A15	1979 210 and 310 auto. wagon
L18	1974 710 1974 620 Pick-up
L20	1974–76 610 1975–77 710 1975–77 620 Pick-up 1977 200SX
L20B	1978–79 510 1978–79 620 Pick-up 1978–79 200 SX
L24	1977–79 810
L26	1974 260Z
L28	1975–78 280Z 1979 280ZX

TUNE UP SPECIFICATIONS

The following specifications are published from the latest information available. This data should be used only in the absence of a decal affixed in the engine compartment.

★When using a timing light, disconnect vacuum hose or tube at distributor and plug opening in tube or hose so idle speed will not be affected.

▲Before removing wires from distributor cap, determine location of the No. 1 wire in cap, as distributor position may have been altered from that shown at the end of this chart.

Year/Engine	Spark Plug		Distributor		Ignition Timing★			Carb. Adjustment	
								Hot Idle Speed	
	Type	Gap Inch	Point Gap Inch	Dwell Angle Deg.	Firing Order Fig. ▲	Timing BTDC ㉑	Mark Fig.	Std. Trans.	Auto. Trans.
1974									
A13	BP5-ES	.033	.020	49–55	A	5°	D	800	650
L18	B6-ES	.030	.020	49–55	B	12°	D	800	650
L20	B6-ES	.030	.020	49–55	B	12°	D	750	650
L26	BP6-ES	.033	.014 ⑲	—	C	③	E	750	600
1975									
A14④	BP5-ES	.033	.020	49–55	A	10°	D	700	650
A14⑤	BP5-ES	.033	.012 ⑲	—	A	⑥	D	700	650
L20④⑦	BP6-ES	.034	.020	49–55	B	12°	D	750	650
L20⑧⑦	BP6-ES	.034	.012 ⑲	—	B	12°	D	750	650
L20④⑧	BP6-ES	.034	.020	49–55	B	12°	D	750	650
L20⑤⑧	BP6-ES	.034	.020	49–55	B	10°	D	750	650
L28④	B6-ES	.033	.012 ⑲	—	C	7°	E	800	700

Continued

TUNE UP SPECIFICATIONS—Continued

| Year/Engine | Spark Plug | | | Distributor | Ignition Timing★ | | | Carb. Adjustment | |
| | Type | Gap Inch | Point Gap Inch | Dwell Angle Deg. | Firing Order Fig. ▲ | Timing BTDC [21] | Mark Fig. | Hot Idle Speed | |
								Std. Trans.	Auto. Trans.
1976									
A14[4][9]	BP5-ES	.033	.020	49–55	A	10°	D	700	—
A14[5][9]	BP5-ES	.033	.012 [16]	—	A	8°	D	700	—
A14[4][10]	BP5-ES	.033	.020	49–55	A	10°	D	—	650
A14[5][10]	BP5-ES	.033	.012 [16]	—	A	8°	D	—	650
L20[4][7]	BP6-ES	.033	.020	49–55	B	12°	D	750	650
L20[5][7]	BP6-ES-11	.041	.012 [16]	—	B	12°	D	750	650
L20[4][8]	BP6-ES	.033	.020	49–55	B	12°	D	750	650
L20[5][8]	BP6-ES-11	.041	.012 [16]	—	B	10°	D	750	650
L28[4]	B6-ES	.033	.012 [16]	—	C	7°	E	800	700
L28[5]	B6-ES	.033	.012 [16]	—	C	10°	E	800	700
1977									
A14[4][9]	BP5-ES-11	.041	.020	49–55	A	10°	D	700	—
A14[5][9]	BP5-ES-11	.041	.012 [16]	—	A	10°	D	700	—
A14[4][10]	BP5-ES-11	.041	.020	49–55	A	8°	D	—	650
A14[5][10]	BP5-ES-11	.041	.012 [16]	—	A	10°	D	—	650
L20[4][9][13]	BP6-ES-11	.041	.020	49–55	B	10°	D	600	—
L20[5][9][13]	BP6-ES-11	.041	.012 [16]	—	B	12°	D	600	—
L20[4][10][13]	BP6-ES-11	.041	.020	49–55	B	12°	D	—	600
L20[5][10][13]	BP6-ES-11	.041	.012 [16]	—	B	12°	D	—	750
L20[4][9][14]	BP6-ES	.041	.020	49–55	B	12°	D	600	—
L20[5][9][14]	BP6-ES-11	.041	.012 [16]	—	B	12°	D	600	—
L20[4][10][14]	BP6-ES-11	.041	.020	49–55	B	12°	D	—	600
L20[5][10][14]	BP6-ES-11	.041	.012 [16]	—	B	12°	D	—	600
L20[4][8][9]	BP6-ES	.033	.020	49–55	B	12°	D	750	—
L20[5][8][9]	BP6-ES-11	.041	.012 [16]	—	B	10°	D	750	—
L20[4][8][10]	BP6-ES	.033	.020	49–55	B	12°	D	—	650
L20[5][8][10]	BP6-ES-11	.041	.012 [16]	—	B	12°	D	—	650
L24	BP6-ES-11	.041	.012 [16]	—	C	10°	E	700	600
L28	BP6-ES-11	.041	.012 [16]	—	C	10°	E	800	700

TUNE UP SPECIFICATIONS—Continued

The following specifications are published from the latest information available. This data should be used only in the absence of a decal affixed in the engine compartment.

★When using a timing light, disconnect vacuum hose or tube at distributor and plug opening in tube or hose so idle speed will not be affected.

▲Before removing wires from distributor cap, determine location of the No. 1 wire in cap, as distributor position may have been altered from that shown at the end of this chart.

Year/Engine	Spark Plug		Distributor		Ignition Timing ★			Carb. Adjustment	
								Hot Idle Speed	
	Type	Gap Inch	Point Gap Inch	Dwell Angle Deg.	Firing Order Fig. ▲	Timing BTDC [21]	Mark Fig.	Std. Trans.	Auto. Trans.
1978									
A14[4][9]	BP5-ES-11	.041	.012 [15]	—	A	10°	D	700	—
A14[10][9]	BP5-ES-11	.041	.012 [15]	—	A	5°	D	700	—
A14[10]	BP5-ES-11	.041	.012 [15]	—	A	[17]	D	—	650D
L20B	BP5-ES-11	.041	.012 [15]	—	B	12°	D	600	600D
L28	BP6-ES-11 [12]	.041	.012 [15]	—	C	10°	F	800	700D
L24	BP6-ES-11 [12]	.041	.012 [15]	—	C	[17]	F	700	650D
1979									
A14[4][9]	BP5-ES-11	.041	—	—	A	10°	D	700	—
A14[10][9]	BP5-ES-11	.041	—	—	A	5° [18]	D	700	—
A14[10]	BP5-ES-11	.041	—	—	A	[17]	D	—	650D
A15[13]	BP5-ES-11	.041	—	—	A	[17]	D	—	650D
L20B[20][9]	BP5-ES-11	.041	.012 [15]	—	B	[1]	D	600	—
L20B[20][10]	BP5-ES-11	.041	.012 [15]	—	B	12°	D	—	600D
L20B[13][9]	BP5-ES-11	.041	.012 [15]	—	B	[2]	D	600	—
L20B[13][10]	BP5-ES-11	.041	.012 [15]	—	B	12°	D	—	600D
L20B[8]	BP5-ES-11	.041	.012 [15]	—	B	12°	D	600	600D
L28	BP6-ES-11	.041	—	—	C	10°	F	800	700D
L24	BP6-ES-11	.041	—	—	C	10°	F	700	650D

①—Except Calif. 11° BTDC; Calif. 12° BTDC.
②—Except Calif. 9° BTDC; Calif. 12° BTDC.
③—Man. trans. 8° BTDC; auto. trans. 15° BTDC.
④—Except Calif.
⑤—California.
⑥—Man. trans. 10° BTDC; auto. trans. 8° BTDC.
⑦—610 & 710.
⑧—Pick-up.
⑨—Manual trans.
⑩—Auto. trans.
⑪—Except Calif. 12° BTDC; Calif. 10° BTDC.
⑫—Optional: BR6ES-11.
⑬—200SX.
⑭—710.
⑮—Distributor air gap.
⑯—Exc. Calif. with catalytic converter.
⑰—Exc. Calif. 8° BTDC; Calif. 10° BTDC.
⑱—Disconnect vacuum hose on distributor side and plug hose.
⑲—210 and 310 wagon with auto. trans.
⑳—510.
㉑—BTDC: Before Top Dead Center.

Continued

TUNE UP NOTES—Continued

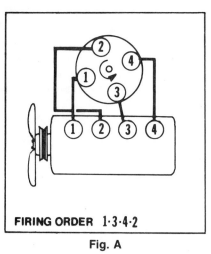

FIRING ORDER 1·3·4·2

Fig. A

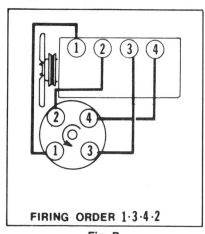

FIRING ORDER 1·3·4·2

Fig. B

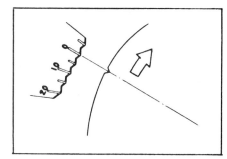

FIRING ORDER 1·5·3·6·2·4

Fig. C

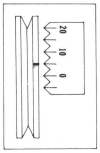

Fig. D

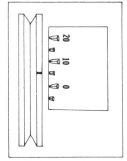

Fig. E

Fig. F

Dodge D-50 • Plymouth Arrow

ENGINE IDENTIFICATION CODE

The engine code is the prefix to the serial number stamped on the right side top edge of the engine block.

52A = 122 cu. in. (2000cc) engine.
54A = 156 cu. in. (2600cc) engine.

TUNE UP SPECIFICATIONS

The following specifications are published from the latest information available. This data should be used only in the absence of a decal affixed in the engine compartment.

★When using a timing light, disconnect vacuum hose or tube at distributor and plug opening in tube or hose so idle speed will not be affected.

▲Before removing wires from distributor cap, determine location of the No. 1 wire in cap, as distributor position may have been altered from that shown at the end of this chart.

Year/Engine	Spark Plug		Distributor		Ignition Timing★			Carb. Adjustment	
	Type	Gap Inch	Point Gap Inch	Dwell Angle Deg.	Firing Order Fig. ▲	Timing BTDC ①	Mark Fig.	Hot Idle Speed	
								Std. Trans.	Auto. Trans.
1979									
4-122	RN9Y	.041	—	—	A	5°	C	650	700
4-156	RN12Y	.041	—	—	B	7°	C	850	850

①—BTDC: Before Top Dead Center.

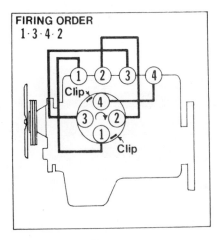

FIRING ORDER
1·3·4·2

Fig. A

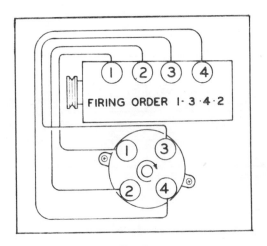

FIRING ORDER 1·3·4·2

Fig. B

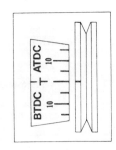

Fig. C

ENGINE IDENTIFICATION

The engine displacement appears on a decal affixed to the valve cover and also on the model plate that's riveted to the body at the right rear corner of the engine compartment.

TUNE UP SPECIFICATIONS

The following specifications are published from the latest information available. This data should be used only in the absence of a decal affixed in the engine compartment.

★When using a timing light, disconnect vacuum hose or tube at distributor and plug opening in tube or hose so idle speed will not be affected.

▲Before removing wires from distributor cap, determine location of the No. 1 wire in cap, as distributor position may have been altered from that shown at the end of this chart.

Year/Engine	Spark Plug		Distributor		Ignition Timing ★			Carb. Adjustment	
	Type	Gap Inch	Point Gap Inch	Dwell Angle Deg.	Firing Order Fig. ▲	Timing BTDC ①	Mark Fig.	Hot Idle Speed	
								Std. Trans.	Auto. Trans.
1974									
All	AG32A	.031	.020	49–55	A	3°	B	700	700D
1975									
All	AG32A	.031	.020	49–55	A	5°	B	700	700D
1976									
All	AFR32	.031	—	—	A	5°	C	700	700D
1977									
4-109 (1800cc)	AGR32	.031	—	—	A	5°	C	800	700D
4-140 (2300cc)	AGRF52	.031	—	—	D	6°	E	800	700D
1978									
4-109	BPRE6S	.031	.020	49–55	A	8°	F	700	—
4-140	BPR5EFS	.031	—	—	D	6°	E	800	700D
1979									
4-122 (2000cc)	BPR5ES	.031	—	—	A	8°	F	650	—
4-140	BPR5EFS	.031	—	—	D	8°	F	800	700D

①—BTDC: Before Top Dead Center.

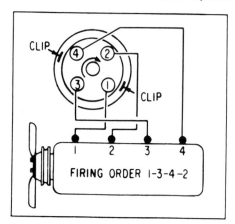

Fig. A

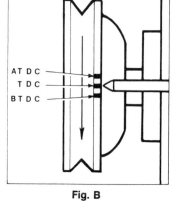

Fig. B

Fig. C

Ford Courier

TUNE UP NOTES—Continued

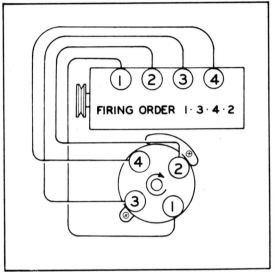

Fig. D

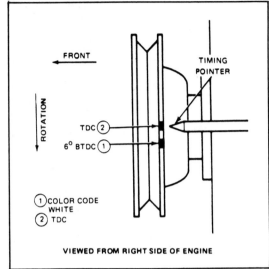

Fig. E

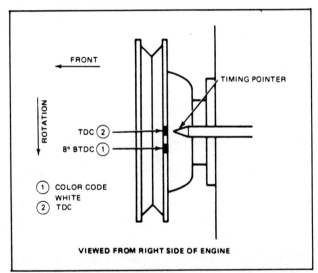

Fig. F

ENGINE IDENTIFICATION

Engine codes are printed on a decal affixed to the valve cover.

Engine	Model
2T-C	1974–79 Corolla (1588cc)
3K-C	1974 and 1977–79 Corolla (1166cc)
4M	1974–76 Mark II 1978–79 Cressida
18R-C	1974 Corona 1974 Celica 1974 Hi Lux pick-up
20R	1975–79 Corona 1975–79 Celica 1975–79 Hi Lux pick-up

TUNE UP SPECIFICATIONS

The following specifications are published from the latest information available. This data should be used only in the absence of a decal affixed in the engine compartment.

★When using a timing light, disconnect vacuum hose or tube at distributor and plug opening in tube or hose so idle speed will not be affected.

▲Before removing wires from distributor cap, determine location of the No. 1 wire in cap, as distributor position may have been altered from that shown at the end of this chart.

Year/Engine	Spark Plug		Distributor		Ignition Timing★			Carb. Adjustment	
								Hot Idle Speed	
	Type	Gap Inch	Point Gap Inch	Dwell Angle Deg.	Firing Order Fig. ▲	Timing BTDC ⑪	Mark Fig.	Std. Trans.	Auo. Trans.
1974									
3K-C	BP5ES-L	.030	.018	50–54	A	5°	B	750	750N
2T-C	BP5ES-L	.030	.018	50–54	A	⑥	C	⑦	⑦
18R-C	⑧	.030	.018	50–54	A	7°	D	650	800N
4M	BP5ES-L	.030	.018	39–43	E	5°	F	700	750N
1975									
2T-C	BP5ES-L	.030	.018	④	A	⑤	C	850	850N
20R	BP5ES-L	.030	.018	50–54	G	8°	H	850	850N
4M	BP5ES-L	.030	.018	38–44	E	⑥	F	800	750
1976									
2T-C	BP5ES-L	.030	.018	50–54	A	10°	C	850	850N
20R	BP5ES-L	.030	.018	50–54	G	8°	H	850	850N
4M	BP5ES-L	.030	.018	38–44	E	③	F	800	750
1977									
3K-C	BP5EA-L	.031	.018	50–54	A	8°	B	750	750
2T-C	BP5ES-L	.032	.018	50–54	A	10°①	C	850	850
20R	BP5ES-L	.031	.018	50–54	G	8°①	H	800	850
1978									
3K-C	BP5EA-L	.031	.012⑩	—	A	8°	I	750	750
2T-C	BP5ES-L	.031	.012⑩	—	A	10°①	J	850	850
20R	BP5ES-L	.031	.012⑩	—	G	8°①	K	800	850
4M	BPR5ES	.031	.012⑩	—	E	10°	M	—	750N

Toyota

TUNE UP SPECIFICATIONS—Continued

The following specifications are published from the latest information available. This data should be used only in the absence of a decal affixed in the engine compartment.

★When using a timing light, disconnect vacuum hose or tube at distributor and plug opening in tube or hose so idle speed will not be affected.

▲Before removing wires from distributor cap, determine location of the No. 1 wire in cap, as distributor position may have been altered from that shown at the end of this chart.

Year/Engine	Spark Plug		Distributor		Ignition Timing★			Carb. Adjustment	
								Hot Idle Speed	
	Type	Gap Inch	Point Gap Inch	Dwell Angle Deg.	Firing Order Fig. ▲	Timing BTDC ⑪	Mark Fig.	Std. Trans.	Auto. Trans.
1979									
3K-C	BP5EA-L	.031	.012⑩	—	A	8°	L	750	750
2T-C	BP5EA	.030	.012⑩	—	A	10°①	J	850	850
20R	BP5EA-L	.030	.012⑩	—	G	8°	K	800	850
4M	BPR5EA-L	.030	.012⑩	—	E	②	M	—	750N

①—Disconnect sub diaphragm hose on vehicles with HAC system.
②—Except California cars, 10° BTDC; California cars, 8° BTDC.
③—Except California cars, 10° BTDC; California cars, 5° BTDC.
④—Single point distributor, 50-54°; dual point distributor, primary points 57°, secondary points 50-54°.
⑤—Single point distributor, 10° BTDC; dual point distributor: primary 12° BTDC; secondary 19-25° BTDC.
⑥—Except California cars, 5° BTDC; California cars, 10° BTDC.
⑦—Except California cars, 750 man. trans., 800 auto. trans.; California cars, 850 man. trans., 850N auto. trans.
⑧—Except California cars, BP6ES; California cars, BP5ES-L.
⑨—BP5ES-L or BP5EA-L.
⑩—Distributor air gap.
⑪—Before Top Dead Center.

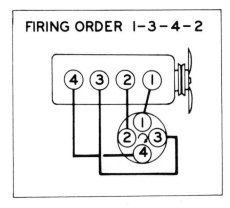

FIRING ORDER 1-3-4-2

Fig. A

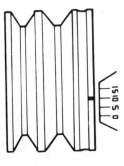

Fig. B

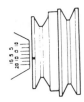

Fig. C

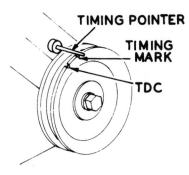

TIMING POINTER
TIMING MARK
TDC

Fig. D

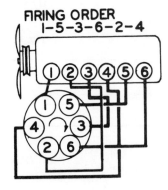

FIRING ORDER 1-5-3-6-2-4

Fig. E

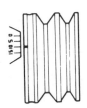

Fig. F

Continued

Toyota

TUNE-UP NOTES —Continued

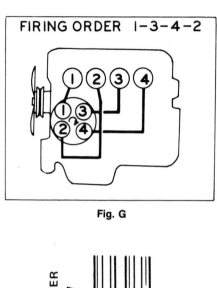

Fig. G

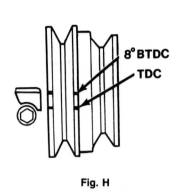

Fig. H

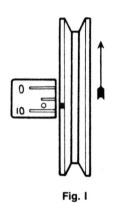

Fig. I

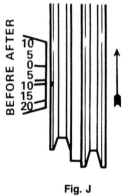

Fig. J

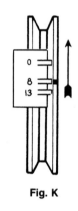

Fig. K

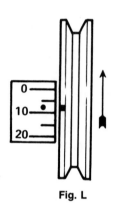

Fig. L

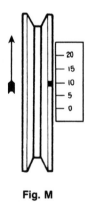

Fig. M

Volkswagen

ENGINE IDENTIFICATION

ENGINE CODE LOCATION: The engine code letters are the prefix to the engine number.

Beetle: The engine code is located on a pad on the crankcase near the front of the alternator mount.

Bus: The engine code is stamped on a pad on the front of the crankcase near the ignition coil.

Rabbit/Scirocco: The engine code is stamped on a pad on the front of the engine block near the rear of the alternator.

Year	Model	Engine Code
1974	Beetle	AH
	Bus	AW
	Rabbit/Scirocco	—
1975	Beetle	AJ
	Bus	AW, ED
	Rabbit/Scirocco	FC, FG
1976	Beetle	AJ
	Bus	GD
	Rabbit/Scirocco	FN
1977	Beetle	AJ
	Bus	GD
	Rabbit/Scirocco	CK, EE, EF
1978	Beetle	AJ
	Bus	GD
	Rabbit/Scirocco	CK, EH, FX
1979	Beetle	AJ
	Bus	GD, GE
	Rabbit/Scirocco	CK, EH, EJ

TUNE UP SPECIFICATIONS

The following specifications are published from the latest information available. This data should be used only in the absence of a decal affixed in the engine compartment.

★When using a timing light, disconnect vacuum hose or tube at distributor and plug opening in tube or hose so idle speed will not be affected.

▲Before removing wires from distributor cap, determine location of the No. 1 wire in cap, as distributor position may have been altered from that shown at the end of this chart.

Year/Model	Spark Plug		Distributor		Ignition Timing★			Carb. Adjustment	
								Hot Idle Speed	
	Type	Gap Inch	Point Gap Inch	Dwell Angle Deg.	Firing Order Fig. ▲	Timing ATDC ①	Mark Fig.	Std. Trans.	Auto. Trans.
1974									
Beetle⑥	L88A	.024	.018	44–50	A	7½°⑤	B	850	950
Bus	N88	.024	.018	44–50	A	③	③	850	950
1975									
Beetle⑥	L288	.024	.018	44–50	A	④	④	875	925
Bus	N288	.024	.018	44–50	A	5°	E	900	950
Rabbit	N8Y	.026	.016	44–50	F	3°	G	950	950
Scirocco	N8Y	.026	.016	44–50	F	3°	G	950	950
1976									
Beetle	L288	.024	.018	44–50	A	④	④	875	925
Bus	N288	.028	.018	44–50	A	7½°⑤	C	900	950
Rabbit	N8Y	.026	.016	44–50	F	3°	G	950	950
Scirocco	N8Y	.026	.016	44–50	F	3°	G	950	950
1977									
Beetle	L288	.028	.016	44–50	A	5°	B	925	925
Bus	N288	.028	.016	44–50	A	7½°⑤	C	875	925
Rabbit	N7Y	.026	.016	44–50	F	3°	G	950	950
Scirocco	N7Y	.026	.016	44–50	F	3°	G	950	950

TUNE UP SPECIFICATIONS—Continued

The following specifications are published from the latest information available. This data should be used only in the absence of a decal affixed in the engine compartment.

★When using a timing light, disconnect vacuum hose or tube at distributor and plug opening in tube or hose so idle speed will not be affected.

▲Before removing wires from distributor cap, determine location of the No. 1 wire in cap, as distributor position may have been altered from that shown at the end of this chart.

Year/Model	Spark Plug		Distributor		Ignition Timing★			Carb. Adjustment	
								Hot Idle Speed	
	Type	Gap Inch	Point Gap Inch	Dwell Angle Deg.	Firing Order Fig. ▲	Timing ATDC ①	Mark Fig.	Std. Trans.	Auto. Trans.
1978									
Beetle⑦	L288	.028	.016	44–50	A	5°	B	875	—
Bus	N288	.028	.016	44–50	A	7½°⑤	C	900	950
Rabbit	N8Y	.026	.016	44–50	F	3°	G	900	900
Scirocco	N8Y	.026	.016	44–50	F	3°	G	900	900
1979									
Beetle⑦	L288	.028	.016	44–50	A	5°	B	875	—
Bus	N288	.028	.016	44–50	A	②	②	875	925
Rabbit	N8Y	.028	.016	44–50	H	3°	G	925	925
Scirocco	N8Y	.028	.016	44–50	H	3°	G	925	925

①—ATDC: After Top Dead Center.
②—Except California: 7½° Before top dead center, Fig. C; California, 5° ATDC, Fig. E.
③—Manual Trans., 10° ATDC, Fig. D; auto. trans., 5° ATDC, Fig. E.
④—Manual trans., 5° ATDC, Fig. B; auto. trans., TDC, Fig. B.
⑤—Before top dead center.
⑥—Also includes Super Beetle and Karmann Ghia.
⑦—Convertible.

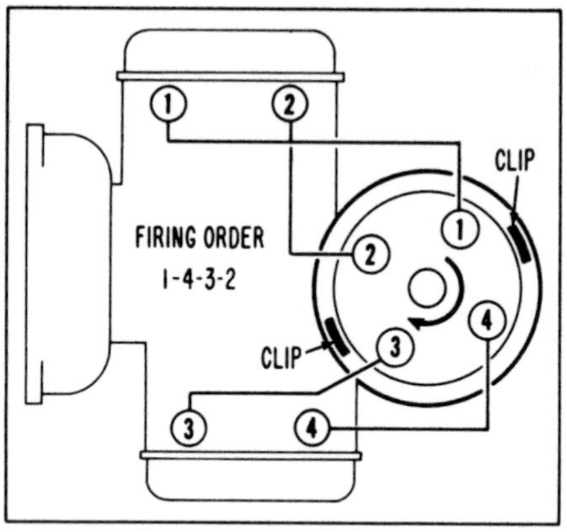

Fig. A

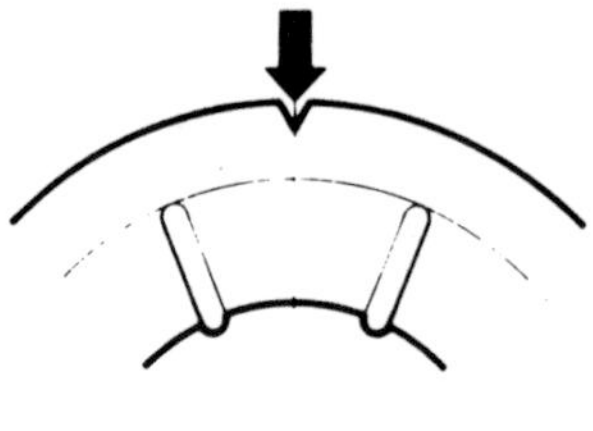

Fig. B

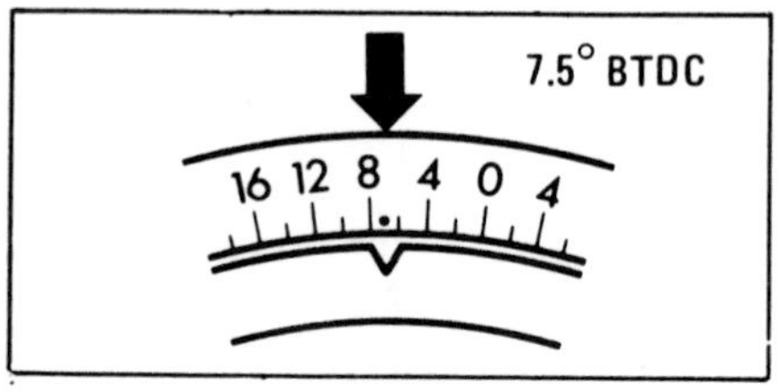

Fig. C

Volkswagen

TUNE UP NOTES—Continued

Fig. D

Fig. E

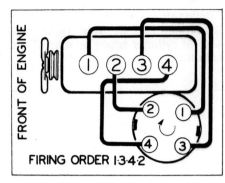

Fig. F

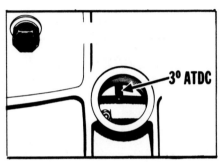

Fig. G

Chevrolet Vans & Trucks

ENGINE IDENTIFICATION

ENGINE NUMBER LOCATION:

SIX CYL.: Pad at front right hand side of cylinder block at rear of distributor.

V8 ENGINES: Pad at front right hand side of cylinder block.

Engines are identified in the following table by the code letters immediately following the engine serial number.

ENGINE CODE NOTES:

A.I.R.—Air Injection Reactor
A.I.R.A.T.—Air Injection Reactor with Automatic Transmission.
C.C.A.I.R.—Cruise Control with Air Injector Reactor.
H.A.P.E.C.—High Altitude Performance Emission Control.
T.H.—Turbo Hydramatic.
2BC—2 barrel carburetor.
NB2—California emission package.

CHEVROLET/GMC
ENGINE CODES

1974

CK TRUCK

Model	Description	Type Descrip.	Model	Description	Type Descrip.
250 - 6 CYLINDER					
C10, K10	T.H. 350 (exc. NB2)	TAA	C10, K10	T.H. 350 w/NB2	TBL
C10	Manual 3-Spd. (exc. NB2, H.D. Clutch)	TAB	C20, 30, K20		TBT
			C10, K10	3-Spd. (exc. H.D. Clutch)	TDB
C10	H.D. Clutch (exc. NB2)	TAC	C10, K10	4-Spd.	TDC
C10, K10	4-Spd., H.D. Clutch w/NB2	TAD	C10	3-Spd. w/NB-2 (exc. H. D. Clutch)	TDD
C20, K20	Manual 3-Spd. (exc. H.D. Clutch)	TAH	C10	4-Spd., NB-2 w/H.D. Clutch	TDF
C20, 30, K20	T.H. 350 - 400	TAJ	C10, K10	T.H. 350	TDU
C20, 30, K20	4-Spd., H.D. Clutch	TAK			
C10, K10	Manual 3-Spd. w/NB2 (exc. H.D. Clutch)	TAL			
292 - 6 CYLINDER					
C20, K20	T.H. 350	THS	C20, 30, K20	Manual Trans.	THU
C30	T.H. 400	THT			
350 - 8 CYLINDER					
C10, K10, 20	4BC, Manual Trans.	TJA	C10, 20, K10, 20	4BC, T.H. 350 (exc. NB2)	TKU
C10, K10	4BC, Manual Trans. (exc. NB2)	TJB	C20, 30, K20	4BC, T.H. 350 - 400	TKY
C20, 30, K20	4BC, Manual Trans.	TJC	C10	4BC, TH350 w/NB-2	TWS
C10, K10	4BC, Manual Trans. w/NB2	TJD	C10, K10	2BC, T.H. 350	TMM
C10, K10	4BC, T.H. 350 w/NB2	TJY	C10, K10	2BC, Manual Trans.	TMR
C10, K10	4BC, T.H. 350 (exc. NB2)	TKT			
454 - 8 CYLINDER					
C10	(exc. NB2)	TRH	C20	(exc. NB2)	TRT
C20, 30	Manual Trans.	TRJ	C20	NB2	TRU
C10	NB2	TRL	C20, 30	T.H. 400	TRW

ENGINE IDENTIFICATION CODES—Continued

G TRUCK

250 - 6 CYLINDER

Model	Description	Type Descrip.	Model	Description	Type Descrip.
G30	Manual Trans.	TAM	G10, 20, 30	T.H. 350	TDT
G30	T.H. 350	TAR	G10, 20	3-Spd. (exc. NB-2, H.D. Clutch)	TDJ
C10, 20, 30	T.H. 350 (exc. NB2)	TAS	G10, 20	3-Spd. w/H.D. Clutch (exc. NB-2)	TDK
G10, 20, 30	Manual Trans. H.D. Clutch	TAT	G10, 20	3-Spd. w/NB-2 (exc. H.D. Clutch)	TDM
G10, 20	Manual Trans. (exc. H.D. Cluch)	TAU	G10, 20, 30	3-Spd., NB-2 w/H.D. Clutch	TDR
G10, 20	T.H. 350 w/NB2	TAW			

350 - 8 CYLINDER

Model	Description	Type Descrip.	Model	Description	Type Descrip.
G10, 20, 30	4BC, Manual Trans. (exc. NB2)	TJM	G30	4BC, Manual Trans.	TKX
G10, 20	4BC, T.H. 350 w/NB2	TJU	G10, 20, 30	4BC, 3-Spd. w/NB-2	TWR
G10, 20, 30	4BC, Manual Trans. w/NB2	TJW	G10, 20, 30	4BC, T.H. 350 w/NB-2	TKL
G10, 20	4BC, T.H. 350 w/NB2	TKR	G10	2BC, T.H. 350	TMK
G10, 20, 30	4BC, T.H. 350 (exc. NB2)	TKS	G10	2BC, Manual Trans.	TML
G30	4BC, T.H. 350	TKW			

1975

CK TRUCK

Model	Description	Type Descrip.	Model	Description	Type Descrip.
250 - 6 CYLINDER					
C10, K10	Manual Trans. (exc. NB-2, C.C.A.I.R.)	TTK	C10, K10	(Manual Trans. w/C.C.A.I.R.) w/NB-2	TTS
C10, K10	T.H. 350 (exc. NB-2, C.C.A.I.R.)	TTL	C10, K10	(T.H. 350 w/C.C.A.I.R.) w/NB-2	TTT
C10, K10	(Manual Trans. w/NB-2) (exc. C.C.A.I.R.)	TTM	C10, K10	(Manual Trans. w/C.C.A.I.R.) (exc. NB-2)	TTU
C10, K10	(T.H. 350 w/NB-2) (exc. C.C.A.I.R.)	TTR	C10, K10	(T.H. 350 w/C.C.A.I.R.) (exc. NB-2)	TTW
292 - 6 CYLINDER					
C20, 30, K20	Manual Trans.	TUF	C30	T.H. 400	TUK
C20, K20	T.H. 350	TUJ			
350 - 8 CYLINDER					
C20, 30, K20	(T.H. 350-400 w/NB-2) w/4BC	TXA	C10	(2BC w/T.H. 350) C.C.A.I.R.	TJG
C20, 30, K20	(4BC w/T.H. 350 - 400) (exc. NB-2)	TXB	C10	(4BC w/T.H. 350) (exc. C.C.A.I.R. NB-2)	TZA
C20, 30, K20	(Manual Trans. w/NB-2) w/4BC	TXC	C10	(2BC w/Manual Trans.) w/C.C.A.I.R.	TJN
C20, 30, K20	(4BC w/Manual Trans.) (exc. NB-2)	TXD	C10	(2BC w/T.H. 350) (exc. C.C.A.I.R.)	TKF
C10	(2BC w/Manual Trans.) (exc. C.C.A.I.R.)	TYC	C10	(4BC w/Manual Trans.) (exc. C.C.A.I.R. NB-2)	TZC
C10	(4BC w/Manual Trans.) w/NB-2 (exc. C.C.A.I.R.)	TYD	C10	(4BC w/T.H. 350) C.C.A.I.R. (exc. NB-2)	TZD
C10, 20, K10, 20	(4BC w/Manual Trans. w/NB-2)	TYW	C10	(4BC w/Manual Trans.) (C.C.A.I.R. w/NB-2)	TZJ
C10, 20, K10, 20	(4BC w/Manual Trans.) (exc. NB-2)	TYX	C10	(4BC w/T.H. 350) (C.C.A.I.R. w/NB-2)	TZK
C10, 20, K10, 20	(4BC w/T.H. 350) w/NB-2	TYY			
C10, 20, K10, 20	(4BC w/T.H. 350) (exc. NB-2)	TYZ			
C10	(4BC w/Manual Trans.) w/C.C.A.I.R. (exc. NB-2)	TKN			
C10	(4BC w/T.H. 350) w/NB-2 (exc. C.C.A.I.R.)	TME			
400 - 8 CYLINDER					
K20	NB-2	TLL	K10, 20	NB-2	TLR
K20	(exc. NB-2)	TLM	K10, 20	(exc. NB-2)	TLS

continued

ENGINE IDENTIFICATION CODES—Continued

454 - 8 CYLINDER

C10	(exc. A.I.R.A.T., A.I.R.)	TRY
C20, 30	(Manual Trans. w/NB-2)	TRZ
C20, 30	(T.H. 400 w/NB-2)	TSA
C20, 30	Manual Trans. (exc. NB-2)	TSC
C20, 30	T.H. 400 (exc. NB-2)	TSD
C10	A.I.R.	TSJ
C10	A.I.R.A.T.	TSM
C10, 20	(exc. NB-2)	TSK
C10, 20	NB-2	TSL

G TRUCK

250 - 6 CYLINDER

G10	Manual Trans. (exc. C.C.A.I.R., NB-2)	TTK
G10	T.H. 350 (exc. C.C.A.I.R., NB-2)	TTL
G10	(Manual Trans. w/NB-2) (exc. C.C.A.I.R.)	TTM
G10	(T.H. 350 w/NB-2) (exc. C.C.A.I.R.)	TTR
G10	(Manual Trans. w/C.C.A.I.R.) w/NB-2	TTS
G10	(T.H. 350 w/C.C.A.I.R.) w/NB-2	TTT
G10	(Manual Trans. w/C.C.A.I.R.) (exc. NB-2)	TTU
G10	(T.H. 350 w/C.C.A.I.R.) (exc. NB-2)	TTW

292 - 6 CYLINDER

G20, 30	T.H. 350	TUL
G20, 30	Manual Trans.	TUM

350 - 8 CYLINDER

G30	(4BC w/T.H. 350 - 400) w/NB-2	TXH
G30	(4BC w/Manual Trans.) w/NB-2	TXJ
G30	(4BC w/Manual Trans.) (exc. NB-2)	TXK
G30	(4BC w/T.H. 350 - 400) (exc. NB-2)	TXL
G10	(2BC w/Manual Trans.) (exc. C.C.A.I.R.)	TYA
G10	(4BC w/Manual Trans.) w/NB-2 (exc. C.C.A.I.R.)	TYJ
G20, 30	(4BC w/T.H. 350) w/NB-2	TYR
G20, 30	(4BC w/Manual Trans.) w/NB-2	TYS
G20, 30	(4BC w/Manual Trans.) (exc. NB-2)	TYT
G20, 30	(4BC w/T.H. 350) (exc. NB-2)	TYU
G10	(4BC w/Manual Trans.) w/C.C.A.I.R. (exc. NB-2)	TMF
G10	(4BC w/T.H. 350) w/NB-2 (exc. C.C.A.I.R.)	TMG
G10	(2BC w/T.H. 350) w/C.C.A.I.R.	TJE
G10	(4BC w/T.H. 350) w/C.C.A.I.R.	TZB
G10	(2BC w/Manual Trans.) w/C.C.A.I.R.	TKE
G10	(2BC w/T.H. 350) (exc. C.C.A.I.R.)	TKG
G10	(4BC w/Manual Trans.) (exc. C.C.A.I.R., NB-2)	TZF
G10	(4BC w/T.H. 350) w/C.C.A.I.R. (exc. NB-2)	TZH
G10	(4BC w/Manual Trans.) (C.C.A.I.R. w/NB-2)	TZL
G10	(4BC w/T.H. 350) (C.C.A.I.R w/NB-2)	TZM

400 - 8 CYLINDER

G30	NB-2	TLD
G30	(exc. NB-2)	TLH
G20, 30	NB-2	TLT
G20, 30	(exc. NB-2)	TLU

1976

CK TRUCK

Model	Description	Type Descrip.	Model	Description	Type Descrip.

250 - 6 CYLINDER

Model	Description	Type Descrip.
C10	4-Spd. (exc. H.D. Chassis)	TBA
C10	T.H. 350 (exc. H.D. Chassis, NB2)	TBB
C10	(3-Spd. w/NB2)	TBC
C10	(T.H. 350 w/NB2)	TBD
C10, K10	T.H. 350	TAS
C10, K10	Manual Trans.	TAT
C10	3-Spd. (exc. H.D. Chassis, NB2)	TAA

Chevrolet Vans & Trucks

292 - 6 CYLINDER

C20, 30, K20 . . . . T.H. 350 (exc. NB2) . . . . THK
C20, 30, K20 . . . . (Manual Trans. w/NB2) . . . . THR
C30 . . . . T.H. 400 (exc. NB2) . . . . THL

C-20, 30, K20 . . . . Manual Trans. (exc. NB2) . . . . THH
C20, 30, K20 . . . . (T.H. 350 w/NB2) . . . . THT
C30 . . . . (T.H. 400 w/NB2) . . . . THU

305 - 8 CYLINDER

UTA
UTB
UTC
UTD

350 - 8 CYLINDER

C10 . . . . (T.H. 350 w/2BC) . . . . TKF
C10 . . . . (3-Spd. w/2BC) . . . . TYC
C10 . . . . (3-Spd. w/NB2) (exc.
          H.D. Chassis) . . . . TWJ
C10 . . . . (T.H. 350 w/NB2) (exc.
          H.D. Chassis) . . . . TJK
C10 . . . . 3 Spd. (exc. H.D. Chassis, NB2) . . . . TKA
C10 . . . . T.H. 350 (exc. H.D. Chassis, NB2) . . TKB
C10 . . . . 4 Spd. (exc. H.D. Chassis) . . . . TKH

C10, 20, K10, 20 . . . . . Manual Trans. (exc. NB2) . . . . TYX
C10, 20, K10, 20 . . . . . T.H. 350 (exc. NB2) . . . . TYZ
C10, 20, K10, 20 . . . . . (Manual Trans. w/NB2) . . . . TYW
C10, 20, K10, 20 . . . . . (T.H. 350 w/NB2) . . . . TYY
C20, 30, K20 . . . . Manual Trans. (exc. NB2) . . . . TXD
C20, 30, K20 . . . . T.H. 350 - 400 (exc. NB2) . . . . TXB
C20, 30, K20 . . . . (Manual Trans. w/NB2) . . . . TXC
C20, 30, K20 . . . . (T.H. 350 - 400 w/NB2) . . . . TXA

400 - 8 CYLINDER

K10, 20 . . . . (exc. NB2) . . . . TLS
K10, 20 . . . . NB2 . . . . TLR

K20 . . . . (exc. NB2) . . . . TLM
K20 . . . . NB2 . . . . TLL

CK TRUCK

454 - 8 CYLINDER

C20, C30 . . . . (4-Spd. w/NB2) . . . . TRZ
C20, C30 . . . . (T.H. 400 w/NB2) . . . . TSA
C20, C30 . . . . 4-Spd. (exc. NB2) . . . . TSC
C20, C30 . . . . T.H. 400 (exc. NB2) . . . . TSD

C10, 20 . . . . (exc. NB2) . . . . TSK
C10, 20 . . . . NB2 . . . . TSL
C10 . . . . (exc. H.D. Chassis) . . . . TSM

G TRUCK

250 - 6 CYLINDER

G10 . . . . T.H. 350 (exc. NB2) . . . . TBB
G10 . . . . (3-Spd. w/NB2) . . . . TBC

G10 . . . . (T.H. 350 w/NB2) . . . . TBD
G10 . . . . 3-Spd. (exc. NB2) . . . . TAA

292 - 6 CYLINDER

G20, 30 . . . . T.H. 350 (exc. NB2) . . . . THK
G20, 30 . . . . (3-Spd. w/NB2) . . . . THR

G20, 30 . . . . 3-Spd. (exc. NB2) . . . . THH
G20, 30 . . . . (T.H. 350 w/NB2) . . . . THT

350 - 8 CYLINDER

G10 . . . . 3-Spd. (exc. NB2) . . . . TKC
G10 . . . . (3-Spd. w/2BC) . . . . TYA
G10 . . . . (T.H. 350 w/2BC) . . . . TKG
G10 . . . . (3-Spd. w/NB2) . . . . TWK
G10 . . . . (T.H. 350 w/NB2) . . . . TJL
G20, 30 . . . . 3-Spd. (exc. NB2) . . . . TYT
G20, 30 . . . . T.H. 350 (exc. NB2) . . . . TYU

G20, 30 . . . . (3-Spd. w/NB2) . . . . TYS
G20, 30 . . . . (T.H. 350 w/NB2) . . . . TYR
G10 . . . . T.H. 350 (exc. NB2) . . . . TKO
G30 . . . . 3-Spd. (exc. NB2) . . . . TXK
G30 . . . . T.H. 350 - 400 (exc. NB2) . . . . TXL
G30 . . . . (3-Spd. w/NB2) . . . . TXJ
G30 . . . . (T.H. 350 - 400 w/NB2) . . . . TXH

400 - 8 CYLINDER

G20, 30 . . . . (exc. NB2) . . . . TLU
G20, 30 . . . . NB2 . . . . TLT

G30 . . . . (exc. NB2) . . . . TLH
G30 . . . . NB2 . . . . TLD

Continued

ENGINE IDENTIFICATION CODES—Continued

1977

CK TRUCK

Model	Description	Type Descrip.	Model	Description	Type Descrip.

250 - 6 CYLINDER

Model	Description	Type Descrip.	Model	Description	Type Descrip.
C10	4-Spd. (exc. H.D. Chassis)	TBA	C10, K10	T.H. 350	TAS
C10	T.H. 350 (exc. H.D. Chassis, NB2)	TBB	C10, K10	Manual Trans.	TAT
C10	(3-Spd. w/NB2)	TBC	C10	3-Spd. (exc. H.D. Chassis, NB2)	TAA
C10	(T.H. 350 w/NB2)	TBD			

292 - 6 CYLINDER

Model	Description	Type Descrip.	Model	Description	Type Descrip.
C20, 30, K20	T.H. 350 (exc. NB2)	THK	C20, 30, K20	Manual Trans. (exc. NB2)	THH
C20, 30, K20, K30	(Manual Trans. w/NB2)	THR	C20, 30, K20	(T.H. 350 w/NB2)	THT
C30, K30	T.H. 400 (exc. NB2)	THL	C30, K30	(T.H. 400 w/NB2)	THU

305 - 8 CYLINDER

Model	Description	Type Descrip.	Model	Description	Type Descrip.
C10	3-Spd.	UTA	C10, 20, K10, 20	Manual Trans. (exc. NB2)	UTF
C10	T.H. 350	UTB	C10, 20, K10, 20	T.H. 350 (exc. NB2)	UTH

350 - 8 CYLINDER

Model	Description	Type Descrip.	Model	Description	Type Descrip.
C10	(H.A.P.E.C.)	TJR	C10, 20, K10, 20	Manual Trans. (exc. NB2)	TYX
C10	(3-Spd. w/NB2)	TWJ	C10, 20, K10, 20	T.H. 350 (exc. NB2)	TYZ
C10	(T.H. 350 w/NB2) (exc. H.D. Chassis)	TJK	C10, 20, K10, 20	(Manual Trans. w/NB2)	TYW
C10	3 Spd. (exc. NB2)	TWD	C10, 20, K10, 20	(T.H. 350 w/NB2)	TYY
C10	T.H. 350 (exc. H.D. Chassis, NB2, HAPEC)	TKB	C20, 30, K20	Manual Trans. (exc. NB2)	TXD
C10	4 Spd. (exc. H.D. Chassis)	TWF	C20, 30, K20, K30	T.H. 350 - 400 (exc. NB2)	TXB
			C20, 30, K20, K30	(Manual Trans. w/NB2)	TXC
			C20, 30, K20, K30	(T.H. 350 - 400 w/NB2)	TXA

400 - 8 CYLINDER

Model	Description	Type Descrip.	Model	Description	Type Descrip.
K10, 20	(exc. NB2)	TLS	K20, K30	(exc. NB2)	TLM
K10, 20	NB2	TLR	K20, K30	NB2	TLL

454 - 8 CYLINDER

Model	Description	Type Descrip.	Model	Description	Type Descrip.
C20, 30	(4-Spd. w/NB2)	TRZ	C10, 20	(exc. NB2)	TSK
C20, 30	(T.H. 400 w/NB2)	TSA	C10, 20	NB2	TSL
C20, 30	4-Spd. (exc. NB2)	TSC	C10	(exc. H.D. Chassis)	TSM
C20, 30	T.H. 400 (exc. NB2)	TSD			

G TRUCK

250 - 6 CYLINDER

Model	Description	Type Descrip.	Model	Description	Type Descrip.
G10	T.H. 350 (exc. NB2)	TBH	G10	(T.H. 350 w/NB2)	TBK
G10	(3-Spd. w/NB2)	TBJ	G10	3-Spd. (exc. NB2)	TBF

292 - 6 CYLINDER

Model	Description	Type Descrip.	Model	Description	Type Descrip.
G20, 30	T.H. 350 (exc. NB2)	TUA	G20, 30	3-Spd. (exc. NB2)	TUB
G20, 30	(3-Spd. w/NB2)	TUD	G20, 30	(T.H. 350 w/NB2)	TUC

305 - 8 CYLINDER

Model	Description	Type Descrip.	Model	Description	Type Descrip.
G10	3-Spd.	UTC	G10	T.H. 350	UTD

Chevrolet Vans & Trucks

ENGINE IDENTIFICATION CODES—Continued

350 - 8 CYLINDER

G10 .... 3 Spd. (exc. NB2) .... TKC	G20, 30 .... (T.H. 350 w/NB2) .... TYR
G10 .... (H.A.P.E.C.) .... TJS	G10 .... T.H. 350 (exc. NB2, H.A.P.E.C.) .... TKD
G10 .... (3-Spd. w/NB2) .... TWK	G30 .... 3-Spd. (exc. NB2) .... TXK
G10 .... (T.H. 350 w/NB2) .... TJL	G30 .... TH. 350 - 400 (exc. NB2) .... TXL
G20, 30 .... 3-Spd. (exc. NB2) .... TYT	G30 .... (3-Spd. w/NB2) .... TXJ
G20, 30 .... T.H. 350 (exc. NB2) .... TYU	G30 .... (T.H. 350 - 400 w/NB2) .... TXH
G20, 30 .... (3-Spd. w/NB2) .... TYS	

400 - 8 CYLINDER

G20, 30 .... (exc. NB2) .... TLU	G30 .... (exc. NB2) .... TLH
G20, 30 .... NB2 .... TLT	G30 .... NB2 .... TLD

1978

OPTION & DISPLACEMENT	MODEL USAGE	FEDERAL AUTOMATIC TRANSMISSION	FEDERAL MANUAL TRANSMISSION	CALIFORNIA AUTOMATIC TRANSMISSION	CALIFORNIA MANUAL TRANSMISSION	AUTOMATIC TRANSMISSION HIGH ALTITUDE
LD4 (250)	C10	TAB, TBB, TAS	TAC	TCM	TCL	
	G10	TAH	TAF	TCS	TCR	
	K10	TAM	TAR			
	C20			TCM	TCL	
	G20			TCS	TCR	
	G30			TCS	TCR	
L25 (292)	P10	THJ	THF			
	C20	THJ,THM	THF			
	G20	TUF	TUH			
	K20	THJ,THM	THF			
	P20	THJ	THF,THC			
	C30	THJ	THF			THS
	G30	TUF	TUH			
	K30	THY,THM	THF			
	P30	THM	THC			THS
LG9 (305)	C10	UTX,UTS	UTW,UTR			
	G10	UTU	UTT			
	K10	UTX	UTW			
	C20	UTX	UTW			
	G20					
	K20	UTX	UTW			

OPTION USAGE	MODEL & DISPLACEMENT	FEDERAL AUTOMATIC TRANSMISSION	FEDERAL MANUAL TRANSMISSION	CALIFORNIA AUTOMATIC TRANSMISSION	CALIFORNIA MANUAL TRANSMISSION	AUTOMATIC TRANSMISSION HIGH ALTITUDE
LS9 (350)	C10	TWZ,TKA	TWJ,TWY TJX,TJY TWK	TWK,TYD	TYH TYB,TYJ	TYF
	G10	TKH	TFK	TZB	TZA	TZC
	K10	TLJ	TWY	TZS,TZW	TZT,TZU	
	K10	TLJ	TWY	TZS,TZW	TZT,TZU	
	C20	TWZ	TKL	TZW,TZS	TZU,TZT	
	G20	TYC	TYA	TZB,TZH	TZD,TZF	
	K20	TWZ,TKK	TKL,TWY	TZS,TZW	TZT,TZU	
	P20	TKW,TWZ	TKT	TZR		
	C30	TZK,TKK		TYM		
	G30	TKR	TYA,TKM	TYM,TCL	TYL	
	K30	TKK		TYM,TCL		
	P30	TKW TZY,TWW	TKZ,TKT	TZZ TKU,TWX	TXZ	
LF4 (400)	K10		TLK		TLB,TLA	
	G20	TLZ		TLW,TLX		
	K20	TLK,TLJ		TLB,TLA		
	G30	TLF TKM,TLZ		TLY TLW,TLX		
	K30	TLU		TLC		
LF8 (454)	C10	TSJ,TST		TSS		
	C20	TST,TSH	TSF	TSS,TRF	TRM	
	C30	TSH	TSF	TSB	TRY	
	P30	TRH		TRJ,TRL		

Continued

Chevrolet Vans & Trucks

ENGINE IDENTIFICATION CODES—Continued
1979

Option & Displacement	Model Usage	FEDERAL		CALIFORNIA		HIGH ALTITUDE	
		Automatic Transmission	Manual Transmission	Automatic Transmission	Manual Transmission	Automatic Transmission	Manual Transmission
LE3(250)	C10	TAK	TAJ	TAX, TAD	TAW		
	G10	TAS	TAL	TDW, TAD	TAT		
	K10	TAK	TAJ				
	C20	TAK	TAJ	TAD	TAA		
	G20	TAS	TAL	TAD, TDU	TAT		
	G30	TAS	TAL	TDU	TAT		
L25(292)	P10	TH8	THA		THA		THA
	P20	THB, THH	THA	THH	THA	THH	THA
	C30	THH	THA	THH	THA	THH	THA
	K30	THH	THA	THH	THA	THH	THA
	P30	THH	THA	THH	THA	THH	THA
LG9(305)	C10	TYS, UTB	UYR UTA, TYR				
	G10	UTD	UTC				
	K10	UTB, UYS	TYR				
	C20	UYS	TYR, UYR				
LS9(350)	C10	TBC TJS, TMH	TBA TBB, TMF	TBT	TBR, TBS	TRR, TMC	
	G10	TBK	TBH	TFJ	TBZ	TMD	
	K10	TBC TBF, TJT	TBB, TBD	TBX TBR, TBY	TBU, TBW		
	C20	TFT, TBF TBC, TJT	TBB, TBD	TBS, TFT TBR, TBY	TBU, TBW	TRS TRR, TFT	
	G20	TBM, TBR	TBL, TBJ	TFJ, TFM	TFK TBZ, TFL		TRZ
	K20	TFT, TBC TBF, TJT	TBB, TBD	TBR, TBY TBX, TFT	TBW, TBU	TFT	
	P20	TFZ	TFX	TFZ, TFR	TFX	TFZ	TFX
	C30	TFT TKC	TFS TKB	TFT	TFS	TFT	TFS
	G30	TBM TBK, TFW	TBL TBJ, TFU	TFM TFJ, TFW	TFL TFK, TFU	TFW	TFU
	K30	TFT	TFS	TFT	TFS	TFT	TFS
	P30	TJA TJB, TFZ	TFY, TFX	TJA TJB, TFZ	TFY, TFX	TJA TJB, TFZ	TFY, TFX
LF4(400)	K10	TLD, TLH TTR		TLS, TLR			
	G20	TLM, TLL		TTM, TLT			
	K20	TLH, TLD TTR		TLS, TLR			
	G30	TLM TLL, TTJ		TTJ TTM, TLT		TTJ	
	K30	TLU		TLU		TLU	
LF8(454)	C10	TRR	TRZ	TRR	TRZ	TRR	
	C20	TRR TRU, TRS	TRZ	TRR TRU, TRS	TRZ	TRR TRS, TRU	TRZ
	C30	TRU	TRT	TRU	TRT	TRU	TRT
	P30	TRW, TRX		TRW, TRX		TRW, TRX	

Chevrolet Vans & Trucks

TUNE UP SPECIFICATIONS

The following specifications are published from the latest information available. This data should be used only in the absence of a decal affixed in the engine compartment.

★When using a timing light, disconnect vacuum hose or tube at distributor and plug opening in tube or hose so idle speed will not be affected.

▲Before removing wires from distributor cap, determine location of the No. 1 wire in cap, as distributor position may have been altered from that shown at the end of this chart.

Year/Engine	Spark Plug		Distributor		Ignition Timing★			Carb. Adjustment	
								Hot Idle Speed	
	Type	Gap Inch	Point Gap Inch	Dwell Angle Deg.	Firing Order Fig. ▲	Timing BTDC [42]	Mark Fig.	Std. Trans.	Auto. Trans.
1974									
6-250 Light Duty	R46T	.035	.019	31–34	B	8°	G	850	600D
6-250 Heavy Duty	R46T	.035	.019	31–34	B	6°	G	600	600
6-292	R44T	.035	.019	31–44	B	8°	G	600	600
V8-350 145 H.P.	R44T	.035	.019	29–31	A	[5]	G	900	600D
V8-350 Light Duty	R44T	.035	.019	29–31	A	8°	G	900	600D
V8-350 Light Duty	R44T	.035	.019	29–31	A	[6]	G	900	600D
V8-350 Light Duty Calif.	R44T	.035	.019	29–31	A	[13]	G	900	600D
V8-350 Heavy Duty	R43T	.035	.019	29–31	A	4°	G	600	600
V8-454 Light Duty	R44T	.035	.019	29–31	A	10°	G	800	600D
V8-454 Heavy Duty	R44T	.035	.019	29–31	A	8°	G	700	700
1975									
6-250 [8]	R46TX	.060	—	—	C	10°	G	850	[37]
6-250 [9]	R46TX	.060	—	—	C	[22]	G	850	600D
6-292 Light Duty	R44TX	.060	—	—	C	8°	G	600	600N
6-292 Heavy Duty	R44T	.035	.019	31–34	B	8°	G	600	600N
V8-350 Light Duty [7] [13] [23]	R44TX	.060	—	—	D	6°	G	800	600D
V8-350 Heavy Duty [7]	R44T	.035	—	28–32	A	4°	G	600	600
V8-350 Light Duty [13] [24] [25]	R44TX	.060	—	—	D	8°	G	600	600
V8-350 Light Duty [4] [24] [25]	R44TX	.060	—	—	D	2°	G	700	700
V8-350 Light Duty [9] [24]	R44TX	.060	—	—	D	[18]	G	800	600D
V8-350 Light Duty [6] [11] [10]	R44TX	.060	—	—	D	[28]	G	800	600D
V8-400 [9] [12]	R44TX	.060	—	—	D	[18]	G	600	600D
V8-400 [9] [4]	R44TX	.060	—	—	D	8°	G	—	600D
V8-400 [25]	R44TX	.060	—	—	D	[10]	G	700	700
V8-454 [23]	R44TX	.060	—	—	D	16°	G	—	650
V8-454 [25]	R44TX	.060	—	—	D	8°	G	[33]	[33]
1976									
6-250 [8] [23]	R46TS	.035	—	—	C	[27]	G	[39]	[40]
6-250 [8] [26]	R46T	.035	—	—	C	6°	G	600	600
6-250 [9]	R46TS	.035	—	—	C	6°	G	850	[37]
6-292 Light Duty [26]	R44T	.035	—	—	C	8°	G	600	600
6-292 Heavy Duty	R44T	.035	.019	31–34	B	8°	G	600	600
V8-305	R45TS	.045	—	—	D	[16]	G	800	600D
V8-350 Light Duty [7] [8] [23]	R45TS	.045	—	—	D	[20]	G	800	600D
V8-350 [7] [9]	R45TS	.045	—	—	D	6°	G	800	600
V8-350 Heavy Duty [7]	R44T	.035	—	28–32	A	4°	G	600	600
V8-350 Light Duty [23] [24]	R45TS	.045	—	—	D	[28]	G	800	600D
V8-350 Light Duty [24] [26]	R44TX	.060	—	—	D	[29]	G	[33]	[33]
V8-400 [9]	R45TS	.045	—	—	D	8°	G	—	600D
V8-400 [26]	R44TX	.060	—	—	D	[10]	G	700	700
V8-454 [12] [23]	R45TS	.045	—	—	D	[21]	G	—	600D
V8-454 [26]	R44T	.045	—	—	D	8°	G	700	700

Continued

TUNE UP SPECIFICATIONS—Continued

| Year/Engine | Spark Plug | | Distributor | | Ignition Timing★ | | | Carb. Adjustment | |
| | Type | Gap Inch | Point Gap Inch | Dwell Angle Deg. | Firing Order Fig. ▲ | Timing BTDC (42) | Mark Fig. | Hot Idle Speed | |
								Std. Trans.	Auto. Trans.
1977									
6-250(5)(13)(23)	R46TS	.035	—	—	C	(10)	G	750	600
6-250(4)(8)(23)	R46TS	.035	—	—	C	(16)	G	850	600
6-250(9)	R46TS	.035	—	—	C	(23)	G	(41)	(37)
6-250(13)(26)	R46T	.035	—	—	C	6°	G	600	600
6-292	R44T	.035	—	—	C	8°	G	600	600
V8-305(23)	R45TS	.045	—	—	D	(23)	G	(33)	500
V8-305(26)	R44T	.045	—	—	D	6°	G	600	600
V8-350(7)(9)	R45TS	.045	—	—	D	(23)	G	700	500
V8-350 Heavy Duty(7)	R44T	.035	—	—	D	4°	G	600	600
V8-350(9)(24)	R45TS	.045	—	—	D	8°	G	—	650
V8-350 Light Duty(23)(24)	R45TS	.045	—	—	D	(23)	G	700	500
V8-350 Light Duty(4)(24)(26)	R44TX	.060	—	—	D	2°	G	700	700
V8-350 Light Duty(13)(24)(26)	R44T	.045	—	—	D	8°	G	700	700
V8-400(26)	R44T	.045	—	—	D	(10)	G	700	700
V8-454(13)(23)	R45TS	.045	—	—	D	4°	G	600	600
V8-454(26)	R44T	.045	—	—	D	8°	G	700	700
1978									
V6-200	R45TS	.045	—	—	E	8°	I	700	600D
V6-231	R46TSX	.060	—	—	F	15°	H	700	600D
6-250(23)	R46TS	.035	—	—	C	(1)	G	750	(13)
6-250(26)	R46T	.035	—	—	C	6°	G	600	600N
6-292	R44T	.035	—	—	C	8°	G	600	600N
V8-305(9)	R45TS	.045	—	—	D	(19)	G	600	500D
V8-305(23)	R45TS	.045	—	—	D	4°	G	600	500D
V8-305(26)	R44T	.045	—	—	D	6°	G	700	700N
V8-350(9)	R45TS	.045	—	—	D	(30)	G	700	500D
V8-350 Light Duty(23)	R45TS	.045	—	—	D	8°	G	(14)	500D
V8-350 Light Duty(26)	R44T	.045	—	—	D	(23)	G	700	700N
V8-350 Heavy Duty	(3)	(3)	—	—	D	4°	G	600	600N
V8-400(4)(23)	R45TS	.045	—	—	D	4°	G	—	500D
V8-400(26)	R44T	.045	—	—	D	(10)	G	700	700N
V8-454(23)	R45TS	.045	—	—	D	8°	G	700	500D
1979									
V6-200	R45TS	.045	—	—	E	(17)	I	700	600D
V8-231	R45TSX	.060	—	—	F	15°	H	—	(40)
6-250(31)	R46TS	.035	—	—	C	10°	G	750	600D
6-250(32)	R46TS	.035	—	—	C	(33)	G	750	600D
6-292	R44T	.035	—	—	C	8°	G	700	700N
V8-305(9)	R45TS	.045	—	—	D	(34)	G	700	(2)
V8-305	R45TS	.045	—	—	D	6°	G	600	500D
V8-350 Light Duty(23)	R45TS	.045	—	—	D	8°	G	700	500D
V8-350 Light Duty(26)	R44T	.045	—	—	D	4°	G	700	700N
V8-350 Heavy Duty	(3)	(3)	—	—	—	8°	G	600	600N
V8-400(23)	R45TS	.045	—	—	D	4°	G	—	500D
V8-400(26)	R44T	.045	—	—	D	4°	G	—	700N
V8-454(23)	R45TS	.045	—	—	D	(36)	G	700	550D
V8-454(26)	R44T	.045	—	—	D	4°	G	700	700N

Chevrolet Vans & Trucks

TUNE UP NOTES

①—Manual trans. 8° BTDC; auto. trans. except Calif. & hi alt. 8° BTDC; Calif. 10° BTDC; high altitude 12° BTDC.
②—Except high altitude 500D rpm; hi alt. 600D rpm.
③—Exc. Calif. R44T gapped at .045"; Calif. RT44TX gapped at .060".
④—California.
⑤—Man. trans. TDC; auto. trans. 8° BTDC.
⑥—C-, K-10 & 20 Suburban and G-20 & 30 Sportvans auto. trans. 12°; man. trans. except Suburban 8°; man. trans. Suburban 6°.
⑦—2-barrel carb.
⑧—Except El Camino.
⑨—El Camino.
⑩—Exc. Calif. 4° BTDC; Calif. 2° BTDC.
⑪—Exc. Calif. & hi alt. 4° BTDC; Calif. 6° BTDC; hi alt. 8° BTDC.
⑫—Except Calif.
⑬—Auto. trans. exc. Suburban 8°; auto. trans. 6°; man. trans. 4°.
⑭—Except Calif. 600 rpm; Calif. 700 rpm.
⑮—Except Calif. & hi alt. models less A/C 550D rpm; all others 600D rpm.
⑯—Man. trans. 6° BTDC; auto. trans. 10° BTDC.
⑰—Man. trans. 8° BTDC; auto. trans. 12° BTDC.
⑱—Man. trans. 6° BTDC; auto. trans. 8° BTDC.
⑲—Except Calif. 4° BTDC; Calif. 6° BTDC.
⑳—Man. trans. 2° BTDC; auto. trans. 6° BTDC.
㉑—With catalytic converter 12° BTDC; less cat. conv. 8° BTDC.

㉒—With integral intake manifold & all Calif. models 10° BTDC; except Calif. models less integral intake manifold 8° BTDC.
㉓—Light duty emissions, GVWR 6000-lbs. & under.
㉔—4-barrel carb.
㉕—Man. trans. 4° BTDC; auto. trans. 6° BTDC.
㉖—Heavy duty emissions, GVWR 6001-lbs. & above.
㉗—Man. trans. except C-10 4-speed 6° BTDC; auto. trans. all & C-10 4-spd. man. trans. 10° BTDC.
㉘—Except Calif. 8° BTDC; Calif. 6° BTDC.
㉙—Except Calif. 8° BTDC; Calif. 2° BTDC.
㉚—Except Calif. & hi alt. 6° BTDC; Calif. & hi alt. 8° BTDC.
㉛—C-, G- & K-10 series.
㉜—C- & G-20, 30 series.
㉝—Except Calif. 10° BTDC; Calif. man. trans. 6° BTDC; auto. trans. 8° BTDC.
㉞—Except hi alt. 4° BTDC; hi alt. 8° BTDC.
㉟—El Camino 700 rpm; Exc. El Camino 600 rpm.
㊱—K-10, 20 & G-20, 30 4° BTDC; C-10, 20 8° BTDC.
㊲—Except Calif. 550 rpm; Calif. 600 rpm.
㊳—Except Calif. 600 rpm; Calif. 700 rpm.
㊴—Except Calif. man. trans. 900 rpm; Calif. man. trans. 1000 rpm.
㊵—Except Calif. auto. trans. 550D rpm; Calif. auto. trans. 600D rpm.
㊶—Less A/C 750 rpm; with A/C 800 rpm.
㊷—BTDC: Before Top Dead Center.

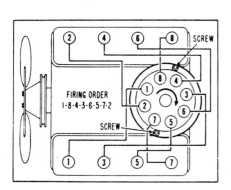

Fig. A

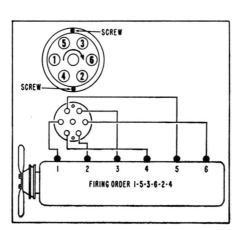

Fig. B

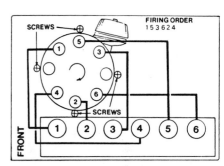

Fig. C

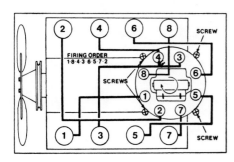

Fig. D

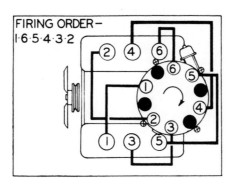

Fig. E

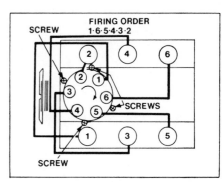

Fig. F

Continued

TUNE UP NOTES—Continued

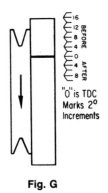

Fig. G

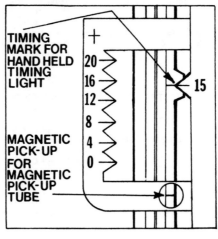

Fig. H

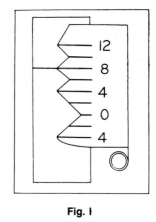

Fig. I

Dodge • Plymouth Vans & Trucks

ENGINE IDENTIFICATION

ENGINE NUMBER LOCATION:

1974–79 SIX: Right front of block below cylinder head.
1974–79 318, 340, 360: Left front of block below cylinder head.
1974–79 V8-400, 1974–75 V8-440: Upper right front of cylinder block.
1976–79 V8-440: Top of block left bank next to front tappet rail.

ENGINE IDENTIFICATION CODE

1974–79: Engines are identified by the cubic inch displacement found within the engine number stamped on the pad (2nd to 4th digit).

Engine codes also are listed on the vehicle identification plate attached to the driver's side door body latch post. 1974–77 models use the 5th digit of the V.I.N. number to denote the engine model. 1978–79 models use the 4th element of the V.I.N. number to denote the engine model.

Engine Code	Engine Type
A	440-3
B	225-1
C	225-2
D	440-1
E	318-1
F	360-2 2bbl.
G	318-3
J	400-1
K	360-3
T	360-4 4bbl.

TUNE UP SPECIFICATIONS

The following specifications are published from the latest information available. This data should be used only in the absence of a decal affixed in the engine compartment.

★ When using a timing light, disconnect vacuum hose or tube at distributor and plug opening in tube or hose so idle speed will not be affected.

▲ Before removing wires from distributor cap, determine location of the No. 1 wire in cap, as distributor position may have been altered from that shown at the end of this chart.

Year/Engine	Spark Plug		Distributor		Ignition Timing ★			Carb. Adjustment	
								Hot Idle Speed	
	Type	Gap Inch	Point Gap Inch	Dwell Angle Deg.	Firing Order Fig. ▲	Timing BTDC ㉟	Mark Fig.	Std. Trans.	Auto. Trans.
1974									
6-225 ⑬	N11Y	.035	—	—	A	⑰	E	800	750
V8-318 ⑬	N11Y	.035	—	—	B	⑲	F	750	750
V8-360 ①⑲⑬	N12Y	.035	—	—	B	⑳	F	800	750
V8-360 ①㉑⑬	N12Y	.035	—	—	B	2½°	F	—	750
V8-360 ㉟⑬	N12Y	.035	—	—	B	TDC	F	750	750
V8-400 ①⑬	J13Y	.035	—	—	C	7½°	I	750	750
V8-400 ㉟⑬	J11Y	.035	—	—	C	2½°	I	750	750
V8-440 ①⑬	J11Y	.035	—	—	C	㉒	I	700	700
V8-440-1 ⑬	J11Y	.035	—	—	C	7½°	I	700	700
1975									
6-225 ⑫⑬	BL11Y	.035	—	—	A	TDC③	D	800	750
6-225 ⑬⑬	BL11Y	.035	—	—	A	TDC	D	700	700
V8-318 ⑫⑬	N11Y	.035	—	—	B	㉓	G	750	750
V8-318-1 ⑫⑬	N11Y	.035	—	—	B	㉔	G	750㉙	750㉙
V8-360-1 ⑬	N12Y	.035	—	—	B	㉚	G	750㉙	750㉙
V8-440 ⑩	J11Y	.035	—	—	C	8°	J	700	700

Continued

TUNE UP SPECIFICATIONS—Continued

Year/Engine	Spark Plug		Distributor		Ignition Timing ★			Carb. Adjustment	
								Hot Idle Speed	
	Type	Gap Inch	Point Gap Inch	Dwell Angle Deg.	Firing Order Fig. ▲	Timing BTDC [37]	Mark Fig.	Std. Trans.	Auto. Trans.
1976									
6-225-1[12]	BL11Y	.035	—	—	A	[23]	D	750	750N
6-225[1][13]	BL11Y	.035	—	—	A	TDC	D	750	750N
V8-318[12][13]	N11Y	.035	—	—	B	[23]	G	750	750N
V8-318[13][16]	N11Y	.035	—	—	B	[11]	G	750	750N
V8-318-1[12]	N11Y	.035	—	—	B	[23]	G	750[29]	750[29]
V8-318-1[13]	N11Y	.035	—	—	B	[11]	G	750	750N
V8-360-1[12]	N12Y	.035	—	—	B	[2]	G	—	700N
V8-360-1[13]	N12Y	.035	—	—	B	[30]	G	700	700N
V8-400-1[12]	J11Y	.035	—	—	C	2°	I	—	700N
V8-440-1	J11Y	.035	—	—	C	8°	I	700	700N
1977									
6-225[12]	RBL15Y	.035	—	—	A	[4]	D	750	750
6-225-1[13]	RBL11Y	.035	—	—	A	TDC	D	700	700
V8-318[12]	RN11Y	.035	—	—	B	[7]	G	750	750
V8-318-1[13]	RN11Y	.035	—	—	B	[24]	G	750[29]	750[29]
V8-360[12]	RN12Y	.035	—	—	B	6°	G	—	700
V8-360-1[13]	RN12Y	.035	—	—	B	TDC	G[14]	750	750[29]
V8-400-1[12]	RJ11Y	.035	—	—	C	2°	I[10]	700	700
V8-400-1[6][13]	RJ11Y	.035	—	—	C	8°	I	700	700
V8-440[13]	RJ11Y	.035	—	—	C	8°	J	700	700
1978									
6-225[12]	RBL16Y	.035	—	—	A	8°	L	750	750
6-225[21][27]	RBL16Y	.035	—	—	A	8°	L	750	750
6-225[13]	RBL11Y	.035	—	—	A	TDC	L	700	700
V8-318[5][12]	RN11Y	.035	—	—	B	12°	H	750	750[31]
V8-318[26]	RN11Y	.035	—	—	B	[11]	H	750	750
V8-360[5][12]	RN12Y	.035	—	—	B	6°	H	750	750[31]
V8-360[5][13]	RN12Y	.035	—	—	B	[16]	H	750[29]	750[29]
V8-360[6][13]	RN12Y	.035	—	—	B	[33]	H	800[34]	800[34]
V8-400[13]	OJ11Y	.035	—	—	C	2°	K	700	700
V8-440[27][21]	OJ11Y	.035	—	—	C	8°	H	—	750
V8-440[13]	OJ11Y	.035	—	—	C	8°	H[10]	700	700
1979									
6-225-1[12]	RBL16Y	.035	—	—	A	12°	L	675	675
6-225-1[5]	RBL16Y	.035	—	—	A	8°	L	800	800
V8-318[5][12]	RN11Y	.035	—	—	B	12°	H	680	680
V8-318-4[6][12]	RN11Y	.035	—	—	B	[36]	H	750	750
V8-318-4[6][27]	RN11Y	.035	—	—	B	6°	H	750	750
V8-360-2[5][12]	RF10	.035	—	—	B	10°	H	750	750
V8-360-4[6][27]	RF10	.035	—	—	B	[23]	H	[9]	[9]
V8-360-4[6][13]	RF10	.035	—	—	B	4°	H	—	700
V8-440-4[13]	OBL9Y	.035	—	—	C	8°	H[10]	—	700

Dodge • Plymouth Vans & Trucks

TUNE UP NOTES

① — Light duty.
② — Exc. Calif. 6° BTDC; Calif. 4° BTDC.
③ — Calif. vehicles built after Sept. 1975 with auto. trans. set at 2° ATDC.
④ — Exc. Calif. 2° BTDC; Calif. w/auto. trans. 2° ATDC; Calif. w/man. trans. TDC.
⑤ — 2-barrel carb.
⑥ — 4-barrel carb.
⑦ — Exc. hi alt. w/auto. trans. 2° BTDC; hi alt. w/auto. trans. 6° BTDC.
⑧ — Exc. Calif. 12° BTDC; Calif. 8° BTDC.
⑨ — Exc. Calif. 700; Calif. 750.
⑩ — On B Series & Voyager models, timing mark located on torque converter.
⑪ — 2° ATDC.
⑫ — Light duty emissions.
⑬ — Heavy duty emissions.
⑭ — On B Series & Voyager models with air pump, timing mark located on torque converter.
⑮ — With electronic ignition.
⑯ — Exc. Calif. 4° BTDC; Calif. TDC.
⑰ — Dist. #3755056 2½° BTDC; others TDC.
⑱ — Dist. #3755021 2½° BTDC; others TDC.
⑲ — Except Calif.
⑳ — Man. Trans. 2½° BTDC; auto. trans. 5° BTDC.
㉑ — California.
㉒ — Exc. Calif. 10° BTDC; Calif. 5° BTDC.
㉓ — Exc. Calif. 2° BTDC; Calif. TDC.
㉔ — Exc. Calif. 2° ATDC; Calif. TDC.
㉕ — Exc. Calif. 4° BTDC; Calif. 10° BTDC.
㉖ — Light & medium duty emissions.
㉗ — Medium duty emissions.
㉘ — Heavy duty.
㉙ — Calif. 700 rpm.
㉚ — Exc. Calif. TDC; Calif. 4° BTDC.
㉛ — High alt. models 750 rpm.
㉜ — 1-barrel carb.
㉝ — Exc. Calif. 4° BTDC; Calif. 6° BTDC.
㉞ — Calif. 750 rpm.
㉟ — Light duty, medium duty & heavy duty emissions.
㊱ — Man. trans. 6° BTDC; auto. trans. 8° BTDC.
㊲ — BTDC: Before Top Dead Center.

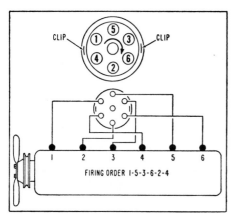

Fig. A

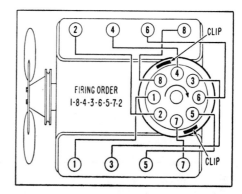

Fig. B

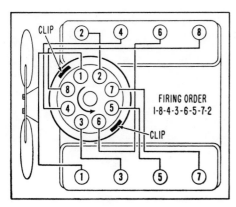

Fig. C

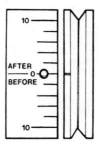

Fig. D

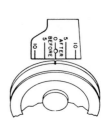

Fig. E

Continued

TUNE UP NOTES—Continued

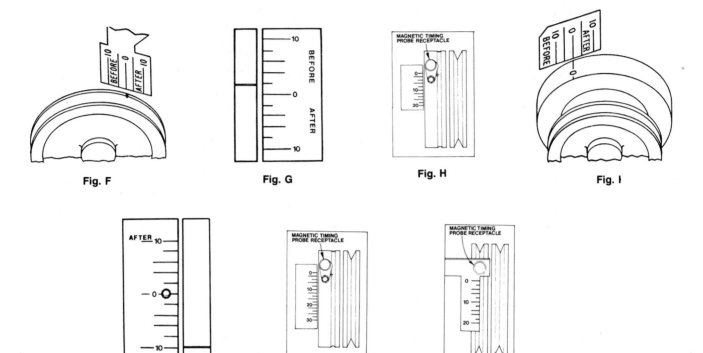

Fig. F

Fig. G

Fig. H

Fig. I

Fig. J

Fig. K

Fig. L

Ford Vans & Trucks

ENGINE IDENTIFICATION

The engine displacement appears on a decal affixed to the engine valve cover. The engine code appears as the fourth character in the vehicle identification number on the Vehicle Rating Plate. On cowl and windshield vehicles, the Rating Plate is mounted on the right side of the cowl top panel under the hood. On all other vehicles, the Rating Plate is mounted on the rear face of the left front door.

FORD ENGINE CODES

Year	Engine	Engine Code
1974	6-200	T
	6-240	A
	6-300	B
	V8-302	G
	V8-360	Y
	V8-390	H
	V8-460	J
1975–76	6-300	B
	V8-302	G
	V8-351	H
	V8-360	Y
	V8-390	M
	V8-460①	A
	V8-460	J
1977	6-300	B
	V8-302	G
	V8-351	H
	V8-400	S
	V8-460	J
	V8-460	A
1978	6-300	B
	6-300②	C
	V8-302	G
	V8-351	H
	V8-400	S
	V8-460①	A
	V8-460	J
1979	6-300	B
	6-300③	K
	V8-302	G
	V8-351	H
	V8-400	S
	V8-460①	A
	V8-460	J

NOTES:
①—Econoline
②—Econoline 3x6 Fuel Economy
③—Heavy Duty

Continued

TUNE UP SPECIFICATIONS

The following specifications are published from the latest information available. This data should be used only in the absence of a decal affixed in the engine compartment.

★When using a timing light, disconnect vacuum hose or tube at distributor and plug opening in tube or hose so idle speed will not be affected.

▲Before removing wires from distributor cap, determine location of the No. 1 wire in cap, as distributor position may have been altered from that shown at the end of this chart.

Year/Engine	Spark Plug		Distributor		Ignition Timing★			Carb. Adjustment	
	Type	Gap Inch	Point Gap Inch	Dwell Angle Deg.	Firing Order Fig. ▲	Timing BTDC ㊼	Timing Mark Location	Hot Idle Speed	
								Std. Trans.	Auto. Trans.
1974									
6-200	BRF-82	.034	—	—	D	6°	Damper	750	550D
6-240	BRF-42	.034	—	—	H	6°	Damper	850	650D
6-250⑪	BRF-82	.034	.025	33	D	6°	Damper	750	600D
6-300⑦	BTRF-42	.044	—	—	H	6°	Damper	㊷	550D
6-300	③	③	—	—	H	10°	Damper	600	550D
V8-302⑪	BRF-42	.034	.017	26–30	B	6°	Damper	⑰	⑰
V8-351W-2 bbl.⑪	BRF-42	.034	.017	26–30	B	6°	Damper	—	600D
V8-351C-2 bbl.⑪	ARF-42	.044	.017	26–30	B	10°	Damper	—	650D
V8-351-4 bbl.⑪	ARF-42	.034	㊽	26–31	B	㊽	Damper	1000	800D
V8-360④	BRF-42	.044	—	—	C	⑰	Damper	⑰	⑰
V8-360	BRF-42	.034	—	—	C	⑰	Damper	⑰	⑰
V8-360⑦	BRF-42	.054	—	—	C	㊹	Damper	850	⑰
V8-390④	BRF-42	.044	—	—	C	⑰	Damper	⑰	⑰
V8-390	BRF-42	.034	—	—	C	⑰	Damper	⑰	⑰
V8-460④	ARF-52	.054	—	—	B	10°	Damper	—	650D
V8-460	ARF-42	.044	—	—	B	10°	Damper	—	650D
1975									
6-300	BTRF-42	.044	—	—	H	12°	Damper	700	550D
V8-302⑦	ARF-42	.044	—	—	B	6°	Damper	900	⑰
V8-351⑦⑪	ARF-42	.044	—	—	C	12°	Damper	—	650D
V8-360	BRF-42	.044	—	—	C	㊾	Damper	850	650D
V8-390⑦	BRF-42	.044	—	—	C	6°	Damper	—	650D
V8-460⑦⑪	ARF-42	.044	—	—	B	14°	Damper	—	650D
1976									
6-300⑦	㊼	.044	—	—	H	10°⑯	Damper	600	600D
6-300④⑬	BRF-31	.030	.024	33–39	H	10°	Damper	600	—
V8-302④⑦⑫	ARF-52	.044	—	—	B	6°	Damper	800	—
V8-302④⑦⑫	ARF-52	.044	—	—	B	8°	Damper	—	600D
V8-302④⑦⑬	ARF-42	.044	—	—	B	12°	Damper	850	—
V8-302④⑦⑬	ARF-42	.044	—	—	B	18°	Damper	—	650D
V8-302④⑦⑬	ARF-42	.044	—	—	B	6°	Damper	850	—
V8-302④⑦⑬	ARF-42	.044	—	—	B	12°	Damper	—	650D
V8-302④⑦⑬	ARF-52	.044	—	—	B	12°	Damper	800	—
V8-302④⑦⑬	ARF-52	.044	—	—	B	18°	Damper	—	650D
V8-302⑦⑬⑭	ARF-52	.044	—	—	B	8°	Damper	850	—
V8-302⑦⑬⑭	ARF-52	.044	—	—	B	4°	Damper	850	—
V8-302⑦⑬⑭	ARF-52	.044	—	—	B	12°	Damper	—	650D
V8-351⑦	ARF-32	.044	—	—	C	12°	Damper	650	650D
V8-351⑦	ARF-42	.044	—	—	C	14°	Damper	650	650D
V8-351⑦⑪⑬	ARF-42	.044	—	—	C	8°	Damper	—	675D
V8-351⑦⑪⑭	ARF-42	.044	—	—	C	6°	Damper	—	650D
V8-360⑦	BRF-42	.044	—	—	C	⑯	Damper	㊷	㊽
V8-390⑦	BRF-42	.044	—	—	C	⑨	Damper	650	650D
V8-460⑦	ARF-52	.044	—	—	B	12°	Damper	—	650D

Ford Vans & Trucks

TUNE UP SPECIFICATIONS—Continued

The following specifications are published from the latest information available. This data should be used only in the absence of a decal affixed in the engine compartment.

★When using a timing light, disconnect vacuum hose or tube at distributor and plug opening in tube or hose so idle speed will not be affected.

▲Before removing wires from distributor cap, determine location of the No. 1 wire in cap, as distributor position may have been altered from that shown at the end of this chart.

Year/Engine	Spark Plug		Distributor		Ignition Timing★			Carb. Adjustment	
								Hot Idle Speed	
	Type	Gap Inch	Point Gap Inch	Dwell Angle Deg.	Firing Order Fig. ▲	Timing BTDC [53]	Mark Fig.	Std. Trans.	Auto. Trans.
1977									
6-300[1]	[17]	.044	—	—	H	6°	Damper	[17]	[17]
6-300[6]	[17]	.044	—	—	H	[10]	Damper	[17]	[17]
6-300[13]	[17]	[17]	—	—	H	10°	Damper	[17]	[17]
V8-302[11]	ARF-52	.050	—	—	E	2°	Damper	600	600D
V8-302[19]	[17]	.044	—	—	E	[20]	Damper	[17]	[17]
V8-302[6]	[17]	.044	—	—	E	[17]	Damper	[17]	[17]
V8-351M[11]	[21]	[21]	—	—	F	[17]	Damper	—	650D
V8-351M[6]	ARF-42	.044	—	—	F	[22]	Damper	800	650D
V8-351M[5]	ARF-42	.044	—	—	F	[17]	Damper	650	650D
V8-351W[11]	ARF-52	.050	—	—	F	[17]	Damper	—	625D
V8-351W[1]	ARF-52	.044	—	—	F	[17]	Damper	—	[50]
V8-351W[23]	ARF-42	.044	—	—	F	[24]	Damper	—	[17]
V8-400[11]	[8]	[8]	—	—	F	[17]	Damper	—	600D
V8-400[6]	ARF-42	.044	—	—	F	6°	Damper	—	650D
V8-400[5]	ARF-42	.044	—	—	F	[23]	Damper	—	650D
V8-460	[17]	.044	—	—	B	12°	Damper	—	[17]
1978									
6-300	BSF-42	.054	—	—	H	10°	Damper	700	550D
V8-302	ASF-42	.044	—	—	E	6°	Damper	[17]	[17]
V8-351M[14]	ASF-42	.044	—	—	F	10°	Damper	800	650D
V8-351M[12][4]	ASF-42	.044	—	—	F	6°	Damper	750	—
V8-351M[4][13]	ASF-42	.044	—	—	F	14°	Damper	—	600D
V8-351W[4][13]	ASF-42	.044	—	—	F	8°	Damper	—	600D
V8-351W[4][12]	ASF-42	.044	—	—	F	6°	Damper	900	—
V8-351W[13][14]	ASF-42	.044	—	—	F	6°	Damper	—	700D
V8-400[4]	ASF-42	.044	—	—	F	12°	Damper	—	650D
V8-400[14]	ASF-42	.044	—	—	F	10°	Damper	—	650D
V8-460	ASF-42	.044	—	—	B	12°	Damper	—	600D

Continued

TUNE UP SPECIFICATIONS—Continued

| Year/Engine | Spark Plug | | Distributor | | Ignition Timing ★ | | | Carb. Adjustment | |
| | | | | | | | | Hot Idle Speed | |
	Type	Gap Inch	Point Gap Inch	Dwell Angle Deg.	Firing Order Fig. ▲	Timing BTDC [55]	Timing Mark Location	Std. Trans.	Auto. Trans.
1979									
6-300[12][26]	BSF-42	.044	—	—	H	6°	Damper	700[52]	—
6-300[13][26]	BSF-42	.044	—	—	H	10°	Damper	—	550D[52]
6-300[27]	BRF-42	.044	—	—	H	12°	Damper	700[52]	700D[52]
V8-302[23]	ASF-42	.044	—	—	E	[28]	Damper	700[52]	600D[52]
V8-302[29]	ASF-42	.044	—	—	E	[30]	Damper	700[52]	600D[52]
V8-351M[12][31]	ASF-42	.044	—	—	F	[32]	Damper	650[52]	—
V8-351M[13][31]	ASF-42	.044	—	—	F	6°	Damper	—	550D[52]
V8-351M[6]	ASF-42	.044	—	—	F	[33]	Damper	650[52]	550D[52]
V8-351M[29]	ASF-42	.044	—	—	F	[34]	Damper	650[52]	550D[52]
V8-351M[35]	ASF-42	.044	—	—	F	[36]	Damper	650[52]	550D[52]
V8-351W[1]	ASF-42	.044	—	—	F	10°	Damper	600[52]	600D[52]
V8-351W[37]	ASF-42	.044	—	—	F	[38]	Damper	600[52]	600D[52]
V8-351W[39]	ASF-42	.044	—	—	F	[40]	Damper	600[52]	600D[52]
V8-351W[41]	ASF-42	.044	—	—	F	6°	Damper	650[53]	650D[53]
V8-400[29]	ASF-42	.044	—	—	F	[34]	Damper	650[52]	550D[52]
V8-400[51]	ASF-42	.044	—	—	F	3°	Damper	600	600D
V8-460	ASF-42	.044	—	—	B	[43]	Damper	—	650D[54]

[1]—E-100.
[2]—Cylinder numbering (front to rear): Right bank 1-2-3-4; left bank 5-6-7-8.
[3]—BRF-31, .030-inch, BRF-42, .034-inch.
[4]—Except California.
[5]—F-150, 250, 350.
[6]—F-100.
[7]—Breakerless ignition.
[8]—ARF-52, .050-inch. ARF-52-6, .060-inch.
[9]—Exc. Calif. auto. trans. 16° BTDC; Calif. auto. trans. 14° BTDC.
[10]—Calif. man. trans. & all auto. trans. models 6° BTDC; man. trans. exc. Calif. see note [17].
[11]—Ranchero.
[12]—Man. Trans.
[13]—Auto. trans.
[14]—California.
[15]—With auto. trans. @ 700 rpm; with man. trans. @ 600 rpm.
[16]—Exc. Calif. 6° BTDC.
[17]—Must refer to engine decal due to running production changes.
[18]—E & F-150, 250, 350.
[19]—Bronco.
[20]—Man. trans. see note [17]; auto. trans. 8° BTDC.
[21]—ARF-52 & ASF-52 .050-inch; ARF-52-6 .060-inch.
[22]—Man. trans. 10° BTDC; auto. trans. exc. Calif. see note [17]; Calif. 8° BTDC.
[23]—E-150, 250, 350.
[24]—Man. trans. 6° BTDC; auto trans. exc. Calif. 8° BTDC; Calif. see note [17].
[25]—Exc. Calif. 12° BTDC; Calif. see note [17].
[26]—E & F-100, 150, 250.
[27]—E & F-350.

[28]—Man. trans. 4° BTDC; auto. trans. 6° BTDC.
[29]—F-100, 150.
[30]—Man. trans. 6° BTDC; auto. trans. 8° BTDC.
[31]—Bronco.
[32]—Calif. models w/3.50 axle ratio 8° BTDC; all others 10° BTDC.
[33]—Man. trans. 10° BTDC; auto. trans. exc. Calif. 6° BTDC; Calif. 10° BTDC.
[34]—Man. trans. 10° BTDC; auto. trans. 6° BTDC.
[35]—F-150.
[36]—Man. trans. 6° BTDC; auto. trans. 12° BTDC.
[37]—E-150.
[38]—Man. trans. 4° BTDC; auto. trans. exc. Calif. 10° BTDC; Calif. 8° BTDC.
[39]—E-250.
[40]—Man. trans. 4° BTDC; auto trans. 12° BTDC.
[41]—E-350.
[42]—Except Calif. 750; Calif. 700.
[43]—E-250, 14° BTDC; E-350, 8° BTDC.
[44]—Man. trans. 6° BTDC; auto. trans. 3° BTDC.
[45]—Man. trans. 6° BTDC; auto. trans. 18° BTDC.
[46]—Man. trans. .020"; auto. trans. .017".
[47]—E-, F-150, 250; 350: BTRF-42.
[48]—Except Calif. 650; Calif. 600.
[49]—Man. trans. 6° BTDC; auto. trans. see note [17].
[50]—Except Calif. 650D; Calif. 700D.
[51]—F-350.
[52]—For A/C-TSP equipped models, A/C compressor electromagnetic clutch de-energized.
[53]—A/C off where equipped.
[54]—E-250: where A/C equipped, energize A/C electromagnetic clutch.
[55]—BTDC: Before Top Dead Center.

Ford Vans & Trucks

TUNE UP NOTES—Continued

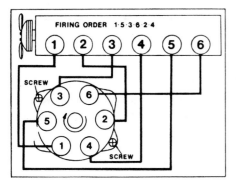

Fig. A

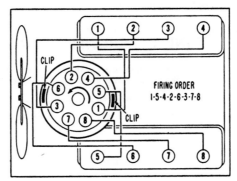

Fig. B

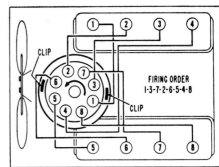

Fig. C

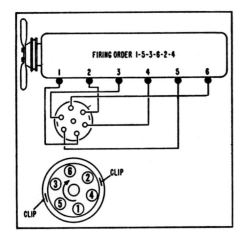

Fig. D

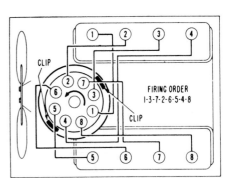

Fig. E

Fig. F

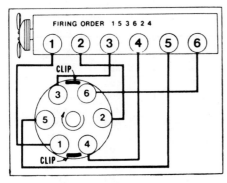

Fig. G

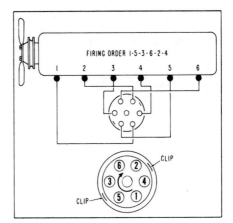

Fig. H

ENGINE IDENTIFICATION

Engine codes and location: see
CHEVROLET.

TUNE UP SPECIFICATIONS

The following specifications are published from the latest information available. This
data should be used only in the absence of a decal affixed in the engine compartment.

★When using a timing light, disconnect vacuum hose or tube at distributor and plug opening in tube or hose so idle speed will not be affected.

▲Before removing wires from distributor cap, determine location of the No. 1 wire in cap, as distributor position may have been altered from that
shown at the end of this chart.

| Year/Engine | Spark Plug | | Distributor | | Ignition Timing★ | | | Carb. Adjustment | |
| | Type | Gap Inch | Point Gap Inch | Dwell Angle Deg. | Firing Order Fig. ▲ | Timing BTDC (59) | Mark Fig. | Hot Idle Speed | |
								Std. Trans.	Auto. Trans.
1974									
6-250	R46T	.035	.019	31–34	B	⑨	I	⑰	600
6-292	R44T	.035	.019	31–34	B	8°	I	600	600
V8-350①⑩	R44T	.035	.019	28–32	C	⑬	I	900	600D
V8-350①⑥⑪	R44T	.035	.019	28–32	C	③	I	900	600D
V8-350①⑦⑪	R44T	.035	.019	28–32	C	④	I	900	600D
V8-350②⑪	R44T	.035	.019	28–32	C	4°	I	600	600
V8-454①	R44T	.035	.019	28–32	C	10°	I	800	600D
V8-454②	R44T	.035	.019	28–32	C	8°	I	700	700
1975									
6-250	R46TX	.060	—	—	D	10°	I	850	㊽
6-292	㊾	⑰	.019	28–32	㊹	8°	I	600	600N
V8-350 Light Duty	R44TX	.060	—	—	E	6°	I	800	600D
V8-350 Heavy Duty⑬	R44TX	.060	—	—	E	⑲	I	600	600
V8-400⑥	R44TX	.060	—	—	E	4°	I	700	700
V8-400⑦	R44TX	.060	—	—	E	2°	I	700	700
V8-454 Light Duty	R44TX	.060	—	—	E	16°	I	—	650
V8-454 Heavy Duty	R44TX	.060	—	—	E	8°	I	㊾	㊾
1976									
6-250 Light Duty㉑	R46TS	.035	—	—	D	㉒	I	㊿㉜	—
6-250 Light Duty㉓	R46TS	.035	—	—	D	㉔	I	—	㉛㉝
6-250 Heavy Duty	R46T	.035	—	—	D	6°	I	600	600
6-292	R44T	.035	.019	31–34	㊹	8°	I	600	600
V8-305	R45TS	.045	—	—	E	8°	I	800	600D
V8-350⑳	R45TS	.045	—	—	E	6°	I	800	600
V8-350㉓	R45TS	.045	—	—	E	㉖	I	800	600D
V8-350 Light Duty㉗	R45TS	.045	—	—	E	㉘	I	800	600D
V8-350 Heavy Duty㉗	R44TX	.060	—	—	E	⑲	I	600	600
V8-400⑳	R45TS	.045	—	—	E	8°	I	—	600D
V8-400㉗	R44TX	.060	—	—	E	㉙	I	700	700
V8-454	R44T	.045	—	—	E	8°	I	700	700

GMC

TUNE UP SPECIFICATIONS—Continued

The following specifications are published from the latest information available. This data should be used only in the absence of a decal affixed in the engine compartment.

★When using a timing light, disconnect vacuum hose or tube at distributor and plug opening in tube or hose so idle speed will not be affected.

▲Before removing wires from distributor cap, determine location of the No. 1 wire in cap, as distributor position may have been altered from that shown at the end of this chart.

Year/Engine	Spark Plug		Distributor		Ignition Timing★			Carb. Adjustment	
								Hot Idle Speed	
	Type	Gap Inch	Point Gap Inch	Dwell Angle Deg.	Firing Order Fig. ▲	Timing BTDC (59)	Mark Fig.	Std. Trans.	Auto. Trans.
1977									
6-250 Light Duty (30)	R46TS	.035	—	—	D	(14)	I	(53)	600
6-250 Heavy Duty	R46T	.035	—	—	D	6°	I	600	600
6-250 (20)	R46TS	.035	—	—	D	(32)	I	(54)	(48)
6-292	R44T	.035	—	—	(44)	8°	I	600	600
V8-305	(68)	.045	—	—	E	(33)	I	(57)	500D
V8-350 (20)	R45TS	.045	—	—	E	8°	I	—	650
V8-350 Light Duty (27)	R45TS	.045	—	—	E	(28)	I	700	500
V8-350 Heavy Duty (27)	(46)	(34)	—	—	E	(19)	I	700	700
V8-400	R44T	.045	—	—	E	(29)	I	700	700
V8-454 Light Duty	R45TS	.045	—	—	E	4°	I	700	700
V8-454 Heavy Duty	R44T	.045	—	—	E	8°	I	700	700
1978									
V6-200	R45TS	.045	—	—	A	8°	G	700	600D
V6-231	R46TSX	.060	—	—	F	15°	H	700	600D
6-250 (13)	R46TS	.035	—	—	D	(33)	I	750	(59)
6-250 (16)	R46T	.035	—	—	D	6°	I	600	600N
6-292	R44T	.035	—	—	D	8°	I	600	600N
V8-305 (36)	R45TS	.045	—	—	E	(37)	I	600	500D
V8-305 (13)	R45TS	.045	—	—	E	4°	I	600	500D
V8-305 (16)	R44T	.045	—	—	E	6°	I	700	700N
V8-350 (36)	R45TS	.045	—	—	E	(38)	I	700	500D
V8-350 Light Duty (13)	R45TS	.045	—	—	E	8°	I	(49)	500D
V8-350 Light Duty (16)	(46)	.045	—	—	E	(19)	I	700	700N
V8-350 Heavy Duty	R44T	(34)	—	—	E	4°	I	600	600N
V8-400 (7)(13)	R45TS	.045	—	—	E	4°	I	—	500D
V8-400 (16)	R44T	.045	—	—	E	(29)	I	700	700N
V8-454	R45TS	.045	—	—	E	8°	I	700	500D
1979									
V6-200	R45TS	.045	—	—	A	(39)	G	700	600D
V6-231	R45TSX	.060	—	—	F	15°	H	—	(51)
6-250 (40)	R46TS	.035	—	—	D	10°	I	750	600D
6-250 (41)	R46TS	.035	—	—	D	(42)	I	750	600D
6-292	R44T	.035	—	—	D	8°	I	700	700N
V8-305 (38)	R45TS	.045	—	—	E	(43)	I	700	(8)
V8-305	R45TS	.045	—	—	E	6°	I	600	500D
V8-350 Light Duty (13)	R45TS	.045	—	—	E	8°	I	700	500D
V8-350 Light Duty (16)	R44T	.045	—	—	E	4°	I	700	700N
V8-350 Heavy Duty	R44T	.045	—	—	E	8°	I	600	600N
V8-400 (13)	R45TS	.045	—	—	E	4°	I	—	500D
V8-400 (16)	R44T	.045	—	—	E	4°	I	—	700N
V8-454 (13)	R45TS	.045	—	—	E	(5)	I	700	550D
V8-454 (16)	R44T	.045	—	—	E	4°	I	700	700N

continued

TUNE UP NOTES

①—1500 series, 2500 series Vandura & Sprint.
②—2500 series (except Vandura) & 3500 Series.
③—Man. trans. except Suburban 8° BTDC; Suburban 6° BTDC; auto. trans. except Suburban & Rally Wagon 8° BTDC; Suburban & Rally Wagon 12° BTDC.
④—Except Suburban w/auto. trans. 4° BTDC; Suburban w/auto. trans. 6° BTDC.
⑤—K-1500, 2500 & G-2500, 3500 4° BTDC; C-1500 & 2500 4° BTDC.
⑥—Except Calif.
⑦—Calif.
⑧—Except hi alt. 500D; hi alt. 600D.
⑨—Series 10, 8° BTDC; Series 20-30, 6° BTDC.
⑩—2-barrel.
⑪—4-barrel.
⑫—Man. trans. TDC; auto. trans. 8° BTDC.
⑬—Man. trans. exc. Suburban 8° BTDC; man. trans. Suburban 6° BTDC; auto. trans. 12° BTDC.
⑭—Exc. Calif. .045"; Calif. .060".
⑮—Light duty emissions, GVWR 6000 lbs. & under.
⑯—Heavy duty emissions, GVWR 6001 lbs. & above.
⑰—Less H.E.I. .035"; with H.E.I. .060".
⑱—Series 15-35.
⑲—Exc. Calif. 8° BTDC; Calif. 2° BTDC.
⑳—Sprint.
㉑—Manual trans.
㉒—Exc. 1500 w/4-spd. trans. 6° BTDC; 1500 w/4-spd. trans. 10° BTDC.
㉓—Auto. trans.
㉔—Sprint 12° BTDC; 1500 exc. Calif. 10° BTDC; 1500 Calif. 4° BTDC.
㉕—2-barrel carb. 1500 Series.
㉖—Man. trans. 2° BTDC; auto. trans. 6° BTDC.
㉗—4-barrel carb. 1500, 2500 & 3500 Series.
㉘—Exc. Calif. 8° BTDC; Calif. 6° BTDC.
㉙—Exc. Calif. 4°BTDC; Calif. 2° BTDC.

㉚—Exc. Sprint.
㉛—Man. trans. 6° BTDC; auto. trans. exc. Calif. 12° BTDC; Calif. 10° BTDC.
㉜—Auto. trans. exc. Calif. 8° BTDC; man. trans. & Calif. auto. trans. 6° BTDC.
㉝—Man. trans. 8° BTDC; auto. trans. exc. Calif. & hi alt. 8° BTDC; Calif. 10° BTDC; hi alt. 12° BTDC.
㉞—Except Calif. .045"; Calif. .060".
㉟—Except Sprint 6° BTDC; Sprint 8° BTDC.
㊱—Caballero.
㊲—Except Calif. 4° BTDC; Calif. 6° BTDC.
㊳—Except Calif. & hi alt. 6° BTDC; Calif. & hi alt. 8° BTDC.
㊴—Man. trans. 8° BTDC; auto. trans. 12° BTDC.
㊵—C-, G- & K-1500 Series.
㊶—C- & G-2500 & 3500 Series.
㊷—Except Calif. 10° BTDC; Calif. man. trans. 6° BTDC; auto. trans. 8° BTDC.
㊸—Except hi alt. 4° BTDC; hi alt. 8° BTDC.
㊹—Less H.E.I. Fig. B; with H.E.I. Fig. D.
㊺—Less H.E.I. R44T; with H.E.I. R44TX.
㊻—Exc. Calif. R44T; Calif. R44TX.
㊼—Series 15, man. trans. 850; series 25-35, man. trans. 600.
㊽—Except Calif. 550; Calif. 600.
㊾—Except Calif. 600; Calif. 700.
㊿—Except Calif. 900; Calif. 1000.
(51)—Except Calif. 550D; Calif. 600D.
(52)—Sprint exc. Calif. man. trans. 850.
(53)—Sprint exc. Calif. auto. trans. 550D; Sprint Calif. auto. trans. 600D.
(54)—Less A/C 750; with A/C 800.
(55)—Except Calif. man. trans. 750; Calif. man. trans. 850.
(56)—Except Sprint R44T; Sprint R45TS.
(57)—Sprint 700; except Sprint 600.
(58)—Except Calif. & hi alt. models less A/C 550D; all others 600D.
(59)—BTDC: Before Top Dead Center.

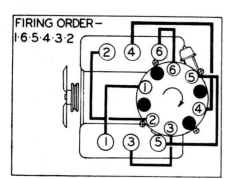

Fig. A

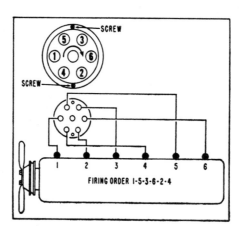

Fig. B

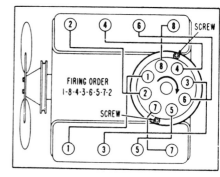

Fig. C

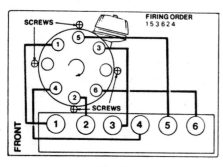

Fig. D

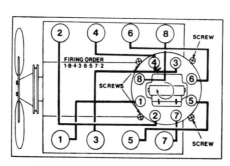

Fig. E

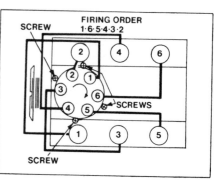

Fig. F

GMC

TUNE UP NOTES—Continued

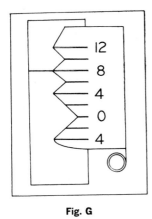

Fig. G

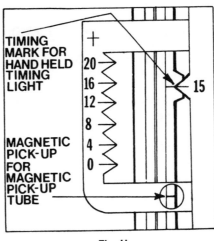

TIMING MARK FOR HAND HELD TIMING LIGHT

MAGNETIC PICK-UP FOR MAGNETIC PICK-UP TUBE

Fig. H

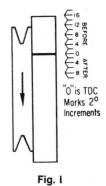

Fig. I

ENGINE IDENTIFICATION

ENGINE CODE: The prefix to the engine serial number identifies the engine model.

ENGINE NUMBER LOCATION

FOUR CYLINDER—left side, upper front on crankcase.

SIX CYLINDER—right side of crankcase near distributor.

V8s—right bank, upper front on crankcase.

TUNE UP SPECIFICATIONS

The following specifications are published from the latest information available. This data should be used only in the absence of a decal affixed in the engine compartment.

★When using a timing light, disconnect vacuum hose or tube at distributor and plug opening in tube or hose so idle speed will not be affected.

▲Before removing wires from distributor cap, determine location of the No. 1 wire in cap, as distributor position may have been altered from that shown at the end of this chart.

Year/Engine	Spark Plug		Distributor		Ignition Timing ★			Carb. Adjustment	
								Hot Idle Speed	
	Type	Gap Inch	Point Gap Inch	Dwell Angle Deg.	Firing Order Fig. ▲	Timing BTDC ⑧	Mark Fig.	Std. Trans.	Auto. Trans.
1974									
4-196	UJ10Y	.030	—	—	⑦	4°	B	500	500N
6-258	N12Y	.035	—	—	D	3°	E	700	700N
V8-304	J6	.030	.017	25–29	A	TDC①	B	700	700N
V8-345	RJ10Y	.030	—	—	A	TDC①	B	700	700N
1975									
4-196	RJ10Y	.030	.008②	26–32	⑦	TDC	B	500	500N
V8-304	RJ10Y	.030	—	—	A	TDC①	B	700	700N
V8-345	RJ10Y	.030	—	—	A	TDC①	B	700	700N
1976									
4-196	RJ10Y	.030	—	—	⑦	TDC	B	550	550N
V8-304	RJ10Y	.030	—	—	A	TDC①	B	675	675N
V8-345	RJ10Y	.030	—	—	A	TDC①	B	650	650N
1977									
4-196	RJ10Y	.035	—	—	⑦	TDC	B	550	550N
V8-304	RJ6	.030	—	—	A	3°①	B	④	④
V8-345	RJ6	.030	—	—	A	4°①	B	⑤	⑤
1978									
4-196	RJ10Y	.035	—	—	⑦	TDC	B	550	550N
V8-304	RJ6	.030	—	—	⑥	3°①	B	④	④
V8-345	RJ6	.030	—	—	⑥	4°①	B	⑤	⑤

International Scout

TUNE UP SPECIFICATIONS—Continued

The following specifications are published from the latest information available. This data should be used only in the absence of a decal affixed in the engine compartment.

★When using a timing light, disconnect vacuum hose or tube at distributor and plug opening in tube or hose so idle speed will not be affected.

▲Before removing wires from distributor cap, determine location of the No. 1 wire in cap, as distributor position may have been altered from that shown at the end of this chart.

Year/Engine	Spark Plug		Distributor		Ignition Timing★			Carb. Adjustment	
	Type	Gap Inch	Point Gap Inch	Dwell Angle Deg.	Firing Order Fig. ▲	Timing BTDC ⑧	Mark Fig.	Hot Idle Speed	
								Std. Trans.	Auto. Trans.
1979									
4-196	RJ10Y	.035	—	—	⑦	TDC	B	700	700N
V8-304	RJ10Y	.035	—	—	C	TDC①	B	700	700N
V8-345	RJ10Y	.035	—	—	C	TDC①	B	700	700N

①—Connect timing light to No. 8 spark plug.
②—Clearance between end of trigger wheel tooth and sensor.
③—Except Calif. TDC; Calif. 5° BTDC.
④—Except Calif. 675; Calif. 625.
⑤—Except Calif. 675; Calif. 650.
⑥—Early 1978 fig. A; late 1978 with integral distributor fig. C.
⑦—Timed at #1 cylinder front of engine. Firing order: 1-3-4-2.
⑧—BTDC: Before Top Dead Center.

FIRING ORDER 1·8·4·3·6·5·7·2

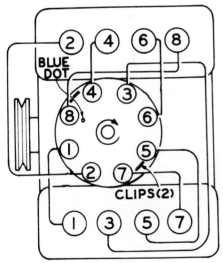

Fig. A

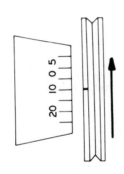

Fig. B

FIRING ORDER 1·8·4·3·6·5·7·2

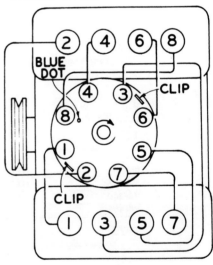

Fig. C

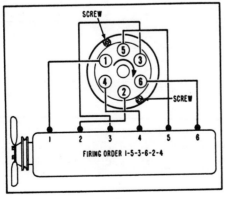

FIRING ORDER 1-5-3-6-2-4

Fig. D

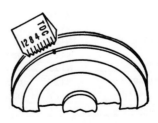

Fig. E

ENGINE IDENTIFICATION

The engine identification tag is attached to the right bank cylinder head cover (V8), or right side of the block between the No. 2 and No. 3 cylinders (six-cylinder). The letter (4th character) in the code identifies the engine type.

Year	Engine	Engine Code
1974–76	6-232	E
	6-258	A
	V8-304	H
	V8-360-2V	N
	V8-360-4V	P
	V8-401	Z
1977–78	6-232	E
	6-258-1V	A
	6-258-2V	C
	V8-304	H
	V8-360-2V	N
	V8-360-4V	P
	V8-401	Z
1979	6-258	C
	V8-304	H
	V8-360	N

TUNE UP SPECIFICATIONS

The following specifications are published from the latest information available. This data should be used only in the absence of a decal affixed in the engine compartment.

★When using a timing light, disconnect vacuum hose or tube at distributor and plug opening in tube or hose so idle speed will not be affected.

▲Before removing wires from distributor cap, determine location of the No. 1 wire in cap, as distributor position may have been altered from that shown at the end of this chart.

Year/Engine	Spark Plug		Distributor		Ignition Timing★			Carb. Adjustment	
								Hot Idle Speed	
	Type	Gap Inch	Point Gap Inch	Dwell Angle Deg.	Firing Order Fig. ▲	Timing BTDC 23	Mark Fig.	Std. Trans.	Auto. Trans.
1974									
6-232	N12Y	.035	.016	31–34	A	5°	D	600	—
6-258	N12Y	.035	.016	31–34	A	3°	D	600	550D[18]
V8-304	N12Y	.035	.016	29–31	B	5°	C	750	—
V8-360	N12Y	.035	.016	29–31	B	5°	C	750	700D[18]
V8-401	N12Y	.035	.016	29–31	B	[3]	C	650	600D[18]
1975									
6-232	N12Y	.035	—	—	A	5°	E	700[19]	—
6-258	N12Y	.035	—	—	A	3°	E	[20]	[20]
V8-304	N12Y	.035	—	—	B	5°	C	750	—
V8-360, 401	N12Y	.035	—	—	B	2½°	C	750	700D
1976									
6-232	N12Y	.035	—	—	A	8°	E	600	—
6-258 [6]	N12Y	.035	—	—	A	8°	E	—	[2]
6-258 [7]	N12Y	.035	—	—	A	6°	E	600	—
V8-304 [5][6]	N12Y	.035	—	—	B	10°	C	—	700D
V8-304 [7]	N12Y	.035	—	—	B	5°	C	750	—
V8-304 [1][6]	N12Y	.035	—	—	B	5°	C	—	700D
V8-360, 401 [5][6]	N12Y	.035	—	—	B	8°	C	—	700D
V8-360, 401 [1][6]	N12Y	.035	—	—	B	5°	C	—	700D
V8-360, 401 [7]	N12Y	.035	—	—	B	5°	C	750	—

Jeep

TUNE UP SPECIFICATIONS—Continued

The following specifications are published from the latest information available. This data should be used only in the absence of a decal affixed in the engine compartment.

★When using a timing light, disconnect vacuum hose or tube at distributor and plug opening in tube or hose so idle speed will not be affected.

▲Before removing wires from distributor cap, determine location of the No. 1 wire in cap, as distributor position may have been altered from that shown at the end of this chart.

Year/Engine	Spark Plug		Distributor		Ignition Timing ★			Carb. Adjustment	
								Hot Idle Speed	
	Type	Gap Inch	Point Gap Inch	Dwell Angle Deg.	Firing Order Fig. ▲	Timing BTDC ㉓	Mark Fig.	Std. Trans.	Auto. Trans.
1977									
6-232⑧	N12Y	.035	—	—	A	5°	E	850	—
6-232⑨	N12Y	.035	—	—	A	10°	E	600	—
6-258⑤⑦⑧⑩	N12Y	.035	—	—	A	3°	E	850	—
6-258①⑦⑩	N12Y	.035	—	—	A	6°	E	850	—
6-258⑨⑩	N12Y	.035	—	—	A	10°	E	600	550
6-258⑥⑧⑩	N12Y	.035	—	—	A	8°	E	—	700
6-258⑪	N12Y	.035	—	—	A	6°	E	650	550
V8-304⑦	RN12Y	.035	—	—	B	5°	C	750	—
V8-304①⑥	RN12Y	.035	—	—	B	5°	C	—	700
V8-304⑤⑥	RN12Y	.035	—	—	B	10°	C	—	700
V8-360⑦	RN12Y	.035	—	—	B	5°	C	750	—
V8-360, 401⑥	RN12Y	.035	—	—	B	8°	C	—	700
1978									
6-232⑧	N13L	.035	—	—	G	5°	E	850	—
6-232⑨	RN13L	.035	—	—	G	10°	E	600	—
6-258④⑦⑩	N13L	.035	—	—	G	3°	E	850	—
6-258⑩⑫	N13L	.035	—	—	G	8°	E	850	550D
6-258⑨⑩	RN13L	.035	—	—	G	10°	E	600	550D
6-258⑪	N13L	.035	—	—	G	6°	E	650	550D
V8-304⑦	N12Y	.035	—	—	H	5°	C	750	—
V8-304①⑥	N12Y	.035	—	—	H	5°	C	—	700D
V8-304⑤⑥	RN12Y	.035	—	—	H	10°	C	—	700D
V8-360⑦	N12Y	.035	—	—	H	5°	C	750	—
V8-360, 401⑥	N12Y	.035	—	—	H	8°	C	—	700D
1979									
6-258⑦⑩	㉑	.035	—	—	G	⑬	E	700	—
6-258⑥⑩	㉑	.035	—	—	G	8°	E	—	600D
6-258⑪⑭	㉑	.035	—	—	G	8°	E	700	600D
6-258⑪⑮	㉑	.035	—	—	G	⑯	E	700	600D
V8-304	㉒	.035	—	—	H	⑰	C	750	600D
V8-360	㉒	.035	—	—	H	8°	C	800	600D

①—California.
②—Except Calif. 500D; Calif. 700D.
③—Exc. heavy duty, 5° BTDC; heavy duty, 2½° BTDC.
④—Exc. Calif. & hi alt.
⑤—Exc. Calif.
⑥—Auto. trans.
⑦—Manual trans.
⑧—Exc. hi alt.
⑨—High altitude.
⑩—1-barrel carb.
⑪—2-barrel carb.
⑫—Man. trans. Calif.; auto. trans. exc. hi altitude.

⑬—Exc. Calif. & hi alt. 3° BTDC; Calif. 8° BTDC; hi alt. 10° BTDC.
⑭—CJ models.
⑮—Cherokee, Wagoneer & truck models.
⑯—Man. trans. 6° BTDC; auto. trans. 4° BTDC.
⑰—Man. trans. 5° BTDC; auto. trans. 8° BTDC.
⑱—Disconnect TCS wires at solenoid valve.
⑲—Calif. 600.
⑳—Without EGR, man. trans. 700; with EGR, man. trans. 650; man. trans. Calif. 600; auto. trans. 500.
㉑—Exc. hi alt. N13L; hi alt. RN13L.
㉒—Exc. hi alt. N12Y; hi alt. RN12Y.
㉓—BTDC: Before Top Dead Center.

continued

Jeep

TUNE UP NOTES—Continued

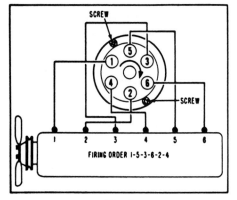

Fig. A

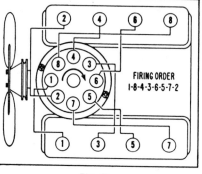

Fig. B

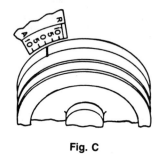

Fig. C

Fig. D

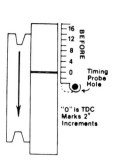

Fig. E

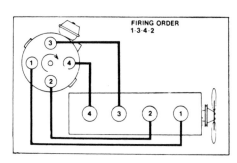

Fig. F

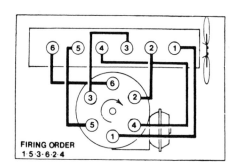

Fig. G

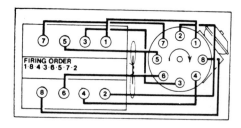

Fig. H

CONVERSION TABLE

INCH FRACTIONS AND DECIMALS TO METRIC EQUIVALENTS

Inches (Fractions)	Inches (Decimals)	m m	Inches (Fractions)	Inches (Decimals)	m m	Inches (Fractions)	Inches (Decimals)	m m
—	.0004	.01	—	.4331	11	31/32	.96875	24.606
—	.004	.10	7/16	.4375	11.113	—	.9843	25
—	.01	.25	29/64	.4531	11.509	1	1.000	25.4
1/64	.0156	.397	15/32	.46875	11.906	—	1.0236	26
—	.0197	.50	—	.4724	12	1-1/32	1.0312	26.194
—	.0295	.75	31/64	.48437	12.303	1-1/16	1.062	26.988
1/32	.03125	.794	—	.492	12.5	—	1.063	27
—	.0394	1	1/2	.500	12.700	1-3/32	1.094	27.781
3/64	.0469	1.191	—	.5118	13	—	1.1024	28
—	.059	1.5	33/64	.5156	13.097	1-1/8	1.125	28.575
1/16	.0625	1.588	17/32	.53125	13.494	—	1.1417	29
5/64	.0781	1.984	35/64	.54687	13.891	1-5/32	1.156	29.369
—	.0787	2	—	.5512	14	—	1.1811	30
3/32	.094	2.381	9/16	.5625	14.288	1-3/16	1.1875	30.163
—	.0984	2.5	—	.571	14.5	1-7/32	1.219	30.956
7/64	.1093	2.776	37/64	.57812	14.684	—	1.2205	31
—	.1181	3	—	.5906	15	1-1/4	1.250	31.750
1/8	.1250	3.175	19/32	.59375	15.081	—	1.2598	32
—	.1378	3.5	39/64	.60937	15.478	1-9/32	1.281	32.544
9/64	.1406	3.572	5/8	.6250	15.875	—	1.2992	33
5/32	.15625	3.969	—	.6299	16	1-5/16	1.312	33.338
—	.1575	4	41/64	.6406	16.272	—	1.3386	34
11/64	.17187	4.366	—	.6496	16.5	1-11/32	1.344	34.131
—	.177	4.5	21/32	.65625	16.669	1-3/8	1.375	34.925
3/16	.1875	4.763	—	.6693	17	—	1.3779	35
—	.1969	5	43/64	.67187	17.066	1-13/32	1.406	35.719
13/64	.2031	5.159	11/16	.6875	17.463	—	1.4173	36
—	.2165	5.5	45/64	.7031	17.859	1-7/16	1.438	36.513
7/32	.21875	5.556	—	.7087	18	—	1.4567	37
15/64	.23437	5.953	23/32	.71875	18.5	1-15/32	1.469	37.306
—	.2362	6	—	.7283	18.256	—	1.4961	38
1/4	.2500	6.350	47/64	.73437	18.653	1-1/2	1.500	38.100
—	.2559	6.5	—	.7480	19	1-17/32	1.531	38.894
17/64	.2656	6.747	3/4	.7500	19.050	—	1.5354	39
—	.2756	7	49/64	.7656	19.447	1-9/16	1.562	39.688
9/32	.28125	7.144	25/32	.78125	19.844	—	1.5748	40
—	.2953	7.5	—	.7874	20	1-19/32	1.594	40.481
19/64	.29687	7.541	51/64	.79687	20.241	—	1.6142	41
5/16	.3125	7.938	13/16	.8125	20.638	1-5/8	1.625	41.275
—	.3150	8	—	.8268	21	—	1.6535	42
21/64	.3281	8.334	53/64	.8281	21.034	1-21/32	1.6562	42.069
—	.335	8.5	27/32	.84375	21.431	1-11/16	1.6875	42.863
11/32	.34375	8.731	55/64	.85937	21.828	—	1.6929	43
—	.3543	9	—	.8662	22	1-23/32	1.719	43.656
23/64	.35937	9.128	7/8	.8750	22.225	—	1.7323	44
—	.374	9.5	57/64	.8906	22.622	1-3/4	1.750	44.450
3/8	.3750	9.525	—	.9055	23	—	1.7717	45
25/64	.3906	9.922	29/32	.90625	23.019	1-25/32	1.781	45.244
—	.3937	10	59/64	.92187	23.416	—	1.8110	46
13/32	.4062	10.319	15/16	.9375	23.813	1-13/16	1.8125	46.038
—	.413	10.5	—	.9449	24	1-27/32	1.844	46.831
27/64	.42187	10.716	61/64	.9531	24.209	—	1.8504	47

INCH FRACTIONS AND DECIMALS TO METRIC EQUIVALENTS/continued

Inches Fractions	Inches Decimals	m m	Inches Fractions	Inches Decimals	m m	Inches Fractions	Inches Decimals	m m
1-7/8	1.875	47.625	—	3.0709	78	—	4.7244	120
—	1.8898	48	—	3.1102	79	4-3/4	4.750	120.650
1-29/32	1.9062	48.419	3-1/8	3.125	79.375	4-7/8	4.875	123.825
—	1.9291	49	—	3.1496	80	—	4.9212	125
1-15/16	1.9375	49.213	3-3/16	3.1875	80.963	5	5.000	127
—	1.9685	50	—	3.1890	81	—	5.1181	130
1-31/32	1.969	50.006	—	3.2283	82	5-1/4	5.250	133.350
2	2.000	50.800	3-1/4	3.250	82.550	5-1/2	5.500	139.700
—	2.0079	51	—	3.2677	83	—	5.5118	140
—	2.0472	52	—	3.3071	84	5-3/4	5.750	146.050
2-1/16	2.062	52.388	3-5/16	3.312	84.1377	—	5.9055	150
—	2.0866	53	—	3.3464	85	6	6.000	152.400
2-1/8	2.125	53.975	3-3/8	3.375	85.725	6-1/4	6.250	158.750
—	2.126	54	—	3.3858	86	—	6.2992	160
—	2.165	55	—	3.4252	87	6-1/2	6.500	165.100
2-3/16	2.1875	55.563	3-7/16	3.438	87.313	—	6.6929	170
—	2.2047	56	—	3.4646	88	6-3/4	6.750	171.450
—	2.244	57	3-1/2	3.500	88.900	7	7.000	177.800
2-1/4	2.250	57.150	—	3.5039	89	—	7.0866	180
—	2.2835	58	—	3.5433	90	—	7.4803	190
2-5/16	2.312	58.738	3-9/16	3.562	90.4877	7-1/2	7.500	190.500
—	2.3228	59	—	3.5827	91	—	7.8740	200
—	2.3622	60	—	3.622	92	8	8.000	203.200
2-3/8	2.375	60.325	3-5/8	3.625	92.075	—	8.2677	210
—	2.4016	61	—	3.6614	93	8-1/2	8.500	215.900
2-7/16	2.438	61.913	3-11/16	3.6875	93.663	—	8.6614	220
—	2.4409	62	—	3.7008	94	9	9.000	228.600
—	2.4803	63	—	3.7401	95	—	9.0551	230
2-1/2	2.500	63.500	3-3/4	3.750	95.250	—	9.4488	240
—	2.5197	64	—	3.7795	96	9-1/2	9.500	241.300
—	2.559	65	3-13/16	3.8125	96.838	—	9.8425	250
2-9/16	2.562	65.088	—	3.8189	97	10	10.000	254.000
—	2.5984	66	—	3.8583	98	—	10.2362	260
2-5/8	2.625	66.675	3-7/8	3.875	98.425	—	10.6299	270
—	2.638	67	—	3.8976	99	11	11.000	279.400
—	2.6772	68	—	3.9370	100	—	11.0236	280
2-11/16	2.6875	68.263	3-15/16	3.9375	100.013	—	11.4173	290
—	2.7165	69	—	3.9764	101	—	11.8110	300
2-3/4	2.750	69.850	4	4.000	101.600	12	12.000	304.800
—	2.7559	70	4-1/16	4.062	103.188	13	13.000	330.200
—	2.7953	71	4-1/8	4.125	104.775	—	13.7795	350
2-13/16	2.8125	71.438	—	4.1338	105	14	14.000	355.600
—	2.8346	72	4-3/16	4.1875	106.363	15	15.000	381
—	2.8740	73	4-1/4	4.250	107.950	—	15.7480	400
2-7/8	2.875	73.025	4-5/16	4.312	109.538	16	16.000	406.400
—	2.9134	74	—	4.3307	110	17	17.000	431.800
2-15/16	2.9375	74.613	4-3/8	4.375	111.125	—	17.7165	450
—	2.9527	75	4-7/16	4.438	112.713	18	18.000	457.200
—	2.9921	76	4-1/2	4.500	114.300	19	19.000	482.600
3	3.000	76.200	—	4.5275	115	—	19.6850	500
—	3.0315	77	4-9/16	4.562	115.888	20	20.000	508
3-1/16	3.062	77.788	4-5/8	4.625	117.475	21	21.000	533.400

INDEX

basic, 20–21
battery service, 28
carburetor service, 106
charging system service, 36
compression service, 54
cooling system service, 128
distributor service, 66
fuel system service, 100
oil system service, 124
starting system service, 44
vacuum service, 58
Torino. *See* Ford, compact and intermediate models
Toronado. *See* Oldsmobile
Toyota
    engine identification, 276
    tune up specifications, 276–78
Tradesman. *See* Dodge vans and trucks
Trailduster. *See* Dodge vans and trucks
transmission oil, checking, 128
trucks. *See* Chevrolet; Dodge; Ford, etc.
tune up
    basic maintenance and, 22–24
    engine parts and, 12
    fundamentals of, 11–24
    mileage and, 13
    schedules, 11
    See also battery; cooling system; vacuum, etc. *and
        names of car manufacturers*

U

universal joint, 20, 21

V

vacuum, 51, 56–62
    basic maintenance and, 24
    cranking engine, 56, 57, 59
    engine-running test, reading, taking, 56, 57, 58
    gauge, connecting, 56, 57, 58
    ignition
        disconnecting, 56, 57, 59
        reconnecting, 56, 57, 60
    PCV valve
        connecting, 56, 57, 60
        plugging, 56, 57, 59
    preparation for servicing, 57
    remote starter switch, installing, 56, 57
    rocker arm valve cover, installing, 61–62
    steps in servicing, 56, 57

throttle plate
    closing, 56, 57, 59
    opening, 56, 57, 60
tools, 58
See also compression
vacuum gauge, connecting, 56, 57, 58
vacuum line, 12
vacuum motor, 12
vacuum-type flapper valves, testing heated-air intake
    system with, 106
Valiant. *See* Plymouth
valves. *See* EGR; PCV
Vandura. *See* GMC vans and trucks
vans. *See* Chevrolet; Dodge; GMC, etc.
Vega. *See* Chevrolet Vega
Ventura. *See* Pontiac
Versailles. *See* Lincoln Versailles
Volare. *See* Plymouth
Volkswagen
    engine identification, 279
    Rabbit (diesel), service procedures for, 138–41
    tune up specifications, 279–81
voltage drop test, 26, 27, 32
voltage regulator, 12, 16
    quick-check, 34, 35, 38
    replacing, 38
    types of, 38
voltmeter, 19
Voyager. *See* Dodge vans and trucks

W

Wagoneer. *See* Jeep
warming up engine, compression service and, 52, 53, 54
warranties, battery, 32
water pump, 12
    inspecting, 126, 127, 131
    servicing, 131
whine, engine problems and, 134
whistle, engine problems and, 135
wiring, inspecting, charging system service and, 34, 35, 37
wrenches
    adjustable, 20, 21
    combination, 21
    ratchet, 20, 21

Z

Zephyr. *See* Mercury, compact and intermediate models